Internationalizing Internet Studies

Routledge Advances in Internationalizing Media Studies

EDITED BY DAYA THUSSU, *University of Westminster*

Internationalizing Internet Studies

Beyond Anglophone Paradigms

**Edited by Gerard Goggin
and Mark McLelland**

Routledge
Taylor & Francis Group
New York   London

First published 2009
by Routledge
270 Madison Ave, New York NY 10016

Simultaneously published in the UK
by Routledge
2 Park Square, Milton Park, Abingdon, Oxon, OX14 4RN

Routledge is an imprint of the Taylor & Francis Group, an informa business

Transferred to Digital Printing 2009

© 2009 Taylor & Francis

Typeset in Sabon by IBT Global.

Library of Congress Cataloging in Publication Data

Internationalizing Internet studies / edited by Gerard Goggin and Mark McLelland.
    p. cm. — (Routledge advances in internationalizing media studies ; 2)
    Includes bibliographical references and index.
    ISBN-13: 978-0-415-95625-3
    ISBN-10: 0-415-95625-0
    1. Cyberspace. 2. Internet. 3. Language and languages. 4. Communication and culture—Technological innovations. I. Goggin, Gerard, 1964– II. McLelland, Mark J., 1966–
    HM851.I5693 2009
    306.440285'4678—dc22
    2008016087

ISBN10: 0-415-95625-0 (hbk)
ISBN10: 0-415-87842-X (pbk)
ISBN10: 0-203-89142-2 (ebk)

ISBN13: 978-0-415-95625-3 (hbk)
ISBN13: 978-0-415-87842-5 (pbk)
ISBN13: 978-0-203-89142-1 (ebk)

Contents

PART III
Islam, Modernity, and the Internet

PART IV
Asian Cybercultures

Figures

Tables

Part I

Rethinking Internet Studies?

1 Internationalizing Internet Studies
Beyond Anglophone Paradigms

Gerard Goggin and Mark McLelland

INTRODUCTION

In the Almond coffee shop in Roppongi, a popular haunt for teenagers in Tokyo, a group of young girls are chatting excitedly while playing with their *keitai* (mobile phones), taking and swapping photos, as well as downloading movie times and reviews and sending instant messages to absent friends advising them of the group's current location. Suddenly, one girl asks the others to be quiet and listen to a new music track coming across the café's FM radio system. This is the track she had mentioned to them earlier—what is it? Who is it by? No one seems to know. One girl takes her phone, points it in the direction of the music, and hits a menu button. The song's artist and title is immediately displayed on her screen. "I *told* you it was a new track by Gackt," she says excitedly, as she hits another menu button that takes her to a popular *chaku-mero* site where she can download the song's chorus as her new ring tone.

Meanwhile, half way around the globe in the Occupied Territories, a teenage Palestinian girl is sitting in an Internet center established by an international aid organization. She has heard from her parents and friends about the Internet and how it is the gateway to a whole world of opportunity and has come along to give it a try. However, after staring at the screen for a few minutes, she has no idea where to begin. A friendly visitor from the United States, who happens to be on the next machine, leans over to give her advice on how to set up an e-mail account. "Which language would you prefer, English or Arabic?" she inquires. "I can't understand either," replies the girl. "I can't read at all."

These two teenage girls live worlds, or even ages, apart. The term "digital divide" does not seem adequate to describe the chasm that separates their respective interactions with the world of communication technology. As Tawil-Souri (Chapter 3, this volume) points out, simply setting up Internet facilities in disadvantaged areas of the globe does very little to empower local populations that lack the cultural and social capital to render such facilities intelligible and useful. In relation to new media, young Palestinian girls are extraordinarily disadvantaged.

In the case of Japan, however, the teenage girls in question are the products of a society wherein they are not simply positioned as consumers of new technologies, but are part of a youth culture stretching back to the 1980s that has driven these new technologies forward and given them their current shape. As Mizuko Ito points out, in Japan (and, to an extent, in other Asian societies) mobile communications technologies were not "conceived by an elite and noncommercial technological priesthood and disseminated to the masses," but emerged out of Japanese consumers' love of "gadget fetishism and technofashion," and the market was driven, not by a business elite, but rather grew out of the existing pager culture of teenage Japanese girls.[1] The agency of Japanese girls stretches beyond simple consumer choice: as Manabe (Chapter 20, this volume) shows, the choices they make have actually altered the way in which the Japanese music industry is organized and how it develops and markets its products.

Obviously, these two very different stories make it necessary to underline the cultural specificity of Internet technology, its design, functions, uses, and meanings—and to emphasize its role as "an artifact located in a specific national context."[2] Ito points out that technologies are not universal; rather, it is necessary to attend to "the heterogeneous co-constitution of technology across a transnational stage."[3] Contemporary world societies comprise very different "technoscapes" that differ markedly from US and European locations, and Internet studies need to attend to these local differences. One purpose of this collection is to add to the growing recognition that communications technologies with a "global" reach also are situated in very local cultures of use.[4]

RETHINKING THE INTERNET AS INTERNATIONAL

From the mid-1990s onward, the Internet has shifted fundamentally from its coordinates in English-speaking countries, especially North America, to become an essential medium in a wide range of countries, cultures, and languages. According to 2007 statistics,[5] the Chinese language is used by 14.3 percent of all Internet users, followed by Spanish at 8 percent, and Japanese at 7.7 percent. At 29.5 percent and falling, the percentage of English-language users is now a minority in terms of overall online language use. Furthermore, at 123 million,[6] China has the largest number of Internet users of any country other than the United States. Given China's massive population and the rapid pace of its economic reforms, it can be anticipated that mainland China will soon be home to the largest number of Internet users of any country.

However, communications and media scholarship, especially in the Anglophone world, has not registered the deep ramifications of this shift in emphasis from English to non-English language users online or the challenges it poses to the concepts, methods, assumptions, and frameworks used to study the Internet. Despite the fact that there is also a large body of work being produced by scholars in non-English-speaking cultures and locales, hardly any of this work is being translated, and it has had little impact on the theorization of the developing fields of Internet and cognate, if short-lived, fields such as web studies.

So far, there is no single monograph or edited collection that introduces and explores the implications of the fact that the Internet is an international phenomenon. The most often used survey books—such as *The Internet in Everyday Life* (2002), or the edited collections *Web.Studies* (2nd ed., 2004) and *The Cybercultures Reader* (2nd ed., 2007)[7]—contain some reference to the diffusion of the Internet globally, but do not focus upon or systematically chart what is now most salient and significant about the Internet: its great cultural and linguistic variety, and the breadth and difference of its uses and applications. In these surveys, there are some useful studies and discussions of Internet use in non-Anglophone environments, but these observations remain peripheral to the bulk of research that focuses on research in English into English-language cyberspaces.

While there have been some earlier studies focusing on language use,[8] these investigations were undertaken when the Internet was still concentrated in wealthier, Western countries, and when the mobile Internet applications that became so popular in East Asia—or technologies such as blogs, wikis, podcasting, and so on—were unknown (and certainly not on the horizon of scholars, let alone users).[9] Research into languages that do not utilize the Roman-based alphabet remains particularly lacking in the literature.[10] Yet, as Gavrilovic (Chapter 10, this volume) points out, in the case of Serbian on the Internet the choice of script is both contentious and politicized. In the case of Chinese, too, there are two very different ways of writing characters that divide the People's Republic of China and Taiwan and lead to encoding problems in cross-strait communication (See Martin's and He's chapters 18 and 19, respectively, this volume). Issues of orthography (and the technical means to input, transmit, and display different scripts) thus have complex cultural, political, and historical dimensions for many languages.

Recently there has been both a growing sense of the multilingual nature of the Internet, and some important work grappling with this. Notably, there has been a special journal issue on the multilingual nature of the web and multimedia.[11] Also, there is now an important collection looking at language and the Internet more broadly, Brenda Danet and Susan C. Herring's *The Multilingual Internet*.[12] However, the focus of both of these works is primarily sociolinguistic—and to a significant extent, both are informed by the tradition of work surrounding the concept of computer-mediated communication, a different starting point from our own work, which is guided by ideas about the Internet suggested by media and cultural studies and social studies of technology. Thus, our collection has a different focus: we have set out to bring together understandings of culture, politics, community, use, and the social shaping of technology in order to suggest the profound implications of internationalization on how we approach the Internet.

There is a growing interest in Internet development in specific societies, with important studies from a number of countries and regions becoming available.[13] However, there still remain a preponderance of studies about, or framed upon, Anglophone Internet experience, histories, and cultures, particularly that of North America. In the literature, generally, the United States is all too often taken as "the supposed vanguard of the information society,"[14] and there has been little attempt to generate a discussion between scholars working on different language cultures or to develop modes of analysis that do not take Anglophone models as their starting point.[15] Indeed, commenting on the collection, *Japanese Cybercultures*, Gauntlett complains of the complacency of Western scholars, pointing out that:

> we assume that people in other countries, using other languages, are probably doing things with Internet technology that are *pretty similar* to those applications that we are familiar with. This book shows how wrong that assumption is.[16]

Ito, too, complains of the Western-centric approach of most Anglophone researchers, noting that although Japanese researchers are well acquainted with Anglophone social science theory, "the reverse flow is relatively rare," and as a consequence, studies of "the Internet" that rely solely upon Anglophone theory run the risk of being parochial at best.[17] At worst, such accounts underpin notions of the Internet—as well as key assumptions that shape Internet studies—that generalize on the basis of quite particular experience. What might be recognized as specific experiences of Internet technologies, in particular their cultural developments and representations are taken as general.[18] The strong version of this claim is borne out, for instance, in Paasonen's (Chapter 2, this volume) genealogy of "cyberspace," where she points out that this "defining" metaphor for the online environment has failed to gain currency in Finland.

In Western countries like the United States, the United Kingdom, and Australia, Internet uptake was very rapid from the mid-1990s, since the penetration rate of personal computers (PCs) in these countries was already very high. In the United States, for instance, in the 1990s, a number of factors—including the prevalence and relative affordability of PCs and the generally advanced nature of the infrastructure and high bandwidth available—encouraged rapid development of particular forms of Internet cultures that became highly visible both online and in the media. These early, largely US-based Internet cultures gave rise to certain ideas and ideologies that have been highly influential in how the Internet has been understood (one thinks of the role of theorists, such as Howard Rheingold or *Wired* magazine, for instance).[19] Despite the ensuing critical interrogation of such ideas of the Internet, especially their utopian and dystopian antinomies, conceptions about what the Internet signifies that are rooted in patterns of development and use that are actually quite specific to US conditions still remain—but are not generally recognized as such.

For instance, a whole popular debate and critical literature on blogging quickly emerged, yet many of the assumptions and set-pieces in this—such as the discussion of the relation of mainstream news and journalism to blogging, or what blogging portends for public spheres and general culture—are deeply fashioned upon quite specific blogospheres, not least the North American.[20] However, one of the most populated blogospheres is that of mainland China. Haiqing Yu points out that some 14.2 percent of China's 123 million Internet users maintain a blog, and that many of these blogs are characterized not so much by "citizens' resistance" but rather by a playful and "deliberate misuse and misinterpretation of mainstream ideology."[21] She suggests that Chinese bloggers enjoy the medium as a kind of "entertainment for entertainment purpose," which conflicts with the orthodox party position of "education through entertainment." Although Western journalists commonly regard these bloggers as being engaged in an adversarial relationship with state authorities, Yu suggests that the bloggers themselves do not regard their activities in such black and white terms. Rather, what is so pleasurable for bloggers, she suggests, is the potential that the medium offers for "moments of tactical and light-hearted resistance." South Korea also has a large and culturally distinct blogosphere. As Yoo (Chapter 14, this volume) points out:

> Korean blogs function as a socialization tool rather than as a venue for social activism . . . blogs in Korea are used more for interaction with others and passing the time than grassroots journalism.

In Iran, too (see Chapter 13 this volume), blogging has proven popular among conservative figures, including political and especially religious leaders, to the extent that holy city of Qom has been dubbed the "IT Capital of Iran."

Furthermore, as contributors to this volume powerfully demonstrate, those interested in the Internet have yet to recognize the existence of legions of bloggers in languages such as Persian, Arabic, Indonesian, Tamil, or Korean, or in multiethnic and multilingual nations such as Iran, India, or Sri Lanka (for discussions on several of these topics, see Chapters 12, 13, 14, and 16, this volume). This is not to mention how bloggers are constituting and participating in new transnational public spheres across global faiths (Chapter 12, this volume) or sexual, linguistic, and cultural communities (Chapter 18, this volume).

To provide another example, when it comes to instant messaging, we may be aware of a number of studies and, indeed, ideas about this technology (synonymous with Microsoft® Messenger, for instance) and associated cultural practices, but what do we know about instant messaging in China, and the hugely popular software QQ (Chapter 17, this volume)? In the craze for social media and software, and buzz around Web 2.0, are our ideas of consumer-generated content and the new productive role of the user predetermined by particular discourses and cultures of use around Western social software, photo-sharing, and video-sharing sites (for which MySpace, flickr, and YouTube might be paradigmatic today)—or should we approach new versions of the Internet with the Korean Cyworld in mind?

THE INTERNET'S DIFFERENT HISTORIES

The process of the internationalization of the Internet makes some striking differences in how the Internet has taken shape in different countries, places, cultures, and societies much more prominent. For instance, in the West, access to the Internet began—and has largely remained—PC-based. However, in other countries, particularly China, Korea, and Japan (which now has one of the world's highest populations of Internet users), PC penetration was relatively low. This is to do with the specific orthography of character-based scripts. Japan and China never went through the same kind of office automation phase characteristic of Western countries because it was very difficult to create simple machines, such as typewriters, to reproduce their scripts (Japanese uses about 2,000 characters in daily life; Chinese over 10,000). The advent of PCs in the mid-1980s helped solve this problem, but there were considerable technical hurdles to overcome in developing a programming language that could handle so much data.[22] Japanese, for instance, uses three different scripts (four if you include roman) and Chinese can be written in two very different character styles—traditional (used in Taiwan, Hong Kong) and simplified (used in PRC and Singapore).

Despite the global spread of the Internet, it is still strongly influenced by its history in the United States. The Internet was originally developed in the United States as a military communications platform and later developed into a mechanism for sharing research data among scientists. Then, it gradually developed into a communications tool for researchers at universities and other research facilities in general. The original programming languages relied on roman script, and the vast majority of early communication was conducted in English. The input and digital transmission of non-roman scripts was a significant problem for programmers for many years. The situation greatly improved with the advent of Unicode.[23] However, there is still the issue of the input device: even today, the QWERTY keyboard remains the main input system for most of the world's different languages. The very architecture of the machine/human interface thus requires that users of different scripts familiarize themselves with roman type.

The historical dominance of English has resulted in numerous other problems for non-English users. Technical computer language, for instance, because of the primacy of US companies such as IBM and Apple, has been developed in English. This leads to problems when computer interfaces are translated into other languages. Nokia, for instance, found it difficult to come up with a Hindi interface when marketing their mobile phones in India, noting that "the terms call divert, data, fax, call register, prepaid credit, incoming call alert, and infrared, don't have good Hindi analogs."[24] Also, research shows how general search engines, such as Google and AltaVista, which were developed using algorithms based on roman script, are comparatively less able to comprehend queries in non-roman scripts, particularly Chinese, since they cannot identify word segments (Chinese is written with no spaces between the characters). [25]

However, the use of character-based scripts is not necessarily a handicap—although characters take longer to input, they take up less display space. Thus it is possible to display more complex messages on a phone's screen in Chinese characters than it is in roman script, making for a richer and more sophisticated short-messaging culture. In Chinese, for instance, popular fiction can be downloaded and read on the small screen. These issues of reshaping technology to allow for use of diverse non-roman scripts and languages, especially those of substantial customer "segments" in the prized "emerging" markets, are a key concern of leading technology companies, many of which are now basing at least some of their research and development in these countries (notably China and India).

In Japan, where prior to the late 1990s, there was not a widespread culture of PC use, it was not desktop computers that were the most popular platform for Internet access, but rather a range of mobile devices—particularly mobile phones—which were Internet-enabled as early as 1999.[26] As Manabe (Chapter 20, this volume) describes, Japanese phone carriers introduced 3G, which offers broadband Internet access over mobile phones, in 2001—three years before Verizon rolled out its 3G platform in the United States. As of March 2006, 3G accounted for 53 percent of all mobile subscribers in Japan. Likewise, polyphonic ringtones, or *chaku-mero* as they are called in Japan, were released only three years ago in the United States, but had been developed by Japanese karaoke companies by 1996 and were commonplace in Japan by 1999. Camera phones, too, were common throughout Japan by 2001, two years before they were first marketed in the United States. Hence, despite a slower start, Japan emerged as a leader in mobile Internet access and has much more sophisticated hardware (and software) available than in Australia or even Europe and the United States, thus challenging the model that sees the United States as "the supposed vanguard of the information society."[27] As Eunice Yoon points out, "The iPhone is so yesterday in Asia."[28]

Korea also came into the Internet age in a particular manner. Thanks to a range of factors, including Korea's topography and population distribution (almost three-quarters of the population live in seven major cities that are dense with high-rise apartment complexes equipped with high-speed

Internet lines) and early government initiatives, Korea has been celebrated as one of the most broad-banded countries in the world. One of the commonly observed features of Korean Internet culture has been the café-like *bangs*, venues for sociability and online gaming.[29] Another key aspect of Korean Internet culture is that the majority of the population own Internet-enabled mobile phones. Korean users are among the most proactive in the world in creating their own online web content. Particularly important is Cyworld's "mini-hompy." These are personalized web pages that can be easily updated with text, pictures, video, and sound. In Korea, it is normal for young people to update their mini-hompys several times a day with news and images about whom they have met and what they are doing. Friends visit each other's hompys to find out what is going on (see Chapters 14 and 15, this volume). As work by Larissa Hjorth has shown, when Korean students move from their home environment—characterized by high levels of network bandwith and media convergence in order to study abroad—they are bewildered by the comparatively poor network services provided in supposedly advanced nations such as Australia that make it impossible to replicate their home Internet environment while overseas.[30] Cases such as this must surely make us rethink the Internet as a truly "international" phenomenon.

Accessing the Internet via a small mobile device is going to be very different from accessing it via a PC—different hardware both enables and disables certain kinds of use and creates particular kinds of Internet experiences. Similarly, the wider telecommunications environment of different societies (such as Korea and Australia), which is determined as much by population densities and natural topography as by government policies and strategies, has an enormous impact on the kinds of electronic cultures that develop around the Internet.

Therefore, when thinking about "the Internet" it is important to remember that we are dealing with a range of different histories and experiences, and that we should not generalize based on "our" use of the Internet to that of other people, even other people in our own communities. It is not really possible to talk about "the Internet" as if it were a single phenomenon or has a simple history.

THE IMPLICATIONS FOR INTERNET STUDIES

One of the important contributions of Internet studies as a field has been the recognition of the Internet as a diverse assemblage of technologies, applications, and cultural practices. Against the tendency to black-box the Internet, to see it still infused with the impulse of early encounters and scholarship as something unified in its forms, Internet studies has contributed insights. In particular, that while there certainly are things that can be said about the Internet as a whole, it is crucial to come to grips with the very different sorts of communicative structures and cultures of use that characterize, say, email lists, as opposed to web-based chat or instant messaging. Therefore we see the important work that is undertaken to describe, analyze, and theorize particular Internet forms, and how users are arranged, publics and audiences are created, and relations of consumption and production are reconfigured. What are the types and genres of blogs, for instance? What are the effects and politics of different collaborative software, such as Wikis? Here we see exploration of the various particular "cultures" of the Internet that contribute to a broader, ongoing assessment of questions relating to the Internet and culture at more general levels.

We think this kind of nuanced approach to studying the Internet has yielded much. What we think is now imperative, and we hope is indicated in this collection, is the need to take this work further still by recognizing the very different shaping of "big" and "little" cultures of the Internet in particular contexts—and by reformulating general assumptions and concepts of the Internet informed by knowledge of these diverse international Internets.

The field of Internet studies has probably not been helped in this task by some of the influential ways that the Internet was imagined during its rise to prominence in the 1990s. We are thinking here of the preoccupation with theorizing the Internet as a singular cyber "space," as "virtual," or as "deterritorialized" and "borderless." Surprisingly, perhaps, the Internet was imagined as the eminent global technology, yet its actual international instantiations were not being realized. There is a fascinating revisionist account yet to be written of the history of these concepts of the Internet. With this in mind, it is instructive to contrast the field of Internet studies with that of mobile phone studies. The study of the mobile phone really emerged in earnest in the 2000s, whereas the field of Internet studies was already taking shape in various forms in the mid-1990s. There is something quite striking about the themes, concepts, and methods of mobile studies and their focus on, say, mobiles and communication, the social implications of mobiles, place and mobiles, mobiles and the body, and mobiles and fashion.[31] To be sure, mobile studies draw more heavily from, say, sociology and ethnography, than Internet studies has done (at least initially). Also, the mobile phone itself, while permitting communication and interaction among people who are widely dispersed, has also been associated with the intimate and personal, and the irruption of this into the public. Deixis here has been a salient theme in mobiles—with one of the most common utterances of the user being, "where are you now?" While still dominated by researchers, organizations, and institutions from wealthier countries, especially Europe, mobile studies does have a strong, if still quite incomplete, recognition of the international development of the mobile.

Such critiques of Internet studies have been made from a range of perspectives, many of which we have found influential. Cultural movements of the Internet itself have often been the most effective and prompt resources for alternative conceptions, as, for instance, in the phenomenon Geert Lovink theorizes as "critical Internet cultures."[32] Important work on race and the

Internet, for instance, has called attention to the social and political constitution of the Internet and its colonizing and oppressive logics, and how this either excludes or overlooks significant groups of users.[33] Debates on access, use, and representation figured under the North American rubric of "digital divide" also raised questions about what the Internet was assumed to be. Then the growing social and civil society movements around control for the Internet and telecommunications infrastructures, codes, and cultures, that coalesced around flashpoints such as "information superhighway" debates, domain-name regulation, and then the grandly-titled World Summit of the Information Society (WSIS; see Goggin [Chapter 4], this volume), eventually saw actors in other parts of the world than the United States and Europe figure into the definition of the Internet. Other accounts of the shaping of the Internet are increasingly being contributed from other literatures and disciplines, such as the field of development and Information and Communication Technologies.

DIRECTIONS FOR FUTURE RESEARCH

Despite the rapid development of the Internet as a multilingual environment, English is likely to remain the most influential online language, even as the percentage of traffic in English continues to diminish relative to newly emergent languages such as Chinese and Spanish. The power of English is, after all, apparent in the architecture of the Internet: uniform resource locators and domain names are still technically rooted in roman script,[34] the QWERTY keyboard remains the main human/machine interface for many languages, coding problems remain for the transfer and display of non-roman scripts, and existing search engines work best for English-language queries. Furthermore, a disproportionate amount of the world's information is stored in English: a glance at the number of articles in Wikipedia, for instance, shows that at 1.7 million, there are more than three times as many entries in English as there are in German, which has the second largest number.[35] However, despite the clear importance of attending to the Internet's Anglophone origins, in this introduction we have been arguing that it is necessary for Internet studies to take greater account of developments in the non-Anglophone world and to qualify the conception of the Internet as a "global" technology with increased recognition of its very local histories and cultures of use.[36]

There are signs that this broader perspective is increasingly being taken up both on the conference circuit and in the number of collections and individual papers being published that focus on non-Anglophone cultural spheres.[37] International meetings, such as the 2005 International Conference on Mobile Communication and Asian Modernities[38] in Hong Kong and the Internationalizing Internet Studies[39] workshop held as part of the Association of Internet Researchers Annual Conference in Australia in

2006, proved valuable forums for promoting discussion among researchers working on a range of non-Anglophone Internet environments.

At these events, concern was expressed regarding the ongoing dominance of US-based research within the developing field of Internet studies. When viewed from outside, the mainstream of North American Internet studies can appear rather self-involved, with its unquestioned assumption that the most interesting and most important sites for Internet analysis are US-based (or at least English-language based). This is underlined by the fact that the general surveys and collections designed to give an overview of "cyberculture" or Internet studies discussed earlier tend only to include a few selections of work from outside the Anglophone world, giving the impression that this work is tagged on rather than central to the way in which these overviews have been conceived. Given that the world's most richly funded research institutions, the most influential university presses, and the biggest market for English-language publications in the humanities and social sciences are all located within a single nation, this US-centrism has real implications for those working outside this Anglophone "center."[40]

Indeed, many Internet researchers working "outside" the Anglophone world sometimes find it a challenge to publish their work because US-based publishers presume that the market for such work will be limited since the majority readership (that is, within the United States) will be unfamiliar with the material and unlikely to set it as course material. These "Anglo-American gatekeepers" are also generally only likely to respond to publications that "address intellectual questions of interest to them and their colleagues," although these questions might be quite peripheral to the interests of the author and his or her regional readership.[41] All too often, "articles that do not have traction with Anglo-American scholars" are rejected by major publishers.[42]

It is also very difficult to convince publishers to go to the "extra expense" of typesetting non-roman scripts since they consider this information redundant to most Anglophone readers, despite the fact that Chinese characters, for instance, are intelligible across the cultural spheres of China, Japan, and Korea. There is a lack of recognition that English is a second language for many of the world's most highly educated people (who are likely readers of such academic texts) and that monolingualism is a characteristic only of *native* English-speaking academics.

Moreover, those working on non-Anglophone Internet cultures, particularly those in Asia, have reported difficulties in receiving useful feedback on work submitted to mainstream Anglophone journals. Not only does such work seem to take longer to review, but given the very small number of people working in English on Japanese, Chinese, and particularly Korean Internet cultures, it can be very difficult to locate peer reviewers with the necessary background. All too often, reviewers with general (read Anglophone) expertise are chosen and are not always best placed to give constructive feedback. The US-dominated academic and publishing system necessarily results in a highly uneven distribution of scholarly and cultural capital, since media studies scholars from Helsinki to Tokyo who wish to gain an international audience for their work have no choice but to acquire an understanding of the way in which Internet studies is framed in the Anglophone world. Yet, reverse flows of influence from the "margins" to the "center" seldom take place.

It is possible for media studies scholars working in English (both as the language of research as well as publication) to build successful careers while remaining almost completely ignorant of the global diversity of non-Western (and also non-American Western) Internet cultures and histories. We still live in a scholarly environment in which North American Internet cultures and theoretical paradigms are often presumed to be primary and general, while non-American cultures, both Western and non-Western, are framed as particular and secondary. We hope that an increase in conferences, workshops, edited collections, and other projects will enable transnational dialogues that challenge the current theoretical primacy of Anglophone theory and experience, but equally importantly begin to build cross-linkages among emerging media studies researchers who work within and on non-Anglophone cultures from all over the world. Clearly this volume has affiliations with broader work in cultural and media studies that also seeks to acknowledge and reflect upon the international nature of contemporary global developments.[43] The collection presented here, arising from just such a workshop entitled "Internationalizing Internet Studies," is offered as a step in this direction.

ACKNOWLEDGMENT

We gratefully acknowledge the support of the Australian Research Council Cultural Research Network, and its members, which made this project possible. We also wish to thank Alice Crawford for compiling the book's index.

NOTES

1. Mizuko Ito, Daisuke Okabe, and Misa Matsuda, eds., *Personal, Portable, Pedestrian: Mobile Phones in Japanese Life* (Cambridge, MA: MIT Press, 2005), 9.
2. Misa Matsuda, "Discourses of Keitai in Japan," in *Personal, Portable, Pedestrian: Mobile Phones in Japanese Life,* ed. Mizuko Ito, Daisuke Okabe, and Misa Matsuda (Cambridge, MA: MIT Press, 2005), 37.
3. Mizuko Ito, introduction, to *Personal, Portable, Pedestrian: Mobile Phones in Japanese Life,* ed. Mizuko Ito, Daisuke Okabe, and Misa Matsuda (Cambridge, MA: MIT Press, 2005), 7.
4. For instance, Kristóf Nyíri, ed., *A Sense of Place: The Global and the Local in Mobile Communication* (Vienna: Passagen Verlag, 2005); Peilin Luo, Leopoldina Fortunati, and Shanhua Yang, eds., *New Technologies in Global Societies* (Singapore: World Scientific, 2006).

5. "Top Ten Languages Used on the Net," http://www.internetworldstats.com/stats7.htm (accessed May 4, 2007).

6. Source, Internet World Stats, figures as of June 2006, "China: Internet Usage Stats and Telecommunications Market Report," http://www.internetworldstats.com/asia/cn.htm (accessed May 8, 2007).

7. Barry Wellman and Caroline Haythornwaite, eds., *The Internet in Everyday Life* (Oxford, UK: Blackwell, 2002); David Gauntlett and Ross Horley, eds., *Web.Studies*, 2nd ed. (London: Arnold, 2004); David Bell and Barbara M. Kennedy, eds., *The Cybercultures Reader*, 2nd ed. (London: Routledge, 2007).

8. Donna Gibbs and Kerri-Lee Krause, eds., *Cyberlines: Languages and Cultures of the Internet* (Melbourne, Australia: James Nicholas Publishers, 2000); Susan Herring, ed., *Computer-Mediated Communication: Linguistic, Social, and Cross-Cultural Perspectives* (Amsterdam: J. Benjamins, 1996).

9. Chris Berry, Fran Martin, and Audrey Yue, eds., *Mobile Cultures: New Media in Queer Asia* (Durham, NC: Duke University Press, 2003).

10. Yukiko Nishimura, "Linguistic Innovations and Interactional Features of Casual Online Communications in Japanese," *Journal of Computer Mediated Communication* 9, no. 1 (2003), http://jcmc.indiana.edu/vol9/issue1/nishimura.html

11. Daniel Cunliffe and Susan Herring, eds., "Minority Languages, Multimedia and the Web," special issue, *The New Review of Multimedia and Hypermedia* 11, no. 2 (2005).

12. Brenda Danet and Susan C. Herring, eds., *The Multilingual Internet: Language, Culture, and Communication Online* (New York: Oxford University Press, 2007).

13. An indicative, and certainly not exhaustive, list includes: Rasha A. Abdulla, *The Internet in the Arab World: Egypt and Beyond* (New York: Peter Lang, 2007); Neil Blair, *Inuit in Cyberspace: Embedding Offline Identities Online* (Copenhagen: Museum Tusculanum Press, 2003); Gerard Goggin, ed., *Virtual Nation: The Internet in Australia* (Sydney: University of New South Wales Press, 2004); Daniel Miller and Don Slater's study of Trinidad Internet, in their *The Internet: An Ethnographic Approach* (London: Routledge, 2000); Cecilia Ng and Swasti Mitter, eds., *Gender and the Digital Economy: Perspectives from the Developing World* (Thousand Oaks, CA: Sage, 2005); Zixue Tai, *The Internet in China: Cyberspace and Civil Society* (London: Routledge, 2006); Deborah Wheeler, *The Internet in the Middle East: Global Expectations and Local Imaginations in Kuwait* (Albany: State University of New York Press, 2006); Yongming Zhou, *Historicizing Online Politics: Telegraphy, the Internet, and Political Participation in China* (Stanford, CA: Stanford University Press, 2006).

14. Ito, introduction, 3.

15. Paul Kei Matsuda, "Negotiation of Identity and Power in a Japanese Online Discourse Community," *Computers and Composition* 19 (2002): 39–55; Nishimura, "Linguistic Innovations,"

16. David Gauntlett, "Preface," in Nanette Gottlieb and Mark McLelland, *Japanese Cybercultures*, (London: Routledge, 2003)xii; emphasis in the original.

17. Ito, introduction, 4. See also Matsuda, "Negotiation of Identity,"

18. For recognition of the importance of the local in the Internet, see Rafael Capurro, Johannes Frühbauer, and Thomas Hausmanninger, eds., *Localizing the Internet: Ethical Aspects in Intercultural Perspective* (München: Fink Verlag, 2007).

19. Howard Rheingold, *The Virtual Community: Homesteading on the Electronic Frontier* (Reading, MA: Addison-Wesley, 1993); Kevin Kelly, *New*

Rules for the New Economy (New York: Viking, 1998). See Geert Lovink's critique of *Wired* magazine's cyberoptimism in *Dark Fiber: Tracking Critical Internet Culture* (Cambridge, MA: MIT Press, 2002).

20. Exceptions include Axel Bruns and Joanne Jacobs, eds., *Uses of Blogs* (New York: Peter Lang, 2006); and Geert Lovink, *Zero Comments: Blogging and Critical Internet Culture* (New York: Routledge, 2007).

21. Yu Haiqing, "Blogging Everyday Life in Chinese Internet Culture," *Asian Studies Review*, 31 no. 4, 423-433 2007.

22. Nanette Gottlieb, *Word-Processing Technology in Japan: Kanji and the Keyboard* (Oxford: RoutledgeCurzon, 2000).

23. Gottlieb, *Word-Processing Technology in Japan*, 186–187; also, cf. extended discussion in the introduction to Danet and Herring's *Multilingual Internet*.

24. Katja Konkka, "Indian Needs—Cultural End-User Research in Mumbai," in *Mobile Usability: How Nokia Changed the Face of the Mobile Phone*, ed. Christian Lindholm, Turkka Keinonen, and Harri Kiljander (New York: McGraw-Hill, 2003), 108.

25. Haidar Moukdad and Hong Cui, "How Do Search Engines Handle Chinese Queries?" *Webology* 2, no. 3 (2005), http://www.webology.ir/2005/v2n3/a17.html

26. Gottlieb and McLelland, *Japanese Cybercultures*, 3–4.

27. Ito, introduction, 3.

28. Eunice Yoon, "The iPhone is so yesterday in Asia," CNN, www.cnn.com (January 13, 2007).

29. Heejin Lee, Robert O'Keefe, and Kyounglim Yun, "The Growth of Broadband and Electronic Commerce in South Korea: Contributing Factors," *The Information Society* 19 (2003): 81–93.

30. Larissa Hjorth, "Home and Away: A Case Study of Cyworld Minihompy by Korean Students Studying Abroad," *Asian Studies Review*, 31 no. 4 397-407 2007, in press.

31. Barry Brown, Nicola Green, and Richard Harper, eds., *Wireless World: Social, Cultural and Interactional Issues in Mobile Communications and Computing* (London: Springer-Verlag, 2001); Richard Harper, Leysia Palen, and Alex Taylor, eds., *The Inside Text: Social, Cultural and Design Perspectives on SMS* (Dordrecht, The Netherlands: Springer, 2005); Leopoldina Fortunati, James E. Katz, and Raimonda Riccini, eds., *Mediating the Human Body: Technology, Communication, and Fashion* (Mahwah, NJ: Lawrence Erlbaum, 2003); James E. Katz and Mark Aakhus, eds., *Perpetual Contact: Mobile Communication, Private Talk, Public Performance* (Cambridge: Cambridge University Press, 2002); James E. Katz, ed., *Machines That Become Us: The Social Context of Personal Communication Technology* (New Brunswick, NJ: Transaction, 2003); Heather Horst and Daniel Miller, *The Cell Phone: An Anthropology of Communication* (Oxford: Berg, 2006).

32. See Geert Lovink, *Dark Fiber*.

33. Beth E. Kolko, Lisa Nakamura, and Gilbert B. Rodman, eds., *Race in Cyberspace*. (New York: Routledge, 2000); Lisa Nakamura, *Cybertypes: Race, Ethnicity, and Identity on the Internet* (New York: Routledge, 2002); Linda Leung, *Virtual Ethnicity: Race, Resistance and the World Wide Web* (Burlington, VT: Ashgate, 2005); Mark McLelland, "'Race' on the Japanese Internet: Discussing Korea and Koreans on 2-channeru," *New Media & Society*, in press.

34. "[I]t is not possible for the Domain Name System (DNS) as it stands to incorporate full Unicode script encoding to be used in top-level domains,"

declare Danny Butt and Norbert Klein, in their "Internet Governance and Socio-Cultural Inclusion," *Internet Governance: Asia-Pacific Perspectives*, ed. Danny Butt (Bangkok: UNDP Asia-Pacific Development Information Programme), 78; Butt and Klein emphasize that "the internationalization of domain names is a cultural issue. There remain serious problems with both the ability of the DNS system to handle non-roman domain names, as well as inadequate procedures to facilitate this occurring." (p. 82).

35. See "List of Wikipedias," http://meta.wikimedia.org/wiki/List_of_Wikipedias (accessed May 7, 2007).

36. Here we would point to long-standing work on cross-cultural, intercultural, and ethical dimensions of technology, communication, and culture represented in the "Cultural Attitudes toward Technology and Communication" international conferences and associated work, such as Charles Ess, ed., *Culture, Technology, Communication: Towards an Intercultural Global Village* (Albany: State University of New York Press, 2001); Charles Ess and Fay Sudweeks, eds., special issue on "Culture and Computer Mediated Communication," *Journal of Computer-Mediated Communication* 11, no. 1 (2005), http://jcmc.indiana.edu/vol11/issue1/; M. Thorseth and Charles Ess, eds., *Technology in a Multicultural and Global Society* (Trondheim, Norway: Norwegian University of Science and Technology, 2005).

37. For instance, Raul Pertierra and Ilpo Koskinen, eds., *The Social Construction and Usage of Communication Technologies: European and Asian Experiences* (Singapore: Singapore University Press, 2007).

38. See conference website, http://enweb.cityu.edu.hk/mobile_comm/

39. See workshop website, http://www.capstrans.edu.au/about/projects/inter-internet-studies.html

40. This argument references the debate around the positioning of "Asian" sexualities in an academic field dominated by European and US-based theory and theorists developed by Peter Jackson, Fran Martin, Mark McLelland, and Audrey Yue. See "About AsiaPacifiQueer: Responding to Disciplinary Exclusion," http://apq.anu.edu.au/about.php

41. Colin Day, "Enabling Intra-Asian Conversation," *Academic Publishing Today* Summer (2007), 7, http://www.iias.nl/nl/icas5/ICAS5_2007_07.pdf.

42. Ibid.

43. Ackbar Abbas and John Nguyet Erni, eds., *Internationalizing Cultural Studies: An Anthology* (Malden, MA: Blackwell, 2005); Daya Thussu, ed., *Internationalizing Media Studies* (New York: Routledge, 2009).

2 What Cyberspace?
Traveling Concepts in Internet Research

Susanna Paasonen

The figure of cyberspace, first introduced by cyberpunk author William Gibson in his 1982 short story *Burning Chrome* (or, depending on the interpretation, his 1984 novel, *Neuromancer*), was soon adapted to describe the communicative and experiential possibilities of the Internet. More than a medium, the Internet of the early 1990s was seen to open up a space, an alternative reality, or a society of the mind invested with novel possibilities of networking and exchange.[1] While cyberspace made its way to, and established its position in, discourses both popular and academic in English-speaking countries—North America in particular—the term did not gain similar transparency elsewhere. In my native country of Finland, cyberspace translations and various "cyber" prefixes were used up until the mid-1990s, but the term has since become somewhat anachronistic and is infrequently used. Consequently, "cyberculture studies" require conceptual analysis and contextualization when discussed in the Finnish university classroom. In such moments of translation and reflection, research terminology loses its transparency: being made strange by local terminology, it is reframed as specific, limited, and even problematic.

Derived from *cybernetics*—the study of communications and control in machines and organic systems—cyberspace is examplary of how terminology travels across national and disciplinary boundaries, crossing different genres and contexts of writing and publishing in the process. As terms travel, they are reworked, debated, and redefined. Drawing on Mieke Bal's work on traveling concepts, this chapter investigates the travels and meanings of cyberspace as a research concept, as well as the kinds of shifts that have occurred during its voyages from casual use to research practices and back again.[2] Using the Finnish context as a point of departure and comparison, the chapter investigates the applicability of Anglo-American conceptualizations and the kinds of Internets that they give rise to.

WHAT'S IN A NAME?

Ways of making new media familiar depend on the chosen terminology, metaphors, and associations through which the possibilities and meanings of the medium are envisioned and depicted. While some of these framings are soon forgotten, others become part of the general lexicon. To use one example, as mobile phones (then bulky and hardly entirely portable) were first introduced in Finland in the 1980s, they were referred to not only as "travel phones" (*matkapuhelin*)—a term still in general use—but also as "shoe phones" (*kenkäpuhelin*), in reference to the fantastic telecommunication technologies employed by the 1960s TV secret agent, Maxwell Smart. Whereas the English terms *mobile phone* and *cell phone* refer to mobility and telephone technology, the Finnish language favors pet names, such as *känny* and *kännykkä* (liberally translated as "little hand"), which were originally introduced by Nokia staff in reference to extensions of a child's hand.[3] Similar pet names are in use in various European languages—in German, mobile phones are also known as "little hands" (*händchen*) and in Italian as "little phones" (*telefonino*). These formulations point to ways in which communication technology has been appropriated and personalized in practices of everyday life.[4]

Naming new media is also a means to domesticate it, to make it familiar. Terminologies applied contribute to certain understandings concerning the media in question and frame it in specific ways. The term *Internet*, "the network of networks," refers to a wide range of different, historically specific technical solutions, innovations, and uses (and is therefore a highly contingent point of reference). The word "Internet" gradually came into use in the 1980s as an umbrella term for the various existing networks, applications, and their interconnections, and for the uses of the Transmission Control Protocol/Internet Protocol (TCP/IP) protocol in particular.[5] Perhaps due to the technical connotation of the Internet, various abbreviations and considerably more imaginative synonyms have been launched since the late 1980s. In addition to nets, networks, and webs used to describe the operating principles of decentralized communication and information exchange, the Internet has been wrapped in various metaphorical terminologies, such as information superhighways, oceans of data, and cyberspace. Its uses again have been conceptualized through tropes of mobility and travel: one is said to "go" and "be" online, "visit" sites, "navigate"—and, especially in the 1990s—to "surf." As Internet scholar Lisa Nakamura points out, Internet use has been figured through a vocabulary of tourism, fun, adventure, and leisure.[6] This terminology differs from the ways of discussing previous forms of "new media," such as television, radio, or telephone. While all these media have been associated with the possibilities of overcoming and bridging geographical distance, ease of communication, and radical transformations in the availability of information, they have not—perhaps with the exception of the "ether" of early twentieth century radio amateurs—been conceptualized as spaces in themselves.[7]

Spatial metaphors frame the uses and experiences of the Internet, as well as the medium itself, but with considerable lingual and cultural differences. Cyberspace remains a general term in English and a key concept of Internet research. Yet, this is not the case on an international level. The term has certainly been translated, as the European examples *cyberrymd* (Swedish), *cyber espace* (French), *ciberespacio* (Spanish), or *Cyberraum* (German) illustrate, but it is not synonymous with the Internet in research, journalism or quotidian discourses. As I discuss below in more detail, in the context of Finland, researchers writing in languages other than English do not routinely resort to cyberspace when conceptualizing Internet-related phenomena.

Metaphors—both spatial and other—construct and shape the reality they describe: they are productive in a performative sense.[8] Scholars participate in giving shape to the Internet thorough their ways of describing the medium. Terms and metaphors are not neutral words used instrumentally or interchangeably for describing existing phenomena—and this is even less the case when these words are used as research concepts. Concepts "distort, unfix, and inflect" the object they represent while also providing a common language for discussions concerning it (Bal, *Travelling Concepts*, 22). My argument, then, is not that the framings and terms discussed in this chapter are somehow false or inaccurate and should be replaced with better ones. Rather, my interests lay in investigating the implications and frames of reference of traveling concepts that are more or less faithful to their native regions.

SUPERHIGHWAYS AND FRONTIERS

Beginning in the early 1990s—and especially since the introduction of graphic web interfaces in 1993—the Internet was wrapped in various metaphors of manifest regional specificity. The Vice President of the United States, Al Gore, launched the term *information superhighway* to describe the networking possibilities of the Internet. The National Information Infrastructure initiative aimed to transform the lives of the American people and contribute to national economic growth.[9] The information superhighway metaphor accentuated mobility through analogies to familiar forms of transport, and the creation of the national road network; like highways, the Internet would bind the continent in one network while eventually stretching across the globe and supporting democracy and welfare all over the world.[10]

Variations of the information superhighway metaphor have been applied internationally. The analogy of the Internet and open roads is recognizable in such iconic representations as the front cover of Bill Gates' 1996 book *The Road Ahead* (also envisioning a networked world), which shows the Microsoft CEO dressed casually in black with his hands in his pockets, standing on an open road with a flat, and characteristically American, landscape stretching out behind him.

A popular term among politicians and businessmen alike, the information superhighway was certainly not the only Internet metaphor launched in the early 1990s. The deeply American metaphor of the electronic frontier created an analogy to the "Wild West." The West's first settlers, also known as pioneers, headed out to the patches of land allocated to them, occupied land previously belonging to the native population, and lived without a set social structure—a state often translated as freedom. In American popular culture, the Western frontier is nothing short of a mythical national symbol of freedom, adventure, and possibility. As David Silver points out, texts written by activists, writers, and scholars in the early 1990s were heavy with references to the "American pioneer spirit" and its revitalization online. Writers like John Perry Barlow, Howard Rheingold, and Douglas Rushkoff applied the frontier terminology when describing the pioneering users exploring the unknown borderlands of the Internet—as already suggested by the subtitle of Rheingold's 1993 book on virtual communities, *Homesteading on the Electronic Frontier* (Silver, "Looking Backwards, Looking Forwards," 21). The terminology of pioneers and frontiers creates analogies to past events, national mythology, and romanticized, selective narratives concerning them, while framing the Internet as a terrain of adventure, freedom, and community independent of governmental regulation (Chun, *Control and Freedom*, 51).[11] In doing so, they also create hierarchies separating the explorers, pioneers, and early arrivals from newcomers.[12]

Considering the speed of modem connections in the early and mid-1990s, the experience of command lines, or the heavily textual feel of the first browser interfaces, the analogue between Internet users and settlers on the Western frontier may have been feeble. Yet, the point of metaphors is not to reflect the existing state of affairs inasmuch as it is to frame this state in a certain way. Information superhighways implying speed and global reach or frontiers connoting unlimited possibilities worked to fuel interest toward information networks among private users, companies, and governmental bodies alike, in line with the general Internet hype of the decade.

ENTER CYBERSPACE

John Perry Barlow—a former lyricist for The Grateful Dead, Internet consultant, and lobbyist for freedom of speech online—has been exceptionally active in the production of Internet metaphors. In 1990, Barlow served as one of the founders of the Electronic Frontier Foundation and he also claims to have been the first to apply the metaphor of cyberspace to the Internet—cyberspace being the most widespread and influential of 1990s metaphors used for figuring the Internet. Cyberspace, as coined by Gibson, is a disembodied parallel reality reached via neural connections in which all the world's data is stored. Dangerous yet fascinating, cyberspace enables flying and adventure: it is a novel frontier that Barlow associates with individual freedom and expression. If the electronic frontier made use of a historical parallel, the metaphor of cyberspace was inspired by cyberpunk fiction—but with a necessarily no less explicit American emphasis. In his 1996 "Declaration of the Independence of Cyberspace," Barlow emulated the US Declaration of Independence while arguing for the sovereignty of cyberspace: like Gore's information superhighway, Barlow's cyberspace was embedded in a fundamentally national rhetoric.

In the early 1990s, cyberspace was used to describe both virtual reality applications and the Internet, and the boundary between the two was also blurred in cinematic depictions of immersion in virtual environments, starting with Disney's *Tron* (1982), and continuing in motion pictures as varied as *Lawnmover Man* (1992), *Lawnmover Man II: Beyond Cyberspace* (1996), *Hackers* (1995), and the *Matrix* trilogy (1999–2003). Potential conceptual slippage did not impede on the use of cyberspace as a research concept in studies of so-called new media.[13] Gibson's fictions have been particularly inspirational in terms of Internet research and development: cyberspace has been interpreted as social theory, a vision of future technology worth striving toward, and even as a "self-fulfilling prophecy" that will come into being as computers are connected to the Internet (Shields, "Looking Backwards, Looking Forwards", 67; cf. Chun, *Control and Freedom*, 42).[14] Although cyberspace may not be the most fitting term for describing the experiences of email, search engines, video downloads, or databases, it enjoys continuing popularity among scholars.

Cyberspace was established as a research concept in studies of new media largely dominated by North American voices and perspectives. Cyberspace is used to refer to the trans- and multilocal networks of online communication, the accessibility of data, and experiences thereof. It marks the differences between the Internet and previous media technologies, but equally denotes the virtual nature of contemporary media culture from television to simulated environments (Burrows, "Cyberspace as Social Theory", 240).[15] The notion of cyberspace both encapsulates and assumes the division of "online" and "offline" to the degree that the former becomes an alternative reality of sorts. This division has again worked to draw attention away from the contexts and conditions of Internet use while bringing to the forefront forms of online communication and interaction (and various kinds of online communities in particular). As artificial as the online/offline divide may be, it has been highly influential in the development of Internet research, methods of framing studies, and phrasing research questions.[16] The appeal and influence of cyberspace terminology in the English-speaking academia is largely due to transparency it has gained through reiteration. In the course of reiteration, its links to dystopian cyberpunk fiction and the declarations and manifestos of the early 1990s have been loosened, and as cyberspace was established as a research term, its specificities and limitations were rendered less striking. The figure of cyberspace comes with a legacy that is, nevertheless, partly effaced as the term has been reapplied and appropriated as research concept. Given its extended use, the figure of cyberspace has had more considerable and enduring impact than those of the information superhighway or the electronic frontier. These have remained descriptions and labels rather than research concepts.

Addressing the applicability of research concepts, Peter Hitchcock argues that their validity depends on whether they describe the phenomenon studied or whether they also have some explanatory power.[17] The division of description and explanation is rather difficult to make with cyberspace, given that the concept works to frame and give shape to the object that it describes. Furthermore, cyberspace is partial as both a descriptive and explanatory concept. Since research concepts are preferably explicit, clear, and defined (Bal, *Travelling Concepts*, 22), the malleability of cyberspace debilitates its explanatory force. The term cyberspace has been used casually in literary and cinematic fiction, gaming, advertising, journalism, and research. Due to such travels, it can be seen as exemplary of the conflation of words, concepts, and labels, as discussed by Mieke Bal. According to Bal, the overlap of casual and theoretical language contributes to both "reluctance to discuss 'meaning' as an academic issue" and to the overextended use of concepts (Bal, *Travelling Concepts*, 26–27). Something of this kind seems to be at play with the notion of cyberspace. Cyberspace is a plastic concept, and because of its plasticity, it has limited descriptive force concerning the Internet. When used as labels in the sense of not explaining or specifying the phenomenon studied, but merely naming it, concepts "lose their working force; they are subject to fashion and quickly become meaningless" (Bal, *Travelling Concepts*, 23, 33). In both cases, the concept is deprived of its power of conceptualization. Cyberspace has possibly traveled a bit *too* much from one forum of discussion, writing, and publication to another and back, and become analytically ineffective in the process.

Cyberspace was fashionable and widely used as a label in the mid-1990s, a period that also saw an avalanche of other neologisms and cyber prefixes, such as cybersociety, cyberlove, cybersex, and cybergeneration. Meanwhile, teen fashions paraded cyber styles and logos on T-shirts, pants, bags, and hairdos. Cybercultural imaginations entered mainstream popular culture, while scholars weaved cyberpunk visions and promises of forthcoming technology together with cultural theory, often in highly speculative ways (Mäkelä, "Virtuaalitodellisuus," 147). Cyber terminology was central to the popularization of the Internet and helped to frame the medium as exciting, novel, and techno-futuristic, with support from contemporary print and screen fiction (Chun, *Control and Freedom*, 37). At the same time, the Internet was made familiar to the general public on the policy level. Information society discourses of the 1990s may have had techno-futuristic tones, but they were still a far cry from the cyberspace visions circulated in journalism and studies of new media alike.

INFORMATION INTENSITY: THE CASE OF FINLAND

Finland was not an early adopter of the Internet. International network connections were established from the United States to other NATO countries in the 1970s, whereas Finland—a neighboring country suspicious of the Soviet Union—got its FUNET (Finnish University Network) in 1984, some fifteen years after the launch of ARPANET. In the early 1990s, Finland experienced a deep economical recession (partly brought forth by the collapse of the Soviet Union, an important trading partner). Nokia, formerly known for manufacturing telephone cable, car tires, and rubber boots, became the symbol of the possible future, as the otherwise declining national economy was literally dependent on its success in mobile communications. This resulted in certain optimism toward new technology, as well as the linking of Nokia with the national economy and technology with the Finnish national image. Marja Vehviläinen has analyzed the uses of "hero figures" like the former Nokia CEO, Jorma Ollila, and Linus Torvalds, "the father of Linux," in the articulation and construction of technological nationalism and in presenting the nation as technologically advanced, innovative, and competitive.[18] In the late 1990s and early 2000s, American journalists visiting Finland crafted stories of this high-tech "Japan of Europe." Finnish media carefully followed newspaper and magazine articles depicting Finland as a technological wonderland, while Manuel Castells co-authored a book celebrating the Finnish information society model and its local applications.[19]

In Finland, the information society and new media technologies have been very much national projects. The case is not unique, as such. As the Finnish Ministry of Education promoted computer literacy as a means of national success in the mid-1990s, Estonia, a neighboring country that had been online since 1991, launched an initiative known as "Tiger's Leap" (*Tiigrihüppe*), aimed at equipping school children with ICT skills and helping Estonia to overcome the economical and cultural gap to the West created by forty years of Soviet rule. In both instances, ICT became a sign of things to come, a tool for the future as well as a means of national self-promotion for small countries bordering the Baltic Sea.

In Finland, as in the other Nordic countries, the information society has been a dominant frame for the Internet. Throughout the 1990s, national and local information society agendas and strategies were launched for wiring the public schools and libraries, for increasing the use of computers and the Internet among different demographic groups, and for crafting those users into appropriately computer-savvy citizens. Notions of progress through technology became ingrained both in strategy and policy documents and journalism covering these developments.[20] With their information society projects and high percentages of Internet users, Finland, Sweden, and Denmark battled over the title of the "most wired country" in the late 1990s (Finland eventually lost the battle, with Sweden reigning supreme). Finnish information society agendas and strategies of the 1990s focused on national competitiveness in terms of technological access and user skills. The focus on content was a later concern, pronounced in initiatives such as "Content Finland," undertaken in 1999 and aimed at making Finland an internationally leading country in content production. Public efforts were made for creating services in Finnish (a marginal language by any standard, spoken by some six million people globally), however the creation of a "Finnish Internet" has not been a pronounced concern.[21] Finland is a bilingual country, where Swedish is (at least technically) understood by most citizens, but services in English are perhaps even more accessible to the younger generation: Habbo Hotel is among the success stories of Finnish Internet, but Finns make equal use of MySpace, YouTube, or Blogger. On a national level, the Internet and mobile communications have both worked as a means of profiling the nation and projecting a certain kind of national image.

The central role of information society projects in Finland echoes a broader use of information as a key term in computer-mediated communications. In Finnish, computers, known in the past decades as "electronic brains" and "calculators," translate literally as "information/knowledge machines" (*tietokone*) and computing as "information processing" (*tietojenkäsittely*).[22] Information society terminology has been easy to align with this already established terminology, which frames ICT uses in terms of exchange, searching, and information management. This highly rational framing corresponds to the information-intense citizens mastering ICTs as part of their civic skills, as presupposed and envisioned in information society agendas.

Information society has been at the core of Finnish Internet research in which democracy, citizenship, and the public sphere have remained central concerns.[23] In addition, research has revolved around questions of everyday use and domestication of the media—the latter also being a strong research paradigm on a Nordic level.[24] Research projects have investigated the local uses of information and communication technologies in rural and urban areas, focusing on the ways in which people negotiate the role of media technology in their everyday lives as tools, objects, and areas of expertise.[25] Both of these research paradigms are concerned with questions of agency and context: rather than addressing online phenomena as occurring in "cyberspace," they focus on social contexts and conditions of Internet use, and the different locations and agencies of Internet users as citizens. The division of online and offline, as implied in the terminology of frontiers or cyberspace, is ill-fitted with the highly local ways in which Internet uses have been discussed and studied.

All in all, the Internet and mobile communications have been "domesticated" in Finland. Over 70 percent of adult Finns use the Internet, while mobile phone penetration is well over 90 percent of the entire population. Mobile phones are used for buying tickets for public transportation, getting quick loans with high interest rates, participating in late-night television chat shows, and managing personal relationships (in 2006, it was announced that the Finnish Prime Minister met his girlfriend through an online dating service and later broke off the relationship via SMS). The Internet has been similarly familiarized as a site for banking, purchasing fishing licenses, and selling off extra children's clothing. There are some similarities to the mobile cultures of Korea and Japan, yet it is noteworthy that, in spite of the welfare society model still prevalent in Finland, there have been virtually no public investments in general broadband infrastructure or access. Public institutions have been equipped with computers, but the spread of high-speed Internet connections and Wi-Fi has been largely left to the private sector. This has resulted in unequal access to broadband connections in the less-populated rural areas of the country (comprising the majority of its acreage), as well as to a general lack of free wireless services. In Helsinki, the capital, some buses and trams have free wireless connection courtesy of the city, while Wi-Fi access in cafés and public spaces, like parks, is sponsored by companies. The "information-intense citizen" is, then, first and foremost a consumer-citizen participating in the national information society project by using and subscribing to commercial services and purchasing consumer electronics.

TRANSLATING "THE INTERNATIONAL"

Internet, information networks, and the web were the primary terms used for the emerging network media in Finland in the 1990s. Translations of cyberspace (*kybertila* or *kyberavaruus*) were used in Finnish journalism and new media textbooks but, some exceptions aside,[26] there were no aims to establish it as an analytical concept. Rather, the notion of cyberspace has been an object of analysis and critique.[27] Cyber terminology soon went out of fashion in journalism, everyday speech, and academic studies alike, while the general domestication of the Internet became evident in the terminology used. The Net was translated (or, perhaps better, transliterated) somewhat diminutively as *netti* and Web as *webbi*, following the casual lexicon used with mobile communications. This terminology was normalized in both quotidian and academic speech, connoting ICT as something familiar, mundane, and approachable.

Meanwhile, cyberspace is no longer part of the language in journalism, research, computing, or programming, but has a slightly anachronistic appeal as a word that was trendy in the 1990s. During its travels to and in Finland, the term has become worn and somewhat quaint. The case is, of course, different in the United States and elsewhere in Anglophonic academia. While the term itself may be used with less vigor than it was ten years ago, it remains a central research concept. Reading Anglophonic Internet research in Finland necessitates translation and contextualization since their conceptualizations do not quite "travel" and are difficult to align with the local terminology. I suspect the situation to be similar in a range of other language environments.

Questions of conceptual travel, translation, and contextualization have become evident to me when teaching courses on Internet research and online communication in Finnish universities. There are few textbooks available, and these tend to be in English: studies of Internet research, then, necessitate studies of largely North American texts, case studies, and terminology. To use one example, the volume edited by Thomas Swiss in 2000, *Unspun: Key Concepts for Understanding the World Wide Web*, features contributors from the United States, Canada, and United Kingdom, and thinks through scholarly debates and conceptual histories from these regional contexts. Using this book for teaching Internet research elsewhere, however, necessitates not only translation, but also a reconsideration of the conceptual histories of the featured keywords—cyberspace included—and their relation to research that has taken place outside English-speaking academia. Overviews on the development of Internet research have had an equally strong Western and English-speaking bent.[28] The situation seems to be changing in some recent publications, such as the 2006 anthology, *Critical Cyberculture Studies*.[29] It nevertheless seems clear that the "disappearance of geography" and the "reorganization of space" diagnosed in relation to information and communication technologies[30] is yet to occur in the definition of the key concepts and overviews on the scholarly history of Internet research.

English-speaking academics often appear nonchalant in terms of the linguistic specificity of their chosen research concepts. In the Finnish classroom, the concept of cyberspace evokes debate and even confusion: it seems strongly associated with cyberpunk fiction, quaint and distant from the Finnish terminology currently in use. The appeal of cyberterminology is, however, equally evident. After reading textbooks in English, cyberterminology tends to find its way into student essays and other assignments, often with little conceptual reflection concerning its applicability to discussions at hand. In these moments, local conceptual practices and dominant research paradigms (namely information society research and contextual studies of new media) are replaced by cyberspace discourse that has, after having been recycled in English for well over a decade, reached a transparent and normative status due to which it apparently no longer *needs to be* an object of critical reflection. This results in a conceptual leap and a clash of different interpretative frameworks.

The dominant position of Anglophonic conceptualizations is hardly surprising, given the US influence in the development of Internet technology and content, as well as the general dominance of English in academia. In her analysis of the North American dominance and international translations of queer theory, Joanna Mizielinska provocatively argues that scholars arriving from regions considered "marginal" are expected to reproduce international—that is, American—scholarship, rather than to question or contribute to it, and therefore basically to confirm its rightness.[31] Theory formation and the definition of key concepts are far too often left to scholars representing the imagined center, while the rest of us are left with the task of applying these. In queer theory, as in Internet research, American scholarship tends to dominate to the degree of being conflated with the international: "'We' all name American tools, concepts and challenges as 'ours'" (Mizielinska, 93). Mizielinska provides numerous examples of such intellectual hegemony and its patronizing tendencies, which render some international case studies interesting and others less so. Academics from Eastern or North Europe are, for example, often asked to refer to more general, familiar, or "interesting" cases than the local ones they have been analyzing. This generally means replacing them with American ones. Scholars writing in and about areas and cultures more or less "off-center" are recurrently reminded of their positions and the particularity of their perspectives. This diverts attention away from the simple fact that *all* perspectives and examples are specific (Mizielinska, 94–98). As astutely pointed out by Kaarina Nikunen, generalizations are not general inasmuch as they are blind toward their own particularity.[32] The example of cyberspace and its varying degrees of conceptual transparency helps to make evident the particularity of research contexts—the particularity of North American research included. Local Internet histories and concepts question the analytical power of generalizations while also making the directions and stances from which these can be made in the first place visible.

In the early 1990s, the notion of cyberspace conflated cyberpunk fiction, virtual reality applications, and information networks in its visions of alternative experiential and communication environments (Mäkelä, "Virtuaalitodellisuus"). A similar idea remains alive in applications such as the currently popular—and widely publicized—Second Life, yet the concepts in use have undergone transformations. The more recent terminology, such as Web 2.0, semantic Web, and mobile or wireless Internet, is decidedly technical and descriptive in nature, referring to transformations brought forth by user-generated content such as Wikis, blogs, and social software (following the logic of upgrades) as well as, the logic of linking, categorizing and accessing information through different platforms. None of the terms explicitly envision alternative spaces or virtual worlds separate from the more human ones: they describe the shape of the medium rather than its potential future developments or user experiences. As online technologies have become increasingly ubiquitous and mobile, the division of online and offline is increasingly artificial and disabling in terms of understanding their uses or meanings. Rather than going online, users and machines alike are perpetually online, hence redefining the meaning of the very notion.

The mobility associated with wireless communications is a case apart from the leisurely terminology of surfing that was popular in the 1990s. In its newer variations, tropes of mobility imply that online technologies are neither fixed to specific sites of access, nor the incorporation of online technologies in everyday life. Focus on context and location, as pronounced in Finnish studies on online technologies, may be helpful in terms of understanding these developments. While the term *cyberculture* aims to describe exactly this kind of meshing of human and machine, offline and online, it also remains connected to the discursive legacy—and baggage—

of cyberdiscourse envisioning monolithic or placeless cyberspaces.[33] Individual scholars making use of cyberspace terminology are also subscribing to histories, assumptions, and associations that they may not acknowledge or even agree with—such as the fundamental division of the online and the offline. In other words, cyberspace is invested with meanings that are in excess to what it is assumed to stand for (Paasonen, *Figures of Fantasy*, 204.) Linking to other texts and debates, cyberspace comes with a conceptual history that again influences the ways in which individual texts making use of the terminology are interpreted. Due to such conceptual baggage, concepts cannot be applied innocently (Mizielinska, "Queering Moominland," 92).

It can be argued that cyberspace is no longer seen as synonymous with the Internet by anyone other than scholars writing in a certain language. The concept has not failed to travel, but it seems to have failed to transform in the process. Internationally, its travels have been bumpy: it has often been discarded not long after its initial translation and replaced with other concepts. Cyberspace is illustrative of how a concept may be in wide use in some places, and far more exotic in others. Acknowledging such conceptual specificity does not mean noting that "things may be different elsewhere" as a vague afterthought or disclaimer. Rather, it requires a consideration of how different hierarchies and norms are produced in Internet research literature, and how research concepts are coined, defined, and used.

Internet research remains a young field with an international association less than a decade old, and negotiations are still actively underway concerning its possibilities and definitions.[34] Terrain remains open to alternative perspectives and conceptualizations. Local conceptualizations, such as the ones addressed in this chapter, can function as critical reserves in the process, questioning and making the governing terminology strange and shifting the emphasis toward less US-specific and more context-sensitive formulations.

NOTES

1. Michael Benedikt, ed., *Cyberspace: The First Steps* (Cambridge, MA: MIT Press, 1991); John Perry Barlow, "A Declaration of the Independence of Cyberspace," http://www.eff.org/~barlow/Declaration-Final.html (1996), hereafter cited in text.
2. Mieke Bal, *Travelling Concepts in the Humanities: A Rough Guide* (Toronto: Toronto University Press, 2002), hereafter cited in text.
3. Pasi Mäenpää, *Narkissos kaupungissa: Tutkimus kuluttaja-kaupunkilaisesta ja julkisesta tilasta* (Helsinki: Tammi, 2005), 267.
4. See chapters by Yoo (Chapter 14), Hjorth (Chapter 15), and Manabe (Chapter 20) in this volume.
5. Wendy Hui Kyong Chun, *Control and Freedom: Power and Paranoia in the Age of Fiber Optics* (Cambridge, MA: MIT Press, 2006), 63–65, hereafter cited in text. Currently "the Grid" is similarly discussed as a novel network of networks, or the "next generation" of the Internet.

6. Lisa Nakamura, "'Where Do you Want to Go Today?' Cybernetic Tourism, the Internet and Transnationality," in *Race in Cyberspace*, ed. Beth E. Kolko, Lisa Nakamura, and Gilbert B. Rodman (New York: Routledge, 2000), 15–26.

7. Susanna Paasonen, *Figures of Fantasy: Internet, Women and Cyberdiscourse* (New York: Peter Lang, 2005), 66–69, hereafter cited in text.

8. George Lakoff and Mark Johnson, *Metaphors We Live By* (Chicago: University of Chicago Press, 1981), 10, 41.

9. See Yogesh Malhotra, Abdullah Al-Shehri, and Jeff J. Jones, "National Information Infrastructure: Myths, Metaphors And Realities," brint.com, http://www.kmbook.com/nii/ (1995).

10. David Silver, "Looking Backwards, Looking Forwards: Cyberculture Studies," in *Web.Studies: Rewiring Media Studies for the Digital Age*, ed. David Gauntlett (London: Arnold, 2000), 21, hereafter cited in text.

11. Cameron Richards, "Computer Mediated Communication and the Connection Between Virtual Utopias and Actual Realities," in *Proceedings: Cultural Attitudes Towards Communication and Technology '98*, ed. Charles Ess and Fay Sudweeks (Sydney, Australia: University of Sydney, 1998), 173–184.

12. Barbara Warnick, *Critical Literacy in a Digital Era: Technology, Rhetoric, and the Public Interest* (Mahwah, NJ: Lawrence Erlbaum Associates, 2002), 80.

13. Tapio Mäkelä, "Virtuaalitodellisuus uuden median populaarikulttuurina," in *Populaarin lumo: mediat ja arki*, ed. Anu Koivunen, Susanna Paasonen, and Mari Pajala (Turku, Finland: University of Turku), 147–169; Rob Shields, "Cyberspace," in *Unspun: Key Concepts for Understanding the World Wide Web*, ed. Thomas Swiss (New York: NYU Press, 2000), 68, hereafter cited in text.

14. Roger Burrows, "Cyberspace as Social Theory: William Gibson and the Sociological Imagination," in *Imagining Cities: Scripts, Signs, Memory*, ed. Sallie Westwood and John Williams (London: Routledge, 1997), 235–248; Tim Jordan, *Cyberpower: The Culture and Politics of Cyberspace and the Internet* (London: Routledge, 1999), 22–23.

15. Margaret Morse, *Virtualities: Television, Media Art, and Cyberculture* (Bloomington: Indiana University Press, 1998).

16. See Elizabeth H. Bassett and Kate O'Riordan, "Ethics of Internet Research: Contesting the Human Subjects Research Model," *Ethics and Information Technology* 4 (2002): 235, 241.

17. Peter Hitchcock, *Oscillate Wildly: Space, Body, and Spirit of Millennial Materialism* (Minneapolis: University of Minnesota Press, 1999), 7.

18. Marja Vehviläinen, "Teknologinen nationalismi," in *Suomineitonen hei! Kansallisuuden sukupuoli*, ed. Tuula Gordon, Katri Komulainen, and Kirsti Lempiäinen (Tampere, Finland: Vastapaino, 2002), 211–229.

19. Manuel Castells and Pekka Himanen, *Information Society and the Welfare State: The Finnish Model* (Oxford: Oxford University Press, 2002).

20. cf. Jari Aro, "Tietoyhteiskunta: epookkiteoriaa, retoriikkaa vai yhteiskuntateoriaa?," in *Näkökulmia tietoyhteiskuntaan*, ed. Kari Stachon (Helsinki, Finland: Gaudeamus, 1997), 22–42.

21. cf. Respective chapters on local language cultures by Cunliffe (Chapter 7), Gottlieb (Chapter 5), and Micó and Masip (Chapter 8) in this volume.

22. Jaakko Suominen, *Sähköaivo sinuiksi, tietokone tutuksi: tietotekniikan kulttuurihistoriaa* (Jyväskylä, Finland: University of Jyväskylä, 2000).

23. See Helena Tapper, "Tietoyhteiskunta ja kansalainen," in *Tietoyhteiskunnan harha*, ed. Rauno Seppänen (Kuopio, Finland: Puijo, 1998), 13–29; Sinikka Sassi, "The Controversies of the Internet and the Revitalization of Local Political Life," in *Digital Democracy: Issues of Theory and Practice*,

ed. Kenneth L. Hacker and Jan Van Dijk (London: Sage, 2000), 90–104; Tapio Häyhtiö, "Tietoyhteiskunta identiteettiprojektina: demokraattinen kansalaisuus verkossa," *Politiikka* 46 (2004): 277–291.
24. See Thomas Berker, Maren Hartmann, Yves Punie, and Katie J. Ward, eds., *Domestication of Media and Technology* (London: Open University Press, 2006).
25. Päivi Eriksson and Marja Vehviläinen, eds., *Tietoyhteiskunta seisak-keella: teknologia, strategiat ja paikalliset tulkinnat* (Jyväskylä, Finland: SopHi, 1999); Johanna Uotinen, Sari Tuuva, Marja Vehviläinen, and Seppo Knuuttila, eds., *Verkkojen kokijat: paikallista tietoyhteiskuntaa tekemässä* (Helsinki: Kansanrunouden tutkijain seura, 2001); Marja Vehviläinen, "Gendered Agency in Information Society: On Located Politics of Technology," in *Women and Everyday Uses of the Internet: Agency & Identity*, ed. Mia Consalvo and Susanna Paasonen (New York: Peter Lang, 2002), 275–291; Johanna Uotinen, *Merkillinen kone: Informaatioteknologia, kokemus ja kerronta* (Joensuu, Finland: Joensuun yliopisto, 2005); Sari Tuuva-Hongisto, Noora Talsi, and Johanna Uotinen, eds., *Hei ihmistä varten! Teknologiapolitiikka, kansalaislähtöisyys ja arki* (Helsinki: Kansanrunouden tutkijain seura, 2006); Virve Peteri, *Mediaksi kotiin: Tutkimus teknologioiden kotouttamisesta* (Tampere, Finland: Tampere University Press, 2006).
26. Kari A. Hintikka, "Uusi media—viesintäkanava ja elinympäristö," in *Johdatus uuteen median*, ed. Minna Tarkka, Kari A. Hintikka, and Asko Mäkelä (Helsinki, Finland: Edita, 1996), 2–18.
27. Ilkka Mäyrä, "Internetin kulttuurinen luonne: kaaosherroja ja verkonkutojia," in *Johdatus digitaaliseen kulttuuriin*, ed. Aki Järvinen and Ilkka Mäyrä (Tampere, Finland: Vastapaino, 1999), 95–190; Sonja Kangas, "MUD—verkon sosiaaliset tilat," in *Johdatus digitaaliseen kulttuuriin*, ed. Aki Järvinen and Ilkka Mäyrä (Tampere, Finland: Vastapaino, 1999), 147–164; Hannu Eerikäinen, "Kyberdiskurssi: ruumis, sukupuoli ja transsendenssin kaipuu," *Synteesi* 19 (2000): 46–69;
28. For example, Jonathan Sterne, "Thinking the Internet: Cultural Studies Versus the Millennium," in *Doing Internet Research: Critical Issues and Methods for Examining the Net*, ed. Steve Jones (London: Sage, 1999), 257–288, hereafter cited in text; David Silver, "Internet/Cyberculture/Digital Culture/New Media/Fill-in-the-Blank Studies," *New Media & Society* 6 (2004): 55–64.
29. David Silver and Adrianne Massanari, eds., *Critical Cybercultural Studies* (New York: NYU Press, 2006).
30. Mike Featherstone, *Undoing Culture: Globalization, Postmodernism and Identity* (London: Sage, 1995); Paul Virilio, *La bombe informatique* (Paris: Galilée, 1998).
31. Joanna Mizielinska, "Queering Moominland: The Problems of Translating Queer Theory Into a Non-American Context," *SQS* 1 (2006): 95, hereafter cited in text.
32. Kaarina Nikunen, *Faniuden aika: kolme tapausta tv-ohjelmien faniudesta vuosituhannen vaihteen Suomessa* (Tampere, Finland: Tampere University Press, 2005), 350.
33. Daniel Miller and Don Slater, *The Internet: An Ethnographic Approach* (Oxford: Berg, 2000), 1.
34. Sterne, "Thinking the Internet." See also Nancy K. Baym, ed., "Special Issue: ICT Research and Disciplinary Boundaries: Is 'Internet Research' a Virtual Field, a Proto-Discipline, or Something Else?" *The Information Society* 21 (2005).

3 Americanizing Palestine Through Internet Development

Helga Tawil-Souri

INTERNET DREAMS

In a small, rural village in the West Bank, I stop by an IT4Youth Internet center. A few kids have been invited to try out the center before its grand opening in a week's time. A group of teenage girls is in the Internet Room. Raucous and excited, they hop from one computer to another to see what each is doing. Next to me is a girl of perhaps fifteen, sitting quietly by herself. She hesitantly interrupts my typing. "Can you help me?" she shyly asks. "What I am supposed to do?" She had been sitting there not daring to touch the mouse or keyboard. I ask her what she wants to do: check her e-mail, read the news, go to a particular site, play games, chat with a friend. . . . After a moment of silence, she asks, "How can I get an e-mail address?" I rattle off some options—Hotmail, Yahoo!, MSN—none of which seem familiar to her. I pull up the Hotmail website, and tell her she can sign up for free by following the instructions on the screen. As I return to typing my e-mail, she interrupts me: "I don't read English." I apologize for my insensitivity and search for an Arabic-language e-mail site. I pull one up and tell her to follow the instructions. Although I do not mean to be rude but rather being in a rush, I return to my computer. Out of the corner of my eye, I notice her paralysis. I ask her if she is stuck on choosing a screen name. "Well, uh," she replies, "I don't read Arabic either."

It was April 2003. The violence, economic destitution, and political upheaval of the Second Intifada were the norm, and yet Internet centers were sprouting up all over the West Bank and the Gaza Strip. This particular village had been under strict closure for almost three years—hardly anyone could get in or out, and curfews were implemented daily. I had come with the IT4Youth team as part of my research on Palestinian internet development. Female, young, living in a rural area, without access to education or the Internet, this young girl was the perfect "target audience" for the center, whose goal was to shrink to digital divide among Palestinians and between Palestinians and the rest of the world, and to empower the youth, especially girls, by providing them with opportunities heretofore unavailable.

On the eve of the center's grand opening, a few days after my encounter with the girl, one of the team members shared his vision of the project:

> This center gives [the population] hope . . . they have no idea what the center is about. They have never seen the Internet, some don't even understand what a computer is. But they all think it's a good thing . . . and I couldn't agree more . . .

Making his way back into the center, he added, "This is for the improvement of the nation." Over the course of my fieldwork, between 2003 and 2006, this was a statement that I would hear across gender, class, religious, and political lines. My colleague's view suggested that Palestinians needed to hold on to something outside the political arena to give them (political) hope; that the national struggle itself must adopt the ways of the West—or at least integrate itself with the West—in order to strengthen itself economically, and consequently, politically.

When I returned to this village in the summer of 2005 it was easy to track down the same girl. A few months shy of her eighteenth birthday, she was now engaged to a distant cousin. She embarrassingly told me that although she had gone a few more times to the center, she never did learn how to read, let alone use the computer. Hers is perhaps an unsurprising ending—with the odds of illiteracy against her it seemed unlikely that the Internet was going to make much difference in her life.

I met others whose stories had different endings. One nineteen-year-old from the same village had taken many courses offered at the center—from typing to video editing, and hardware to web design—and with the skills she gained, moved to Ramallah for a job. She had been away from home for almost a year, making enough money as an assistant at a foreign nongovernmental organization (NGO) to send back home and allow herself a few shopping sprees besides. Her story would be cited by those at IT4Youth to exemplify success, but at the price of social costs: she feared that, like other motivated, independent, young women, her future would eventually come down to a choice between career and family.

While both of these young women grew up in the same village, the role of the Internet in each of their lives has been as divergent as their futures seem (other significant conditions in their lives notwithstanding). However, the divergence is representative of the contradictions at the heart of Internet development: Does it propagate social and class differences already existent in society? Is it a universal force for social and economic "progress"? Is it about gaining access to Western modernity, and doing so at the expense of "traditional" values? I would set out to understand whether the Internet was a "modernizing" tool and an important aspect of the national struggle by analyzing the forces behind its growth.

THE CASE OF IT4YOUTH

IT4Youth describes itself as a nonprofit project aimed at enhancing the learning skills and employability of Palestinian youth, especially girls and young women, through the creation of in-school computer labs and regional IT centers open to the public. The program is a collaborative mission between two NGOs, the Welfare Association[1] and International Youth Foundation (IYF),[2] with additional funding from the US Agency for International Development (USAID), the Intel Corporation, Hewlett-Packard (HP), and other mostly US-based corporations. IT4Youth's goal is to "build a 'digital bridge,' reducing the digital divide and helping to create a level educational playing field for Palestinian youth."[3] By offering opportunities for training and retraining, it hopes to develop a pool of IT-proficient youth and lay a foundation for the development of a national IT industry.

IT4Youth is certainly not the only Internet development project in the Palestinian Territories, but it is exemplary for many reasons. First, it is funded by US-based NGOs with strong ties to US-based multinational corporations operating in the West Bank and Gaza Strip with local employees. Second, it could only have come into existence as a result of the 1993 and 1995 Oslo peace process (when Palestinian statehood seemed possible), and as such, justifies itself as necessary for state building. Third, it sees its role as being one of direct influence over Palestinian social structure, seeking to bring progress and improvement economically, politically, and socially by "modernizing" the population. Fourth, although positioning itself as a state-building project, it does not have any direct affiliation with the Palestinian Authority. Fifth, given that its funding originates primarily from outside the Territories, it is part of a larger trend in Palestinian development competing with, and marginalizing, indigenous grassroots and civic institutions.[4] Lastly, while the project is a nonprofit endeavor, its goal is that within four years, a profit must be made and the center must become economically sustainable, with a stipulation that it must purchase any computer products from Intel- and HP-approved sources.

IT4Youth provides fertile ground for an analysis on the role of the Internet in non-Western societies and the process of development. Thus, the objectives of this chapter are not only to heighten awareness of local Internet practices in order to widen the field of Internet Studies to include those marginalized—whether technologically or otherwise—but also to analyze the relationship between communication technology, development, and the expansion of capitalism.

BEHIND INTERNET GROWTH

Unlike in other developing countries or Middle Eastern contexts, the Palestinian government has had little direct involvement in pursuing a managed IT strategy. Internet development has been driven by foreign private donors and mostly American NGOs, with tacit approval by the Palestinian Authority (PA). Between 1994 and 2004, IT funding in the Territories amounted to more than US$150 million, not including the over US$100 million that went directly into upgrading the communications infrastructure.[5] The Second Intifada, which erupted in September 2000, while devastating politically and economically, propelled phenomenal growth in the Internet and IT sectors. Closures, curfews, and checkpoints forced Palestinians to find alternative solutions to overcome problems of physical separation. Cellular phone calls, text messaging, e-mails, and Internet chat sessions became the most affordable way of staying in contact with friends and relatives. The Internet also became a means for people to share experiences of the incursions with web surfers all around the world, continue their education through outreach programs, and for social life.[6] In short, the Second Intifada opened the way for making the Internet "one of the few growth industries in the Palestinian economy."[7]

The Palestinian communications technology infrastructure up to this point had been essentially unchanged since the 1940s, primarily because of Israel's unwillingness to upgrade the connection to the increasingly sophisticated Israeli backbone. Personal computers and Internet use before 1995 was practically nonexistent; international telephone connections were forbidden prior to the Oslo agreements. In the wake of the peace talks, Palestinians found themselves with international phone and Internet access. Internet centers and cafes sprouted up around the Territories, with for-profit and nonprofit access programs launched in schools, refugee camps, urban centers, and rural areas. By 2001, there were 60,000 Internet users, a number that rose to 105,000 in 2002,[8] to over 225,000 in 2003, which is about a tenth of the population,[9] and finally reaching up to more than one-third of the population by the end of 2005.[10] While other Arab nations would boast faster growth rates, one must remember that, especially since 2000, much of the growth in the Palestinian Territories was occurring against the backdrop of worsening economic conditions.

TOWARD A DIGITAL DIVIDE?

The popularity and use of the Internet in Palestinian society has not been universal. There is a clear divide manifesting itself along class and geographical lines. For the most part, the Internet and other new media technologies are more popular among the elite: urban, middle- and upperclass, educated, and employed citizens. Certainly the elite class has used the Internet in a variety of ways, some of which are dedicated to improving economic and political conditions in Palestine. The Internet is used for a variety of business purposes (to bolster an Internet industry within the country or to make connections with the outside world) or to start English-language blogs to raise global awareness about everyday political conditions.[11] Using the Internet for the greater cause of the national struggle has more often fallen into the hands of diasporic Palestinians living in the West.[12]

However, the IT4Youth center is a good site from which to examine more "popular" uses, as users have not always been afforded the same privileges. For those with access—namely through centers, such as IT4Youth, that are found throughout the Territories—the Internet has not become a life-changing experience, except for a relative few, such as the young woman described above who gained employment due to her new IT skills. Moreover, to say that the Internet has played a role in the national struggle gives it much more power than it deserves, and negates the slew of variables standing in the path of the Palestinian national project (from the role of Israeli policies to the role of foreign aid, and from the corruption of the Arafat-run PA regime to the almost globally ostracized Hamas government). Based on in-depth interviews, observations, and usage statistics at IT4Youth and other Internet centers, it may be safe to say that the new medium is equivalent to a social network used as an online dating service and entertainment tool, but rarely as an economic necessity or for the political struggle.

The most popular use of the Internet is communication with others—an important aspect, given the difficulty that most Palestinians experience when trying to travel outside of their towns, let alone internationally. As one young man, who was a regular user of the IT4Youth center, explained in 2005, "I use the Internet mostly to chat with my friends. Many of them are here, but I've made a few friends among Palestinians abroad." Or as another young woman explained, she had been using the Internet to "meet" young Arab men, chatting virtually with members of the opposite sex, many of whom were in other nations. Since gender relations are largely defined in "traditional" means, commingling with members of the opposite sex is looked down upon, especially in rural areas or poorer neighborhoods. The Internet enabled transgression of gender, and often geographical, lines.[13]

For younger users, the Internet has been a fun tool, a means of playing games—some of which have "pro-Arab" political/ideological undertones, such as Hizballah's *Special Force* or Dar Al-Fikr's *Under Ash* and *Under Siege*.[14] As one computer center owner in Bethlehem lamented, "Kids only come here to play games, not improve any skills that will benefit them in the future, like improving their English or learning new things." When the owner removed the games from the computer's hard drives, most of the kids stopped coming, and he eventually succumbed to their needs. While difficult to generalize because of the lack of user surveys and research done in the Palestinian Territories, from observations with Internet users, it seemed the technology was more often used as a communicative or fun tool than for economic benefit or political mobilization. Except for a very few number of elites, the Internet was not an integral part of daily life.

THE AMERICANIZATION OF IT DEVELOPMENT

The fact that the Internet has become integral to human life for some more than others has not curbed the perceived importance of having access to the network in the most remote parts of the world, such as the abovementioned village. A guiding assumption of developmental projects is that the Internet is a site of empowerment—economically, socially, and politically. In the Palestinian context, Internet development projects reaffirm this assumption lock, stock, and barrel. Introducing the Internet to the Territories, in the view of projects like IT4Youth, also has larger goals, such as modernizing the Palestinians, ensuring their status as "developed" in the new world order, and as a means to pursue effective state building. More importantly, such a vision is compatible with the growing presence of American corporations and NGOs in the Territories speaking the language of "modernization" and "integration into the global economy."

Of concern here is that Internet development in the Palestinian context—with similarities reverberating globally—is nothing short of the Americanization of Palestinian society. A number of factors allude to this process: the (perceived and real) need for competence in the English language, the increasing number of American NGOs and high-tech firms in the Territories—and subsequent reliance on them to develop the IT/Internet sector—the expansion of American capital, and finally, the uncritical adoption of neoliberal strategies for development dictated by what is commonly referred to as the *Washington Consensus.*

First, in the virtual realm, there is no denying the need for competence in the English language. While there are certainly Arabic-language sites and a growing presence of both Arabs and Arabic content on the Web (about 100 million of the more than 12 billion websites are in Arabic), Arabic users account for less than 2 percent of total world use, with an average penetration rate in Arabic countries of 10 percent[15], and there is still a strong-rooted assumption that to use, or rather fully utilize the potential of, the Internet requires English proficiency. This was reflected in interviews and observations with users across all genders, ages, or socioeconomic status. As one young man browsing the Web in Arabic explained:

> Of course there are Arabic websites, but we all know that the world of the Internet is the world of English . . . Sure we go to Arabic sites, but think about it, even to chat, the software is in English, so somebody has to be familiar with the basics, how to read instructions or know which button to click on.

His friend interrupted to add:

> Even when we chat we use English words. Or we use the English alpha-
> bet and write things phonetically to sound Arabic . . . I think to use the
> Internet without knowing English is to miss a lot [sic].

Among IT4Youth users, the argument was often the same, that without
knowledge of English, the Internet was limited and limiting. As one team
member explained:

> In one instance we were giving them courses on fixing hardware. There
> are no words in Arabic to describe motherboard, modem, hard drive . . .
> there weren't even any manuals in Arabic. Everything we were given by
> HP was in English . . . Anyone who wanted to take that course had to
> have some level of English . . . We discovered it was the same in every
> course, making digital music or learning to surf the Internet. English is a
> must. Yes maybe not a fluent English, but certain words and phrases.

In response to this, the IT4Youth center offered English-language classes. English was believed to be the predominant language of the Internet. Moreover, for
many centers (whether for-profit or not), English was a necessity operationally,
whether in writing grant applications to receive funds from foreign (mostly
American) donors and corporations, setting up computers and installing software, or in basic programming. As one center owner in Ramallah explained:

> I hired my friend of mine to do our website. I knew he was a great de-
> signer, but I had no idea that to make a website you need to know English
> . . . Now I know html programming cannot be done in Arabic. So he
> couldn't do it. He was a great designer, but he barely knew English . . .
> You cannot survive in this hi-tech business without English!

Second, Americanization is taking place in the material realm through
the dominance of American NGOs and corporations as the forces behind
Internet development. The presence of American institutions is palpable,
whether in USAID-funded projects dedicated to IT or the dozens of training and certification centers sponsored by Microsoft and Cisco. Perhaps no
institution has played as significant a role in directing state-building efforts
in the Palestinian Territories as USAID, setting the stage for infrastructure development and institution building, one example of which are projects aimed at Internet development. The organization has been involved in
every type of Internet development project in the Palestinian context.

Internet development in the Territories led by American institutions has
come in three forms, and is aimed at different age groups.[16] First, school-based
computer centers and local Internet centers targeted at the youth, such as the
IT4Youth project, have been running since 2000. By the end of 2005, there

were over thirty such computer programs in elementary and high schools, only five of which were not built, financed, or controlled by an American institution (although, needless to say, their computers originated in the United States). There were also six projects building nonprofit, community Internet centers for children and the youth, ranging from IT4Youth to the Intel Club House, all of which were relying on American high-tech firms and funded in large part by USAID. Second, training and vocational programs in the form of corporate-sponsored certification programs, computer science programs at universities, and the creation of technical schools were targeting the teen and young adult population. Herein, the Territories have been home to thirteen privately run Cisco Academies, eight Oracle certification programs, seven Microsoft certification programs, and a number of joint projects between American high-tech firms (namely Microsoft, Cisco, Oracle, and Intel) to build vocational schools in the West Bank and the Gaza Strip. The creation of computer science departments at the various universities in the Territories has also been funded by American hi-tech firms. Third, the Palestinian and Israeli governments have joined forces with the World Bank, United Nations Development Program (UNDP), USAID, and US high-tech firms to build multibillion dollar technology incubators as means to provide low-wage computer jobs and encourage entrepreneurship for an export market. In every sector of Internet development, the majority of projects have been driven by the interests of American nonprofit and for-profit organizations.

Concomitant with the dominance of American institutions is the expansion of American capital—whether in investments in the Territories, in flows of money to and from the Territories, or in reliance on the US dollar for most transactions. This is yet another facet of Americanization, most palpable in the Internet domain, since capital originates from and makes it way back to the United States and US-based high-tech firms. As Adel Samara notes:

> In general, the PA has adopted a strategy of stimulating private sector development and competition by encouraging the inflow of foreign capital through limiting restrictions of foreign remittances and dealings in foreign currency. This very open policy . . . extends beyond the Palestinian investment law in encouraging foreign over local capital.[17]

The adoption of open-door policies with no protection or limitations on foreign capital has become the decision not only of the PA, but of donors, NGOs, and international organizations (many of whom are American or controlled by Americans) that push an agenda of economic liberalization. In fact, the entirety of the Palestinian Territories:

> has been subordinated to the prescriptions of international financial institutions . . . Unlike other formerly colonized countries, the PA's economy may be alone in having been designed from its very beginning by the policies and prescriptions of globalizing institutions.[18]

This is perpetuated especially as peace processes and negotiations continue to be sponsored by the United States (the main controller of globalizing financial institutions such as the World Bank), resulting in policies that are globally, not internally, oriented. Thus, Palestine becomes a node in the global expansion and exchange of American capital.

Lastly, and perhaps most importantly, Americanization is occurring by virtue of the ideology of neo-liberalism that envelops Internet development. Specifically, the Washington Consensus of development has come to be seen as the only path for national growth and progress. Development projects and agencies in the Territories have unquestioningly adopted the logic of liberalization, deregulation, privatization, and the unwinding of the welfare state as the natural course of things, often conflated with the process of globalization. Alternative forms of economic development are practically inconceivable (although ostracized from the global funding calculus, even Hamas recognizes the need for foreign aid in sustaining Palestine, and does not suggest that development pursue a different ideological path). For example, one Welfare Association executive managing IT projects, including IT4Youth, explained:"

> the objective is to grow the Palestinian economy to be a modern component in the larger global system . . . Globalization is here and we cannot close our eyes, fold our hands, do nothing about it and accept being left out."

The underlying belief is that modernization is equal to global capitalism, which national progress itself is contingent upon. The means by which to quickly become part of the new global order is the Internet; in the words of one the IT4Youth team members:

> progress has to be economic . . . We must modernize in terms of develop away from an agricultural society to an industrial, or service and information economy.

INTERNET DEPENDENCY

It is important to recognize that the changes taking place in the Territories, as well as in Internet growth, have happened at a particular time in history, and therefore are charged with a particular ideology. The reconfiguration of the global economy post-1991 led to anxieties among the Palestinian elites and eventually the PA as to where they would fit in the new world economic order. Furthermore:

> the political triumph of the United States meant, too, the victory of a special brand of economic neo-liberalism—what came to be called the Washington Consensus—especially as a recipe for others to adopt . . .

The heads of [. . .] the PLO were no exception in facing increasing pressure based on larger economic changes way beyond their control.[19]

For Palestinian leaders, and those involved in development projects alike, "globalization" signaled a process of world economic restructuring that threatened to widen the gap between the haves and have-nots, as determined by access to new IT and the direct foreign investment associated with it.[20]

While the global context may provide an understanding—and justification—for the need for Internet development, as well as recognition of the global need to jump on the hi-tech bandwagon, my concern is that these processes of Americanization have led to a deepening dependency on the Western core. This dependency may stand in the way of the benefits and objectives of Internet development—bridging the digital divide within Palestinian society and outside it, ensuring women's futures, economic growth, integration into the global capitalist economy, and as means to strengthen the national political struggle.

Even when their proponents make society-changing claims, Internet development projects usually have a narrow focus, posited to be about improving prospects for wider access to information and communication networks on the assumption that this is enough to enable political and economic "progress." Such assistance initiatives strive to address issues such as:

> poor telecommunications infrastructure; government regulation and censorship; poor knowledge about the opportunities for economic and social development afforded by information technologies . . . ; the prohibitive cost of hardware and connection for individuals and organizations; and a lack of technical expertise, training and capacity, and requisite skills for using the Internet.[21]

Funding is contingent on the host government's willingness to liberalize the telecommunications sector, adopt cost-based tariff setting for Internet services, and allow the unrestricted flow of information; a second phase works to develop the local Internet training capacity.[22] Internet development projects, such as IT4Youth, that focus on youth empowerment and those that establish technology incubators are examples of such efforts to force the government (whether through the Ministry of Education in the first case, or through direct involvement in the latter) to restructure the Palestinian economy according to external demands. The assumption that Palestinian society will improve through Internet access or high-tech training is taken for granted, as is the belief that growing an IT industry can only happen through the liberalization of the sector and through the influx of foreign capital and know-how. Such programs argue for "a measurable link between political and economic freedom and access to the Internet," and claim that "clearly the Internet has a substantive role to play in the process of democratization and economic development."[23] These claims are exemplary of the

Washington Consensus, with its premise that underdeveloped nations must learn to be "in the game," whatever that game may be at a particular time in economic history.

With the increasing globalization of information technologies, many developing countries look to the Internet as a means to "leap-frog" over developed countries to establish their own niche markets in high-tech areas. These new expressions of modernization indeed argue that it is *necessary* to give up any idea of building a self-reliant economy and concentrate instead on the creation of highly efficient sectors capable of directly competing in the world markets—in this case, of creating a viable Palestinian Internet sector. As one development scholar noted:

> new governments were faced with the task, for the first time, of ad-ministering their countries . . . the populations of the developing world looked to their new rulers, now their own kind and not foreign, for a promise of better things and for the means to obtain them . . . Some sought help from international agencies, such as the World Bank, from their former colonial power, which had ruled them and from economic advisers both imported and home-grown. Their aim was to diminish rapidly the difference in the levels of economic attainment, standard of living, technical sophistication and economic independence between their country and that of the "western" industrialized world. This was regarded as a goal which was not only attainable but as one which could be reached quickly.[24]

Developing countries—or more accurately, the elites who control develop-ment strategies in developing nations—uncritically adopt the claims of the Internet's ability to jump-start a nation's economic capacity. From a purely financial perspective, however, development focused on IT (or any part of that industry/sector) cannot provide real economic benefit to the societies concerned: those in developing countries still remain largely without the expertise to maintain the systems, or the income to take advantage of trade deals. Profits are repatriated offshore and the society in question ends up no better off. In fact, it can become worse off as it becomes a hostage to monopolistic practices and increasingly dependent on its foreign supplier (in the case of IT4Youth, American high-tech firms). Such deals may very well leave the country more dependent on others to provide essential infra-structure services and sustain its niche market than before. Everard has described the ensuing dependence thus:

> developing countries outsource technical and managerial skills to reap what benefits they can from being plugged into the global system. While some will find at least short-term niche markets, there are dangers that even such growth in service countries as some developing countries . . . may be short-lived, leaving greater debt and opportunity costs in its wake.[25]

Since its grand opening in mid-2003, IT4Youth has had to hire experts from the United States, overpay for its Intel- and HP-approved hardware, and generally run up huge debts. As one of the managers explained in early 2006:

> we could only buy computers from HP . . . and only from specific vendors. It didn't matter that we could find much cheaper components elsewhere, or imagine that we would want to buy some from a Palestinian company, no way. We had to follow IYF and USAID orders . . . This meant we paid hundreds of shekels more than we could have had we been allowed to buy on the open market.

It was a similar story when there were technical issues that needed to be fixed; some of the team members thought of hiring a young man from the village (who had been trained at the center) to upgrade systems and tend to fixing hardware. As one team member explained:

> they in the US [IYF] said no, you can't hire a local. We will send you someone. So of course first we have to wait for this guy to come here . . . it takes him five months . . . and then, what, we paid him so much money that it was more than our whole budget for maintenance for the whole fiscal year! . . . and later, of course, he wasn't here when things broke down again.

The irony, of course, is that the very goal of training locals to obtain Internet and technical skills were not to be used for the center. The center kept receiving directives from its donors as to where to buy equipment, who to hire for simple hardware needs, and how much to pay for such services— and all of these would be American sources. The same trend existed in other forms of Internet development, whether in dependence on American hitech firms to provide computers for university students, American-trained experts to teach courses in the academies, or the reliance on American capital to fund high-tech incubators.

Ironically, the very striving for modernity through Internet technology is undertaken to show that the societies in question are becoming free from their (former) "masters." The symbols of modernity that drive such development projects are inextricably linked to Western cultural value systems. As such, invoking the "information society" as an icon of modernization and a mark of Western industrial development becomes a new form of (re)colonization, reinforcing a world of contact and influence between radically asymmetrical economies. This is not a recent phenomenon, as development and communication technologies have a long colonial legacy: in the mid-nineteenth century, communications networks, such as the telegraph, shipping, and railroads, were regarded as instruments of surveillance and direction by the colonizers.[26] One can make the same argument about the

Internet, whereby the "developed" nation controls the direction of development while also increasing surveillance methods through new communications technology.[27] The relationship stemming from Internet development between the developing nation and its "supplier" is one of "mercantile colonization,"[28] influenced by the history of the Internet, itself created under the economic constraints of capitalism. Here then, Internet development serves the purpose of sustaining certain power relations (and the IT4Youth project) along with the Cisco Academies and high-tech incubators, and it symbolizes how capitalist production extends into the farthest reaches of the global "periphery."

The Internet is an important element in the process of global capital expansion,[29] and thus carries capitalism's contradictions: its liberating and progressive forces and its oppressive and tragic consequences (allowing one young woman to jump start a career while keeping the other in a state of illiteracy and poverty). On one hand, Internet development creates possibilities for some to benefit economically and perhaps politically. On the other hand, it undermines the potential for actual development and economic sustainability, and must be understood as a process that economically subjugates and dominates Third-World peoples. Internet development does not provide real economic benefit, but results in further global polarization, whereby peripheries such as the Palestinian Territories become governed by the West's financial and technological interests and turn into dependent peripheries. Internet development as analyzed in the Palestinian context is "cause and effect" of capitalist expansion, precluding the achievement of the very goals of development and further deepening the dependency and subjugation to Western aid. Moreover, the goal of integrating a technologically literate Palestinian workforce into the global economy reduces human beings to the status of the commodity of labor power, and must be recognized as an integral part of the destructive aspects of capitalism—the latest stage in mercantile colonialism and Western "progress" that negates indigenous needs.

For some scholars, the question is how to make sense of seemingly opposing processes; for example, how are we to make sense of Internet growth in the Palestinian Territories given the latter's "backwardness"? For example, Tehranian and Tehranian pose the challenge as such:

> If there is a new world order [. . .] it can be better understood in terms of the paradoxes of a situation in which we are increasingly witnessing dazzling technological and economic breakthroughs without corresponding social, political and normative innovations . . . the challenges lie [. . .] in trying to bridge the widening chasms between the exploding technological opportunities, the currently unfulfilled human needs, and the social systems that attempt to fulfill them.[30]

However, these authors seem to miss an important point. The "widening chasms" are very much due to the logic of deepening global polarization.

While Internet development may actually strengthen the practice of the free market and of "dazzling technological breakthroughs," it does not mean that the third world will become the first world, but rather that the third world will be incorporated into a relationship with the first world based on inequality and exploitation, creating a more callous world.

While the Internet may link users globally and enable information to flow across borders, location still matters in shaping both the creation of the infrastructure needed and online activities. It is equally important to recognize offline activities that determine the development and expansion of the Internet. Moreover, while Internet development brings with it liberating, democratizing, and positive possibilities, in this case it also creates a form of unequal exchange between the industrialized West and the Palestinians that is reflective of the larger trends of unequal development inherent in global capitalism. While its uses hold promises of "progress," its development, as in Palestine, is also the latest expression of modernization theories, which state that it is necessary to give up building a self-reliant economy and concentrate instead on the creation of a particular sector that can supposedly compete in the global market.

CONCLUSION

Looking beyond the Palestinian Territories, IT4Youth, the Cisco and Oracle Academies and technology incubators are not unique. There are projects similar to IT4Youth all around the world (in fact, the project itself exists in South Africa), Cisco and Microsoft certification programs exist in almost every country, and many regions (cities or nations) attempt to lure hi-tech firms and increase local employment by building "free-trade" zones. These projects share some important aspects: they originate in the West, take the Western model of development as the one to emulate and strive for, and they attempt to "catch up," if not at times "leap frog," the West economically by establishing niche markets (often in Internet/IT). Thus, Internet development is symbolic of a global trend of adopting the mainstream perspective of "development," of the hegemony of the "Washington Consensus" for neo-liberal economic growth models, and the perceived need to have to integrate as quickly as possible into the global marketplace. While the Internet certainly holds uses for economic and national success, Internet development is also part and parcel of the "forces of globalization": with it comes the promises and ills of neo-liberal economic strategies, the dreams and nightmares of an "information society," and the dominance of the West.

While the Palestinian example, like others, may be unique, it offers challenges and contributions to the field of Internet studies. The economic imperatives behind Internet development are crucial in examining the technology's ability to create new politics, to afford those marginalized new kinds of global or virtual linkages. For those who are still excluded from the global information village, the question remains as to whether their inclusion must come with offline costs, and how painful those may be. We have come to recognize that cultural dimensions of Internet use differ widely depending on local context, but Internet expansion must also be counterposed with transnational and global influences, whether manifested as problems of language, the hegemony of "development," or the ideology of global capitalism. Only then can a truly international understanding of the Internet emerge.

NOTES

1. The Welfare Association is the premier Palestinian funding agency or NGO. A "Westernized" agency, both in terms of its professionalization and ideological belief in neo-liberal values, the Welfare Association is a private, non-profit foundation established in 1983 by a group of Palestinian diaspora leaders to support development in the Territories. It is the largest Palestinian NGO in terms of budget, employees, presence, and number of projects. By 2000, it emerged as a leading Palestinian development organization (by which time it had dispersed approximately $100 million).
2. Based in the United States, the IYF runs programs in sixty countries with the aim of improving the conditions and prospects of young people through the networking of companies, foundations, and civil society organizations to "scale up" existing programs in education and technology. The majority of IYF's funding and its projects are tailored to the needs of the project's corporate partners (mostly Western high-tech firms), creating a "branded program that matches a company's giving interests and core business needs" (http://www.iyf.org).
3. IT4Youth website, http://www.it4youth.com
4. Helga Tawil Souri, "Marginalizing Palestinian Development: Lessons Against Peace," *Development* 49, no. 2 (2006): 75–80.
5. PASSIA, "Palestine Facts," http://www.passia.org/index_pfacts.htm (retrieved on June 2, 2004).
6. Amira Hass, "Israel's Closure Policy: An Ineffective Strategy of Containment and Repression," *Journal of Palestine Studies* 31, no. 3 (2002): 5–20; Joshua Mitnick, "To Reach Past Curfews, Palestinians Go Online," *New York Times*, February 18, 2004, Section W, 1, Column 3; Laila El Haddad, "Intifada Spurs Palestine Internet Boom," *Al-Jazeera*, December 11, 2003; Joseph Federman, "Palestinian Turn to Internet to Cope with Israeli Restrictions," *USA Today*, November 18, 2003, http://www.usatoday.com/tech/news/2003–11–18-palestine-online_x.htm
7. Mitnick, "To Reach Past Curfews."
8. The World Bank Group, "West Bank and Gaza Update: West Bank and Gaza Strategic Outlook," http://lnweb18.worldbank.org/mna/mena.nsf/Attachments/West+Bank+and+Gaza+Update+APril+2002/$File/May+2002+update.pdf (April 2002); The World Bank Group, "Four Years—Intifada, Closures and Palestinian Economic Crisis: An Assessment," http://siteresources.worldbank.org/INTWESTBANKGAZA/Resources/wbgaza-4yrassessment.pdf (October 2004).
9. Internet World Stats, "Internet Usage in the Middle East," http://www.internetworldstats.com/ (September 30, 2004).

10. Palestinian Control Bureau of Statistics (PCBS), *Palestinians at the End of Year 2004* (Ramallah: PCBS, 2005).

11. For example, the Raising Yousuf blog created by Gaza-based journalist Leila Al-Haddad, http://a-mother-from-gaza.blogspot.com/.

12. For example, http://www.electronicintifada.com.

13. Using the Internet for cross-gender communication is popular across the Arab world. See, for example, Deborah Wheeler, *The Internet in the Middle East: Global Expectations and Local Imaginations in Kuwait* (Albany: State University of New York Press, 2006).

14. Helga Tawil Souri, "The Political Battlefield of Pro-Arab Video Games on Palestinian Screens," in "Mediated Politics in the Middle East," ed. Annabelle Sreberny, and Gholam Khiabany, special issue, *Comparative Studies of South Asia, Africa, and the Middle East* 27, no. 3 (2007): 536-551

15. Internet World Stats, "Internet Usage in the Middle East," http://www.internetworldstats.com/ (September 30, 2006).

16. Helga Tawil Souri, "Move Over Bangalore, Here Comes . . . Palestine? Western Funding and 'Internet Development' in the Shrinking Palestinian State," in *Global Communications: Toward a Transcultural Political Economy*, ed. Paula Chakravartty and Yuezhi Zhao (Boulder, CO: Rowman and Littlefield), 2007, 263-284.

17. Adel Samara, "Globalization, the Palestinian Economy, and the 'Peace Process,'" *Journal of Palestine Studies* 29, no.2 (2000): 20–34.

18. Samara, "Globalization," 21.

19. Baruch Kimmerling and Joel Migdal, *Palestinians: The Making of a People* (New York: Free Press), 323–324.

20. See Jonatha Nitzan and Shimshon Bichler, *The Global Political Economy of Israel* (Sterling, VA: Pluto Press, 2002) for analysis of the transformation of the Israeli political economy in response to the "forces" of globalization and new technologies.

21. Dana Ott and Melissa Rosser, "The Electronic Republic? The Role of the Internet in Promoting Democracy in Africa," in *The Internet, Democracy and Democratization*, ed. Peter Ferdinand (Portland, OR: Frank Cass, 2000), 144.

22. See Ott and Rosser, "The Electronic Republic?", and the websites of USAID and IYF.

23. Ott and Rosser, "The Electronic Republic?", 152.

24. Quoted in Jerry Everard, *Virtual States: The Internet and the Boundaries of the Nation-State* (New York: Routledge, 2000), 39.

25. Everard, *Virtual States*, 42.

26. cf. Tom Standage, *The Victorian Internet* (New York: Walker and Company, 1998); and Brian Winston, *Media Technology and Society. A History: From the Telegraph to the Internet* (London: Routledge, 1998).

27. For a discussion on Israeli surveillance over Palestinian society using methods developed through new technologies, see Elia Zureik, "Constructing Palestine Through Surveillance Practices," *British Journal of Middle Eastern Studies* 28, no. 2 (2001): 205–227.

28. Everard, *Virtual States*, 40.

29. See Dan Schiller, *Digital Capitalism: Networking the Global Market System* (Cambridge, MA: The MIT Press, 1999); Frank Webster, *Theories of the Information Society* (London: Routledge, 1995); Manuel Castells, *The Rise of the Network Society* (Cambridge: Blackwell, 1996).

30. Majid Tehranian and Katherine Tehranian, *Restructuring for World Peace: On the Threshold of the Twenty-First Century* (Cresskill, NJ: Hampton Press, 1992), 122.

4 The International Turn in Internet Governance
A World of Difference?

Gerard Goggin

INTRODUCTION

An important aspect of the internationalization of the Internet is the widening struggle over governance, policy, and the shaping of the technology. Because the Internet is now used by billions of people in countries around the world, from the mid-1990s onward, there has been growing pressure for a pluralization of voices and interest in key institutions, from technical standards setting, to domain names and numbers, to general questions of democracy, and to how the Internet can be accessed, used, and determined by all. In this chapter, I review the international turn in Internet governance, how it has unfolded, who it represents and includes, and what linguistic, social, and cultural values it inscribes in the technology.

First, I look at the key institutions of Internet governance, especially Internet Corporation for Assigned Names and Numbers (ICANN), World Wide Web Consortium (W3C), and others, describing the transformations and struggles associated with these in the period of commercial, mass Internet (from 1992 onward). Secondly, I examine the phenomenon of the World Summit on the Information Society (WSIS), which saw the venerable International Telecommunications Union (one of the very first international organizations, established in the middle of the nineteenth century) offer a forum for international debates on government and civil society and the direction of the Internet. Thirdly, I assess to what extent the international trend of the Internet's use, consumption, and significance has been successfully registered in governance and policy processes. Finally, I reflect on the implications of the politics of the international turn in Internet governance for wider discussions on internationalizing Internet studies.

CRISIS IN INTERNET GOVERNANCE: DOMAIN NAMES AND ICANN

For roughly the first three decades of the Internet's history, relatively decentralized, effective mechanisms and bodies to handle administration, technical development and standards, and governance matters had evolved.[1]

In 1979, the US Department of Defense's Defense Advanced Research Projects Agency (DARPA; http://www.darpa.mil) established the Internet Configuration Control Board. The program manager at DARPA responsible for this at the time was the now legendary figure in Internet development, Vint Cerf.[2] The Internet Configuration Control Board was disbanded and replaced with the Internet Advisory Board (IAB) in 1984, which was renamed the Internet Activities Board in 1986. In 1992, the Internet Society (ISOC; www.isoc.org) was formed by a number of widely respected figures, with the aim of providing an institution to coordinate and resource various technical and governance activities. The IAB successfully proposed that its activities take place under the auspices of this new organization. As part of this new charter, it became the Internet Architecture Board, the name it retains today (www.iab.org). The brief of the IAB is to oversee the architectural aspects of Internet activities, Internet standards processes, and also to appoint a crucial figure in the Internet community, the Request for Comment (RFC) editor.

The IAB oversees the working groups of the Internet Engineering Task Force (IETF; http://www.ietf.org/). The IETF describes itself as:

> a large open international community of network designers, operators, vendors, and researchers concerned with the evolution of the Internet architecture and the smooth operation of the Internet. It is open to any interested individual.[3]

Here we see a defining characteristic of the Internet community and its governance as it developed, especially through the 1970s and 1980s: the core principle of openness of process. Witness how the IETF mission statement opens:

> The goal of the IETF is to make the Internet work better . . . The IETF will pursue this mission in adherence to the following cardinal principles:
> Open process—any interested person can participate in the work, know what is being decided, and make his or her voice heard on the issue . . .
> Technical competence—the issues on which the IETF produces its documents are issues where the IETF has the competence needed to speak to them, and that the IETF is willing to listen to.[4]

The Internet community, as embodied by various working groups of IETF, such as the IAB, the ISOC, and other affiliated organizations and institutions, sought to make the development of the Internet, especially in relation to technical standards and directions, open to whomever wished to join in, and was recognized as having sufficient technical expertise. A key element that allowed such openness to take a concrete form remains the RFC series. The first RFC was issued by Jon Postel on April 7, 1969. Postel, a personification of the values of Internet community, served as RFC editor for 28 years. An RFC is a memo that contains technical and organizational notes and proposals regarding the Internet (authors must first publish their texts as an "Internet draft"). While not standards themselves, RFCs play an important role in Internet standards development. In a commemorative RFC about the history of RFCs, Cerf recalls:

> When the RFCs were first produced, they had an almost 19th century character to them—letters exchanged in public debating the merits of various design choices for protocols in the ARPANET. As email and bulletin boards emerged from the fertile fabric of the network, the far-flung participants in this historic dialog began to make increasing use of the online medium to carry out the discussion—reducing the need for documenting the debate in the RFCs and, in some respects, leaving historians somewhat impoverished in the process. RFCs slowly became conclusions rather than debates.[5]

There are a number of other bodies involved in the development of the Internet and governance, but much tension and wider public debate centered around the area of addresses. As Milton L. Mueller notes, when the Internet protocol was finally specified in 1981, with it came the creation of an address space.[6] Jon Postel had assumed responsibility for allocating addresses and numbers from 1977 onward, and for many years he retained this role—one individual managing this system (albeit with assistance from colleagues). With the growth of the Internet than ensued, especially with the use of e-mail, the idea of translating addresses into names was developed.[7] An early difficulty related to the need to define top-level domains, which soon raised the issue of designating countries. The first country code designation was ".uk," assigned to one individual to monitor (Andrew McDowell, University College London). Yet, this in itself raised difficulties when Jon Postel adopted the relevant International Organization for Standardization (ISO) standard on country names as top-level domains[8]—and it turned out, too late, that ".gb" was the two letter code stipulated in the ISO standard, not ".uk."[9] We have seen elsewhere in this volume that the assumptions about why a polity qualifies or does not qualify for representation as a "country" or "nation" in Internet governance, especially domain names, has been a hotly contested issue.[10]

Under a long-term contract between DARPA and the Information Sciences Institute (ISI) at the University of Southern California, Jon Postel was given "what would later be called the *policy authority* over name and number assignment," and indeed received funding for this and to carry out other functions as well.[11] (Though in 1987, responsibility for assignment of IP numbers and registry functions was transferred from the ISI to Stanford Research Institute's Defense Data Network–Network Information Center or DDN-NIC.) From 1985 to 1993, Postel delegated the responsibility for country code top-level domains to "responsible" individuals on, essentially, a first-come, first-serve basis:

Significantly, that delegation method tended to bypass completely the institutions in other countries that historically had possessed authority over communication . . . Almost none of these institutions were paying attention to the Internet at this time. Typically, the result was that delegations ended up in the hands of university computer science departments or education and research networking organizations in the named territory.[12]

In 1988, Postel conceived of an organization that embodied this function, and called it the Internet Assigned Numbers Authority (IANA; www.iana. org).[13] There is much more to be said about the way that, at this juncture, Postel, Cerf, and other *éminence grise* sought to fashion and charter various bodies to preserve what they saw as fundamental to the Internet community's modes of governance—and indeed whether their strategy, if it found support or gained authority, would have provided a viable, alternative set of governance arrangements to deal with the Internet's dizzying expansion, commercialization, and internationalization. However, I will pass over many important developments to briefly focus upon the controversial institution that did arise instead, which became the focal point not only for the widening circles of stakeholders with now considerable investments and interests in Internet governance, but also the crucible for a new international social and civil society movement constituted through digital networks.

In the early 1990s, there were a number of developments that combined to see the Internet grow very rapidly. The ban on Internet commerce that had been enforced through acceptable use rules was ultimately lifted by the US government in 1991. Graphic user interfaces made using the Internet much easier for many. The invention of the World Wide Web and its deployment in browsers (Mosaic, Netscape, Internet Explorer, and others) from 1993 onward brought together quite disparate resources in an easy-to-access form. The World Wide Web also popularized the use of domain names rather than Internet Protocol (IP) addresses. Users became accustomed to typing in and remembering uniform resource locators (URLs), the syntax and usability of which relied upon domain names.

The explosive growth and dramatic changes in the nature of the Internet put a great deal of pressure on the practices and institutions that had evolved to administer, distribute, and arbitrate disputes. In particular, attention was focused upon how domain names were managed. The sheer number of requests for domain name registrations made it difficult for registries to keep up, especially when they were still receiving little, if any, recompense for their efforts. With proposals to introduce competition into the provision of domain names, registries were put on a commercial footing, and indeed in the "dot.com" boom of the late 1990s, became lucrative new economy businesses in their own right.

One of the policy issues that became more pressing resulted directly from the commercialization of the Internet. As it become imperative for organizations, especially commercial operations, to have a presence on the Internet, problems emerged with how existing brands and trademarks related to domain names. Simply put, many large corporations expected to be able to own the domain name that corresponded to their registered trademark or products, and did not take kindly to those who had actually registered such domain names, whether for legitimate reasons or as a version of what become called "cybersquatting."

At a more profound level, however, domain names symbolized overarching challenges and debates about control and governance of the Internet. Until the early 1990s, the development of the Internet was bound up not only with assumptions about its public good and educational and governmental character, but also its reliance upon the US government—especially the military—but also on the educational policy agencies and the US higher education and research establishment itself. To be sure, a number of other countries and their scientific, military, research, and educational agencies were also very much involved in the development of the Internet. The Internet community itself was also quite dispersed across the world, limited to a few countries well endowed with advanced technology (mainly Western countries, but also Japan and Australia). Yet, the almost mythical role played by recognized custodians, such as Jon Postel, belied the firm underpinning of the Internet by the United States, as is clear when one delves into the details of the ultimate underwriting of the mandate Postel enjoyed.

As more and more people became interested in, and users of, the Internet through the 1990s, and as it spread to many more countries—in short, as it internationalized, unevenly as it did—it was not surprising that pressure grew for these new users to be represented in how the Internet was governed. In 1994, the traditional custodians of the Internet tried to use ISOC as a body to take formal authority and ownership over numbers and domain names. When the US government responded with a counterclaim, Vint Cerf responded by invoking ISOC as the body best placed to respond to the internationalization of the Internet. Others—notably the regional address registry organizations in Europe and Asia–Pacific—also emphasized the need to take an international perspective. While promoting discussion on the need for new ways to manage domain names, the United States also was reluctant to fully embrace a genuine international approach in the creation of new governance bodies. Therefore, this was one important element in what became a furious debate over domain names.

Once the US government became concerned about the future of domain management, and then-President Clinton's policy advisor, Ira Magaziner, became deeply involved, it issued a so-called "green paper," and then white paper, calling for a new, nonprofit corporation to assume responsibility for domain name and address policy—and for such a body to arise from private sector consensus. With many twists and turns along the way, this consensus failed, but the US government decided to proceed with a contentious proposal for the establishment of a body called ICANN (www.icann.org). Established in September 1998 in less than propitious circumstances, ICANN went through a series of difficult battles over how its membership would be represented.

ICANN's initial aspirations were global and democratic in tenor, but the problem was that it was an organization that had been created without agreement on its fundamental principles and structure. Initially, its Membership Advisory Committee[14] recommended a proposal that allowed an "at-large" membership of individuals who would each have one vote for board members in both regional and global categories. ICANN management tried to abandon this proposal, but then backed down, and an "at-large election" took place, which saw the election of non-ICANN-endorsed candidates, who were indeed outright opponents of the organization's policies. However, management and the board "acted to contain the elected board members and minimize their impact." Not surprisingly, the dissent over ICANN's less-than-democratic approach to governance continued, with its most visible form perhaps being the creation of a watchdog, ICANNWatch (www.icannwatch.org). Despite such a legitimacy crisis, ICANN has consolidated its role. In September 2006, ICANN signed a new agreement with the US Department of Commerce, which claimed to move a step closer to genuine, independent governance.

What is evident from the debate over domain names in the 1990s, which resulted in the creation of the awkward compromise of ICANN, is the considerable interest from a range of contributors, even those from civil society, in apparently narrow technical, administrative, and governance matters concerning the Internet.[15] It is fair to say, however, that only a relatively small subsection of civil society contributors maintained an interest in debates about domain names. Yet, domain names have become a legitimate and important part of a very wide range of debates about who controls the Internet. This breadth and depth of public concern about Internet governance came to light through the watershed events associated with WSIS.

INTERNET GOVERNANCE ON THE WORLD STAGE: THE PROMISES AND TRIBULATIONS OF WSIS

We might recall that the governance and participation processes and institutions of the Internet were initially quite small, decentralized, informal, and relatively uncontentious, being as they are the provinces of the technically informed researchers and engineers. The development of the Internet, and its governance, were reliant upon one country in particular: the United States. There is a striking contrast between Internet governance as it developed and transformed in the late 1990s and tele-communications.

In telecommunications we see the legacy of the twentieth-century struc-ture and organization via national carriers and administration. Technical standards, international coordination, and policy matters were dealt with by one of the first modern international organizations, the International Telecommunications Union (ITU). Founded in 1865 as the International Telegraph Union, the ITU is one of the specialist agencies of the United Nations (UN) and is headquartered in Geneva. The membership of the ITU comprises countries ('member states'), but companies and other organizations can also hold associate or 'sector member' status, allowing them to participate in particular activities of interest, such as technical standardization. The ITU became something of a byword for its exhaus-tive, consultative, top-down standardization development, often con-trasted with the nimble, speedy, bottom-up, Internet community efforts. In the 1990s, the ITU was reshaped with the decisive victory of private interests over the former public operators of telecommunications. Hence the ITU now reflected the power of new market entrants into telecommu-nications, as well as the new dynamics represented by privatized, former government carriers. The role of governments had decisively shifted from operator, standards-setter, and regulator rolled into one post-telegraph telecommunications agency to a residual, last-resort determinant of pol-icy and regulation.

What was intriguing about WSIS was the re-emergence of the ITU as the lead agency of a UN effort to hold a world discussion on Internet, ICTs, and development. The ITU had, for some time, taken an active interest in telecommunications and development through a number of high-profile initiatives in the 1990s. Elsewhere, the issues of Internet and development had received considerable attention, and been widely debated, especially with the coining of the term *digital divide*. The idea of WSIS was first proposed in 1998, and the importance of the availability of new technol-ogy benefits to all was included in the UN Millenium Declaration.[16] In 2001, the UN General Assembly ratified the idea of WSIS,[17] and gave lead responsibility for its organizing to the ITU, later acknowledging that:

> Information and communication technologies are among the critical determinants for creating a global knowledge-based economy, acceler-ating growth, raising competitiveness, promoting sustainable develop-ment, eradicating poverty and facilitating the effective integration of all countries in the global economy.[18]

In 2002, the ITU identified three objectives and nine themes for WSIS. As well as access, ICTs for social and economic development, security, and training, the role of different sectors (government, business, civil society), and others, the last two themes were:

- Cultural identity and linguistic diversity, local content, and media development; and
- Identifying and overcoming barriers to the achievement of an information society with a human perspective.

As Marc Raboy and Norman Landry observe:

> the ITU's initial documentation on the WSIS suggests a fundamentally technology-centred approach to the issues of the information society.[19]

An essential part of the first phase of the WSIS process was the Preparatory Committees (PrepComs). The role of nonstate actors in these Prep-Coms was vexed because they were positioned as observers and advisors, with governments dominating—despite a declaration endorsing a multistakeholder approach.[20] On the one hand, WSIS represented an important innovation in global governance, with the UN seeking to integrate nonstate actors, especially civil society and the private sector (who were accorded recognition as individual organizations, not just through peak bodies). On the other hand, this initiative unfolded in a force field, where governments and powerful corporations still reigned:

> For the first time, a UN Summit has been given an organizational structure [to] bring together representatives of member States, the private sector, civil society and various UN agencies . . . [however] the organizers' willingness ran counter to the States' way of seeing things . . . [21]

In response, civil society organized quickly, with many alliances, coalitions, and initiatives. Notably, there was the campaign for Communication Rights in the Information Society (www.crisinfo.org), launched by a number of important groups, not the least of which was an organization that pioneered the Internet, the Association for Progressive Communications (APC).[22]

There is no space here for a detailed discussion of the two phases around the grand meetings in Geneva and Tunisia, or for assessments of the outcomes, let alone the follow-ups. Instead, I want to briefly reflect on the significance of WSIS for discussions of the internationalizing Internet.

What was striking about WSIS was that the debates were not restricted to narrow understandings of the digital divide—the discussions were very comprehensive indeed. Further, there were genuine, if deeply problematic, efforts to incorporate disadvantaged countries, groups, and actors. There is widespread sense that WSIS was a failure, and considerable disappointment regarding this. I certainly agree with critics that the key models that guided WSIS embodied political positions and significant limitations that proved

fatal, as Communication Rights in the Information Society organizer, Seán
Ó Siochrú, argues:

> The failure of the WSIS Declaration and Action Plan is a reflection of the
> extremely limited room for manoeuvre available within the compromised
> "information society" debate. It is an expression of the limitations of
> the neo-liberal model, of a failure of imagination and political will by
> governments incapable of questioning its basic tenets, and of a refusal of
> powerful countries to consider alternative paradigms . . . This is the final
> position, the ultimate stalemate, of a specific conception of the informa-
> tion society that had its defining moment a decade earlier, but was then
> securely and exclusively tied to the market-driven agenda.[23]

Yet, WSIS has an important legacy. It is no exaggeration to say that a global
movement arose through a shared focus on ensuring that the diversity and
importance of civil society concerns and their voices were recognized in the
WSIS deliberations. There were a wealth of responses to generating discussion, documentation, proposals, and interventions on behalf of civil society
into the WSIS processes. Also created was a large popular, policy, and academic literature on WSIS.[24] This body of work not only dwarfs the corresponding analysis of Internet governance elsewhere, it is literature in which
nontechnical disciplines are featured, notably media and communications
studies. There are a number of reasons for this, one of which is because
of the connections that might be drawn between the 1970s preoccupation
with New World Information and Communication Order, and international
responses, and organizing, and that of WSIS.[25] The two key milestones here
were the 1980 MacBride Report and the 1984 Maitland Report.[26]

Also highly visible were innovative uses of the Internet to organize, document knowledge and concerns, and circulate information. The Internet was
also used to inform those interested in international civil society of the min-
ute-by-minute development of WSIS PrepCom meetings and the summits
themselves. WSIS provided a handy theater for the development and representation of international concerns about the shaping, spread, implications,
and control of Internet and associated technologies. As Raboy observes:

> The WSIS is therefore above all a space of confrontation between oppos-
> ing communicational paradigms. The opposition to the current dominant
> model has been reorganized in a new political space where civil society is
> called upon to be increasingly present. The WSIS exemplifies, therefore,
> the important trends emerging in global governance, encouraging civil
> society to participate more actively in defining a new global public sphere
> and to integrate more deeply to developing transnational public policy.[27]

The lightening rod for civil society concerns was governance. The failure
of the 2003 summit to agree on Internet governance saw the formation of

the Working Group on Internet Governance. Thus, one outcome of WSIS was that Internet governance did broaden, explicitly seeking to be more inclusive. This was nicely evoked when the redoubtable Cerf, in his role as Chairman of ICANN, opened the first Internet Governance Forum in Athens in late 2006, and declared:

> It is equally important that we preserve the global interoperability of the Internet even as we strive to make it more inclusive of all the world's languages. Already, UNICODE is helping us to record and present information in many of the world's languages on web pages and in massive databases. There is a strong interest in the existing and nascent Internet community to have the ability to register domain names written in the characters used in their preferred languages and therein lies a huge technical challenge.[28]

CONCLUSION: GOVERNANCE STRUGGLES AND THE INTERNATIONALIZING INTERNET

Most of the chapters in this book chart the take-up of the Internet in various settings around the world, and together suggest the importance of doing justice to the international character of this technology. As many of the contributors note, part and parcel of the everyday use and appropriation of the Internet in particular contexts is a desire to fashion the technology so that it meets the needs of users and their societies. This has had direct implications on how the Internet is governed.

Therefore, the case of the Catalan community shows that limitations of the design of the domain-name system, in which upper-level domains are organized around nation-states—but that particular polities and societies might wish to have their online identity recognized, even though their claim to national status is problematic, in the eyes of dominant ways of understanding and listing nations. The orthography, grammar, and customs attached to particular language communities, such as Welsh, Asian languages, or languages using Cyrillic scripts, is still not adequately registered in the range of codes, standards, applications, and protocols that comprise the Internet and associated technologies, and so a mix of sociotechnical activities need to be undertaken by representatives and advocates for those groups.

My focus in this chapter has been to shift away from detailed studies of Internet consumption, use, and imagining in order to consider instead the governance debates that have played out on a global level. There are a number of conclusions I would suggest when thinking about the theme of internationalizing Internet studies.

First, it is clear that the internationalizing dynamic of Internet diffusion has revealed a set of issues for the design of governance and policy arrangements (as well as challenges for the design of the technology itself). Through the two pivotal case studies discussed here, domain-name governance and WSIS, we can see how new actors emerged in Internet technology processes—with new expectations that enlarged the field of action and complicated its *dramatis personae*, assumptions, structures, and routines. While these governance issues are still very much alive, we can see that they, at least partly, arose because of demands that Internet governance match its multifarious users better—and especially that the Internet move beyond the special relationship with one country (the United States), and find a satisfactory, if novel, form to capture the demands for participation of a range of governments, private sector actors, nongovernmental organizations, individual Internet users, as well as those prior custodians of Internet technology and community.

Second, if this exercise became tricky with ICANN, it became immensely more so with WSIS, and the very large notions of governance, equality, development, cultural citizenship, and so, by which Internet governance was amply framed. Questions well-known to those involved in international policy, treaties, and organizations such as the UN, were visited on Internet governance: who speaks, in what languages, who decides, how the powerless and marginalized are addressed, and how do we meet claims to democracy and development, as well as technical collaboration and interworking. While WSIS was still dominated by the interests of the most powerful and wealthy countries and classes, it nonetheless allowed the formulation and discussion of many of the questions raised in this volume, which had previously been on the fringe of Internet policy and governance discussions.

Third, through the domain-name governance debates, but especially through WSIS, new forms of collective action at the international level emerged. These used the Internet, its practices, affordances, and cultures to constitute (or at least reconstitute) a global social movement—one that centered on claims and actions concerning the Internet. Some have argued that, if nothing else, WSIS evidences a global civil society or global public sphere, springing forth from the conditions of globalization and the new network technologies that characterize this.[29] From a different perspective, theorists such as Ned Rossiter seek to understand such movements as "organized networks" (as opposed to "networked organizations"), characterized by the new modes of Internet and digital cultures.[30] These are important developments and debates that we need to engage in as we consider the forms and implications of the Internet's internationalization for governance, power, and the place of citizens, users, and consumers.

NOTES

1. For details on Internet governance, particularly regarding domain names, see Daniel J. Paré, *Internet Governance in Transition: Who is the Master of this Domain?* (Lanham, MD: Rowman & Littlefield, 2003); Milton L. Mueller, *Ruling the Root: Internet Governance and the Taming of Cyberspace*

(Cambridge, MA: MIT Press, 2005). For a succinct primer that explains the basics of Internet technology, see also, Roger Clarke, "An Internet Primer: Technology and Governance," in *Virtual Nation: The Internet in Australia*, ed. Gerard Goggin (Sydney, Australia: University of New South Wales Press), 13–27. Materials that are helpful for a broad understanding of historical and contemporary Internet policy are: Brian Kahin and Janet Abbate, eds., *Standards Policy for Information Infrastructure* (Cambridge, MA: MIT Press, 1995); Brian Kahin and James H. Keller, eds., *Coordinating the Internet* (Cambridge, MA: MIT Press, 1997); Sandra Braman, ed., *The Emergent Global Information Policy Regime* (New York: Palgrave Macmillan, 2004). On Internet governance in regional settings, see Indrajit Banerjee, ed., *The Internet and Governance in Asia: A Critical Reader* (Singapore: Asian Media Information and Communication Centre and Nanyang University, 2007).

2. IAB, "A Brief History of the Internet Advisory / Activities / Architecture Board," http://www.iab.org/about/history.html
3. Internet Engineering Task Force, "Overview of the IETF," http://www.ietf.org/overview.html
   On the IETF, see Susan Harris, "The Tao of IETF—A Novice's Guide to the Internet Engineering Task Force," RFC 3160, Internet Society, http://www.ietf.org/rfc/rfc3160.txt (August 2001).
4. Harald Alvestrand, "A Mission Statement for the IETF," RFC 3935, http://www.ietf.org/rfc/rfc3935.txt (October 2004).
5. Vint Cerf, "RFCs—The Great Conversation," in RFC Editor et al., "30 Years of RFCs," RFC 2555, ftp://ftp.rfc-editor.org/in-notes/rfc2555.txt (April 1999).
6. Mueller, *Ruling the Root*, 76; see also Jon Postel, "Assigned Numbers," RFC 790, ftp://ftp.rfc-editor.org/in-notes/rfc790.txt (September 1981); and Information Sciences Institute, "Internet Protocol;" RFC 791, ftp://ftp.rfc-editor.org/in-notes/rfc791.txt (September 1981).
7. Zaw-Sing Su and Jon Postel, "The Domain Naming Convention for Internet User Applications," RFC 819, ftp://ftp.rfc-editor.org/in-notes/rfc819.txt (August 1982).
8. International Organization for Standardization (ISO), "ISO 3166 Code Lists," http://www.iso.org/iso/en/prods-services/iso3166ma/02iso-3166-code-lists/index.html; Jon Postel and Joyce Reynolds, "Domain Requirements," RFC 920, ftp://ftp.rfc-editor.org/in-notes/rfc819.txt (October 1984).
9. Mueller, *Ruling the Root*, 79.
10. Micó and Masip, Chapter 8 in this volume; see also Peter Gerrand, "Cultural Diversity in Cyberspace: The Catalan Campaign to Win the New .cat Top Level Domain," *First Monday* 11, no. 1 (2006), http://www.firstmonday.org/issues/issue11_1/gerrand/index.html
11. Mueller, *Ruling the Root*, 81.
12. Ibid., 89.
13. On the curious nature of IANA as a confected entity, see Paré, *Internet Governance in Transition*, 17–18; and Mueller, *Ruling the Root*, 93–94. IANA first appeared in RFC 1083, listing Postel's colleague, Joyce K. Reynolds, as its contact (Internet Activities Board, "IAB Official Protocol Standards," RFC 1083, http://www.isi.edu/in-notes/rfc1083.txt [December 1988]). As Mueller suggests, such inventions and the language in which they were presented "reflected the technical community's growing conception of itself as an autonomous, self-governing social complex" (*Ruling the Root*, 93).
14. Mueller, *Ruling the Root*, 200.
15. Mueller offers a useful list of eleven types of stakeholders engaged in Internet governance struggles about domain names, including "civil society and civil liberties organizations" (*Ruling the Root*, 166–167).

16. UN General Assembly, Fifty-Fifth Session, *United Nations Millennium Declaration,* Resolution A/RES/55/2, http://www.itu.int/wsis/docs/background/resolutions/55–2.pdf (adopted September 18, 2000). In my description of WSIS, I am indebted to the ITU's official archive (http://www.itu.int/wsis/index.html), as well as various unofficial archives, a short list of which includes: the WSIS Papers project (http://wsispapers.choike.org/); WSIS blogs.org (http://www.edwebproject.org/wsisblogs/); the Heinrich Böll Foundation's WSIS Web site (http://worldsummit2003.org/), and the oppositional WSIS? We Seize (http://www.geneva03.org/). I have also drawn upon Marc Raboy and Normand Landry's excellent *Civil Society, Communication, and Global Governance: Issues from the World Summit on the Information Society* (New York: Peter Lang, 2005).

17. UN General Assembly, Fifty-Sixth Session, *World Summit on the Information Society,* Resolution A/RES/56/183, http://www.itu.int/wsis/docs/background/resolutions/56_183_unga_2002.pdf (adopted December 21, 2001). This was the first resolution on WSIS adopted by the UN General Assembly.

18. UN General Assembly, Fifty-Sixth Session, *Meeting of the General Assembly Devoted to Information and Communication Technologies for Development,* Resolution A/RES/56/258, http://www.itu.int/wsis/docs/background/resolutions/56–258.pdf (adopted January 31, 2002).

19. Raboy and Landry, *Civil Society, Communication, and Global Governance,* 13.

20. Ibid., 17–19. The original resolution encouraged "effective contributions from and the active participation of all relevant United Nations bodies . . . and encourages other intergovernmental organizations, including international and regional institutions, nongovernmental organizations, civil society and the private sector to contribute to, and actively participate in, the intergovernmental preparatory process of the Summit and the Summit itself" (Resolution A/RES/56/183).

21. Ibid., 30.

22. See CRIS Campaign, *Assessing Communication Rights: A Handbook,* http://www.crisinfo.org/pdf/ggpen.pdf (September 2005).

23. Ó Siochrú, "Will the Real WSIS Please Stand Up?"

24. For example, see Rhonda Breit and Jan Servaes, eds., *Information Society or Knowledge Societies?: UNESCO in the Smart State* (Penang, Malaysia: Southbound, 2005); Jan Servaes and Nico Carpentier, eds., *Towards a Sustainable Information Society: Deconstructing WSIS* (Bristol, U.K.: Intellect, 2006); WSIS Papers, *Information Society for the South: Vision or Hallucination? Briefing Papers Towards the World Summit on the Information Society* (Montevideo, Uruguay: Instituto del Tercer Mundo, 2005), http://www.choike.org/nuevo_eng/informes/3592.html

25. For a discussion of the 1970s and 1980s "communication debate," and also accounts of the "information society" and how these histories influenced WSIS, see Seán Ó Siochrú, "Will the Real WSIS Please Stand Up?: The Historic Encounter of the 'Information Society' and the 'Communication Society,'" *International Communication Gazette* 66 (2004): 203–224.

26. The MacBride Report: International Commission for the Study of Communication of Communication Problems, *Many Voices, One World* (Paris: UNESCO, 1980). The Maitland Report: International Telecommunications Union, *The Missing Link: Report of the Independent Commission for World-Wide Telecommunications Development* (Geneva: ITU, 1984). Also available online at http://www.itu.int/osg/spu/sfo/missinglink/index.html. For perspectives on the MacBride report 25 years later, see "25 Years of the MacBride Report: International Communication and Communication

Policies," special issue, *Quaderns del CAC*, http://www.portalcomunicacion.com/informe_macbride/eng/home.asp For a useful discussion of what has occurred since the Maitland Report, especially in light of WSIS, see Tim Kelly, "Twenty Years of Measuring the Missing Link," http://www.itu.int/osg/spu/sfo/missinglink/kelly-20-years.pdf (October 2005).

27. Marc Raboy, "The WSIS as a Political Space in Global Media Governance," *Continuum: Journal of Media & Cultural Studies* 18, no. 3 (2004): 357.

28. Vint Cerf, "Opening Remarks," (presented at the Internet Governance Forum, Athens, Greece 30 October–2 November, 2006), available at http://www.icann.org/announcements/announcement-1–30oct06.htm

29. Raboy, "The WSIS as a Political Space."

30. Ned Rossiter, *Organized Networks: Media Theory, Creative Labour, New Institutions* (Rotterdam: NAi; Amsterdam: Institute of Network Cultures, 2005).

Part II

Language Communities Online

5   Language on the Internet in Japan

Nanette Gottlieb

INTRODUCTION

This chapter discusses two aspects of language use on the Internet in Japan: what languages are used on websites and why, and innovative uses of the Japanese language itself in computer-mediated communication (CMC), including mobile messaging. While language use on the web in Japan, in terms of the selection of languages, is conservative overall with a strong monolingual bent, as dictated by national language policy, infrastructure, and cultural considerations, ludic use of the Japanese language itself online is multifaceted and far from conservative.

The Internet was developed using encoding technology not suited to languages that do not use the Roman alphabet. Convergence, therefore, at first seemed likely. Early views were that the Internet would become a linguistically homogenizing force, with English as its *lingua franca*, and in the mid-1990s the language of around 80 percent of websites was indeed English. Graddol predicted, however, that the proportion of English on the Internet would fall to around 40 percent over the following decade,[1] and, in fact, his estimate has been exceeded. A web poll based on data from Nielson/Net Ratings, the International Telecommunications Union, the Computer Industry Almanac and other sources[2] states that English was used by only 30 percent of the online population in 2006. The prestige of English as the global language of commerce, higher education, diplomacy, development, and many other fields remains strong, of course, but its overall share of language use in cyberspace has definitely declined. In the "blogosphere," it has already been overtaken by Japanese.[3] Studies on aspects of the multilingual Internet have recently begun to appear, highlighting the diversity of the languages used and the divergent practices found online.[4]

We must remember, though, that while multilingualism on the Internet has undoubtedly increased, it remains restricted. "Greater diversity does not mean that all languages are equal," Block notes.

> Bigger is still better in the pecking order of world languages as much of
> the proportional weight wrested away from English has been in favor

of a few major national languages. Thus Japanese, German, Chinese, French, Spanish, Russian and other languages of the economically advantaged nations of the world have managed to establish a strong presence on the Internet. . . . [5]

The list of the top ten languages used on the web, compiled by Internet World Stats, bears this out: the top six, in descending order, are English, Chinese, Japanese, Spanish, German, and French.[6] Chinese and Japanese, with character-based orthographies that many initially believed could not serve for electronic use, had risen by 2006 to the position of the second (13.8 percent) and third (8.3 percent) most commonly used languages on the web, respectively. Languages with smaller, less influential populations of speakers are likely to establish only a minor online presence, and any critical evaluation of the multilingual nature of the Internet needs to bear this in mind.

THE LANGUAGE OF THE JAPANESE WEB

"When cultures participate on the Internet, their websites are among the most visible forms of nationalism."[7] Japan is no exception. An enabling factor here is, of course, the capacity to access large amounts of information in the national language, an aspect usually linked with economic power: UNESCO-supported research indicates that while richer countries like Japan are able to access information in their own language, poorer ones may have to rely on English sources.[8] Indeed, Internet access itself, regardless of language, is closely correlated with the wealth of countries, as Khiabany and Sreberny (Chapter 13, this volume) note.

Japan has an old and venerated national language, a high literacy rate, does not recognize community languages in its language policies, and exhibits no perceived pressing need to teach and use foreign languages other than English as a language of international communication. Its minority groups have been perforce assimilated over time and speak Japanese. The domestic publishing industry is one of the largest in the world, and a thriving translation industry means that most information is readily available in Japanese not long after it has appeared in other languages. The constitution, like those of Australia, the United States, and the United Kingdom, contains no provisions relating to language; that Japanese is the national language is taken as a given. All this probably means that the Internet, and particularly the web, in Japan will remain largely monolingual, except for the instrumental use of English and a few other languages.

Although Japan was a relatively late starter in personal computer (PC)-based Internet uptake, a situation that it very quickly remedied around the mid-1990s, it now leads the world in the mobile Internet. The path to this pinnacle was not easy in linguistic terms, because the nature of the writing system—a blend of two phonetic scripts with ideographic characters long ago borrowed from China—necessitated the development of a much more complex electronic input–output system than was needed in the West. This put Japan about twenty years behind the United States and other countries in introducing word processing, but once the technology was on the market, uptake was swift. With stand-alone word processors rapidly replaced by PCs after the opening of the market to US-made Compaq clones in 1992, Japan soon established a substantial and rapidly increasing Internet presence using its own language.[9] Infrastructure considerations and policy indecision also played their parts in the slow start, of course, but without the resolution of the script-related issues, the Internet in Japan would perforce have used either romanized Japanese or English. Today, however, as Manabe (Chapter 20, this volume) points out, substantial numbers of users are able to access the "i-mode" Internet through the screens of mobile phones either in addition to or as a substitute for using PCs to access conventional websites.[10]

Can the Internet be construed as a globalizing force in Japan or not? Its uptake there does, of course, enable global interactions on personal, governmental, commercial, and other levels. At the level of language use, however, its function in this respect is limited to the barely there; that is, if "globalizing" is taken to mean "linguistically homogenizing": English-language sites account for only a very small part of the Japanese web. Cyberspace is a source of external influence and provides an overarching cosmopolitan arena for intercultural communication, but local cultural boundaries remain strong and fixed rather than being erased by that influence.[11] Language is probably the strongest factor here: when Japanese, for example, is marked as the norm and English as useful but foreign, the latter is unlikely to be used on websites for anything other than pragmatic or aesthetic reasons. English does pop up quite frequently as a design feature on websites, and a large number of English loanwords such as *"intaanetto"* (Internet) and *"pasukon"* (PC), written with the phonetic katakana script used for foreign loanwords, reflect both the influence of computerization on the language and the willingness in Japan to borrow words from other languages. However, English is not used widely on the Japanese web as a medium of communication. Japanese itself is not used worldwide as a language of diaspora or a legacy of colonialism to the extent that other languages are. Its use on the Internet conforms largely to the national borders of Japan.

Halavais' 1998 study of 4,000 websites and the destinations of their hyperlinks provides some empirical evidence for this. Despite the much-touted borderless nature of the Internet, this study found that entrenched cultural practices are not easily abandoned simply because the technology enables it: network usage patterns on the sites studied more often than not conformed to national borders; that is, sites most often linked to other sites within the same country. The study found that, in the case of Japan, the web was "relatively inward-linking:" 74.6 percent of its links were to other sites in Japan, with by far the greatest proportion of its external links being with the United States. "National cultures," the study concluded, "continue to exert a substantial influence on how [Internet] connections are made."[12]

It seems safe to assume from the factors discussed above, the restricted geographical spread of Japanese speakers, and the Halavais study that the Japanese-language web is accessed mainly by users in Japan itself or by Japanese living overseas. The difficulty of confirming this properly through empirical research highlights a methodological problem in Internet studies related to languages: while servers hosting webpages keep logs of where accesses (hits) originate, they do not usually keep records of the nature of any data transferred between the server and the user's browser. Even the access logs themselves can be problematic, as it is often not possible to tell from the address exactly where a user is located geographically: an address ending in .jp does not necessarily mean that the user is in Japan itself, since some Japanese companies use .jp in the web addresses for their overseas operations as well.[13] Halavais lists the two major problems with measuring information flow on the Internet: how to define where the Internet ends, and the fact that the Net is a distributed network, making it difficult to determine the relationship between information flow and the total amount of flow, and the relationship between information flow and users.[14] Methodologies vary: Sue Wright, in her introduction to an initial report on UNESCO's Initiative B@bel project, which promotes multilingualism on the Internet, espouses a user-questionnaire methodology, rather than a mechanical count-the-hits approach, which may not accurately reflect language use.[15] A UNESCO-supported Language Observatory Project, launched in 2003, is meant to "provide means for assessing the usage level of each language in cyberspace," periodically putting out statistical profiles.[16] Once this collaborative project is operational, it will be theoretically and practically possible to say how many webpages are written in any given language.

The use of languages on the Japanese Internet, then, insofar as they are able to be observed, reflects the adherence to national borders discussed above. The language of e-mail, chat rooms, and websites is overwhelmingly the national language. Japan is a textbook case of what Paolillo calls "pre-existing bias" with regard to language use on the Internet,[17] a term he has adopted from a framework developed by Friedman and Nissenbaum[18] for identifying bias in computer systems. Pre-existing bias exists independently of technology and refers to the institutional and attitudinal dimensions within which the technology operates. Its sources include:

> the historical distribution of language populations, economic arrangements favoring larger languages, and institutional policies of national states.

Pre-existing bias in Japan means that minority languages are regarded as more or less inconsequential in terms of government support. Where

Korean and Chinese appear on government websites, as discussed below, it is usually as an instrumental means of ensuring smooth travel or acculturation. Japanese is the juggernaut; the only other contender in terms of government, commercial, and other access is English, and even that appears only on a limited range of sites.

This is because language ideology is and always has been a powerful force in modern Japan, where language policy is informed by a view of Japanese as a key component of both individual and national identity. A highly influential ethnocentric and essentialist literary genre known as *Nihonjinron* (theories of what it means to be Japanese), which underpinned much of the governmental, academic, and cultural writing on Japanese society during the post-war period and is still influential today, pushed this line hard, portraying the language as somehow different from all other languages, while at the same time insisting on Japan's linguistic homogeneity.[19] In this deeply entrenched view, race, language, and culture are inextricably tied together. Today, however, Japan faces a compelling set of challenges brought about by post-1980 social and technological developments, specifically, increased globalization-induced immigration, the consequences of character-capable software for literacy, and the explosion of Internet availability on mobile phones. The evolution of policy to accommodate these changes is likely to be slow in coming.

The ongoing conflation of national identity with national language carries over to the Internet. The same is true, of course, for other countries. In many of the countries that we might think of as examples, politico-economic structures, such as the European Union, perforce lead to the use of member languages more widely than is the case with Japan, whose major international relationship is with the United States. Japan's growing immigration levels[20] may lead to a change in language expectations over the coming decades, but this has not yet made any significant inroads on the national psyche.

Ricento conceptualizes three stages in the development of language policy: the early stage, where language was viewed as both a pragmatic resource and a tool for nation-building; the 1970s and 1980s, when the neutral view of language gave way to a critical awareness of the ideological trappings of language policy; and the present stage, in which the focus is on global flows and identity interactions.[21] Japan is now in this third stage, while its existing language policies are largely derived from the first. The spread of a language's use depends to a large extent on the existence of official language policies in wide-reaching and pertinent public fields such as government and education. The Internet, however, is not as easily controlled by such policies. Language policy in Japan, at least at the national level, has not yet begun to come to grips with emerging multilingualism, let alone develop a policy regarding the Internet, even if the parameters and objectives of such a policy could be defined.

It has been suggested that UNESCO could work in the future toward sensitizing member states to the importance of voluntary policies promoting multilingualism on the Internet. The absence of language policies is seen as a critical gap that can be closed by developing "a veritable policy on digital content that obviously includes a language policy for the digital world,"[22] though it is not clear what such a policy would look like in actual practice. In the case of Japan, it may now be time to seek, as Katsuragi has proposed, the development of a "language policy framework;"[23] that is, an overarching set of policies that complements language policies and sets out the guiding ethos for language issues within the society. This might eventually include the Internet.

For the present, however, language use on the Japanese Internet in the main reflects the entrenched "one-country, one-language" mindset, with the instrumental exception of web sites offering multilingual information for tourists or new arrivals and those with established international links. Ellis, describing language choice when presenting information online, lists the options in terms of the audience: local (who has access and can use it) and global (who in the world wants to know). In cyberspace, people use the official language, the national language (used by the majority), and the local language(s) (used by a minority).[24] The options here are the same for Japan as for any other country in which the national language is not a world language: Japanese for local content and English (in the main) for international outreach on a limited and predictable range of sites (e.g., government, higher education, tourism, some commercial sites, some support group sites, and some scholarly and pop-culture sites).

The most proactive official use of other languages on the web, apart from language teaching sites, is found at local government level, where there are instrumental benefits to facilitating integration of non-Japanese residents into the community. The website of Tokyo's Kita-ku Ward Office, for example, alerts foreign newcomers to the existence of hard-copy bilingual residents' handbooks and provides information on living in the ward in Japanese, English, Chinese, and Korean.[25] A quick survey of the top-level web pages of the 23 special wards of central Tokyo reveals that (in addition to Japanese) 20 offer web pages in English and 11 supplement that with Chinese and Korean. Katsushika Ward offers Chinese only, and Taito-ku (home of several major national museums) adds information pages in French and German to the other four options. Shinjuku Ward offers an online video on living in the area in English, Chinese, and Korean; Suginami and Edogawa Wards both offer multilingual online handbooks (English, Chinese, and Korean) of the same kind. The web site of the Tokyo Metropolitan Government itself provides for Japanese, English, Chinese, and Korean users, as well as cell phone access.[26]

These language offerings reflect the insignificant place of foreign languages other than English within national language policies. A suggestion for overcoming this was made several years ago in a Prime Minister's Commission on Japan's Goals in the Twenty-First Century discussion paper, which contained two language-related recommendations. The one that garnered all the attention was the suggestion that, as mastery of English was an essential element in global literacy, then in addition to strengthening education in that language, consideration might be given in the long term to making it an official second language of Japan. Overshadowed was a paragraph in the section dealing with "neighborly relations," which observed that:

> we should . . . dramatically expand our programs of Korean and Chinese language instruction. In addition, we should develop a sense of neighborliness by providing multilingual information displays at major locations throughout Japan that include Korean and Chinese alongside English.[27]

The above brief survey of ward web sites indicates that the second aim—that of providing multilingual information displays—has been achieved online by around 50 percent of Tokyo's special wards. Signs in Chinese and Korean also greet arrivals at major airports and other facilities.[28] The incorporation of regional languages into the school curriculum, however, has not seen any great degree of progress. The use of languages other than Japanese on government web sites thus reflects the low profile they are accorded compared to the national emphasis on English as the foreign language of choice.

INNOVATIVE USES OF JAPANESE ONLINE

We turn now to the nature of the changes in written Japanese observable in older forms of CMC, such as chat rooms and bulletin boards, and newer forms, such as mobile text messaging. Mobile phone (*keitai*) messaging is especially important in Japan, where:

> a broad consensus has been formed that the usage of keitai, including especially the myriad wireless Internet applications, is central to the transformation of the Japanese information society, a process significantly distinct from the development of computer-based Internet in other countries.[29]

At the end of March 2006, mobile phone subscribers accounted for almost 96.5 million of the approximately 128 million people in Japan.[30] Since a distinctive feature of keitai use in Japan is its heavy reliance on mobile e-mail, with younger users preferring to send text messages rather than use their phones to make voice calls,[31] we can expect to see much more research forthcoming on the kind of language used in this medium.

The Japanese writing system lends itself well to play because the interplay of the three scripts[32] allows variation and surprise through tweaking the accepted conventions. For example, one of the two phonetic scripts might be substituted for the other to impart an unexpected brio, much like the use of different fonts allows in English. Unsurprisingly, therefore, in the studies undertaken of language use in CMC, unconventional uses of orthography play as big a part as unconventional uses of language itself.

This is particularly true with text messages. During the early 1990s, text messages sent by pagers became a common means of communicating among students; after 1996, the mobile phone replaced the pager. Fujimoto notes that while many aspects of the pager and mobile phone as information and communication devices were developed by American, British, and northern European companies, the evolution of these devices in Japan has taken a distinctive trajectory, and that Japan is now a major exporter of what he calls "keitai culture" (which includes i-mode mobile Internet messaging, photo and movie e-mail, unconventional digital font styles, and a host of associated items).[33]

Keitai text messaging is dominated by women in their teens and twenties.[34] Low service prices make this an economically attractive way of staying in touch. One contributing factor to the reliance on text messaging rather than voice calls is that in countries such as Japan where public transport is the main means of getting around, people develop skills in using mobile messaging faster than in societies where the car is king (e.g., the United States).[35] In this regard, the social norm in Japan of "no voice, e-mail okay" in public places, particularly on trains, also plays a part.[36] Not surprisingly, in such text messages, as in online chat rooms, the tone is casual and colloquial, featuring use of onomatopoeia, childish expressions, regional dialect, and emoticons from the handset's built-in offerings.[37]

Emoticons play a role in Japan as elsewhere in CMC. They are known in Japanese as *kaomoji* (face characters) or *emoji* (picture characters). Many dictionaries of *kaomoji*, either hard-copy or online, have been published since 1993; some can be downloaded from web sites directly onto the user's computer.[38] In mobile phones, they are built in. As in English, emoticons often substitute for words, usually conveying information about nonverbal emotional aspects of communication that the user may not wish to spell out and, therefore, function as abbreviations to save time and energy in key strokes. Such symbols help to disambiguate meaning.[39] Katsuno and Yano liken their use in chat rooms to the language of *manga*, now used in cyberspace, and point to the rich field of cultural intertextuality, which has led to the phenomenon.[40]

Recent years have seen a phenomenon known as *gyaru moji* (gal talk) in text messaging. One version of this divides characters into their component parts and arranges them in a predetermined codified manner. For example, phrases appear in a straight line with word spaces indicated by punctuation. Spaces between words are not a feature of written Japanese, but are necessary in this version to decode the message. Another version uses characters that are just slightly wrong in some way, relying on the context and the intended reader's assumed knowledge to provide the meaning, just as email or text messages in English use, for example, "2nite" for "tonight." Messages may also include roman letters, typographic or mathematical symbols, Greek letters, and others. This type of language play is very popular among teenage girls using cell phones, hence the name "gal talk." It functions as a form of codification that protects privacy and indicates membership of an in-group of friends. One web site, *Gyaru Moji Henkan* (Gal Talk Conversion),[41] converts user input into *gyaru moji*, offering three degrees of scrambling of the original text, which can then be sent straight to a friend's cell phone. Inputting 三時に会いましょう (*sanji ni aimashō*, let's meet at three), for example, turns into 三時に会ぃまUょぅ, with a "mild" scramble; that is, the only difference is that one of the phonetic symbols has been replaced with a capital U and two of the others have been made smaller. The same phrase given the "all-out" option returns 三時レ二会レヽмaUょぅ: the first phonetic symbol, formerly hiragana "ni" に, is now レ二 (a combination of the two katakana symbols pronounced "re" and "ni"); the hiragana "i" ぃ in "aimashō" has likewise been scrambled into レ; the hiragana "ma" ま has been romanized to MA; again the "shi" し hiragana symbol has been replaced with a capital U; and the final hiragana symbol has been made smaller.

Miller characterizes this type of linguistic innovation by a small group of young women as a challenge to the dominant models of gendered language and behavior. Through transgressing society's gender-related linguistic expectations in this way, she argues, *kogals*—"the mainstream media label used to describe young women between the ages of 14 and 22 who project new types of fashion, behavior, and language"—constitute a distinctive subcultural group and "symbolize the ongoing redefinition of women in late capitalism."[42] In Japan, where expectations of language use have always carried a heavy moral and symbolic freight of cultural nationalism, concern over perceived *kotoba no midare* (disarray in the language) is frequently discussed in the media and in books. "Gal talk" writing practices tie in with this perception, earning the usual headshakes from older people, who may tend to view language use as a barometer of society's moral health. Users, however, simply see it as "cool." Because it is a restricted code by its very nature, we are unlikely to see a more generalized adoption of these innovations.

Language play found in messages posted at Channel 2 (*2-channeru*), a well-known unmoderated Japanese web site, which is often controversial because of the outspoken nature of some postings, has also been investigated. Analyzing a corpus of data taken from Channel 2 glossaries and from posted messages that deviate from standard usage, Nishimura[43] has classified unusual linguistic practices into three groups:

- Using characters (ideographs) phonetically to spell out words with the same pronunciation but different meanings, i.e., a type of "kanji punning" enabled by the large number of homophones in Japanese. The character 鯖, meaning "mackerel" and pronounced "saba," for example, may be used as a shortcut for the word "saabaa" (server, a loanword from English usually written in katakana). Characters may also be used phonetically for speed, special connotations, or euphemisms: avoiding the use of the character 死, meaning "death," for example, by substituting it with another character with the same pronunciation but a different meaning, so that the expression "shine" (drop dead) is written 市ね, rather than 死ね, using the character for "city" instead.

- Playing with symbols (usually in the katakana script) that are very similar in shape, replacing one with another that is visually almost identical, but represents a different sound, e.g., using ソ (so) instead of ン (n).

- What Nishimura calls "conventionalized errors;" that is, inadvertent literacy errors (such as using, in good faith, the wrong character for a word), which are then adopted for their entertainment value, or typing errors.

Nishimura later extended her investigation of online language use to a study of linguistic features of CMC. Investigating bulletin boards on fan sites, she found that most of the features identified by Danet in English-language CMC (which included multiple punctuation, eccentric spelling, added emphasis, vocalizations of laughter, or weeping) were also found in Japanese, using similar strategies, if not always exact, correspondences. Where an English message might include an asterisk for emphasis as in, for example, "I'm really *angry* at you," in Japanese, katakana script would replace a word normally written in hiragana for the same purpose (e.g., ヨロシクお願いします instead of よろしくお願いします). The repetition of an English syllable as in "hahahahahaha" to indicate laughter occurs in Japanese as ふふふ (fufufu).[44]

As the three studies outlined above show, what we are seeing now in Japan is a very deliberately undertaken manipulation of the orthography, often combined with the features of informal spoken Japanese, in order to achieve conciseness, style, and wit. Brevity is the great virtue of characters when compared to phonetic scripts: the word "watashi," meaning "I," for example, may be written with one character 私, but requires three symbols—わたし—to write in hiragana. Language play has always been a feature of written Japanese; what we are seeing now is this tradition moving into new areas mediated by electronic technologies. As Nishimura found in the case of the Channel 2 usages and Miller found in the case of the kogals, language play of this sort functions as an identity marker within a subcultural community. Habuchi extends this:

> the new forms of communication enabled by keitai influence the acknowledgment of the self" in that "there has never been a technology like keitai that has so completely achieved a one-on-one connection between the user and the device.[45]

CONCLUSION

This chapter has shown that language use on the Internet in Japan is in one sense conservative, reinforcing national preoccupations with language, and in another sense reactive, in that what use of foreign languages there is on the public web occurs as a result of perceived instrumental needs. The well-worn national parameters are Japanese for everyday use, English for sites likely to have a wide international reading, and regional languages for specific domains relating to non-Japanese residents and tourists. This confirms both Halavais' speculation that language use on the Internet largely conforms to national borders and Wright's observation that:

> groups with prestige standard written languages are increasingly able to use these language for all their various information gathering and interactive activities on the Internet.[46]

However multilingual the Internet may become in terms of the number of languages used online, Japan exemplifies a major world player whose information needs can be met through the use of its own language both online and off, and that is unlikely to change.

In a second dimension, though, that of language play online, the use of Japanese on the Internet can be far from conservative. The features of CMC in informal settings, such as bulletin boards and e-mail or text messages, replicate the tendency to informality and use of spoken discourse features also found in other language communities. In Japan, users tweak, manipulate, and otherwise play with standard orthographic conventions online, subverting norms in order to strengthen in-group solidarity and create subcultural identities for themselves. While such language play is certainly not conservative, it is also not particularly new, although the subcultural aspect may be intensified by the technology. These practices build on the long tradition permitted by the nature of the Japanese writing system, as often seen in the text of advertisements or invitations. Over the last fifteen years, the practice has moved online, where it will no doubt continue to flourish.

NOTES

1. David Graddol, *The Future of English?* (London: The British Council, 2000), 61.
2. "Internet Users by Language," http://www.internetworldstats.com/stats7.htm (accessed August 8, 2006).
3. A Technorati survey found that, in March 2006, Japanese-language blogs accounted for 37 percent of the total (cf. 31 percent in English); the report also noted that Japanese bloggers appeared to write shorter blogs more often, possibly because blog entries were being sent from mobile phones. David Sifry, "State of the Blogosphere, April 2006 Part 2: On Language and Tagging," http://www.sifry.com/alerts/archives/000433.html
4. See, for example, Brenda Danet and Susan Herring, eds., "The Multilingual Internet: Language, Culture and Communication in Instant Messaging, Email and Chat," *Journal of Computer-Mediated Communication* 9, no. 1 (2003), http://jcmc.indiana.edu/vol9/issue1/

5. David Block, "Globalization, Transnational Communication and the Internet," *IJMS: International Journal on Multicultural Societies* 6, no. 1 (2004): 35, http://www.unesco.org/shs/ijms/vol6/issue1/art2

6. "Internet Users," http://www.internetworldstats.com/stats7.htm

7. Carolyn Wei and Beth Kolko, "Resistance to Globalization: Language and Internet Diffusion Patterns in Uzbekistan," *New Review of Hypermedia and Multimedia* 11 (2005): 212.

8. Sue Wright, "Thematic Introduction," *IJMS: International Journal on Multicultural Societies* 6, no. 1 (2004): 10, http://www.unesco.org/shs/ijms/vol6/issue1/art1

9. See Nanette Gottlieb, *Word-Processing Technology in Japan: Kanji and the Keyboard* (Richmond, UK: Curzon Press, 2000) and Nanette Gottlieb, *Language and Society in Japan* (Cambridge: Cambridge University Press, 2005).

10. More people accessed the Internet through cell phones than through PCs in 2005 (Ministry of Internal Affairs and Communication, *Jōhō Tsūshin Hakusho Heisei 18nenban* [White paper on communications, 2006]),http://www.johotsusintokei.soumu.go.jp/whitepaper/ja/h18/pdf/18honpen.pdf

11. Soraj Hongladarom, "Global Culture, Local Cultures and the Internet: The Thai Example," *AI & Society* 13 (1999): 389–481.

12. Alexander Halavais, "National Borders on the World Wide Web," *New Media & Society* 2 (2000): 16, 22.

13. Jim Breen, "Re: Query About Japanese Internet Sources," e-mail to author (June 6, 2006).

14. Halavais, "National Borders," 9–10.

15. Wright, "Thematic Introduction," 8.

16. Yoshiki Mikami, Ahamed Zaki abu Bakar, and Virach Sonlert-Lamvanich, "Language Diversity on the Internet: An Asian View," in *Measuring Linguistic Diversity on the Internet*, ed. UNESCO Institute for Statistics (Montreal: United Nations Educational, Scientific and Cultural Organization, 2005), 101. Also available online at http://unesdoc.unesco.org/images/0014/001421/142186e.pdf

17. John Paolillo, "Language Diversity on the Internet," in *Measuring Linguistic Diversity on the Internet*, ed. UNESCO Institute for Statistics (Montreal: United Nations Educational, Scientific and Cultural Organization, 2005), 50 Also available online at http://unesdoc.unesco.org/images/0014/001421/142186e.pdf

18. Batya Friedman and Helen Nissenbaum, "Bias in Computer Systems," in *Human Values and the Design of Computer Technology*, ed. Batya Friedman (Stanford, CA: CSLI Publications, 1997), 21–40.

19. The influence of this genre was at its height in the 1980s and 1990s. Although other views of Japan have arisen to challenge it, it remains influential.

20. Immigration, though still small in comparison with other countries, has increased significantly since the 1980s, and is likely to continue to rise. In 2004, the population included nearly two million registered foreigners, along with an estimated quarter of a million undocumented foreign residents (overstayers).

21. Thomas Ricento, *Ideology, Politics, and Language Policies: Focus on English* (Amsterdam: John Benjamins, 2000).

22. Daniel Pimienta, "Linguistic Diversity in Cyberspace—Models for Development and Measurement," in *Measuring Linguistic Diversity on the Internet*, ed. UNESCO Institute for Statistics (Montreal: United Nations Educational, Scientific and Cultural Organization, 2005), 27. Also available online at http://unesdoc.unesco.org/images/0014/001421/142186e.pdf

23. Takao Katsuragi, "Japanese Language Policy from the Point of View of Public Philosophy," *International Journal of the Sociology of Language*, 175/176 (2005): 41–54.
24. Simon Ellis, "Monitoring Language Diversity," http://portal.unesco.org/ci/en/ev.phpURL_ID=19199&URL_DO=DO_TOPIC&URL_SECTION=201.html (2005).
25. See "Kita City Official Home Page," http://www.city.kita.tokyo.jp/
26. Eighteen of the twenty-three wards mentioned provide cell phone versions of their web sites.
27. Prime Minister's Commission on Japan's Goals in the Twenty-First Century, "The Frontier Within: Individual Empowerment and Better Governance in the New Millennium," http://www.kantei.go.jp/jp/21century/report/overview.html (2000).
28. See Peter Backhaus, *Linguistic Landscapes* (Clevedon: Multilingual Matters, 2007).
29. Manuel Castells, Mireia Fernandez-Ardevol, Jack Linchuan Qiu, and Araba Sey, *The Mobile Communication Society: A Cross-Cultural Analysis of Available Evidence on the Social Uses of Wireless Communication Technology* (Los Angeles: Annenberg Research Network on International Communication, 2004), 103. Also available online at http://arnic.info/WirelessWorkshop/MCS.pdf
30. Ministry of Internal Affairs and Communication, *Jōhō Tsūshin*.
31. Tomoyuki Okada, "Youth Culture and the Shaping of Japanese Mobile Media," in *Personal, Portable, Pedestrian: Mobile Phones in Japanese Life*, ed. Mizuko Ito, Daisuke Okabe, and Misa Matsuda (Cambridge, MA: MIT Press, 2005), 49.
32. There are five if Arabic numerals and the occasional use of romanization are included.
33. Kenichi Fujimoto, "The Third-Stage Paradigm," in *Personal, Portable, Pedestrian: Mobile Phones in Japanese Life*, ed. Mizuko Ito, Daisuke Okabe, and Misa Matsuda (Cambridge, MA: MIT Press, 2005), 87.
34. Misa Matsuda, "Discourses of *Keitai* in Japan," in *Personal, Portable, Pedestrian: Mobile Phones in Japanese Life*, ed. Mizuko Ito, Daisuke Okabe, and Misa Matsuda (Cambridge, MA: MIT Press, 2005), 35.
35. Castells et al., *The Mobile Communication Society*, 38.
36. Daisuke Okabe and Mizuko Ito, "*Keitai* in Public Transportation," in *Personal, Portable, Pedestrian: Mobile Phones in Japanese*, ed. Mizuko Ito, Daisuke Okabe, and Misa Matsuda, *Life* (Cambridge, MA: MIT Press, 2005), 207.
37. I. Nakamura, "Keitai mail no ningen kankei," in *Nihonjin no Jōhō Kōdō 2000*, ["Human Relationships and *keitai* E-Mail," in *Japanese Information Behavior 2000*] (Tokyo: University of Tokyo Press, 2001), 285–303. Cited in "Discourses of *Keitai*," 35.
38. Hirofumi Katsuno and Christine Yano, "Face to Face: On-Line Subjectivity in Contemporary Japan," *Asian Studies Review*, 26 (2002): 211.
39. Brenda Danet, *Cyberpl@y: Communicating Online* (Oxford: Berg, 2001), 62.
40. Katsuno and Yano, "Face to Face," 213.
41. Gyaru "Moji Henkan," http://mizz.lolipop.jp/galmoji/
42. Laura Miller, "Those Naughty Teenage Girls: Japanese Kogals, Slang, and Media Assessments," *Journal of Linguistic Anthropology* 14 (2004): 225, 226.
43. Yukiko Nishimura, "Establishing a Community of Practice on the Internet: Linguistic Behaviour in Online Japanese Communication," in *Proceedings of the 29th Annual Meeting of the Berkeley Linguistics Society*, ed. Berkeley Linguistics Society (Berkeley, CA: Berkeley, 2004), 340–347.

44. Yukiko Nishimura, "Linguistic Innovations and Interactional Features of Casual Online Communication in Japanese," *Journal of Computer-Mediated Communication* 9, no. 1 (2003), http://jcmc.indiana.edu/vol9/issue1/nishimura.html

45. Ichiyo Habuchi, "Accelerating reflexivity," in *Personal, Portable, Pedestrian: Mobile Phones in Japanese Life*, ed. Mizuko Ito, Daisuke Okabe, and Misa Matsuda (Cambridge, MA: MIT Press, 2005), 179.

46. Wright, "Thematic Introduction," 12.

6 More than Humor
Jokes from Russia as a Mirror of Russian Life

Eugene Gorny

INTRODUCTION

Humor is one of the most important elements of culture. Humor reflects an immediate reaction of people to various life phenomena. Being a form of communication that makes people laugh or evokes feelings of amusement and happiness,[1] humor can make even unpleasant or painful situations acceptable or tolerable. Although humor seems to be a pan-human universal, it is also culturally specific inasmuch as it is based on language and culture. Humor is, therefore, "a key to understanding societies, as it reflects collective fears, ideologies, and social power."[2] National humor is one of the most powerful means of maintaining national identity through shared feelings and understandings.

The Internet altered traditional ways of dissemination of information, including humor, by allowing global reach and instant access. This chapter tells the story of the website, Jokes from Russia[3]—the most comprehensive, uncensored collection of Russian humor on the web. It argues that the online collection of such seemingly frivolous stuff, such as jokes, has performed a quite serious cultural function of "virtual (re)unification"[4] of Russians both in Russia and abroad on the basis of shared language, values, and sense of humor.

This is also a story of the Russian Internet, which has received relatively little attention in English-language scholarship. Western Internet studies, until recently, have almost completely ignored non-English segments of cyberspace and made their generalizations on the basis of the Anglo-American Internet. This bias has been recently admitted as a problem, which David Silver acknowledges as "a Western, English-speaking slant" in cyberculture/Internet studies.[5] There is a growing understanding of the need for "de-Westernizing media studies"[6] as well as Internet studies[7]. Hopefully, this study can contribute to a wider program of research into non-Anglophone uses and interpretations of the Internet, which is the key goal of this volume.

ONLINE HUMOR

This chapter addresses the issue "cyber humor," which has attracted the attention of Internet researchers very recently.[8] Shifman has formulated two research questions related to this topic:

a) To what extent does the Internet function as a mediator of traditional humorous forms and topics, and to what extent does it facilitate new humorous forms and topics?

b) How do the new forms and topics of online humor relate to fundamental characteristics of the Internet, such as interactivity, multimedia, and global reach?

These questions are instrumental to this chapter. However, we believe that the study of online humor *per se* should be supplemented by the study of the sociocultural context in which humor is generated and disseminated. This chapter also explores themes developed in the author's work elsewhere, such as the role of cultural identity and the social context as a shaping force of Internet culture; the correlation between personal and collective creativity on the Internet; the opposition between official and non-official media; and issues of censorship and free speech.[9]

To understand the role that Jokes from Russia has played on the Russian Internet, the social and cultural situation in the country should first be considered. The authoritative political regime and the underdevelopment of civic institutes in Russia led to the function of the public sphere being partially performed by literature. The traditional literature-centric nature of Russian culture has been reflected on the Russian Internet. The first Russian websites were devoted to literature and culture rather than technology or politics. The first Russian interactive projects were literary games, such as *Bouts-rimés*.[10] The consolidation of the Russian net community occurred around the online literary contest Teneta[11] and the "herald of net culture," Zhurnal.ru.[12] Writers have been among the most common users of the Russian-language segment of LiveJournal.[13] Jokes from Russia, to which users contribute jokes, real-life stories, and material from other literary genres, is among the most popular websites on the Russian Internet. The prominent role of literature and the abundance of literature-related websites is a striking characteristic of the Russian Internet, which seems to have no direct parallel in the West.[14]

Jokes (*anekdoty*), especially political ones, played a prominent role in the Soviet culture by giving people a way to express their real thoughts and feelings in a hypocritical environment dominated by Communist ideology. Under Stalin, one could be sent to the labor camp for ten years or even sentenced to death for telling a political joke; they could be treated as "anti-Soviet propaganda," which, according to Article 58 (Russia Soviet Federated Socialist Republic [RSFSR] Penal Code), was a capital offence. In later years, the attitude toward anekdoty softened, and even members of the Politburo and activists of the Communist Party indulged in telling anti-Soviet jokes. Anekdoty have become the major genre of Soviet/Russian urban folklore. Any significant event in domestic or international life was immediately echoed by fresh jokes transmitted from mouth to mouth and circulated all over the country. Of course, anekdoty includes not only political jokes, but also many other thematic groups and subgenres of jokes.[15] All these categories can be found on the Jokes from Russia website. "Some of the jokes are timeless, but many are commentaries on contemporary Russian life," notes an American observer.[16] Political jokes are not among the most popular ones. However, many jokes are in direct response to what is happening in the country.[17]

"Jokes are Russian sex"—this aphorism, popular at one point among Russian users, emphasized the disproportionate role that jokes have played in Russian Internet culture. The aphorism can be traced back to Leonid Delitsyn's article.[18] In his 1996 study of the online advertising market, Delitsyn found out that the most visited websites on the English-language Internet were sexually oriented. For example, Playboy.com provided erotic content that was second in number of views only to Netscape.com, which gave away its web browser for free. The Playboy website attracted a quarter of a million visitors daily, who generated five million hits. Other sex-related websites ranged from amateur hardcore to those requiring various systems of age verification. They generated high traffic and, correspondingly, could earn money by showing banner advertisements. Trying to find a prospective market for online advertising in Russia, Delitsyn set out to discover analogues to *Playboy* on the Russian Internet—and he failed! Instead, he found out a striking correlation between sex, humor, and literature on the Russian Internet.

> Apparently, at the present moment, the closest analogue to *Playboy* Magazine for the Russian reader is the game server Hussar Club, under whose banner are assembled jokes from Verner, limericks, Manin's bout rimes, works by Tolkienists, jokes about Lieutenant Rzhevski and other entertainments both innocent and "adult." According to my data, currently the most lively Russian entertainment pages are the collections of jokes by Dmitri Verner and Konstantin Okrainets. Russian sex . . . seriously funny! (*Russkij sex . . . anekdot, da I tol'ko!*)

A brief note on terminology used in the study may by useful. The original title of Verner's website may be (and sometimes is) translated as Anecdotes from Russia. However, this may be confusing for the English-language reader. In English, *anekdot* (*anekdoty* in plural) should be translated as "funny story," "short story with a punchline," or "joke" normally told in informal situations in a small circle of people. The website also includes the genre of *istorii*, which literally means "stories," but which is normally very close to "anecdotes" in the English meaning of the word. To escape terminological confusion, throughout the remainder of the chapter, I refer to anekdoty as jokes and to anecdotes as stories.

HISTORY OF THE JOKES FROM RUSSIA WEBSITE

Unlike the West, where the key agents of the Internet development were government and academia, the development of the Internet in Russia in the early 1990s was the result of mostly private initiatives.[19] If private companies created the technological prerequisites for the development of the Internet in Russia, the Russian Internet as a cultural phenomenon was developed by private persons—a relatively small group of young people, most of whom studied or worked in the West (in the United States, Israel, Germany, Estonia, Finland, and so on). They had a high level of creative drive and passion, access to the new technology, and spare time to play with it. They considered the Internet a hobby and a toy rather than work. These individuals felt their unity and energetically collaborated, making up a kind of creative cyber-élite as a group as opposed to passive users. In a few years, they managed to create successful projects of different types (media, online services, digital libraries, art, and entertainment). Through continuous experimentations, they had developed forms and patterns that were socially accepted and became commonly used and reproduced by others. Jokes from Russia is a vivid example of the creative projects of the "heroic period" of the early Russian Internet.

Jokes from Russia was launched on November 8, 1995. It was the second website Dmitri (Dima) Verner ever made; the first was Atomic Data for Astrophysics,[20] which he made a month earlier. Initially, Jokes from Russia was located on the server of the Department of Physics and Astronomy at the University of Kentucky, where Verner worked.[21] In the year after the launch of the website, it had more than one thousand visitors daily and generated about 80 percent of the traffic of the department's webpages.[22] The increase occurred in March 1996 when Alex Farber put a link to Jokes from Russia on his Germany-based website, Russian Literature on the Internet, a then-popular collection of links to Russian literature-related online resources. He also shared his scripts with Verner, and Jokes from Russia became available in different encodings (at that time, there was no standard encoding for Russian pages, and "advanced" websites provided four encodings plus transliteration to facilitate reading for users on different platforms). By autumn 1996, the daily traffic of Jokes from Russia reached one thousand visitors.

The audience grew, and soon Anekdot.ru became the most visited website on the Russian Internet. For more than a year, from April 1997 to August 1998, it held the first place in Rambler's Top 100, a popularity rating of Russian websites.[23] The August 1988 financial crisis gave rise to the development of online news publications, and pushed the Ros Business Consulting (RBC) news agency into first place in Rambler's Top 100. However, Jokes from Russia's traffic has remained extremely high. In 1998, the website had 12,000 visitors daily; that is, one visitor every 7 seconds. It was rated the second in Hitbox.com's international rating of entertainment resources, outstripping the website with photographs of Monica Lewinsky, and was behind only a website featuring nude celebrities' photos.[24] In 1999, it had 200,000

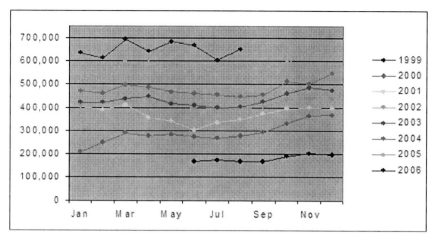

Figure 6.1   Anekdot.ru popularity growth: statistics by unique hosts per month. Data source: Mail.ru (2005), Verner (2005, 2006).

visitors per month, and by 2004 it reached the half million mark. Add to this the 90,000 users who subscribed to receive jokes by e-mail. One can mention that Anekdot.ru permanently occupies the first position in Rambler's Top 100 "Humor" category, gathering approximately two times more visitors than any other website in this field.

GENERAL CHARACTERISTICS OF THE WEBSITE

Let us proceed to the general characteristics of the website and compare them with what can be found elsewhere on the Internet. The most important of these characteristics are completeness, interactivity, and user contributions.

Completeness

The idea of Jokes from Russia as it was being formed at an early stage of the project was to collect and publish online all available Russian anekdoty without any discrimination. In a sense, it denied the oral nature of the genre (*anekdotos* in Greek means "unpublished"). This decision has had far-reaching consequences. In a few years, Anekdot.ru has drastically changed the traditional ways of the circulation of jokes in Russia and, as some people argue, undermined the nature of the genre itself.

The issue of selection was resolved at the very beginning: Verner decided that anekdoty would be a completely uncensored collection of jokes. This would allow the site to adequately represent present-day Russian folklore and, through it, to give an unbiased picture of the zeitgeist. The users supported this position, and it continues to be observed today. This made anekdoty different from the majority of other Russian and foreign humor websites that have followed tastes either of the owner or of the audience.[25] "The main aim of Anekdoty," emphasized Verner, "is not popularity, but objectivity and the completeness of the collection."[26]

Interactivity

The organization of Jokes from Russia was original and did not repeat existing models. American humor websites of the time normally consisted of long static lists of "canonical jokes" in plain text format. Daily issues of fresh jokes rated by users were Verner's innovation, which was later adopted by other Russian and foreign sites.[27] The list of most important innovations included daily updates, the encouragement of user contribution, feedback mechanisms, and a multilevel system of grading and sorting material.

In the beginning, Verner collected jokes from outside sources; later on, the majority of jokes were sent to him by e-mail. When the website was redesigned in late 1996, an interactive form appeared enabling users to post jokes. At the same time the Discussion Club was opened to discuss the censorship issue.[28] These innovations were significant since they gave users an opportunity to become co-producers, rather than passive readers of the website. Discussions in the Discussion Club and, since September 1998, in the bBook of Complaints and Suggestions, in which the most active and concerned part of the audience participated, have influenced the further evolution of the website.

The voting system was suggested by users in the Discussion Club section, and serves a number of functions. As Verner points out, a website aiming at the creation of the most comprehensive collection of modern folklore has to solve several problems simultaneously that, to a certain extent, are in a conflict with each other.[29] On the one hand, one needs to gather and publish everything without any censorship and selection. On the other hand, if one publishes everything in one stream without sorting, then the "signal" becomes choked up with the "noise." People cease sending "valuable" messages if they get lost in "garbage." Therefore, the site should include multistep sorting. As a matter of fact, the initial concept of the site—to publish issues of jokes while avoiding repetition—was already a means of separating the signal from the noise. Later on, when the popularity of Jokes from Russia grew and the site began to receive more than one hundred texts daily, the sorting became more complex. Now, all the texts are divided into "new" and "repeated," "main" and "the rest." An additional sorting of "the rest" is made by forming the "readers' top ten" (*chitatelskaya desyatka*), which results from voting. Therefore, voting (grading the texts) performs several functions at once: a) a way of sorting and separating the most "valuable" messages; b) testing the audience's reaction; and c) providing encouragement to the authors.

With the introduction of interactive elements (guestbooks, voting system, etc.) the Jokes from Russia site turned from a static collection of modern folklore into an open laboratory for creation of new folklore. This made a further development of the collection possible when the pool of known jokes was exhausted. This material, Verner emphasizes, could be used for the analysis of social, psychological, and linguistic processes in contemporary Russia. The combination of the total lack of censorship, the completeness of the collection, and the effective means of grading and sorting material, which prevents the "noise" from stifling the "signal," makes it a valuable instrument of scientific research. However, Verner complains, this material still awaits research.[30]

User Contributions

If the technological structure of the Internet was developed by specialists in computer and information science, then the development of Internet content and social applications has involved direct user participation. The Internet is probably the most participatory medium, allowing users to create content and contribute to the development of the medium itself. "Interactive creativity"[31] and the "hi-tech gift economy"[32] have been essential features of the Internet since its very beginning. Jokes from Russia is a striking example of "how users matter."[33]

While the core staff of Anekdot.ru has always consisted of Verner alone, at various stages, other people were involved in the project on a voluntary basis. Verner's first assistant, who compiled "second tens" from "repeating jokes" since 1997, was Aleksei Tolkachev, a Russian programmer living in the United States, also known as the first Russian LiveJournal user.[34] Arieh Edelstein joined the project in 1998—he began as a compiler of story issues, and then edited the aphorism and poetry sections. In late 1998, a literary salon, edited by Galya Anni, was launched on Anekdot.ru.[35] Since 2005, when Jokes from Russia became an independent enterprise, they have employed a paid staff. However, Jokes from Russia would be impossible without users' contributions. First, users have provided the lion's share of material published on the site—not only jokes in the proper sense, but also stories, poems, caricatures, and megabytes of discussion. Second, users have influenced—and sometimes determined—the ways of the site's development.

THE CREATOR OF JOKES FROM RUSSIA

Although the users' contributions cannot be overestimated, Jokes from Russia would not become what it is without the insight, enthusiasm, and daily work of its originator. In what follows, I analyze Dima Verner's motivation and personal traits, which have allowed him to maintain the website for so many years.

Verner liked to read jokes, and in the mid-1990s, he read them every day in the relcom.humor news group. However, he soon found out that were many repetitions and irrelevant discussions. Moreover, Verner wanted daily issues. Since there was no such page at the time, he decided to make it himself. In his own words, his initial motivation was "curiosity, the interest in the subject, the desire to make something which did not exist." [36]

At first he felt shy about his passion for such an insignificant thing as jokes. He showed his website to a few friends; their judgments were critical: "Half of the jokes are old stuff; three-fourths are not funny." It was then that he decided that he would collect not just "good" jokes, but all jokes without exception or selectivity. A new motivation began to reveal itself: to provide a complete picture of Russian life through jokes. Verner decidedly resisted the idea of his collection being presented as "Jokes from Verner," wanting to emphasize instead its transpersonal and national nature.[37] The scientific objectivity and impersonality, natural for an astrophysicist, became a foundation of Verner's collection of jokes and one of his personal motivations.

Daily issues of jokes attracted the audience and when Verner missed a day, people sent him messages: "What happened? Where is the new issue?" Verner found out that many people needed his website. Thus, a new motivation developed—a *responsibility to the audience*.

When Rambler's Top 100 was launched in March 1997 to measure the popularity of websites on the Russian Internet, Verner decided to participate "for the sport of it." *Emulation and competition with others*—which Kroeber considers the main moving force of the development of "cultural configuration"[38]—entered the scene.

Soon, Verner began to feel that the website distracted him from his main work. In the beginning, he spent about fifteen minutes making an issue; it was enough to scan through fresh news group articles, copy jokes, and paste them in a file. After the website appeared in Rambler's Top 100, he spent three to four hours daily, and his work on the site tended to devour all of his time if he did not control himself enough. He decided to discontinue the project. He declared his decision and immediately received an offer from ISP Cityline to continue the project for money. The *material stimulus*, Verner accepts, was a powerful motivation—especially for his family, which was extremely dissatisfied that he spent his time and energy on such things as jokes.

On June 1, 1997, Jokes from Russia moved to a new server and obtained the domain name anekdot.ru registered by ISP Cityline. From that day on, there was not a single break in Verner's work; the website has been updated every day without breaks, even for holidays and weekends—regardless of his journeys from one country to another, illnesses, and so on. *Persistence, stubbornness, and passion* constitute the basis for one more of Verner's motivations: "To see how long I can stand!"

Next is the motive of *recognition and fame*. Verner has gained recognition among both the Internet audience and professionals.[39] Beyond the Internet, Verner's personal fame is less widespread because the Russian media tend to quote jokes from his website without references. However, articles about Jokes from Russia and interviews with Verner have appeared in the media, and he has been invited often to speak on the radio and television.[40] Verner became a celebrity in Russia.

From this came one more motivation: *the involvement in Russian life and the feeling that Russia needs him*. Verner has been a successful astrophysicist, and is the author of several dozen scientific articles, four of which have a Science Citation Index rating higher than 100.[41] However, he felt that something was missing. This something was Russia, which he missed while in America. Now, the website he created has more than a half million visitors per month, and he feels that he makes a difference:

> It's already the fifteenth year that I have been working abroad. On the Internet, I don't feel that I lost contact with the motherland; my web site is a part of the Runet, it lives by the life of Russia and it influences it (both directly and indirectly—because the site's materials are being republished by the biggest Russian newspapers and magazines, broadcast on the television and radio). In other words, Jokes from Russia is my participation in Russian life, my work for Russia. [42]

Verner's case clearly shows that the motivation for creativity on the Internet (as well as in other domains) is a complex mixture and includes both intrinsic and extrinsic elements. It also has its dynamics—the specific weight of different elements changes over time. Like most Runet creators, Verner started working out of pure love, interest, and the pleasure of doing what he liked; then, when he began to spend more and more time on this, work it gradually became his main activity, and the issue of material reward arose. The combination of intrinsic and extrinsic motivations is typical in the later stages of a creative activity.[43] However, the actual structure of motivation is much more complex; it consists of a variety of elements, ranging from the practical and utilitarian to the most abstract and immaterial. It may be assumed that the actual set of motivational elements varies from one creator to another, but it is the complexity of motivation that enables them to keep working and developing their creative projects.

I asked Verner if his personal qualities, in his view, have played a decisive role in the fact that he began, and is still working on, the website. He replied with a joke—that it has been the mixture of German pedantry and Russian disorganization (*bezalabernost'*). The first means that one carries what one began to its conclusion, and the second that one carries to conclusion not what one began, but something completely different. The serious answer was that to work so many years without any breaks, one needs to have responsibility, patience, and perseverance.

AUTHORS AND AUTHORSHIP

As is the case with folklore, the authors of jokes and stories at Anekdot. ru usually remain anonymous or hide themselves under nicknames and pseudonyms. The most successful authors are known under names such as Philipp, Cadet Bigler, Vadim, Mikhail, Allure, and Rocketeer. None of them get any material reward for their creative work and invent new jokes "for art's sake." A reporter from one Moscow newspaper got in touch (through Verner) with three of these authors.[44] She found out that two of them were lecturers at universities and the third was lieutenant colonel; one lived in Paris, two others in Moscow. Their ages were thirty-seven, forty-eight, and fifty. All of them agreed that the best reward for their work is when they hear jokes they created from their friends. However, it is considered bad form to admit one's own authorship. The authors of jokes believe that knowing the identity of the author kills the joke. Verner himself confessed elsewhere that he invented a few jokes that received high grades from the readers. He was very proud of them, but he refused to reveal which jokes were his. Such is the nature of true folklore the people's creativity. What is important is the thing itself, not authorship or copyright.

AUDIENCE

Initially, the audience of the site consisted mostly of Russians living abroad because they could access the Internet more easily than their compatriots in the Motherland. Jokes from Russia became a part of their daily reading, along with the Moshkov Library;[45] their leading motivation was the "lack of [Russian] reading in the real life."[46] However, when asked if he considers Jokes from Russia as a way of national self-preservation, Verner modestly replied, "Not only my website, but the Russian Internet as a whole helps self-preservation."[47] The predominance of users from abroad was a common trait of the early Russian Internet.

The response from the audience was generally very positive. Verner found out that many people needed his website:

> How does the working day begin for an employee of a St. Petersburg commercial bank and a secretary of the Moscow office of a Western company, a post-graduate at the University of Ohio and a system programmer in London, a visiting professor in Tokyo, and a Russian engineer in a small town in Southern Korea? They sit down at their computer, look through their e-mails and open a fresh issue of Jokes from Russia. A few thousand people in fifty countries throughout the world do the same.[48]

With the growth of the Internet in the Russian metropolis, the structure of the audience has changed. Thus, in 2002, Russia, together with Commonwealth of Independent States (CIS) countries, provided about 75 percent of visitors to Verner's website. Half of the visitors were from Russia, and a half of these were from Moscow. The United States produced the second highest number of visitors, followed by Ukraine, Israel, and Germany. Overall, the geography of visitors included more than one hundred twenty countries,[49] giving an idea about the distribution of the Russian diaspora over the globe.[50]

SOURCES

After 5 years, there have been 55,000 jokes published at Anekdot.ru (about 150,000 if you count variants and repetitions). It might seem that replenishment is impossible—new jokes do not appear by the dozen every day; however, the collection continues to grow. Verner lists several major sources for this growth: author's jokes, translated jokes, and direct reaction to significant Russian and foreign news.[51]

JOKES AND STORIES

During the first year, Verner collected only "traditional" jokes, which have no authorship and that passed the test of oral retelling. Authored jokes, as well as authored anecdotes from everyday life, were not included. However, with the growth of the site's popularity, the visitors began sending, along with traditional jokes, many "real stories," accounts of true anecdotal events. Sometimes they were really amazing; it would have been a pity to lose them, so Verner began to include them in regular issues of jokes. This, in its turn, provoked a chain reaction, and more texts of this genre were submitted, and in September 1997, Verner began to make weekly issues of "real stories." There was plenty of material; users started demanding to have issues of the stories daily, which finally occurred on January 1, 1998. A month later, new sections were introduced—those of *aphorisms* (phrases) and *rhymes* (short, funny poems). When artists, both professional and amateur, began to send their drawings, this resulted in the launch of the *caricature* section. The role of the users in the evolution of the Jokes from Russia website has been extremely high. All of new sections that appeared after jokes emerged unplanned under the influence of the materials posted to the site and the expressed wishes of the users.

Over time, the relative "weight" of the sections within the site has changed, and a shift from jokes to stories occurred. The story section is not homogeneous; it consists of at least three main groups:

The first group is folklore stories in the proper sense, transmitted from one person to another. The most popular have been posted to the site dozens of times, and in order to increase the effect, the storyteller often identifies himself as the story's witness or claims that it occurred with his close acquaintances. Some of these stories were in use in the pre-Internet époque, and some can be traced back to ancient times. The second group is authentic accounts of events that the storyteller really witnessed. The best of them tend naturally to move into the first group and begin their own life, independent of the original storyteller. The third group includes authored short stories, which are usually fiction (but not always) that is disguised as a narrative about real events. One of the favorite activities of the site's visitors is to debate the authenticity of the story. Often the truth is in between: the tale is based on a real occurrence, but is enhanced by the storyteller.

The popularity of stories in comparison with jokes has been continuously growing. This can be seen from both the statistics of visits by sections and the grades put down by readers. Since July 1999, a system of grades has been active on the site that evaluates submissions on a scale from '–2' (terrible) to '+2' (excellent). The average grade shows the degree of success of a given text with the audience.

Many of the stories' authors are people with authentic literary abilities. However, most of them are known only by their pseudonyms. The "stories" section of the website seems practically inexhaustible: something interesting has happened to any person at least once. The policy of Anekdot.ru to publish everything guarantees that no message will be lost. Even if the text is boring and unconvincing, it will be published, if only in the "additional" section. If the editor overlooked a really interesting text and included it in the "additional" section, the readers' grading of texts in this section would "raise" it into the "readers' top ten."

JOKES FROM RUSSIA AS A CHRONICLE

The August 1998 financial crisis, the war in Yugoslavia, Yeltsin's resignation, the closure of NTV by the state—all of these events produced special issues of jokes. The terrorist acts in the United States on September 11, 2001 provoked a real outbreak. People responded with jokes to sporting events (the 2002 Winter Olympiad and World Soccer Championships) as well as to tragic news (the Moscow theater hostage crisis [known as 2002 Nord-Ost seige]; the 2003 shuttle explosion). The war in Iraq produced thirty special issues. As Verner says:

> Sometimes bitter, often cynical, mostly not funny at all, these texts, however, have represented the events and people's reaction to them no worse than the media. In the absence of censorship or any political engagement, Jokes from Russia help to understand what is going on in the country and in the world.[52]

Verner published a few special issues of jokes about the terrorist acts of September 11, 2001 in the United States. He confessed that he hesitated when deciding whether to publish these jokes or not. He wavered between three options: to keep publishing normal issues as if nothing had happened, to shut down the site, or to make a special issue immediately. He chose the last option:

> I was struck by the immediacy of reaction and its mass character. There had been no such response in all of the site's history. And then I made my mind up to publish all these texts right now, in the same order that they came. It seems to me that this should be known and understood as well. No selection was possible. I don't think any of these jokes is funny.[53]

The publication provoked a wave of indignation—on the site and beyond. A man by the name of Alex Fridland, PhD, sent letters to University of Kentucky, as well as to NASA, complaining that Verner used university computers and his working time to disseminate anti-American propaganda.[54] However, in spite of the anti-American spirit of the majority of the jokes, The September 11 Digital Archive sponsored by the Alfred Sloan Foundation and Smithsonian Institute included these texts and the concomitant discussion at Anekdot.ru in its archive.

Verner has been accused often of publishing material that is morally and aesthetically unacceptable. His policy of the total lack of the censorship has sometimes provoked insults and threats against his website and him personally, especially when jokes touched on such sensitive topics as terror and death. But occasionally it has been interpreted in a more balanced way. Somebody wrote in the site's guestbook after the September 11 special issues:

> Who said that Anekdot.ru is an entertainment site? This is a chronicle of recent history. And Verner is a truthful Nestor[55] who would not throw out a word from it (Anni, 2002).

On September 17, a commentary on the jokes about September 11 appeared on the website written in transliteration by a Russian woman who had worked on the seventy-second floor of one of the towers and managed to save her life. She concluded her message with the following words:

> Verner! Guys! Thanks for the silly jokes, even for evil ones! There's no need for tears, they wouldn't help; we'll cry ourselves, if we wish, when the shock is over. These jokes, they are useful, even now. They won't harm the dead, and they really help us, who are alive. So publish, read, laugh, I do it as well. And if I want, if I can and I do so, then all others may do so as well. . . . I'VE SURVIVED AND I'M LAUGHING—LAUGH WITH ME. I have the right to allow you. This is OK, honestly.
>
> Anya

CONCLUSION

As I have outlined in this chapter, the website Jokes from Russia contains the most comprehensive collection of urban folklore that was circulated in the Russian language before the époque of the Internet. It has deeply influenced the process of diffusion of folklore and facilitated creation of new folklore. It is a website created by a private person living abroad "just for fun" that became one of the most visited website on the Russian Internet. Not only was the first Russian website updated daily, it is probably the only website in the world updated daily by the same person for more than ten years, eight of which without any breaks (a fact worthy of the Guinness Book of Records). But it could not succeed without the active contribution of users, who became its co-authors, and the audience of Russians worldwide, who are its grateful readers. The lack of censorship and subjective selection, supplemented by multilevel sorting of the texts by readers, allow adequate representation of modern daily life of Russians. Thus, a one-person creation gave voice to the joking and laughing masses and became an "encyclopedia of Russian life," with all its turmoil and painful problems. Jokes from Russia is also a mirror of the Russian psyche, inasmuch as it reflects humorous reactions of the people to all kinds of domestic and international events. The comprehensive and constantly updated online collection of Russian humor promotes a cultural consolidation of Russians all over the world, and serves an active contributor to Russian culture.

NOTES

1. Wikipedia, "Humour," Wikipedia, http://en.wikipedia.org/wiki/Humour
2. Limor Shifman and Hamutal Ma'apil Varsano, "The Clean, the Dirty and the Ugly: A Critical Analysis of 'Clean Joke' Web Sites," *First Monday* 12, no. 2 (2007), http://firstmonday.org/issues/issue12_2/shifman/index.html
3. "Anekdoty iz Rossii," http://anekdot.ru
4. Henrike Schmidt, Katy Teubener, and Nils Zurawski, "Virtual (Re)Unification? Diasporic Cultures on the Russian Internet," in *Control + Shift: Public and Private Usages of the Russian Internet,* ed. Henrike Schmidt, Kati Teubener and Natalia Konradova, (Norderstedt, Germany: Books on Demand, 2006), 120–146.
5. David Silver, "Internet/Cyberculture/Digital Culture/New Media/Fill-in-the-Blank Studies," *New Media & Society* 6 (2004), 55–64.
6. James Curran and Myung-Jin Park, eds., *De-Westernizing Media Studies* (London: Routledge, 2000).
7. David Gauntlett, ed., *Web.Studies: Rewiring Media Studies for the Digital Age* (London: Edward Arnold, 2000).
8. Giselinde Kuipers, "The Social Construction of Digital Danger: Debating, Diffusing and Inflating the Moral Dangers of Online Humor and Pornography in the Netherlands and the United States," *New Media & Society* 8, no. 3 (2006), 379–400; Limor Shifman, "Cyber-Humor: The End of Humor as We Know It?" (paper presented at the Oxford Internet Institute Seminar, Oxford, UK, March 23, 2006; also available at http://www.oii.ox.ac.uk/collaboration/

?rq=seminars/20060323); and Shifman and Varsano, "The Clean, the Dirty and the Ugly."

9. Eugene Gorny, "Creative History of the Russian Internet" (PhD diss., Goldsmiths College, University of London, 2006).

10. http://centrolit.kulichki.net/centrolit/cgi/br.cgi

11. http://www.teneta.ru/

12. http://www.zhurnal.ru/

13. Eugene Gorny, "Russian LiveJournal: The Impact of Cultural Identity on the Development of a Virtual Community," in *Control + Shift: Public and Private Usages of the Russian Internet*, ed. Henrike Schmidt, Kati Teubener, and Natalia Konradova (Norderstedt: Books on Demand, 2006), 73–90.

14. Henrike Schmidt, "CyberRus. Blicke in die russische Internetkultur und -literatur," http://www.ruhr-uni-bochum.de/lirsk/sphaeren/pages/seite.htm

15. For a comprehensive review of Russian anekdoty, with categorization and examples, see, "Russian Joke," Wikipedia, http://en.wikipedia.org/wiki/Russian_joke

16. Sarah Karush, "wwwhat's online in Russia," *The St. Petersburg Times*, September 25, 1998; also available at http://kulichki.kulichki.net/entsikl/muzeum/raritet8.htm

17. See selected jokes from Anekdot.ru in English the webpage of the National Resource Centre at Harvard University: http://www.fas.harvard.edu/~nrc/teacherresources/humor.htm

18. Leonid Delitsyn, "Sex sells sex . . . i ne tol'ko," *Zhurnal.ru* 3 (1996), http://zhurnal.ru/3/delisex.htm

19. Rafal Rohozinski, "Mapping Russian Cyberspace: Perspectives on Democracy and the Net," http://unpan1.un.org/intradoc/groups/public/documents/UNTC/UNPAN015092.pdf (1999); Eugene Gorny, "Letopis' russkogo Interneta: 1990–1999," http://netslova.ru/gorny/rulet> (2000);Anna Bowles, "The Changing Face of RuNet," in *Control + Shift: Public and Private Usages of the Russian Internet*, ed. Henrike Schmidt, Kati Teubener, and Natalia Konradova (Norderstedt: Books on Demand, 2006), 21–33.

20. http://www.pa.uky.edu/~verner/atom.html

21. http://www.pa.uky.edu/~verner/an.html

22. Dmitri Verner, "Anekdoty NE ot Vernera," *Zhurnal.ru.* 7 (1998), http://www.zhurnal.ru/7/anekdot.html

23. Sergei Parfenov, "Anekdot.ru: 1257 dnej bez edinogo vyhodnogo," Netoscope, http://www.netoscope.ru/news/2000/11/08/764.html (November 11, 2000).

24. Alexsei Tsvetkov, "Transcript of Seventh Continent Programme," http://www.svoboda.org/programs/sc/1998/sc0303.asp (March 3, 1998).

25. See, for example, Shifman and Varsano, "The Clean, the Dirty and the Ugly."

26. Dmitri Verner, "Anekdoty iz Rossii i fol'klor internetovskoj epokhi," Russky Zhurnal, , http://russ.ru/netcult/20030617_verner.html (June 17, 2003).

27. Sergei Aksenov, "Vecher's Vernerom," *InterNet* 24 (2000), http://www.gagin.ru/internet/24/22.html

28. http://anekdot.ru/d0.html

29. Dmitri Verner, "Anekdoty iz Rossii' i fol'klor internetovskoj epokhi," Russky Zhurnal, http://old.russ.ru/netcult/20030617_verner.html (June 17, 2003).

30. Ibid.

31. Tim Berners-Lee, "Realising the Full Potential of the Web" (presentation at the World-Wide Web Consortium Meeting, London, UK, March 12, 1997; also available at http://www.w3.org/1998/02/Potential.html)

32. Richard Barbrook, "The Hi-Tech Gift Economy," *First Monday* 3, no. 12 (1998), http://www.firstmonday.dk/issues/issue3_12/barbrook/

33. Nelly Oudshoorn and Trevor J. Pinch, eds., *How Users Matter: The Co-Construction of Users and Technologies* (Cambridge, MA: MIT Press, 2003).
34. Gorny, "Russian LiveJournal."
35. Parfenov, "Anekdot.ru."
36. Dima Verner, "Re: voprosy po anekdotam," e-mail to author, February 7, 2005.
37. Dima Verner, "Anekdoty NE ot Vernera."
38. Alfred L. Kroeber, *Configurations of Cultural Growth* (Berkeley: University of California Press, 1944).
39. Verner was listed as one of the three most famous figures of Russian Internet in the Celebrities of the Russian Internet online survey in 1999 and 2000. In 2004, he was ranked sixth in the Magnificent Twenty list of the people who made the most significant contribution to the development of the Russian Internet. Jokes from Russia won the title "Humorous Website of the Year" three years in a row (2001, 2002, and 2003) in POTOP (Russian Top) online contest.
40. See the list of these publications and broadcasts at http://www.anekdot.ru/interview.html
41. The Science Citation Index allows a researcher to identify articles that have cited any particular previously published article, articles that have cited the work of any particular author, or to determine which articles have been cited most frequently.
42. Dmitri Verner, e-mail message to the author, February 7, 2005.
43. Richard S. Crutchfield, "Conformity and Creative Thinking," in *Contemporary Approaches to Creative Thinking*, ed. Howard E. Gruber et al. (New York: Athrton, 1962), 120–140; Teresa M. Amabile, *Creativity in Context: Update to the Social Psychology of Creativity* (Boulder, CO: Westview Press, 1996).
44. Mariya Lyamina, "Tajnye anekdoty otcov," *MK-Voskresenie*, , http://syy.narod.ru/wordmk.htm (March 14, 2004).
45. http://lib.ru
46. Verner, "'Anekdoty iz Rossii' i fol'klor internetovskoj epokhi."
47. Maria Govorun, "Anekdot bez broody," *Mir Internet 5*, no. 68 (2002), http://www.iworld.ru/magazine/index.phtml?do=show_article&p=99781682
48. Verner, "Anekdoty NE ot Vernera."
49. Washington ProFile, "'Anekdoty iz Rossii' delayutsya v SShA," Washington ProFile, October 12, 2002, http://www.washprofile.org/Interviews/Verner.html
50. According to Wikipedia, "the term *Russian diaspora* refers to the global community of ethnic Russians. The largest number of Russians outside Russia itself can be found in former republics of the Soviet Union; sizeable Russian-speaking populations also exist in the USA, in the European Union and in Israel. According to Russian government data, there are almost ten million Russians in Central Asian countries (over half of them in Kazakhstan; see Russians in Kazakhstan), 11 million in Ukraine, about one million in the independent republics of the Caucasus, 1.3 million in Belarus, half a million in Moldova, and a million and a half in the three Baltic states that were formerly part of the Soviet Union (800,000 in Latvia, 430,000 in Estonia and 340,000 in Lithuania). The rest of the European Union is home to roughly 200,000 Russian speakers; as many as 850,000 live in the USA. Many Russians also live in Brazil (70,000), Canada (60,000), and Argentina (50,000), as well as Australia and New Zealand (20,000)." (Wikipedia, "Russian Diaspora," Wikipedia, http://en.wikipedia.org/wiki/Russian_diaspora).
51. Verner "'Anekdoty iz Rossii' i fol'klor internetovskoj epokhi."
52. Ibid.

53. Dmitri Verner and Roman Leibov, "Anekdoty i/kak terror: beseda s Dmitriem Vernerom," Russky Zhurnal, http://old.russ.ru/netcult/20010917_verner.html (September 17, 2001).

54. Galina Anni, "Ya vyzhila i smeyus': Chernyj yumor kak lekarstvo ot straha," Novaya Gazeta, http://2002.novayagazeta.ru/nomer/2002/02n/n02n-s25.shtml.

55. An Old-Russian chronicler of the 11th and the early 12th centuries, a monk of Kievo-Pechersky Monastery, who wrote the *Story of Former Years* (Povest' vremennyx let), the first all-Russian chronicle code.

7 The Welsh Language on the Internet

Linguistic Resistance in the Age of the Network Society

Daniel Cunliffe

INTRODUCTION

According to Manuel Castells, the emerging *network society* is characterized by the globalization of economic activities and a new, shared culture emergent in the global media.[1] However, in reaction and opposition to the force of globalization, powerful expressions of diverse "local" identity are also emerging, and many minority and indigenous communities are turning to information technology (IT) as a means of cultural preservation.[2] The global networks are at once channels for globalizing influences and instruments of resistance against those influences.

The experience of "local" cultures coming into contact with powerful external cultures is not a new phenomenon; colonization, trade, and immigration have all been causes. This chapter considers a particular example, that of Wales, which was conquered by the English in the thirteenth century. A strong sense of Welsh identity has endured, at least in part due to the continuing existence of the Welsh language, *Cymraeg*. This chapter examines the relationship between the Welsh speaker and the Internet, the nature of the Welsh-language Internet, and presents examples of the use of the Internet as a direct instrument of Welsh language resistance.

While this chapter focuses specifically on the Welsh language, similar issues are faced by many minority languages, for example, Basque,[3] Catalan,[4] Hawaiian,[5] and Māori,[6] to mention just a few. While the unique contexts of each language will determine the appropriate role for IT (if any), the fundamental issues faced will have much in common.

WALES, WELSH IDENTITY, AND THE WELSH LANGUAGE

Wales was conquered by its neighbor England in the thirteenth century and was subsequently increasingly integrated into the English state (and ultimately into the British state). Despite this, a separate sense of Welsh identity has endured. Present-day Wales is one of the four constituent countries of the United Kingdom. Following a narrow referendum vote in favor of devolution, in 1999 selected powers and responsibilities were transferred from the Secretary of State for Wales to a new National Assembly for Wales, giving Wales a limited form of directly elected government separate from that of the United Kingdom.

Welsh identity has been shaped by its relationship with its economically, politically, and linguistically dominant neighbor, England. The Welsh language, Cymraeg (a Celtic language closely related to Cornish and Breton) which can trace its roots back to the sixth century, has arguably played an important role historically in distinguishing Wales from England, as the two countries' languages are mutually unintelligible. However, Cymraeg has seen a long period of decline. The decennial UK census of 1891 was the first to include a question on language in Wales; it was also the only census in which a majority of people in Wales were recorded as being able to speak Welsh. The majority of the population was already bilingual, with only 30.4 percent of the population being monoglot Welsh speakers.[7] Figures from the 2001 census indicate that 28.4 percent of the population of Wales (aged three years old and over), which is approximately 800,000 people,[8] has at least one language skill in Welsh, though only 16.3 percent have a complete set of language skills. Even though practically all Welsh speakers are now bilingual and possess native-speaker fluency in English, more than 270,000 people in Wales use Welsh on a daily basis.[9] The 2001 census figures show an increase in Welsh speakers compared with the 1991 census, both as a proportion of the population (+1.8 percent) and in number of speakers (+13.3 percent), the first increase since the 1891 census. However, they also show continuing decline in the proportion of Welsh speakers in the traditional Welsh-speaking heartland in the North and West. The role of the Welsh language in contemporary Welsh identity is also complex, as only 45 percent of people born in Wales believe that speaking Welsh is "important" or "fairly important" to being truly Welsh.[10] On the other hand, 88 percent of people in Wales agree that the language is "something to be proud of," and 77 percent agree that it is "an asset to Wales."[11]

The media have played an important role in the construction of Welsh identity and the Welsh nation. While the English language has dominated the media in Wales, a "willingness to embrace"[12] successive media technologies is suggested as one of the secrets to the Welsh language's survival. However, the media have often been a focus for linguistic resistance, including acts of civil disobedience, such as the boycotting payment of the Television License fee, and acts of violence, including the bombing of television transmitters.[13] Compared to the traditional media, the Internet is loosely regulated and relatively low in cost, and Welsh has been used on the Internet " . . . extensively from the outset."[14] Because the Welsh alphabet uses Latin characters, its use online was relatively unproblematic, though initially there were problems with diacritic characters on vowels (particularly the commonly occurring ŵ and ŷ) before these were included within the Unicode standards. An additional feature of the Welsh alphabet is the digraph (letters made up of more than one character; for example, 'ch'), which introduces additional complexity into sort orders and algorithms, as well as letter/character counting.[15]

There is a strong tradition of software localization into Welsh that is often volunteer-based and focused on open-source software, in some cases with financial support from the Welsh Language Board (a statutory organization whose main function is to promote and facilitate the use of the Welsh language). Current software includes: Agored,[16] based on OpenOffice; Gwelywiwr Mozilla,[17] which is a localization of the application suite developed by the Mozilla Foundation; as well as a variety of other software, such as spelling and grammar checkers.[18] There is also a Welsh version of Unix called Cymrux.[19] Commercial software developers in Wales are also providing bilingual and Welsh-language software. In December 2004, the Welsh Language Board and Microsoft launched Welsh-language interface packs for Office 2003 and Windows XP.[20] Both of these are available free of cost, in line with the Board's strategy of free dissemination of Welsh-language IT resources. Also, an organization has been established for those developing Welsh software, Cymdeithas Meddalwedd Cymraeg.[21]

In contrast to traditional media, the there is a tendency to use the Internet as an *instrument* of resistance, rather than being the *subject* of such resistance. However, where language policies exist, there is still the potential for conflict. In 1995, Compuserve's UKForum Wales, which had allowed posts in both Welsh and English, underwent a change of forum manager.[22] The new forum manager was a non-Welsh speaker who decided, without consultation, that the forum would be English only. This provoked protests from both Welsh speakers and non-Welsh speakers, made headline news in *The Western Mail*, and prompted the involvement of the Welsh Language Board. Despite attempts to silence the debate by censoring and deleting posts on the topic in the forum, the forum manager was eventually replaced by a Welsh speaker and an additional space was created in the forum exclusively for posting in Welsh.

IT IN WALES

IT is relatively well established in Wales. In 2005, 51 percent of households owned a computer[23] and 41 percent had an Internet connection.[24] In 2006, there was 98.6 percent broadband coverage for Wales, with 39 percent of households having a broadband connection (18.2 percent of the population), which is ahead of both the UK and European Union averages.[25] However, figures like these mask significant variations in both use and access by age and by social class. In some of the most remote and economically deprived areas of Wales, home Internet access is on the decline, and the rate of Internet access in 2005 was lower than it had been in 2002.[26]

The Welsh Assembly Government places considerable emphasis on IT for the future of Wales. Its e-Wales Division consultation document[27] outlines an ambitious vision in which IT transforms both public services in Wales and the Welsh economy. Therefore, the Welsh language's presence in, or absence from, the IT domain will have significant impact on its long-term maintainability. Discourse on the significance of IT for the Welsh language falls broadly into two camps—one focused on language *status* and another focused on language *use*. As with many minority languages, discourse focused on status is typically based on concepts of modernity, with a presence in IT changing the characteristics associated with a language from traditional to modern, past to present, rural to urban, and emotional to rational.[28]

> The availability of relevant and contemporary services in Welsh, including internet shopping and mobile device technology, would be a clear boost to its status in the eyes of young people.[29]

In 1995, 40 percent of people in Wales disagreed that Welsh was "relevant to modern life,"[30] so an association with modernity through IT may well be important. However, the direct impact of this on actual language use is unclear. Discourse focused on use identifies IT as a new domain that has particular significance for young people and that provides both new opportunities and new threats.

> The field of ICT products remains hardly touched by Welsh production . . . Almost no computer games are available in Welsh, nor other software which interests young people . . . the almost total absence of Welsh from this market is potentially damaging for future use of Welsh by young people.[31]

A report investigating ways to market the Welsh language[32] has identified a particular segment of Welsh speakers labelled "Young Urbans," who are extremely enthusiastic in their attitudes toward the language, and for whom "using Welsh is both modern and fashionable."[33] These Young Urbans are not necessarily from Welsh-speaking families, but have been educated through the medium of Welsh and have chosen to go to Welsh-medium further or higher education. The Young Urbans make a conscious effort to use Welsh, and are distinctive in their use of Welsh in e-mail, texting, new media, and IT in general. The report suggests that Young Urbans are important as potential trendsetters.

THE WELSH SPEAKER'S EXPERIENCE OF THE INTERNET

Given that many minority groups are excluded from IT and the Internet, one of the first questions that should be considered is whether or not Welsh speakers actually use the Internet. Figures for 2004 and 2005 indicate that there is little difference between the percentages of Welsh speakers and non-Welsh speakers in Wales who do not use the Internet:

Table 7.1 Percentage of People in Wales Who "Do Not Access the Internet."[34]

	2004	2005
Fluent Welsh speaker	59	57
Speaks Welsh, but not fluently	48	48
Don't speak Welsh	61	61

These figures suggest that Welsh speakers are no more excluded from the Internet than nonspeakers. However, they do not reveal the amount of use, or whether there are excluded groups among Welsh speakers, perhaps by age, gender or social class, or by location (region or rural/urban). It also does not reveal anything about what Welsh speakers use the Internet for—either as consumers or producers—or what their experience of using the Internet is like.

LANGUAGE ATTITUDES AND LANGUAGE USE

Given that Welsh speakers are using the Internet, their expectations and attitudes toward Welsh online needs to be examined. In a small-scale study, Welsh speakers were asked to rate how important it was that different types of organization provide information in Welsh on their websites.[35] The respondents considered a Welsh-language provision to be important across a range of organizations.

In another small study,[37] Welsh-speaking Head Teachers provided some interesting comments on the use of Welsh (translated from Welsh and made anonymous):[38]

> I believe in the importance of maintaining Welsh as a living language by communicating via the web. We in [Place] are a strong local community of Welsh medium schools but only infrequently use the language online.

> This is a living language in the 21st Century. We must get used to new technology like this and we must get used to using Welsh online!

These studies suggest that Welsh speakers believe that it is important for the Welsh language to have a presence on the Internet, and that this is a necessary requirement for a contemporary language. There is also a sense that the language is still threatened, and an acceptance that part of the responsibility to ensure that the language is used online falls to Welsh speakers themselves.

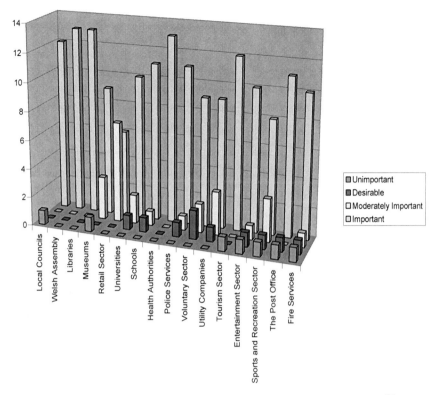

Figure 7.1 Perceived importance of Welsh-language provision on websites.[36]

However, this positive attitude toward the provision of Welsh online does not necessarily translate into actual use of the language online. A study of Welsh speakers in 2005[39] showed that 47 percent had used an English-language website in the previous month, while 13 percent had used a Welsh-language website. It may be tempting to explain this simply in terms of the lack of Welsh-language website provision—Welsh speakers would use Welsh services if they were available. However, it appears that the factors influencing the choice of language are more complex. Respondents in the study reported a lack of awareness of the existence of Welsh-language websites and how to find them. Another factor might be lack of confidence in the language. A correlation was observed between fluency and the use of Welsh-language websites: 18 percent of fluent speakers, 8 percent of those who spoke a fair amount of Welsh, and 3 percent of those who could only speak a little Welsh had used one in the previous month (44 percent had used an English site).

Other factors have been suggested by a small-scale survey of thirteen Welsh speakers.[40] Of the thirteen, one reported modest Welsh reading ability, one competent, and eleven fluent. All thirteen reported fluent English reading ability. When presented with a choice of reading a website in Welsh or English, four said they would always choose Welsh, eight would sometimes choose Welsh, and one would never choose Welsh (this was one of the fluent readers). Factors influencing this choice were: the ability to understand the Welsh vocabulary, the clarity of the Welsh, the mood or ability to concentrate, how information was going to be used, and the support of Welsh-language provision.

They were also asked what would cause them to change from Welsh to English while reading a website: eleven would change from Welsh to English if the Welsh was poorly written, twelve if they encountered unfamiliar Welsh terminology, nine if the content had obviously been translated from English, and twelve if there was less information in the Welsh version. Additional reasons given included: if the Welsh had a strong regional dialect (there are differences in vocabulary and phrase structure, particularly between North and South Welsh), if the Welsh was too formal (written Welsh is often far more formal than spoken Welsh), and to ensure that both language versions included the same content.

Respondents were then asked how likely they were to read webpages on different topics in Welsh and/or English if both were provided on a website (Figure 7.2). These figures show interesting variations in language choice with respect to topic. In the case of a repair manual for a car, no one would "definitely" use Welsh; on the other hand, for visitor information about a local attraction, no one would "probably" or "definitely" use English.

If the language behaviors are this complex, then simple assumptions about the relationship between Welsh-language provisions and Welsh-language use need to be reexamined. Indeed, it may be necessary to reconsider the nature

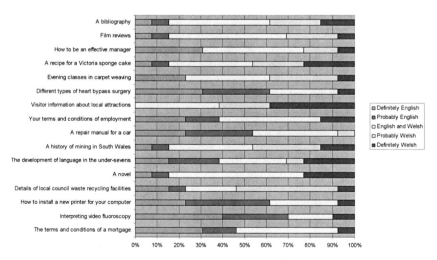

Figure 7.2 Language preference for reading webpages.[41]

of bilingual website design. The conventional approach to bilingual design has emphasized equality of provision. However, it can be argued that equal provision essentially treats the two languages as equal, when in fact one of them is in a minority position. Welsh speakers may need additional support or encouragement to use a Welsh-language provision, particularly given their fluency in English and possible lack of confidence in Welsh. The BBC's Vocab system[42] (cofunded by the Welsh Language Board), which provides pop-up translations for unfamiliar Welsh terms, is an example of providing support rather than just an option to change to English.

THE WELSH-SPEAKING VIRTUAL COMMUNITY

The concept of "community" has traditionally played an important role in Welsh identity, and the Internet has been identified as a means to strengthen existing communities in Wales[43] and to create new virtual Welsh-language communities.[44] It has been suggested that the Internet is also playing a crucial role in the reimagining and reconstruction of a diasporic Welsh identity in the United States.[45]

While these suggestions have not been subjected to detailed investigation, the BBC's Cymru'r Byd, a Welsh-language online news service, provides some suggestive indications for both the sense of community within Welsh-speaking Wales and the sense of Welsh identity in the diaspora.[46] A detailed study of the server logs showed that news relating to the Welsh language, communities, and politics was the most popular, even though this news formed only a minor proportion of the 60 percent of Wales-based news.

> Despite the contemporary, worldwide nature of the service, it appears community issues are still closest to the hearts of the users.[47]

Overall, 24 percent of users were from the Welsh diaspora (including 16 percent from other parts of the United Kingdom). Among the messages of appreciation for the service was one from Patagonia (in Argentina, which has a Welsh-speaking community of several thousand people):

> Thank you for your praiseworthy service. All the Argentine Welsh look at the Online News. It is great to hear about the Old Country. (Translated from Welsh.)[48]

And from the United States:

> It was a great honour for us tonight to listen to Garry Owen reading the "News" so excellently in pure South Wales Welsh. We thank BBC Cymru for this venture that enables exiles like us who live in a small village in the United States to be a little closer to Wales. It was strange

to sit by the computer and listen to accounts of the river Towi and about "Merched y Wawr"—it was as if we were sitting in the kitchen in Cwm Gwendraeth. It will be an honour for us to listen and watch every night the on-line news from Wales. (Translated from Welsh.)[49]

It appears that the Internet is providing new opportunities for asserting and negotiating Welsh identity within an emerging virtual Welsh (and partly Welsh-speaking) community. This virtual Welsh community may become more clearly defined if the campaign for a ".cym"-sponsored top-level domain for the Welsh linguistic and cultural community is successful[50],[51].

THE WELSH-LANGUAGE INTERNET

Arguably one of the main drivers behind Welsh-language content on the web has been the Welsh Language Act.[52] Under the terms of the Act, the Welsh Language Board has statutory powers to require public bodies (for example, local authorities, health trusts, fire and police services, and government agencies) to prepare Welsh Language Schemes. These schemes give details of how an organization will treat English and Welsh equally when delivering services to the public, including online services. While this has produced a significant body of Welsh-language Internet content, the quality of provision has been variable,[53],[54],[55] and the extent to which this material is used is questionable. Figures published in the Wikipedia entry for "Welsh Language" suggested that the Welsh-language web presence had a strong bias toward public bodies.[56] While the empirical basis for this assertion is unclear, it appears to reflect a common perception about the nature of the Welsh-language web. A similar view is expressed in the "Welsh Language" entry on Wicipedia, the Welsh-language version of Wikipedia.[57]

The Welsh Language Board appears to be moving toward the introduction of some form of quality standard with regard to bilingual website design.[58] This may provide an additional impetus to Welsh-language provision on the web, in addition to improving the quality of the provision. However, the Welsh Language Board has limited authority in the private sector and it may be that they are not in a position to influence the services that Welsh speakers wish to use.

The traditional media are also providing online services in Welsh. BBC Wales[59] has had an online presence since 1997. Its online Welsh-language news service, Cymru'r Byd,[60] was launched in 2000, and included video and audio-on-demand. Figures from January 2004[61] showed that Cymru'r Byd was the third most popular website in Wales, after the BBC Wales English site and the icWales site (an English-language news site run by Western Mail and Echo Ltd., publishers of newspapers and magazines in Wales). No other monolingual Welsh website was featured in the top twenty, though the Welsh Language Board's bilingual site was ranked sixteenth. Radio Cymru has broadcast over the Internet since 2005. S4C[62] (a station responsible for all Welsh-language television broadcasting in Wales) has webcast a number of events, including the Urdd Eisteddfod and the Llangollen International Musical Eisteddfod. Both BBC Wales and S4C also provide content for children and materials for learners.

While there are representative Welsh-language sites for most aspects of Internet activity, it is unlikely that there is sufficient provision for most Welsh-speaking Internet users to conduct all of their Internet activities through the medium of Welsh, the provision is patchy and the quality variable. A few sites are available in Welsh only; for example, Pishyn[63] is a Welsh-language dating service; Wicipedia,[64] the Welsh-language Wikipedia, was started in 2003 and now contains just under six thousand articles. A larger number of sites are bilingual to a greater or lesser extent; for example, gwales[65] is a bilingual bookshop run by the Welsh Books Council; jobscymraeg[66] is bilingual site advertising vacancies for bilingual staff; and Stonewall Cymru[67] is a bilingual site campaigning for lesbian, gay, and bisexual rights in Wales. In some cases, there is only token use of Welsh, being little more than a marker of identity.[68] While there has been no systematic study of Welsh-language provisions online, research has looked at civil society sites[69] and party political websites.[70]

There are a number of websites that are clearly engaging in acts of resistance. Cymuned is a pressure group that seeks to defend Welsh-speaking communities against colonization and Anglicization. While the content of their main site[71] is bilingual and contains information on joining the organization, information for the press, policy documents, merchandise, and campaign information, there are also numerous issue-specific sites, some in Welsh, some bilingual. On the site www.wales-4sale.com the intended audience is clearly the English visitor, who may be considering purchasing a holiday home in Wales:

> . . . So before you think of acquiring a house here, may we suggest that, if you come to live here, you have a moral duty to learn the native language of the country—and to use it, too. Or perhaps it would be better, after all, just to come and see us whenever you feel like it. As one of our breezier slogans has it, ENJOY YOUR STAY—THEN GO AWAY—COME AGAIN ANOTHER DAY!

Cymdeithas yr Iaith Gymraeg is another pressure group, but their website[72] is far more orientated to Welsh speakers and contains relatively little content in English—just some news and basic information about the organization. Currently, a particular focus of the site is their campaign calling for new Welsh Language Act, including an e-petition to gather signatures in support of the call. This call has been taken up by sections of the Welsh-language Internet.

FORUMS

Maes-e[73], a well-known Welsh-language forum started in 2003 (currently with just under 2,800 registered users), provides some insight into the range of subjects discussed by Welsh speakers online. The main topic areas are music, computing, melting pot (including food and drink; literature; sports; films television and radio; and culture), current affairs, language, and fun. The specific topics that are most popular (based simply on the number of messages) are sports; contemporary Welsh-language music; films, television and radio; Welsh affairs; gigs; and the future of the Welsh language. Thus the twin themes of Wales and the Welsh language feature strongly, as does the notion of linguistic resistance, with the topic of "Language events" bearing the description, "Protests, lectures, etc."

BLOGS

Morfablog, started in 2001, claims to be the first Welsh-language blog.[74] The blogs included in the Welsh-language blog aggregator Blogiadur[75] (just under eighty blogs) provide a partial overview of the Welsh-language blogosphere. In addition to personal blogs, topics include music (principally Welsh-language music), poetry, television, cinema, various sports, chess, poker, politics, sci-fi, astronomy, technology, and travel. Several blogs are run by people learning Welsh and serve as an opportunity to practice their language skills. While most of the bloggers appear to be based in Wales, there are a number from overseas, the majority of these from the United States. One Welsh-language blog that is not included in Blogiadur is badans,[76] started in 2005. The principal content of badans is pornographic images, which is noteworthy, as there appears to be very little erotic or pornographic online content in Welsh.

Most of the Welsh-language blogs are entirely in Welsh, though there are a few bilingual blogs and some cases where a blogger runs a separate, non-identical blog in Welsh and English. Blogs that are in Welsh sometimes contain a brief note in English introducing the blog or the blogger, often making reference to the Welsh language—"It's in Welsh because it is, and so are we;"[77] or "All of my blog, except this one page, is written in the Welsh language."[78] Within the Welsh-language blogs, English may still be found in the form of quotations, or when used for humorous or sarcastic emphasis.

Many of the blogs contain links to each other on the basis of a shared language rather than shared topics. Some blogs contain links to English-language blogs based on shared topics. There is also an identifiable element of linguistic resistance present on around 15 percent of the blogs, commonly in the form of links to the Cymdeithas yr Iaith Gymraeg call for a new Welsh Language Act, or links to language pressure groups. Entries in blogs sometimes feature language protests as well; Rhys Llwyd,[79] for example, describes the student occupation of the main library at the University of Wales, Aberystwyth, in support of better Welsh-language provision in higher education and the creation of a Welsh-language Federal College. The blog entry includes video clips of the occupation, hosted on YouTube. He also posted pictures of the occupation to maes-e as part of a discussion about the occupation, and filed them under the future of the Welsh-language topic.[80]

SOCIAL NETWORKING SITES

The Welsh language is also used in popular social networking sites such as MySpace, YouTube, del.icio.us, and Flickr. YouTube, Flickr, and del.icio.us feature Welsh-language tags. Where Welsh tags are used, corresponding English tags are also often used, with bilingual tagging perhaps being the norm for general content. Elements of linguistic resistance also exist; Flickr in particular has some interesting groups based around existing pressure groups, but also appears to have fostered new forms of activism. The *scymraeg* group[81] (being a combination of a pun on the English word 'scum' and Cymraeg) collects examples of poorly translated Welsh-language signs—in a particularly notorious example, the English sign read "Pedestrians look right," while the Welsh sign warned pedestrians to look left. While the group operates almost exclusively in Welsh, it does include some information in English, a posting entitled, "For our English (speaking) friends—what this group is about,"[82] which includes:

> Also, I would really like to hear what "non-Welsh speaking Welsh people" think about this issue. I don't believe the Labour Party/Western-Mail-letters-page myth that things like this only matter to the 20% or so of us who speak the language. In fact, I think that's an appalling slander on the 80% who don't, assuming as it does that you don't know the value of your own language/culture/heritage/history/selves. Because this language is yours, even if you've got out of the habit of using it in the last generation, or two, or thirty. (That should cover everyone ;-)

Thus the group is directly addressing nonspeakers, acknowledging a shared value placed on the language as part of Welsh culture. It also suggests that action should be taken to bring these issues to the attention of corporations and shareholders:

> To paraphrase Utah Phillips:
> The Welsh language isn't dying, it's being killed. And those who are killing it have names and addresses.
> And shareholders . . .

CONCLUSIONS

This chapter has examined the relationship between the Welsh speaker and the Internet, and has briefly characterized the Welsh-language Internet. There are many questions that remain unanswered about the Welsh-language Internet and its relationship with the non-Welsh-language Internet as experienced and created by Welsh speakers. Are these parallel Internets, each providing the same functions for its own language community, or does the Welsh-language Internet fulfill specific functions for Welsh speakers? To what extent do Welsh-language producers address a non-Welsh-speaking audience? Is Welsh-language production a deliberate choice meant to address Welsh speakers or to exclude non-Welsh speakers? Is it an act of resistance, or merely an unconscious expression of language preference? Is the use of the Internet as a direct instrument of Welsh-language resistance effective?

In order to achieve the Welsh Language Board's goal of "the normalization of the Welsh language in the world of Information Technology,"[83] it is clearly important to answer these questions and a myriad of related ones. The future of the Welsh language online is likely to mirror the future of the language in the real world and will depend critically on people's determination to use the language. In order to encourage Welsh speakers to use their language online, it will be necessary to develop and maintain a rich Welsh-language presence that is both attractive and valuable to Welsh speakers.

NOTES

1. Manuel Castells, *The Power of Identity* (Oxford: Blackwells, 1997).
2. Laurel Evelyn Dyson, Max Hendriks, and Stephen Grant, eds., *Information Technology and Indigenous People* (Hershey, PA: Information Science Publishing, 2007).
3. Luis Fernandez, "Patterns of Linguistic Discrimination in Internet Discussion Forums," *Mercator Media Forum* 5 (2001): 22–41.
4. Josep Lluis Micó and Pere Masip (Chapter 8, this volume).
5. Mark Warschauer, Keola Donaghy, and Hale Kuamoÿo, "Leokï: A Powerful Voice of Hawaiian Language Revitalization," *Computer Assisted Language Learning* 10 (1997): 349–361.
6. Te Taka Keegan and Sally Jo Cunningham, "Indigenous Language Presence on the Web: The Maori Example" (presented at the Association of Internet Researchers Conference 4.0, Toronto, Canada, October 16–19, 2003; also available online at http://www.cs.waikato.ac.nz/~tetaka/PDF/IndLangPres.pdf)
7. Her Majesty's Stationery Office, "Extract From the 1891 Census," Report on the 1891 Census, http://www.bwrdd-yr-iaith.org.uk/download.php/pID=10688
8. John Aitchison and Harold Carter, *Spreading the Word: The Welsh Language 2001* (Talybont: Y Lolfa Cyf, 2004).
9. Welsh Language Board, "2004 Welsh Language Use Survey," http://www.bwrdd-yr-iaith.org.uk/download.php/pID=67935.6 (2006).
10. Richard Wyn Jones and Dafydd Trystan, "The 1997 Welsh Referendum Vote," in Scotland and Wales: Nations Again?, ed. Bridget Taylor and Katarina Thomson(Cardiff: University of Wales Press, 1999), 65–93.

11. NOP Political and Social, "Public Attitudes to the Welsh Language," (draft report prepared for the Central Office of Information and the Welsh Language Board, 1995; available online at http://www.bwrdd-yr-iaith.org.uk/download.php/pID=18971.2)

12. Grahame Davies, "Beginnings: New Media and the Welsh Language," in *Proceedings of the First Workshop on E-Dentity: Borders and Identities in the Internet Age*, ed. Daniel Cunliffe, Rob Thomson, and Chris Williams (Treforest, Wales: University of Glamorgan, 2005), 15.

13. W.J. Howell Jr. "Bilingual Broadcasting and the Survival of Authentic Culture in Wales and Ireland," *Journal of Communication* 32, no. 3 (1982): 51.

14. Hugh Mackay and Tony Powell, "Connecting Wales: The Internet and National Identity," in *Cyberspace Divide: Equality, Agency and Policy in the Information Society*, ed. Brian D. Loader (London: Routledge, 1998), 215.

15. Welsh Language Board, "Bilingual Software Guidelines and Standards," http://www.bwrdd-yr-iaith.org.uk/download.php/pID=66182.1 (2006).

16. Agored, http://www.agored.com (accessed May 8, 2008).

17. Gwe-lywiwr Mozilla, http://www.gwelywiwr.org (accessed May 8, 2008).

18. Canolfan Bedwyr Language Technology Unit, University of Wales, http://www.bangor.ac.uk/development/canolfanbedwyr/technolegau_iaith.php.en?menu=10&catid=3088&subid=0

19. Cymrix, http://www.cymrux.org.uk (accessed May 8, 2008).

20. Welsh Language Interface Packs for Microsoft Office 2003 and Windows XP, http://www.bwrdd-yr-iaith.org.uk/cynnwys.php?pID=case&nID=39&langID=2

21. Cymdeithas Meddalwedd Cymraeg, http://www.meddalweddcymraeg.org (accessed January 4, 2007).

22. Karen Atkinson and Tony Powell, "Welsh-Language Ban in 'Wales'," *Planet* 116 (1996): 81–84.

23. Office for National Statistics, "Corrected: Family Spending—2004/05 Expenditure and Food Survey," http://www.statistics.gov.uk/downloads/theme_social/Family_Spending_2004–05/FS04–05.pdf (2006).

24. Sarah Richards, "Internet Inequality in Wales: Update 2005," Welsh Consumer Council Report, http://www.wales-consumer.org.uk/research_policy/pdf/WCC34_Internet_Inequality_in_Wales_Update_2005.pdf (2005).

25. Broadband Wales Observatory, *Broadband Benchmark: Quarterly Update (Q1)* no. 1, (2006), http://www.broadbandwalesobservatory.org.uk/broadband-3233

26. Richards, "Internet Inequality in Wales."

27. Welsh Assembly Government, "Towards e-Wales—a Consultation on Exploiting the Power of ICT in Wales," http://new.wales.gov.uk/docrepos/40382/4038231141/403821124/517285/ewalesstrategy_e.pdf?lang=en (July 2006).

28. Patrick Eisenlohr, "Language Revitalization and New Technologies: Cultures of Electronic Mediation and the Refiguring of Communities," *Annual Review of Anthropology* 33 (2004): 21–45.

29. Welsh Language Board, "The Welsh Language Board's Youth Strategy: Increasing the Social Use of Welsh by Young People (11–25)," http://www.bwrdd-yr-iaith.org.uk/download.php/pID=45991.8, 33 (2005).

30. NOP Political and Social, op. cit.

31. Heni Gruffudd, "Planning for the Use of Welsh by Young People," in *Language Revitalization: Policy and Planning in Wales*, ed. Colin H. Williams (Cardiff: University of Wales Press, 2000), 190.

32. NOP World Consumer, FBA Ltd, and Walton Evans Associates, "Changing Behaviour, Usage and Perceptions: Marketing the Welsh Language" (report

prepared for the Welsh Language Board, 2003; available online at http://www.bwrdd-yr-iaith.org.uk/download.php/pID=62040.5), 71.

33. NOP World Consumer, "Changing Behaviour," 137.
34. James Thomas and Justin Lewis, "'Coming Out of a Mid-Life Crisis'?: The Past, Present and Future Audiences for Welsh Language Broadcasting," *Cyfrwng* 3 (2006): 7–40, 28.
35. Rob Thomson and Daniel Cunliffe, "Welsh Identity On-Line," in *Proceedings of the First Workshop on E-Dentity:Borders and Identities in the Internet Age*, ed. Daniel Cunliffe, Rob Thomson, and Chris Williams (Treforest, Wales: University of Glamorgan, 2005), 53–59.
36. Thomson and Cunliffe, "Welsh Identity On-Line," 56.
37. Daniel Cunliffe and Rhys Harries, "Promoting Minority-Language Use in a Bilingual Online Community," *The New Review of Hypermedia and Multimedia* 11 (2005): 157–179.
38. Cunliffe and Harries, "Promoting Minority-Language Use," 169.
39. Beaufort Research, "Living Lives Through the Medium of Welsh Study: Summary Report October–December 2005" (report prepared for the Welsh Language Board, 2006; available online at http://www.bwrdd-yr-iaith.org.uk/download.php/pID=69388.5).
40. Daniel Cunliffe, "Supporting Minority Language Cultures Through Bilingual Web Site Design," in *Proceedings of the 2nd BCS HCI and Culture Workshop*, ed. Karen Gunter, Andy Smith, and Tim French (London: Greenwich University, 2003), 30–36.
41. Thomson and Cunliffe, "Welsh Identity On-Line," 57.
42. BBC Vocab/Geirfa, http://www.bbc.co.uk/cymru/vocab (accessedJanuary 4, 2007).
43. Mackay and Powell, "Connecting Wales."
44. Colin Williams "The Case of Welsh/Cymraeg in Wales," in *Rebuilding the Celtic Languages: Reversing Language Shift in the Celtic Countries*, ed. Diarmuid Ó Néill (Talybont: Y Lolfa Cyf., 2005), 96.
45. Wayne Parsons, "From Beulah Land to Cyber-Cymru," *Contemporary Wales* 13, (2000): 1–26.
46. Davies, "Beginnings: New Media and the Welsh Language."
47. Ibid., 22.
48. Ibid., 18.
49. Ibid.
50. Siôn Jobbins, "Beyond Frontiers," *Agenda* Summer (2006): 59–61.
51. dotCYM, http://www.dotcym.org/
52. Welsh Language Act 1993, c.38; available online at http://www.opsi.gov.uk/acts/acts1993/Ukpga_19930038_en_1.htm
53. Linguacambria Cyf, "Snapshot Survey: Websites of Organisations Complying with Statutory Language Schemes" (report prepared for the Welsh Language Board, 2001; available online at http://www.bwrdd-yr-iaith.org.uk/download.php/pID=1970.6).
54. Daniel Cunliffe, "Bilingual Usability of Unitary Authority Web Sites in Wales," in *Proceedings of The Web in Public Administration, EuroWeb 2001 Conference*, ed. Oreste Signore and Bob Hopgood (Pisa: 2001), 229–244.
55. Cwmni Cymad, "Websites Survey: Websites of Organisations That Have a Statutory Welsh Language Scheme" (report prepared for the Welsh Language Board, 2003; available online at http://www.bwrdd-yr-iaith.org.uk/download.php/pID=6847).
56. "Welsh has a substantial presence on the Internet, but this is strongly biased towards public bodies: the ratio of search engine hit frequencies for Welsh words to their English equivalents tends to be about 0.1% for formal terms

such as *addysg* (education), *cymdeithas* (society) or *llywodraeth* (government), but only about 0.01% for everyday terms such as *buwch* (cow), *eirlaw* (sleet) or *cyllell* (knife)." (Removed from Wikipedia in November 2006 as a result of a "No Original Research" policy.)

57. Wicipedia, "Cymraeg," http://cy.wikipedia.org/wiki/Cymraeg#Cymraeg_ar_y_we (accessed January 22, 2007).
58. Welsh Language Board, "Information Technology and the Welsh Language: A Strategy Document," http://www.bwrdd-yr-iaith.org.uk/download.php/pID=66215.5, 15 (2006).
59. BBC Wales, "BBC Wales Home Page," http://www.bbc.co.uk/wales/ (accessed January 4, 2007).
60. BBC Cymru'r Byd, http://www.bbc.co.uk/cymru/ (accessed January 4, 2007).
61. G. Davis, "Beginnings," 22.
62. S4C Online, http://www.s4c.co.uk/ (accessed January 22, 2007).
63. Pishyn, http://www.pishyn.org/ (accessed January 22, 2007).
64. Wicipedia, http://cy.wikipedia.org/ (accessed January 4, 2007).
65. Gwales Online, http://www.gwales.com/ (accessed January 4, 2007).
66. Jobscymraeg Online, http://www.jobs-cymraeg.com/ (accessed January 22, 2007).
67. Stonewall Cymru Online, http://www.stonewallcymru.org.uk/cymru/default.asp (accessed January 4, 2007).
68. Thomson and Cunliffe, "Welsh Identity On-Line."
69. Daniel Cunliffe and D. Roberts-Young, "Online Design for Bilingual Civil Society: A Welsh Perspective," *Interacting with Computers* 17, no. 1 (2005): 85–104.
70. Daniel Cunliffe, "Party Political Web Sites and Minority Languages: Some Initial Observations from Wales," in *Proceedings of the 5th International Conference on Cultural Attitudes towards Technology and Communication (CATaC 2006)*, ed. Fay Sudweeks, Herbert Hrachovec, and Charles Ess (Tartu, Estonia: 2006), 696–701.
71. Cymuned, http://cymuned.net/ (accessed January 4, 2007).
72. Cymdeithas yr Iaith Gymraeg, http://cymdeithas.org/ (accessed January 22, 2007).
73. Maes-e, http://www.maes-e.com/ (accessed January 4, 2007).
74. Morfablog, "An Open Letter to the Owner of Nat Watch," http://morfablog.com/archif/2005/08/25/an-open-letter-to-the-owner-of-nat-watch/
75. Blogiadur, http://www.blogiadur.com/ (accessed January 4, 2007).
76. Badans, http://badans.blogspot.com (accessed January 4, 2007).
77. Beibl Datblygu, http://www.datblygu.com/ (accessed January 4, 2007).
78. Blog Dogfael, http://blogdogfael.org/ (accessed January 22, 2007).
79. Blog Rhys Llwyd, "Protest Addysg Gymraeg," posted October 27, 2006,http://rhysllwyd.blogspot.com/2006/10/protest-addysg-gymraeg.html (accessed May 8, 2008).
80. Rhys Llwyd, comment on "Rali UMCA (yn fyw o'r lleoliad)," maes-e, comment posted on October 26, 2006, http://www.maes-e.com/viewtopic.php?p=304077#304077 (accessed on May 8, 2008).
81. Scymraeg, http://www.flickr.com/groups/scymraeg/ (accessed January 22, 2007).
82. Scymraeg, "For our English Speaking Friends."/
83. Welsh Language Board, "Information Technology and the Welsh Language," 7.

8 The Fight of a Minority Language Against the Force of Globalization

The Case of Catalan on the Internet

Josep Lluís Micó and Pere Masip

INTRODUCTION

Globalization, which often materializes through new information and communication technologies, is usually considered almost exclusively in economic terms, often as a synonym for global capitalism. However, it is necessary to approach globalization as a complex series of processes; it is a heterogeneous phenomenon that includes transformations in spatial and temporal relationships, social practices, and forms of representation.

It is true that globalization transfers the power of nation-states to the global arena with the promise of a new era of prosperity and improvement, while also producing a cultural standardization with universal cultural symbols:

> a single-commodity world where local cultures and identities are uprooted and replaced with symbols from the publicity and marketing departments of multinational corporations.[1]

Nevertheless, it is also true that globalization produces the opposite effect—it has led to the revival of local cultural identities.[2] Cultural assertiveness and vindication of self-identity have emerged in response to the standardization process. The examples are numerous, and include Catalonia, Scotland, Quebec, Wales, and the Basque country, because, as Manuel Castells points out, the age of globalization is also the age of identity.[3]

A plurality of identities is often a major source of tension and conflict, since there is normally one identity that considers itself to be legitimate and tries—and sometimes succeeds—to impose itself on the others. The feeling of belonging to a community (whether geographical, political, or functional) practically always leads the members of this community to distinguish between "them" and "us."[4] In contrast, the Internet opens the door to multiplicity and the growth of multiple realities and identities,[5] and the concept of cultural, ethnic, or national identity can be dealt with in a different way. Internet society allows the construction of cultural and linguistic identities not based on criteria of territoriality or hierarchy, as in the real world, but based on "will" and "action."[6] Political and geographical barriers can be overcome, thanks to the Internet, and may result in a democracy based on a civil society stronger than the previous one.[7]

Strong cultural or linguistic communities, such as the Spanish community, do not face great difficulties in dealing with globalization, since they have a broad social basis and the support of the media and the state. For minority linguistic communities, the situation is much more difficult, as they do not have this support. Generally, they have neither a state nor large media companies to back them up, and their social basis is limited. Moreover, linguistic diversity is often seen as an inconvenience rather than an asset: European linguistic diversity is an "obstacle to the creation of a European audiovisual space."[8] In a similar vein, in response to the Constitution of the new autonomous government of Catalonia, *Variety*, the major source of information about Hollywood, expressed a fear that the new Minister of Culture might promote the dubbing of films into Catalan (currently, foreign films are dubbed mainly into Spanish only).[9]

Along with traditional media, the Internet acts as a new social agent for constructing and consolidating social identities. However, the Internet has the advantage of not needing the support of big media groups and large economic investments, but rather the participation of social agents and people. Castells claims that if the Internet does end up being controlled by the general public, it might become a tool for democratization. It would lead to greater transparency of governments and more active involvement of individuals in public life. The Internet might even become a platform for denouncing unjust situations that could be easily accessed by the minority groups affected.[10] Castells also describes a social model, which consists of different subjects developing their shared interests, affinities, and so on, on the Internet. As Turkle[11] and Dutton[12] have also claimed, if networks stabilize, virtual communities as intense as real communities may emerge. The Internet allows virtual meeting spaces to be created where citizens with the same interests—linguistic or cultural, for example—can interact regardless of their social and economic status or geographical situation. These cybernetic forums foster exchange, vindication, diffusion, promotion, creation, business, and so on.

The objective of this chapter is to highlight the opportunities provided by the Internet to develop and promote minority languages and cultural identities. In this chapter, we will do so through a specific example: the Catalan language.[13] If it is true that the progress of a language is linked to the use of technology by its speakers,[14] then the Internet can be a very important tool in promoting or revitalizing a language.

Like any other language, Catalan is a means of communication. However, it must also be considered a symbol of identity—and this is precisely why it has become a matter of controversy. The use of Catalan has been repeatedly forbidden throughout contemporary Spanish history. The most recent example, and probably the most widely known internationally, is the persecution of the language under Franco's dictatorship. Although today Catalan is an official language of Catalonia, it shares this status with Spanish, Catalan is still considered by many Spaniards as a nuisance or an anomaly, rather than a symbol of social richness. Even today, the imbalance between the two languages means that Catalan speakers are still forced to demand its use in many fields, including government, culture, education, and everyday life.[15]

In fact, having over seven million speakers is apparently not sufficient for the European Union (EU) to include Catalan among its official languages. It does not appear to matter that, in terms of the number of speakers, it is the ninth most common language in the EU, ahead of Greek, Portuguese, Swedish, Danish, and Finnish. Catalan is not even an official language in the whole of the Spanish state. This situation, as paradoxical as it is unjust, is more striking if we think about the strength of the language on the Internet, where it became, in 2005, the twenty-sixth most used language on the web.[16] It is a language that, since December 2005, has boasted an Internet domain: ".cat."

CATALAN LANGUAGE AND SOCIETY

Catalan is the Romance language native to Catalonia, a territory designated as an Autonomous Community within Spain by the Spanish Constitution. Catalonia, located in the northeasterly part of the Spanish state, covers an area of 31,895 sq km, and has about seven million inhabitants. This population is concentrated in Barcelona and its metropolitan area, where over 4,500,000 people live. Catalan is also spoken over a wider linguistic area that goes beyond the borders of the Autonomous Community, which is known as "the Catalan Lands." Whereas the Catalan Lands form an entity in linguistic terms, this entity is non-existent in political terms. In total, there are about seven and a half million speakers of Catalan, while almost ten million people understand the language.[17]

The Catalan Lands are distributed over four European countries: Spain, France, Andorra, and Italy. In Spain, Catalan is also spoken in the Balearic Islands, in most parts of the Community of Valéncia, and in the Franja de Ponent, a narrow strip of land in Aragón that borders Catalonia. In France, it is also spoken in so-called "Northern Catalonia," a region that includes the areas of Roussillon, Vallespir, Cerdanya, Conflent, and Fonolleda (Département des Pyrenees Orientales). In Italy, the language is used in the town of L'Alguer (Isle of Sardinia). Moreover, Catalan is the only official language in Andorra, a small state in the Pyrenees between Spain and France, which is a full member of the United Nations.

Table 8.1 Catalan Linguistic Area

	Surface Area (km²)	Population	Capital	Country
Catalonia	31,895	6,995,206	Barcelona	Spain
Community of Valencia	23,255	4,692,449	València	Spain
Balearic Islands	4,992	983,131	Palma de Mallorca	Spain
Franja de Ponent	1,812	42,000	Fraga	Spain
Northern Catalonia	4,116	364,000	Perpinyà	France
L'Alguer	224	41,000	L'Alguer	Italy
Andorra	465	52,000	Andorra la Vella	Andorra
Total	66.462	13,169,786		

Sources: Institut d'Estadística de Catalunya, Generalitat de Catalunya; Institut Valencià d'Estadística, Generalitat Valenciana; Institut Balear d'Estadística, Govern de les Illes Balears.

Despite these figures, Catalan finds itself in a delicate situation. As is the case with other languages of similar characteristics, both its survival and its use as a vehicular language are facing great difficulties. The reasons for this are manifold: its non-official status in countries with powerful official languages, such as Spanish and French; the ubiquitous presence of English in many areas of society; and other more recent phenomena, such as immigration.

It is undeniable that the increasing rate of immigration presents another challenge for the Catalan language, although this phenomenon can also be seen as a good opportunity to ensure its survival. Between 1950 and 1975, there was a notable influx of people from the southern and inland regions of Spain into Catalonia; this changed the linguistic characteristics of the region, as the newcomers arrived with Spanish as their mother tongue. Catalonia has also received thousands of non-Spanish citizens, mainly from South America, Asia, and the Maghreb. The immigrants from Latin America are in a position similar to that of the immigrants who arrived between the 1950s and 1970s, and whose command of Spanish made knowledge of Catalan unnecessary for them to cope with everyday life. On the other hand, foreigners coming from other parts of the world can find in Catalan a means of integration.

THE CATALAN MEDIA SYSTEM

The construction of cultural identities in the second half of the twentieth century was closely connected with national communications systems.

The Catalan media market is considered to be of average size by EU standards. However, it is has some specific characteristics that mean it cannot be compared with the markets of other European countries with languages spoken by a similar number of people. Firstly, it must be borne in mind that the power of the Catalan administration regarding the promotion of the Catalan media industry, and the audiovisual industry in particular, is very limited. Basic regulations related to telecommunications and the audiovisual sector are not subject to Catalan political power, but rather to central government and, in addition, EU institutions. Moreover, following the restoration of democracy in 1978, official Catalan institutions did not realize in time the strategic importance of mass media in general, and the audiovisual industry in particular, in sustaining and even promoting the language and the culture in an environment that was becoming more and more complex.

Furthermore, the Catalan media industry is not strong enough to compete with Spanish and international media groups. One consequence of this relative weakness is the penetration of the Catalan communications space by Spanish multimedia groups, which is an upward trend, particularly in the audiovisual sector. Moreover, the major Catalonia-based media companies publish and broadcast mainly in Spanish.

Regarding the press, of the eight newspapers found in all of the usual retail outlets in Catalonia, only three (*El Punt*, *Avui*, and *El Periódico de Catalunya*) are written in Catalan—although *El Periódico de Catalunya* had produced a Spanish edition long before its Catalan edition first printed. The circulation of daily newspapers in Catalan amounts to 25.8 percent of the total circulation in Catalonia, while Spanish-language newspapers account for the remaining 74.2 percent (data from 2003). Free newspapers could further add to this imbalance, for these are mostly written in Spanish.

The data related to television are equally discouraging. Only two of the seven TV channels (TV3 and Canal 33) that provide free, open access are in Catalan.[18] These are public-owned channels financed by the Catalan Government. All other channels broadcast totally in Spanish, except for TV2—the second channel of Spanish public television—which broadcasts 9.8 percent of their programs in Catalan. However, managers of Corporación Radio-televisión Española (RTVE) (the public Spanish Broadcasting Corporation) announced that, in order to reduce the budget deficit, from January 1, 2007 onward, programs in Catalan will be confined to just half an hour per day.[19] No cable or satellite channel broadcasts any programs in Catalan.

Radio is the medium that most contributes to linguistic standardization because of both the large number of stations broadcasting in Catalan and its audience figures (50.5 percent as opposed to 49.5 percent, but with an increase of 19.8 percent over the last five years). Catalunya Radio—a public station—currently plays a leading role in Catalan radio. Its main competitors are Spanish commercial radio stations, with the only exception of Rac1, a new commercial Catalan-speaking radio station.

Finally, as far as the cinema industry is concerned, the position of Catalan is critical. In 2006, the number of films released in Catalan cinemas was 467, of which, scarcely 10 percent were screened in Catalan. Movies that were dubbed, subtitled, or made in Catalan are included in this percentage. This year, fifty-six full-length films produced in Catalonia were screened, thirty of which were filmed in Catalan.[20] All these figures are from Catalonia; in the rest of the Catalan Lands, the number of films screened in Catalan is virtually zero.

CATALAN ON THE INTERNET

The status of Catalan on the Internet is very different from its status in the other fields mentioned previously. In this case, the presence of Catalan on the Internet is an indicator of its vitality, which is conditioned more by levels of economic and social development than by demography.

Catalan has found in the Internet a suitable platform for consolidating and promoting the language and overcoming the economic and political problems of the "real world." For example, in the "real world" there is no single organization for defending the language because the Catalan linguistic area extends over four countries; in Spain, there is a law that bans the existence of a TV network in Catalan that broadcasts to the Catalan Lands. Officially, this prohibition is the result of broadcasting licenses that are issued by regional governments. These licences are only valid to broadcast in the territory within their respective jurisdiction. This decision, however, has a political motivation, which intends to prevent the nationalist sectors (well rooted in Catalonia) from using television to spread pan-catalanist sentiments to other communities (such as the Community of València and the Balearic Islands).

Boosted by social movements, which are basically popular in character and have their origins in civil society, a series of initiatives have appeared in cyberspace to defend and promote Catalan language and culture. Through the Internet, these movements have been able to overcome the incompetence of the governing class, many political controversies, and economic pressure, and they have spread the feeling of identification with the geographical, historical, and linguistic Catalan community.

In 2005, when Catalan became the twenty-sixth most-used language on the Internet, it had positioned itself ahead of some languages that are officially spoken by more people than Catalan in member states of the Organization for Economic Co-operation and Development (OECD) or the EU. Two years earlier, Catalan was the twenty-third most popular language on the web, ahead of languages such as Greek, Arabic, and Indonesian. In its research project, the group, *Softcatalà*, estimated that in 2005, there were about seven million websites in Catalan. That is a relatively low figure, but it reveals a linguistic community that is, at the same time, much more active in the creation of websites than other communities with larger populations.

In fact, the rate of websites per Catalan speaker is 1.09—a percentage that places Catalan nineteenth in the world, ranking ahead of languages such as Spanish (0.41), Russian (0.26), Portuguese (0.25), and Chinese (0.08).[21]

A report on Catalan society by Manuel Castells and Imma Tubella,[22] helps us to understand the reasons why Catalan has such a strong presence on the Internet. According to this report, the segment of the population that has developed a strong Catalan identity uses the Internet more intensively than the sector that does not share these feelings of identity: the first group accounts for 38.4 percent of the population, and the second accounts for 33.4 percent. When comparing both groups' use of the Internet, it was found that 21.9 percent of Catalan people with the wider identity praxis use the Internet for professional purposes (for the other group, the percentage goes down to 17.2 percent). With respect to practical uses, the figures are 29.6 percent and 23 percent, for those with a Catalan identity and those without respectively; for online purchases they are 12.1 percent and 9.4 percent; for educational purposes, 21.3 percent and 17.2 percent; for political or union activities, 4.8 percent and 2.6 percent; and for leisure activities, 30.3 percent and 27.1 percent. The percentages are similar when it comes to searching for news (14.9 percent and 13.4 percent) or technological purposes (11.8 percent versus 11.1 percent). On the contrary, the percentage is slightly lower for the first group when using the Internet for social purposes (20.6 percent and 21.8 percent).

Among Internet users with a marked Catalan identity, the largest group is that of young people. However, Internet users have a different attitude toward the language compared with the average citizen: in speech, web users have a greater tendency to use Catalan. Those people living in Catalonia and who do not use the Internet are mainly Spanish speakers.

The countries with the highest rates of Internet use are also those that show the highest ratio of language speakers to website production. Apart from English, the languages with the highest ratio of language speakers to website production are Icelandic, Estonian, Norwegian, Swedish, Finnish, and Danish. All of them are spoken by a similar number of people as Catalan, but in countries with a high rate of Internet use and, above all, with their own state.

Surveys regularly carried out by the group, Webmásters Independents en Català de Cultura i Ámbits Cívics (WICCAC; www.wiccac.org), show that the web presence of Catalan is erratic, depending on the area. For instance, in market-oriented sectors, the use of Catalan is low to very low. According to WICCAC analysis, the presence of Catalan on websites is highest (between 80–100 percent) io websites of such groups as universities (with 95.24 percent), theaters and dance companies (91.23 percent), or search engines (80.95 percent), among others.[23]

All the universities in the Catalan Lands, except the University of Perpignan, have at least their website in Catalan. In this category, it is worth mentioning the Universitat Oberta de Catalunya (UOC), an educational project conceived in Catalan that has been exported worldwide. The UOC, founded in 1994, offers university courses for undergraduates, graduates, and doctoral students. It is the only all-inclusive university in Spain that is not attendance-based. Here we have another valuable element for the normalization and spreading of Catalan on the Internet, as Catalan is the UOC's vehicle. Its success—the UOC currently has over 20,000 students—makes it clear that good projects produce good results, regardless of the language used. However, the UOC's open nature has led it to offer courses in Spanish to the rest of Spain and Latin America, and it has projects in English, Chinese, and Arabic, as well.

The situation of Catalan in the sector of search engines is also very good. Either as a result of commercial tactics or as a consequence of social mobilizations, most of the main search engines have a version in Catalan. One of the most significant examples is Google, but Alltheweb and Yahoo! also have a Catalan version. Moreover, there is a Catalan section of the Open Directory Project, with 44,000 indexed webpages.

In spite of these figures, there is another less optimistic reality. The use of Catalan is very low (0 percent to 30 percent) or low (between 30 percent and 50 percent) in sectors such as industry, services and government. Heading this dubious ranking we find the car industry, where there are only two companies that have a website in Catalan (2.90 percent). The presence of Catalan is also low in categories such as "large companies and multinationals" (19.44 percent), "transportation" (23.33 percent), "institutions of the Spanish Government and the European Union" (27.08 percent), "temporary work agencies" (34.78 percent), and "telecommunications, electronics, mobile telephony and technology" (39.47 percent). Probably the most paradigmatic example of Catalan exclusion can be found on the websites of the Spanish government, where monolingualism, in Spanish, is almost absolute.

The conclusion can be drawn, therefore, that Catalan has shown itself to be strong enough to face the challenge posed by the Internet in spite of the problems that it still encounters both in social use and in specific areas, particularly in business.

SUCCESSFUL EXAMPLES OF CATALAN ON THE INTERNET

Because of the persecution of Catalan during Franco's dictatorship, and because during the current democratic period, the Spanish authorities have treated it with contempt, many of the Catalan initiatives on the Internet are associated with protest. Obviously, this contrasts with the evolution and presence of Spanish on the Internet, as Spanish people do not need to protest because their culture and language are in a more secure position.

Those concerned with defending Catalan culture and language have found the ideal resource to do so in the Internet. The use of conventional media, such as radio, television, or press, requires an enormous financial investment and, in the case of audiovisual media, a license granted by the Catalanian

Administration. In the case of Internet, there is hardly any financial investment necessary and independence of political power is absolute. The Internet
allows for some of the limitations imposed by the Spanish television laws to
be overcome, enabling all web contents to be available anywhere.

Most of these achievements have their origins in social groups and individuals concerned with the defense of their own culture. In the following
sections, we will focus on the most successful initiatives related to the promotion of Catalan and its use in many spheres of everyday life. We will
use, in part, the taxonomy of Surman and Reilly,[24] who categorize the use
of web technologies by social civil organizations in four different strategic
uses: collaboration, publication, mobilization, and observation.

Collaboration

The marginalization of Catalan in many spheres of everyday life has been the
trigger, in some cases, for the people of the region to collaborate with each
other. One of the best-known cases are the websites that offer guidance to
people who wish to avoid consuming trademark products that are not labeled
in Catalan (Associació en Defensa de l´Etiquetatge en Català [www.adec-cat.
org] and Plataforma per la Llengua [www.plataforma-llengua.org]).

Out of the many examples of collaboration, there is one website in particular worth mentioning: Softcatalà (www.softcatala.org). This is a nonprofit association that supports the use of the Catalan language in new
technologies. Softcalà is made up of students, programming engineers,
philologists, designers, and translators who undertake the work in a nonprofit, cooperative spirit. The idea for this association arose in 1997, and its
promoters decided soon after to provide it with a proper platform to meet
the needs of all those users who want to have a full Catalan experience
in computing. Softcatalà has been responsible for the translation of such
popular software as Open Office, Abiword, Mozilla, Gnome, etc., as well
as the Catalan version of Google.

Publication

According to the Spanish online media census,[25] there is a total of 1,278 news
websites within Spain as a whole, of which 10 percent to 12 percent are written
in Catalan. Although the demographical weight of the population in Catalan-
speaking areas exceeds this percentage, and should therefore be considered as
lower than expected, the fact is that the importance/significance of the press
produced in Catalonia for the Internet goes far beyond strictly quantitative
measures. Therefore, it would not be an exaggeration to claim that, to a large
extent, Catalan media have led the digital press in Spain.

The first Spanish media outlet to make the leap onto the web was the
magazine, *El Temps* (written in Catalan), which developed a digital publication in 1994, first accessible through the private service provider, Servicom,

and, shortly afterward, through the Internet. A year later, three of the most important newspapers published in Catalonia would begin publishing their digital own versions: *La Vanguardia* (www.lavanguardia.es), *El Periódico de Catalunya* (www.elperiodico.es), and *Avui* (www.avui.cat). A few months later, other newspapers—some of which were published in Madrid, such as *ABC* (www.abc.es) or *El Mundo del Siglo XXI* (www.elmundo.es), and others in the Basque country, such as the *Diario Vasco* (www.diariovasco.es)—would follow the same path.

Despite the early move of the main Catalonia-based newspapers to the Internet, some of the most noteworthy and successful initiatives were undertaken by small-size firms, and even individuals. This is the case of La Malla, Racocatalà, Naciodigital, and, in particular, Vilaweb.

The pioneering nature of Catalan media on the Internet is evident through enterprises such as the one undertaken by the journalist, Vicent Partal, who in 1996, founded the first completely electronic medium in Spain: Vilaweb (www.vilaweb.cat). The story of Vilaweb, however, goes back to the year 1995, when Vicent Partal (until then, responsible for the digital version of *El Temps*) created Infopista, a modest directory in Catalan, which, at that time, pooled no more than a hundred resources. A few months later, Infopista had already changed its original purpose and was on its way to becoming a genuine means of communication; that is, the electronic newspaper called Vilaweb.

According to the data of the Oficina de Justificación de la Difusión (Bureau for the Justification of Diffusion), Vilaweb currently has an average of 863,796 monthly visitors.[26] In addition, this new medium has been able to combine the global possibilities of the Internet with the interests of local readers. This means that, since 1997, one hundred local editions have joined the general edition , with contents more closely linked to the social, political, and cultural realities of the web users.[27] The scope of these local Vilawebs can be at a municipal level, at a neighborhood level, or at an international level, as with the Australian Vilaweb (www.vilaweb.cat/www/australia) or the New York Vilaweb (www.vilaweb.cat/www/nyc).

Another good example of the dynamism of the new media in Catalonia was the appearance in 1999 of LaMalla (www.lamalla.net), a local portal written in Catalan promoting audiovisual contents on the web. Although LaMalla is a public-funded portal, its origins lie in a modest initiative led by two journalists, Toni Esteve and Oriol Ferran, who were able to convince the Diputació de Barcelona (an intermunicipal public administration) of the interest and usefulness of the project. Nowadays, LaMalla is a consolidated project focusing on local news and multimedia contents and promoting active audiences. However modest, the innovative nature of the project won it several digital press awards, with the Net Media Award (www.net-media.co.uk) being particularly worthy of mention.

Besides pioneering projects such as Vilaweb, LaMalla, and *Avui*, we should not forget the large number of more modest initiatives undertaken in the last few years, which are becoming more and more visible in cyberspace. Good examples are the cases of Racocatalà (www.racocatala.com) or the group Nació Digital (www.naciodigital.com*)*.

Although its dimensions (much greater) and its nature (public-funded) mean that it cannot be compared with the examples discussed previously, we should also mention here the fine work that the Corporació Catalana de Radio i Televisió (Catalan Broadcasting Corporation) is doing for the normalization of Catalan. Its multimedia division has developed a series of high-quality projects focusing on news (www.telenoticiescat), sports (www.elsesports.cat), children (www.clubsupertres.cat), and leisure activities for young people (www.3xl.cat).

Mobilization

The main obstacles to the full enjoyment of Catalan on the Internet come from big transnational companies and—paradoxically enough—from the Spanish government. The most striking example of the exclusion of Catalan is to be found on the webpages of multinational companies, despite their considerable economic activity in the region. However, over the course of time, some of these companies (including Ikea, Metro, and Carrefour) have ended up "catalanizing" their Internet sites. Popular protest campaigns conducted via e-mail have been crucial to making this decision.

Some controversies in civil life have lead to protests in cyberspace. Internet, e-mail, and mobile phones have played a central role in some of the initiatives in Spain and Catalonia in recent times. These include, for instance, the campaigns against Spanish participation in the Iraq war or the way in which the central government manipulated the news after the terrorist attacks in Madrid on March 11, 2004.

One of the most notable examples of social mobilization is the Associació PuntCat (PuntCat Association; www.puntcat.org), which on September 15, 2006 succeeded in getting Internet Corporation for Assigned Names and Numbers (ICANN) to approve, for the first time, a top-level Internet domain representative of the Catalan language and culture.[28] This decision was the first time a top-level domain (TLD) for a specific language and culture had been granted. Nevertheless, the whole process prior to recognition had not been easy. There was the political opposition of the Spanish Government, at that time in the hands of the conservative Partido Popular, led by José María Aznar,[29] in addition to the requirements and rigor imposed by ICANN.

The race for the ".cat" officially began in March 2004, when the Associació PuntCat made its request to ICANN for a sponsored domain.[30] However, they had started on this journey years before, in effect through Professor Amadeu Abril of the University Ramon Llull. In 1996, Abril had first attempted to obtain recognition for the geographical domain, ".ct," but the request was rejected, as Catalonia was not an independent state, and could not, therefore, be included in the list of country codes held by the International Organization for Standardization, which is responsible for the establishment of territorial codes.

The Associació PuntCat was founded in 2001 with the aim of gaining recognition for the top level domain ".cat" based on language and not territory, as was the case with ".ct." It had the support of more than ninety associations (rather than private individuals or trading corporations) all over the world. In March 2004, the association presented its request for a sponsored TLD backed up by 68,000 supporting messages sent by individuals.

The rest of the story is well known. ICANN accepted the proposal in September 2005, although it first had to overcome an initial reluctance caused by concern about setting a precedent in approving a sponsored top-level domain based on cultural and linguistic criteria. Once it had achieved this, the Associació PuntCat became the Fundació PuntCat (PuntCat Foundation), the body responsible for the management of the domain. The implementation process for the new domain was undertaken gradually. The first phase was limited to institutions directly involved in the promotion of Catalan culture, such as schools, communication media, and publishers, and also to the more than 68,000 people who had given their support.

The second phase began on April 23, 2006. A registry was opened for any individual able to demonstrate a commitment to the promotion of the Catalan language and culture. At the beginning of April, the Fundació PuntCat had received more than 10,000 requests to register. A simple search on Google will reveal more than 3,390,000 pages already with the domain ".cat," which means that it has become much more prominent than other recently assigned domains, such as ".jobs," ".aero," or ".travel."[31]

CONCLUSION

The present chapter had a double objective: on the one hand, its purpose was to give visibility to a small part of the activity and the research on the Internet that is being carried out in Catalonia, and, on the other hand, to highlight the opportunities provided by the Internet to develop and promote minority languages and cultural identities.

Regarding the first point, much research activity and interesting initiatives being carried out around the world are invisible to most scholars. The reason of this "invisibility" is not because of lack of quality, but rather because these activities are not published in English. Research published in languages other than English, even if it is valuable, it is not spread to the international community. This reality does not only prejudice against researchers for whom English is not their mother tongue or who are not fluent enough in English to use material from English-language websites, but also to English-speaking scholars, because they are deprived of knowledge produced in other languages, some of them very influential such as Russian, German, Japanese, or Spanish.

This issue allows us to make more visible a small portion of the research on Internet produced in different parts of the world. It will not solve the problem of the visibility of literature that is not written in English, but it gives the floor to researchers whose daily experience of the Internet is mediated through non-Anglophone languages and cultures, as well as researchers situated within the Anglophone academia whose work focuses on cultures outside North America and Europe.

Regarding the second point, globalization affects all aspects of economic activity, society, and culture. However, it does not mean that local realities should become weaker and disappear; on the contrary, in some cases, minority cultures are gaining strength: the age of globalization is also the age of identity. The example of Catalan demonstrates that these local realities can take advantage of the opportunities that globalization offers.

Generally speaking, Catalan people have understood the essence of the Internet, and they have used the full potential of information technology and the Internet in achieving their goals: spreading their language and culture all over the world, while at the same time making them stronger in the local environment. That is, Internet users have taken advantage of one of the most paradigmatic tools of globalization for preserving and spreading a local element.

If the survival of a language depends on the desire of its speakers to preserve and transmit it to future generations,[32] the case of Catalan proves that the Internet can be a tool of the first order in the defense of a language or culture. However, we cannot give way to euphoria. Weaker cultural and linguistic communities still have many obstacles to overcome in their development. The goodwill of their members is not enough. Nevertheless, there is no doubt that the Internet offers previously unimaginable possibilities.

The Internet allows identity, whether individual or national, to be created without more global cultural uses of it being renounced. First of all, cyberspace offers visibility. It gives some groups, no matter how small, the opportunity to make their voices heard by millions of people all over the world—potentially, at least. In the case of the ".cat" domain, it is linked with a question of prestige as well.

The Internet helps citizens make contact with others who share the same feelings of identity. It no longer matters how far away they are from each other. Through the Internet, they can now work together to defend their shared reality and to fight for individual and collective rights. In that sense, ".cat" has set a precedent for the major use of minority languages on the web. In fact, a group of Galician bodies has already made public its determination to apply for the domain ".gal" as representative of the Galician culture and language,[33] and the Catalan precedent has rekindled campaigns for a TLD for the Welsh community (see Cunliffe, Chapter 7, in this volume).

Beyond these vindications, and despite some difficulties, the Internet seems to be a more transparent platform than other milieus for citizens to develop their everyday activities, and for them to consume, to have fun, and to find information . . . in their own language. In addition, and as the case of Catalan has well proved, when institutions do not take the initiative in these matters, civil society does.

The Internet allows most active citizens to mobilize in defense of their interests. Popular movements using the Internet have stood in for the Catalunya Administration and big corporations in promoting the use of Catalan on the Internet, as well as in all aspects of everyday life. Some remarkable examples are: the Associació en Defensa de l'Etiquetatge en Català and la Plataforma per la Defensa de la Llengua o Softcatalà. Thanks to these popular movements, companies that at first marginalized Catalan have had to change their minds and adopt Catalan, for example, in labeling, websites, communication with customers, or advertising. One of the most recent examples of this is the agreement of mobile companies to use Catalan and to incorporate it in phone menus, services, and user manuals.

Vilaweb, the first completely Catalan online medium, proved that it is possible to consolidate a business (journalism, in this case) on the Internet from a community of speakers relatively few. It is not by chance that the example comes from the world of communication, since the Catalan media have led the digital media press in Spain, but also at the European level. In academia, the role of the UOC has been similar to that developed by Vilaweb.

In spite of the opposition of the Spanish government, the approval of the domain ".cat" has allowed that the Catalan language and culture become more visible, even comparable with other languages that have more speakers, or having the support of a state. In parallel, youngsters have played a determining role. They have become the most active group on the Internet in defense of language and cultures. Because of their age and education, they are the age group most familiarized with the use of the Internet. This is a guarantee that the strategy for the defense of the Catalan language and culture in cyberspace will continue.

NOTES

1. U. Beck, *What is Globalization?* (Cambridge, U.K.: Polity, 2000), 43.
2. Anthony Giddens, *Runaway World: How Globalization is Reshaping Our Lives* (London: Profile, 1999).
3. Manuel Castells, "Indentital local i comunicació global: els ateneus a l'era digital" (lecture, Barcelona, Spain, March 15, 2006).
4. Piérre Lévy. *Cyberdémocratie* (Paris: Éditions Odile Jacob, 2002).
5. Sherry Turkle. *Life on the Screen: Identity in the Age of the Internet* (New York: Simon and Schuster, 1995).
6. I. Tubella "Comunitats flexibles en un món intercultural" (paper presented at the I International Conference on Communication and Reality, Barcelona, Spain, 2000).

7. Lévy, op cit.

8. Jacques Mousseau, *Communication et langages* (1989), 79. Cited by Iñaki Zabaleta in "La comunidad lingüística como universo" (paper presented at the I International Conference on Communication and Reality, Barcelona, Spain, 2000).

9. John Hopewell and Emilio Mayorga, "Catalan Gov't Poses Threat to Hollywood Pix. New Culture Minister May Press for More Catalan Prints," *Variety*, November 29, 2006, http://www.variety.com/article/VR1117954694.html?categoryid=13&cs=1 (accessed December 10, 2006).

10. Manuel Castells. *The Internet Galaxy: Reflections on the Internet, Business, and Society* (Oxford: Oxford University Press, 2001).

11. Turkle, op. cit.

12. William Dutton. *Society on the Line: Information Politics in the Digital Age.* (New York: Oxford University Press, 1999).

13. The Catalan language is a Romance language with Latin roots. By the end of the tenth century, Catalan was already a fully-formed language, clearly distinguishable from its Latin origins. Further information about Catalan history is available at "Catalan, Language of Europe," http://www6.gencat.net/llengcat/publicacions/cle/clee.htm (accessed March 7, 2007).

14. David Crystal. *Language Death* (Cambridge: Cambridge University Press, 2000).

15. Both Catalan and Spanish are official languages in Catalonia, the Community of Valéncia, and the Balearic Islands. However, the situation of Catalan differs depending on the community. In Catalonia, both languages coexist at schools, and all students are bilingual. This is not the case in the Community of Valéncia or the Balearic Islands, where Spanish is the dominant language. Despite the fact that Catalan is the native language of Catalonia, nowadays it is the mother tongue of only 41.6 percent of population, while Spanish is the mother tongue of 50.3 percent. (CIS. "Estudio postelectoral de cataluña. Elecciones autonómicas 2006," http://www.cis.es/cis/opencms/ES/1_encuestas/estudios/ver.jsp?estudio=6198, 2006 (accessed March 7, 2007). For detailed information about the history of Catalan culture and its relations with Spain, see, Albert Balcells, *Catalan Nationalism: Past and Present* (New York: St. Martin's Press, 1996); Daniele Conversi, *The Basques, the Catalans and Spain: Alternative Routes to Nationalist Mobilisation* (Reno: University of Nevada Press, 2000); John Hargreaves, *Freedom for Catalonia?: Catalan Nationalism, Spanish Identity and the Barcelona Olympic Games* (Cambridge: Cambridge University Press, 2000).

16. Jordi Mas, "La salut del català a Internet el 2005," http://www.softcatala.org/articles/article60.htm, 2005 (accessed October 8, 2006).

17. The Spanish language is the only 'official' language in Spain, but there are several Autonomous Communities that have other co-official languages. As well as Catalan, Basque is co-official in the Basque country and Galician in the Autonomous Community of Galicia. Aranès (occitan) is also co-official in Vall d'Aran, a county located in the north of Catalonia, and Bable and Aragonés are protected languages in Asturias and Aragón.

18. Both channels are generalists. Their programming includes: talk shows, sports programs, sitcoms, advertisements, news, movies, soap operas, etc.

19. F. Robles, "El Colegio de Periodistas pide que se mantengan las desconexiones en catalán de TVE," *El País*, December 6, 2006.

20. From January to August. Institut Català de les Industries Culturals, Generalitat de Catalunya, "Dades generals de l'exhibició cinematogràfica a Catalunya (llargmetratges i curts) Període: Gener-Agost 2006,"http://

www20.gencat.cat/docs/CulturaDepartament/ICIC/Documents/Arxiu/ 061113Informe%20Exhibicio%20CADM%20Octubre%202006–1.pdf (accessed March 14, 2006).

21. Mas, op.cit.
22. Manuel Castells et al., "The Network Society in Catalonia," http://www. uoc.edu/in3/pic/eng/pic1.html, 2003 (accessed October 2005).
23. WICCAC, "Baròmetre de l'ús del català a internet," http://wiccac.cat/web-scat_tot.html, 2006 (accessed October 9, 2006).
24. M. Surman and Katherine Reilly, *Appropriating the Internet for Social Change: Towards the Strategic Use of Networked Technologies by Transnational Civil Society Organizations*. (New York: Social Science Research Council, 2003); also available at http://www.ssrc.org/programs/itic (accessed June 9, 2006).
25. Xosé López et al. "Tipología de los cibermedios," in *Cibermedios* ed. R. Salaverría (Sevilla, Spain: Comunicación Social, 2005).
26. OJD Interactiva, http://ojdinteractiva.ojd.es/home.php (accessed September 16, 2006).
27. The full list of local editions of Vilaweb is available at http://www.vilaweb. cat (accessed September 16, 2006).
28. For a detailed history of the campaign to win .cat in English, see, Peter Gerrand, "Cultural Diversity in Cyberspace: The Catalan Campaign to Win the New .cat Top Level Domain," *First Monday* 11, no. 1 (2006), http://www. firstmonday.org/issues/issue11_1/gerrand/index.html (accessed July 15, 2006).
29. According to Peter Gerrand, the Spanish government sent an emissary to Washington to attempt to persuade the US Departments of State and Commerce to block the .cat application.
30. A sponsored TLD is a specialized TLD that has a sponsor representing the narrower community.
31. Search carried out in August 2006.
32. Joshua Fishman, *Reversing Language Shift* (Clevedon: Multilingual Matters, 1991).
33. "Un grup d'entitats de Galícia demanen el domino '.gal'," *El Periódico de Catalunya*, April 12, 2006

9 The German Internet Portal Indernet

A Space for Multiple Belongingness

Urmila Goel

DIFFERENCE-SENSITIVE INTERNET STUDIES

Much has been written about how the Internet can overcome boundaries both geographical and individual.[1] Not only worldwide communication seems possible, but it also seems that users can change their identity online, thus overcoming boundaries faced offline. However, after the initial phase of Internet enthusiasm, many scholars argued that not all boundaries are overcome and others are developed anew.[2] The discussion about the digital divide began, analyzing how certain regions of the world and groups of people are barred from using the Internet. It was acknowledged that there is a "Western" bias not only in the technology, but also in Internet studies.[3] Scholars showed, for example, that boundaries of language and culture remain,[4] Internet spaces are used for exclusionary purposes,[5] and transnational communication is considered a threat by governments.[6] Kolko et al., in particular, argue that virtual communication cannot be seen as independent from offline experiences. The latter are carried over to the online spaces and cannot be overcome totally even by changing one's identity online. Therefore, they argue that, for example, racialized identities matter in virtual space just like in "real" life.[7] In this volume, Khiabany and Sreberny (Chapter 13, this volume) argue that offline differences have to be taken into account if one wants to effectively internationalize Internet studies.

The socially constructed lines of differences of colonialism, racism, gender, heteronormativity, and class, which determine the access of people to resources and power, and are theorized in postcolonial racism, critical whiteness, and gender studies, are the focus of my analysis. In this volume, Tawil Souri (Chapter 3, this volume) shows how "US American" multinationals use their hegemonic power in Palestine for their own commercial interests. But in general, mainstream research[8] seems to be blind to these differences, their interdependencies, and the resulting power inequalities. Gender studies have shown how the implicit norm in "Western" societies, their languages, and also their research, is male and heterosexual, and indeed how the supposedly neutral position is in fact defined as such.[9] Critical whiteness studies[10] analyzes how, in "Western" societies, the generally unmarked "white"[11] position possesses hegemonic power and also functions as a supposedly neutral position that needs no further investigation. As a consequence of these norm settings and the historically established power structures, mainstream research remains dominated by "white" male heterosexual middle class researchers from the "West,"[12]who imagine themselves as neutral observers of their field of research and construct the others as subjective and involved.

This reproduction of hegemonic power structures also can be observed in Internet studies. Most of it is written from a "Western," "white," middle-class perspective, where the male and the Anglophone perspectives are still dominant. I myself am part of the "Western" middle class, hegemonic position and am sufficiently confident working with the English language. However, in my work I hardly reflect on this privileged position, but rather focus on being a young racialized woman from outside the Anglophone world. Thus I also take part in veiling and reproducing these hegemonic positions that privilege me. I rather challenge those positions that put me at a disadvantage, and constantly need to remind myself of my own privileges and how those privileges influence my perspective and research.

Taking academic texts and analyzing their implicit points of reference can illustrate how the reproduction of hegemonic power structures works. If I would take one of my own texts, the neglect of class and "East German" issues would become obvious. Here, however, I will use an (arbitrarily chosen) quote from another author:

> The web, of course, has no central point, no capital city. But most people find their way around by starting with Yahoo! (www.yahoo.com), a massive Web directory compiled by humans, or one of the search engines, such as AltaVista (www.altavista.com).[13]

Arguing that the web has no "central point, no capital city" ignores the fact that web access and the production of web content is not distributed equally across the world and among people. In the early days of the Internet, both access and production were concentrated in the United States; today they are more diversified, as this volume shows, but still display certain clusters that function as centers. From the perspective of a user in India, the Internet has central points, which are located outside her context of life. If she reads this quote, she thus immediately knows that the text refers to somebody else, while a middle-class user in the United States will most probably consider it a general statement. The further claim that "most people" use websites such as www.yahoo.com and www.altavista.com, furthermore implicitly defines "people" as those who know English (using English-language websites) and are likely to be based in the United States (using websites based there). Thus a seemingly innocent formulation like that of this quote reproduces power structures without referring explicitly to them. As in other fields of research, the subjectivities of the Internet scholar's perspectives are hardly reflected and addressed. Mainstream Internet Studies imagines itself as objective and universally applicable. The cases where its analyses do not fit are considered exceptional deviations from the norm, which need to be dealt with as such.

This distinction between the norm and the deviation can be seen when analyzing how academic writing is organized. As an example, I use the very good introduction to Internet studies by Döring,[14] which gives a comprehensive overview over contemporary Internet research. In its detailed list of contents, one can find only one direct reference to unequal power structures in the term "Americanization."[15] The index gives two more references to "Americanization," but none leads to a detailed discussion of the concept. The terms "white," "Europe," "Western," "South," or "developing countries" are not included at all in the index. Racism, like "digital divide," is referred to just once. The quotes for "ethnicity" and "ethnic identity" lead to short paragraphs about the special use "ethnic minorities" can make of the Internet. In line with mainstream perceptions, "whiteness," "Westernness," "middle class," etc., are not marked as something special, rather they remain the unmarked norm. Those marginalized by racist power structures are further marginalized in the structure of the book by being considered as deviations from this unchallenged norm. Döring shows that this can be done differently in the case of heteronormativity, where she displays a much deeper awareness. Not only are there many more references to gender and homosexuality than racism included in the index, the usually unmarked norm heterosexuality is also included. With the tendency to marginalize the marginalized, Döring's book is replicating mainstream Internet studies. Texts can be roughly divided into those dealing with supposedly general topics, like Döring's (linked to the "white," "Western," middle-class male perspective), and those dealing with the others, like the chapters in this volume (those who are outside the unmarked norm).

The distinction between the norm and the deviation can also be seen in the way language is dealt with. If the language of Internet communication is English, then it is not further discussed, as this is considered "normal." If, however, the language is any other, then a need for discussion is claimed. In this volume, for example, Gavrilović (Chapter 10, this volume)—like me—argues that language (in her case, Serbian, and in mine, German) restricts the number of potential users. While this is true, the same also holds true for English, but this fact is hardly ever mentioned. In fact, as the editors elaborate in the Introduction to this volume, English is no longer the dominant language on the Internet, even if it remains dominant in mainstream research.

As Khiabany and Sreberny (Chapter 13, this volume) argue, internationalizing Internet studies implies more than a collection of articles from different locations. It is essential that lines of social differences and their own position within the hegemonic power structure are taken into account. It is not sufficient to acknowledge the digital divide; it has to be understood in relation to the real differences in the physical world and the role those privileged by them play in continually reproducing them. Furthermore, the unequal distribution of resources and power has to be taken into account when analyzing virtual spaces. Rather than considering those outside the norm of the hegemonic power structure as marginal, peripheral, and exceptional, they have to be considered as "normal" in the same way that those within the center of power and the power relations have to be addressed.[16] Analyzing the Internet as an emancipative medium to overcome dominant power structures online—as in chapters in this volume by Cunliffe (Chapter 7, this volume) and Micó and Masip (Chapter 8, this volume)—is one of many ways to do this.

I follow Miller and Slater's ethnographic approach to Internet studies,[17] analyzing the Internet in its offline context. In contrast to them, however, I am not analyzing a particular geographical space, but rather a particular virtual space: the Internet portal http://www.theinder.net, called the Indernet.[18] It is a space I am also linked to personally, as I belong to its target group. Like Miller and Slater, I am exploring my field of research in its complexity and in its interaction with offline spaces, which in my case are mainly located in "Germany." My analysis focuses on the functions that this "German" virtual space fulfils in the context of "national," "ethnic," and "cultural" ascriptions (thus neglecting aspects of gender and class, in particular). Theoretically, it is based on the argument that social identities and groups are not "naturally" given, but are the result of constructions,[19] and that these discursive constructions are part of the hierarchical structuring of societies, through racism in particular.[20] Consequently, I mark these constructed and ambiguous categories in inverted commas. When I argue that "Indians of the second generation" are othered and excluded in "Germany," and that the Indernet is a space to deal with this, I do not consider this an exceptional use of the Internet. It is one of many and, like all others, unique. The editors and users of the Indernet, far from being passive victims of the hegemonic power structures, have agency to deal with this and are innovative in developing strategies, although they are restricted in their social resources. Their use of German as the main language is something "natural" and is not a particular choice. In contrast to the use of Japanese in Gottlieb's analysis (Chapter 5, this volume), it is not a nationalistic statement; it is simply the language most of the editors and users know best and feel most comfortable with. If they had chosen either English or an "Indian" language, this would, in contrast, have been a purposeful decision that needs to be analyzed.

THE INDERNET

The Indernet forms a virtual space of "Indians of the second generation" for "Indians of the second generation" in German-speaking Europe, localized geographically both by the use of language and topics. While referring symbolically to an imagined "India," the users' practical point of reference is the "Germany" that determines their everyday lives.[21] Here, they undergo experiences of othering and exclusion; here they face the demands of univocal "national" belongingness. The Indernet portal provides them with a space in which they can explicitly and implicitly exchange their experiences and, in doing so, negotiate their belongingness in "national," "ethnic," and "cultural" contexts.[22]

The Indernet is an Internet portal like many others. On the Indernet, young "Germans" interact in forums about films, music, parties, and politics. They engage in small talk and flirt with each other. They hang out together and occasionally get involved in flames.[23] In the editorial sections, they can read articles about films, parties, and politics, and they can consult the events calendar for the next party or other cultural events in "Germany." All this they can do in German, the main language of the portal. Most of the editors and users are based in "Germany," some in other German-speaking countries. Jointly they have created "theinder.net—Indien-Portal für Deutschland,"[24] an Internet portal for "Germany."

The Indernet is thus different from other virtual spaces marked as "Indian," which use English as the main language.[25] As German is understood internationally by relatively few people who are marked as "Indian," the Indernet does not allow for transnational communication with "Indians" based in other countries. "Indians" based in "Germany" who want to do that use other virtual spaces, such as the matrimonial website, http://www.shadi.com, or the sports portal, http://www.indianfootball.com.[26] New "Indian" migrants to "Germany," who are neither fluent in German nor familiar with "Germany," use the mailing list GINDS, which caters better to their specific needs.[27] Each of these spaces targets different audiences and fulfils different functions. They are, however, not mutually exclusive. Many users of the Indernet use at least one other "Indian" virtual space.

When I use the term "Germans," as in the previous paragraphs, most would disagree with me and categorize the people I talk of as "Indians," "Indians of the second generation," or "Indo-Germans." Referring solely to the place of their residence is a deviation from the norm of emphasizing the "origin" of a person. In calling the editors and users of the Indernet "Germans," I follow Mecheril's[28] use of the term "German" to describe all those who have lived, live, and will live in "Germany"—those who plan and live their lives there. The term "German" is thus defined independently of citizenship, ancestors, or ascribed "culture." To do so is both a political statement against essentialism and othering as well as the creation and application of an analytical category. Few of the editors and users of the Indernet, however, would use "German" without further qualification as a self-description. Most would rather refer to "India" than to "Germany" when describing themselves in "national," "ethnic," or "cultural" terms.

Even though the Indernet is a virtual space using the German language, and a space where issues of interest in "Germany" are discussed by people I categorize as "Germans," it is defined primarily as an "Indian" space. The domain name theinder.net, as well as the name Indernet, include the German term *Inder*, which in English translates to "Indian." The founders thus are referring to a network of "Indians." In the early descriptions of the project, the target group was accordingly described as: "Our target group is primarily the generation of young Indians living in Germany."[29] In their interviews with me, the editors specified this further as being primarily "Indians of the second generation," and also to some extent, young information technology (IT) professionals from "India." The English slogan "Germany's premier NRI portal"[30] describes the target group as "Non-Resident Indians." Thus it links them both to "India" and to the worldwide "Indian diaspora." This is further emphasized by providing English and Hindi versions of the portal, in addition to the German-language version. The symbolic rather than pragmatic character of the trilinguality becomes apparent when observing that the English version has very little content, and the Hindi version hardly has any. Both versions are not so much online to provide a platform for English and Hindi speakers, but more to establish the fact that the Indernet is part of the "diaspora"[31]—and as one of the founders has told me in the interview, to emphasize that Hindi is the national language of "India."[32] Also, in the interactive elements, German is the dominant language. "Indian" languages like Malayalam, Punjabi, or Bengali are only occasionally used to emphasize regional affiliations. English posts seem to be written mostly by "white" people who want to get in contact with "Indians."[33]

Through its forums and editorial sections, its choice of topics and language, and its structure and design, the Indernet links "Germany" and "India." It is a space for those who are linked both to "Germany" and "India" and are localized in German-speaking Europe. The Indernet is thus a "space of the second generation."

A "SPACE OF THE SECOND GENERATION"

The Indernet functions primarily as a space of the "Indians of the second generation in Germany."[34] This is despite the fact that there are also several active "white" users, many "white" lurkers, and some "Indians of the first generation," who read articles and posts, as well as use the events calendar. An Internet portal like the Indernet consists not only of several more-or-less independent virtual (sub)spaces, which are linked through the same domain address, but also gives space to many different types of users. Most of these users are lurkers, although some post as well. Such users read only the editorial sections, only the forum, only the events calendar, or any combination of these. Some come only once a month, others daily. Through this variety of users, the complexity of the Indernet, and because of the specificity of virtual spaces where only active interaction can be observed, the appropriation of the virtual (sub)spaces by different users for different aims is possible. Accordingly, the Indernet can be simultaneously an own space of the "Indians of the second generation" and an information portal on "India" for "white" users.

My analysis of the Indernet is based on extensive participant observation on- and offline since its creation in 2000, as well as more than sixty interviews with founders, editors, users, and observers. This field research was conducted mainly as part of the research project, The Virtual Second Generation.[35] I started observing the Indernet out of an interest in the "second generation," as one of which I identify myself. The Indernet was the first interactive and dynamic virtual space for "Indians of the second generation." It gained my attention by growing rapidly, surviving major crises, and gaining much public attention of both "Indians of the second generation" and "white" people interested in "India" and "Indians in Germany." The interviews made it possible for me to contextualize what I observed on- and offline, and to discuss interpretations with my interview partners. My analysis can be understood as tessellating a mosaic from the individual pieces I collected through observation and interviews. It is the combination of the different impressions that creates the picture I draw here.[36]

The Indernet was founded in the summer of 2000 by three young men whose parents had migrated from "India" to "Germany" in the 1960s and 1970s. The latter were part of the first major phase of migration. Individual young men came to study or work, and many of them got good jobs and stayed, married "white" German women, or were joined by their "Indian" wives. Some time later, young female nurses—who were recruited by the Catholic Church—migrated in small groups, established (in contrast to the earlier migrants) an own "ethnic" and religious infrastructure, and were, after several years, joined by their husbands from "India." In comparison to the asylum seekers, who came later, both of these groups are legally, socially, and economically privileged. The recent IT migrants are similarly privileged, but have not yet settled down in "Germany."[37]

In total, the residents marked as "Indian" in "Germany" are still a comparatively small group. In 2003, there were about 43,500 Indian citizens, an estimated 17,500 Persons of Indian Origin (PIO) Card holders, and uncounted undocumented "Indians." The biggest ethicized group in "Germany" is formed by those marked as "Turks," who display a similar economic, social, and racialized status as "Asians" in "Britain." "Indians" in "Germany" are comparatively privileged.[38] While they do experience othering and exclusion, in most cases this does not form an existential threat to them. As most "Indians" live scattered throughout "Germany," they had to establish themselves in mainly "white" environments. Many, in an attempt to escape racism, sought to assimilate in the workplace, at school, and other public places, while struggling to preserve their "culture" at home. This attempt to do everything "right," however, necessarily leads to tensions. On the one hand, racist discourses will never let them become "Germans," so their attempts to assimilation are futile. On the other hand, the "German" environment and their interaction with it are so dominant that a "pure Indian culture" cannot be retained. The "second generation" experiences that, while they belong to both contexts, they are not granted unquestioned belongingness to either.[39]

Prior to founding the Internet portal, the three founders of the Indernet were all experimenting with the new Internet technology, and had created personal websites. They had grown up knowing only a few other "Indians of the second generation" and were interested in meeting others who had similar experiences as theirs. When, in the summer of 2000, the conservative opposition reacted to a "Green Card" initiative for foreign IT specialists with a racist campaign, which was soon known as *"Kinder statt Inder,"*[40] the three "Indians of the second generation" had found an issue around which they could create an Internet portal. They took up the German play on words, merging "Indians" and Internet, and named their portal Indernet, they put several cartoons on "Indian" IT specialists and *"Kinder statt Inder"* online, and started their network of the "Indians of the second generation."[41] By using offline networks, the Indernet grew rapidly in content, users, and editors. Over the last six years, new elements were repeatedly introduced, but the basic idea and structure of the portal remained. Already several years back the Indernet had established itself as the major medium of the "second generation," known to people who do not use it—and about which comparatively much is written in other media and research.[42]

The Indernet is a space created by "Indians of the second generation" for "Indians of the second generation." With the term "Indians of the second generation," I categorize those who have been mainly socialized in "Germany" and who, through social or visual markers, are categorized as "Indians" in "Germany." Among these are the children of "Indian" migrants, as well as people who were adopted from "South Asia." There are those who have been brought up by parents who were socialized in "South Asia," as well as those who have had no contact at all with "South Asia" but are marked as "Indians" through (ascribed) "ancestry." This broad and ambiguous definition of the "second generation" was formed in the course of my field research, as it best encompasses all those who feel a sense of natio-ethno-cultural belongingness[43] in "spaces of the second generation," such as at seminars, parties, and on the Indernet. Among those categorized by me through this term, many, but not all, would consider themselves "Indians of the second generation." The term should thus not be understood as a self-description of a homogenous group, but rather as an analytical category,[44] which focuses on the experiences of being socialized in "Germany" and considered "Indian" at the same time.

The *Indernet's* aim, as formulated in December 2000, was to build a network of "Indians of the second generation":

> Our aim is to bring together young Indians, to promote communication among each other, to inform about projects of our members and about the country India as such.[45]

Judging by the names given in the list of members, the profiles in the forum, and the statements in the posts, most of those who leave traces on the Indernet seem to be "Indians of the second generation." From discussions in the forum and my interviews, I get the impression that most users and editors assume that the majority of the users belong to this category. Adapting Mecheril's concept of the "standard German,"[46] one can talk, in this context, of the "standard user." The "standard user" is the shared image of the fictitious ideal type of the Indernet user, independent of who in fact uses it. The editors provide a framework of structure, design, content, and rules catering to this "standard user," and this framework is further developed by the posters. When addressing users, both "Indians of the second generation" and "white" users generally assume them to conform to the image of the "standard user." The editors write articles about issues that they believe the "second generation" is interested in.[47] Thus, the norm of being "Indian of the second generation" on the Indernet is created. A feeling of being among others (natio-ethno-culturally) like oneself is established. Common experiences are imagined and referred to. In the interviews, the Indernet was described to me by most as a space of "Indians of the second generation," where there is no need to explain, where one can build on shared experiences, joke together, and feel a sense of familiarity.

This "space of the second generation" developed in virtual space, as the "Indians of the second generation" in "Germany" live too scattered geographically to easily establish permanent own spaces offline. Its popularity was helped by the fascination of many young "Indians of the second generation" with the medium of the Internet, its easy accessibility with few resources, and the possibility of users creating their own public. The Internet is a natural medium[48] for most of the editors and users. They use it like other media because it is available and because it satisfies a particular need.[49]

A SPACE FOR MULTIPLE BELONGINGNESS

In most spaces other than the Indernet, "Indians of the second generation" experience that they are considered to deviate from the natio-ethno-cultural norm.[50] The unmarked norm in "Germany" is that any person univocally belongs to one "nation," "ethnicity," or "culture." This norm not only informs the legal system—for example, in citizenship law—but also social interactions. Accordingly, most people can hardly think of anyone belonging to more than one natio-ethno-cultural context. Thus, "migrants of the second generation" who have, in Mecheril's terms, a multiple natio-ethno-cultural belongingness are not thinkable by most people as well as mainstream research, and so they are ascribed to their "country of origin." But the "migrants of the second generation" also experience, often primarily, a sense of belongingness to "Germany." As this is not accepted, Mecheril argues that real belongingness, which develops only when the feeling of belongingness on the one side is met by acceptance on the other, cannot develop. "Indians of the second generation" like other "migrants of the second generation," rather than being accepted in their multiple belongingness, are faced with exclusion, othering, and discrimination. Since these form a major part of their experiences, Mecheril develops the term "Other Germans"[51] as an analytical category, thus emphasizing the fact that they are not unquestioningly accepted as "Germans."

On the Indernet, "Indians of the second generation" are not othered on the basis of their multiple natio-ethno-cultural belongingness. Here, the latter is the unnamed norm. Everybody assumes that most editors and users fall within the "second generation." Here, those who can be univocally ascribed to only one natio-ethno-cultural context are the others, the ones who are considered to deviate, those who need to explain themselves. Here, the "Indians of the second generation" are safe from being othered as "Indians of the second generation." Here, they do not have to fear questions that other them natio-ethno-culturally. Here, they can find a refuge from the natio-ethno-cultural othering and discrimination experienced in other spaces.[52] Without explicitly talking about these issues, they can be sure that the others have had similar experiences. Here, they know that such othering and discrimination would not be tolerated but would be immediately sanctioned. Here, they experience that already implicit reference to these experiences are understood by the others. Through this absence of othering and discrimination, as well as the exchange with others who have had similar experiences, the "Indians of the second generation" experience on the Indernet an acceptance of their sense of belongingness that they can hardly experience in other spaces in "Germany." As one of the users told me in the interview:

> I also went through phases, when I was almost depressive, because I thought: "Oh no, where do I belong?" A conflict of identity, when one does not know, where . . . what am I? You look into the mirror and you see somebody with black hair. You go outside, talk to people and when you listen to yourself, you think: "Yes, naturally. For myself I am German." When I listen to myself thus, but as soon as, I don't know . . . there are small things said by others, by friends, small remarks like "How is it done at your place?" Then it is again: "Oh no, I am different after all." And then I found other people with this conflict of identity on pak24 and theinder.net. There one can talk with each other, exchange experiences. A bit of survival training: how does one deal with this?[53]

The Indernet is also different from the spaces created by the parents, who migrated from "South Asia." While these spaces refer to the "India" the parents left decades ago, as well as to an imagined "traditional India" with "high classical culture" and the maintenance of unchanging "traditions,"[54] the spaces of the "second generation" refer to a "modern India." The "Indians of the second generation," who were socialized in "Germany," think like their "white" friends in the dichotomies of "modern" and "traditional," "civilized" and "natural."[55] Like their friends, they have learned to consider "modern" and "civilized" as superior. In their search for a natio-ethno-cultural context they can positively identify with, they accordingly are looking for one they can describe as "modern" and "civilized." The parents' references to "classical culture" and "traditions" do not fulfill this need. On the Indernet and at parties, the basis for positive identification is laid by drawing the picture of an "India" fitting all "modern" developments, being part of an international music scene, excelling in IT, and so on.

Both in the editorial sections and the forum, the Indernet offers information about "India" and "India in Germany." It is accessible, as it is in German and in a form that fits the needs of young users. Furthermore, the information is fitted to their interests and requirements. There are reports on films and parties, as well as on those issues that are often the object of questions from "white Germans." As Battaglia has shown, "migrants of the second generation" are regularly involved in conversations establishing their otherness.[56] They are asked where they come from, are told that they should know the language of their "ancestors," are ascribed a different "mentality," and are considered as experts on their ascribed "origin." But, as most "Indians of the second generation" know little more than their "white" peers about "India," they can hardly fulfill the role of the expert and consequently experience the humiliation of not fulfilling the expectations set for them. On the Indernet, they are provided with information that helps them to survive better as "experts" in these discussions.

In offering "Indians of the second generation" a space of refuge from discrimination and othering, an imagination of belongingness and commonness, as well as something positive to identify with, the Indernet helps "Indians of the second generation" to deal with their experiences of othering in other spaces. By defining the natio-ethno-cultural belongingness on the Indernet as "Indian," it also offers the evocation of univocal belongingness without negating the multiple belongingness experienced by "Indians of the second generation." The Indernet is a space without natio-ethno-cultural othering for "Indians of the second generation," without, however, tackling other forms of othering prevalent in "Germany," such as heteronormativity or class differences. Thus, for example, while the Indernet challenges the "white German" images of "Indian" women, it does not challenge the gender dichotomy as such. Almost all the articles are clearly written within a heteronormative framework; in the forum, sexist and homophobic posts are hardly challenged. One of my interview partners thus stopped using the Indernet after his coming-out, although he was looking for contact with other "Indians of the second generation":

> . . . this was a reason for me to change my usage of the Indernet, because I did not find it [his homosexuality, ug] represented . . . and I often experienced it as very homophobic.[57]

By referring to a "transnational identity" and by offering a space to imagine themselves as "Indians," the Indernet deals with experiences in "Germany." At the same time, it links to an imagined "India" as it is clearly localized in "Germany." "India" is the natio-ethno-cultural context where belonging-ness is looked for and collectively imagined. "India" is the country that is considered to be the "origin" of the "Indians of the second generation." Accordingly, within a framework where univocal natio-ethno-cultural belongingness is considered the norm, "India" is seen as determining the "nationality," the "ethnicity," and the "culture" of "Indians of the second generation." Many "Indians of the second generation" follow this ascription and make it their own.[58] But even if they do so, they remain "Other Germans." They are socialized in "Germany;" German is the language they know best. The Indernet takes account of this by linking the imagination of an "Indian identity" with the German language. The editors and users refer to "India" while they remain localized in "Germany." They deal with the experiences of othering and discrimination there, and from there, imagine what it is to be "Indians." Accordingly, while at a first glance, the topic of the Indernet seems to be "India;" on closer observation and analysis, it shows itself to be "being Indian in Germany."[59]

DEALING WITH OTHERING AND EXCLUSION

In a world shaped by racism, heteronormativity, and class differences, those who fall outside of the norm defined through hegemonic power experience constant othering and exclusion. Martin shows in Chapter 18 (this volume) how women identifying as lesbian and "Chinese" use the Internet to inter-act with others who have similar experiences and to imagine a community. I have shown the same for "Indians of the second generation." In both cases, the spaces of the places of residence, which are shaped through racist and heteronormative discourses, continually reproduce othering. Accord-ingly, those othered look for and develop alternative spaces. In both cases, the virtual spaces cater to multiple belongingness for several seemingly con-tradicting "identities." In contrast to Miller and Slater's analysis of "Trini-dad," neither can refer unambiguously to a geographical space or a sexual identity. In the case of Martin, the women experience othering both in "Chinese" and in "Western lesbian" spaces. In the case of the "Indians of the second generation" they experience othering both in "Germany" and in "India." Thus, both othered groups need to create something new for themselves (compare this with He's discussion in Chapter 19 in this volume about hybridization). Because it requires few resources, the virtual space gives them the possibility to link scattered individuals, of creating an own public, and imagining a community.

A globalized world of equals is a fantasy of those who possess the privileges bestowed by hegemonic power. They do not need to deal with the lines of difference that exclude others. By ignoring the lines and the unequal power structures, and by constructing the idea of equality, they secure their own position and continually reproduce the differences—not least in research. Internet studies need to consider the impact of the lines of differences beyond the question of the digital divide. They need to deal with the diversity of online interactions as a replication of differences in the physical world. Internet scholars (including myself) need to question their own hegemonic position and stop further othering those already othered. It is not a question of center and periphery, of the norm and the exceptional, but of different positions in power structures. All have the same agency, but some have considerably less access to resources and power. To analyze this, Internet studies need to take account of the methods, theories, and approaches developed by postcolonial, racism, critical whiteness, and gender studies. By doing so, such inter- and transdisciplinary Internet studies could set a positive example for other fields of social studies, in particular for those it is closely interacting with.

ACKNOWLEDGMENT

I am indebted to the two editors of this volume, Mark McLelland and Gerard Goggin, for encouragement and critical comments on this paper.

NOTES

1. See Nicola Döring, *Sozialpsychologie des Internet: Die Bedeutung des Internet für Kommunikationsprozesse, Identitäten, soziale Beziehungen und Gruppen* (Göttigen, Germany: Hogrefe, 2003) for an overview of Internet studies. Most of the following examples I discuss are found there.
2. cf. Christian Stegbauer, *Grenzen virtueller Gemeinschaft: Strukturen Internetbasierter Kommunikationsforen* (Wiesbaden, Germany: Westdeutscher Verlag, 2000).
3. See, for example, Döring, *Sozialpsychologie des Internet*, 14.
4. cf. David Morley and Kevin Robins, *Spaces of Identity* (London: Routledge, 1995), 1, as well as Gottlieb, Chapter 5, in this volume.
5. For an example, see, Tara McPherson, "I'll Take My Stand in the Dixie-Net: White Guys, the South, and Cyberspace," in *Race in Cyberspace*, ed. Beth E. Kolko et al. (New York: Routledge, 2000), 117–132.
6. Karim H. Karim, *The Media of Diaspora* (London: Routledge, 2003), 15.
7. Beth E. Kolko et al., *Race in Cyberspace* (New York: Routledge, 2000)
8. I use the term *mainstream research* to describe the unmarked norm of research: that is, research that is generally considered to be the standard, and in relation to which researchers position themselves. This does not necessarily mean that most research falls into the mainstream. The mainstream develops its normative character through being generally considered the norm (compare this to the fictitious "standard German," as developed by Paul Mecheril, *Prekäre Verhältnisse: Über natio-ethno-kulturelle [Mehrfach-] Zugehörigkeiten* [Münster, Germany: Waxmann, 2003], 211–212).

9. Like any other field of research, gender studies are also far from homogenous and experience internal debates. In particular, scholars who are outside the unmarked norm of "white," "Western," heterosexual feminist, have argued that the lines of difference created through heteronormativity, class, and racism also need to be taken into account in gender studies. I am referring in my work, in particular, to the critique of identity politics and the theoretical context developed by Judith Butler—in particular: *Gender Trouble: Feminism and the Subversion of Identity* (New York: Routledge, 1990)—and as discussed in Avtar Brah, *Cartographies of Diaspora: Contesting Identities* (London: Routledge, 1996).

10. For an analysis of "white" research perspectives, see, for example, Maureen Maisha Eggers et al., eds., *Mythen, Masken, Subjekte—Kritische Weißseinsforschung in Deutschland* (Münster, Germany: Unrast, 2005), and Aileen Moreton-Robison, *Talkin' up to the White Women: Indigenous Women and Feminism* (St. Lucia, Australia: UQ Press, 2000).

11. I use "white" as the description of the hegemonic and powerful social positioning as developed in Critical Whiteness Studies. I thus attempt to mark those in the "West" who are normally unmarked, as they are part of the unchallenged norm.

12. "White," male, heterosexual, middle-class researchers are no longer the only researchers of a generally acknowledged reputation. But if there are now "black," female, queer, or lower class researchers who have reached important positions in research, this is not yet threatening the general hegemonic position of "white," male, heterosexual, middle-class researchers. The latter still define the unmarked norm to which the others have to relate.

13. See David Gauntlett, ed., *Web.Studies: Rewiring Media Studies for the Digital Age* (London: Arnold, 2000), 6.

14. See Döring, *Sozialpsychologie des Internet.*

15. In the short section referred to here, one finds, in fact, only one sentence about "Americanisation," and that is linked to Europe (Döring, *Sozialpsychologie des Internet*, 30).

16. Mostly this is not done. For example, Heribert Schatz and Jörg-Uwe Nieland, "Einführung in die Thematik und Überblick über die Beiträge," in *Migranten und Medien: Neue Herausforderungen an die Integrationsfunktion von Presse und Rundfunk*, ed. Heribert Schatz et al. (Wiesbaden, Germany: Westdeutscher Verlag, 2000), as well as Oliver Hinkelbein, *Ethnische Minderheiten, neue Medien und die digitale Kluft: Deutschland ein digitales Entwicklungsland?* (Bremen, Germany: bik, 2004; also available at http://www.digitale-chance.de/transfer/downloads/MD642.pdf), treat migrants as objects rather than agents. Ananda Mitra, "Marginal Voices in Cyberspace," *New Media & Society* 3, no. 1 (2001): 29–48, and also Döring's *Sozialpsychologie des Internet*, ignore the unequal power relations when they consider the Internet to be a space for the marginalized voice.

17. Daniel Miller and Don Slater, *The Internet: An Ethnographic Approach* (Oxford: Berg, 2000).

18. The term *Indernet* as the name of the Internet portal can be found at http://www.indien-netzwerk.de/logo/projekt/projekt-deu.htm (accessed September 6, 2006). It was also used by many of my interview partners.

19. On the constructions of social identities, see, Richard Jenkins, *Rethinking Ethnicity: Arguments and Explorations* (London: Sage, 1997); Anthony Cohen, *The Symbolic Construction of Community* (London: Routledge, 1985); Fredrik Barth, *Ethnic Groups and Boundaries* (Boston, MA: Little, Brown, and Co. 1969); and Rogers Brubaker, *Ethnicity Without Groups* (Cambridge, MA: Harvard University Press, 2004).

20. On racism, see, Stuart Hall, "Rassismus als ideologischer Diskurs," in *Theorien über Rassismus*, ed. Nora Räthzel (Hamburg: Argument, 2000), 7–16; Robert Miles, "Bedeutungskonstitution und der Begriff des Rassismus," in *Theorien über Rassismus*, 17–33; and Mecheril, *Prekäre Verhältnisse*.
21. Compare this with Martin's notion of imagined geographies in Chapter 18 in this volume.
22. cf. Urmila Goel, "Fatima and theinder.net: A Refuge in Virtual Space," in *Import Export—Cultural Transfer—India, Germany, Austria*, ed. Angelika Fitz et al. (Berlin: Parhas Verlag, 2005), 201–207.
23. cf. Döring's *Sozialpsychologie des Internet*.
24. This slogan is found on the home page of the Indernet, http://www.theinder. net/ (accessed September 9, 2006). Translated to English, it would read "theinder.net—India portal for Germany." The Indernet also has an English version, but it is not a direct translation of the German. The quoted slogan in English, for example, reads as "Germany's premier NRI portal," which has a different meaning.
25. Most literature focuses on English-speaking spaces, for example, Amit Rai, "India Online: Electronic Bulletin Boards and the Construction of a Diasporic Hindu Identity," *Diaspora* 4, no. 1 (1995): 31–57; Vinay Lal, "The Politics of History on the Internet: Cyber-Diasporic Hinduism and the North American Hindu Diaspora," *Diaspora* 8, no. 2 (1999): 137–173; Ananda Mitra, "Virtual Commonality: Looking for India on the Internet," in *Virtual Culture: Identity and Communication in Cyberspace*, ed. Steven Jones (London: Sage, 1997), 55–79; Madhavi Mallapragada, "The Indian Diaspora in the USA and around the Web," in *Web.Studies: Rewiring Media Studies for the Digital Age*, ed. David Gauntlett (London: Arnold, 2000), 179–185; Arvind Rajagopal, "Hindunationalism in the US: Changing Configurations of Political Practice," *Ethnic and Racial Studies* 23, no. 3 (2000): 467–496; and Christiane Brosius, "Of Nasty Pictures and 'Nice Guys': The Surreality of Online Hindutva," SARAI Reader 2004: Crisis/Media, http://www.sarai. net/journal/04_pdf/18christiane.pdf
26. The latter's chief editors are based in "Germany" and are also the sports editors of the Indernet.
27. cf. Volker Oberkircher, "Die deutsche Greencard aus der Sicht indischer IT-Experten," in *masala.de: Menschen aus Südasien in Deutschland*, ed. Christiane Brosius and Urmila Goel (Heidelberg, Germany: Draupadi, 2006),161–188.
28. Paul Mecheril, "Die Lebenssituation Anderer Deutscher. Eine Annäherung in dreizehn thematischen Schritten," in *Andere Deutsche: Zur Lebenssituation von Menschen multiethnischer und multikultureller Herkunft*, ed. Paul Mecheril and Thomas Teo (Berlin: Dietz, 1994), 57–94; Paul Mecheril, "Rassismuserfahrungen von Anderen Deutschen—eine Einzelfallbetrachtung," in *Psychologie und Rassismus*, ed. Paul Mecheril and Thomas Teo (Hamburg: Rourohit, 1997), 175–201, and Mecheril, *Prekäre Verhältnisse*.
29. My translation of the German original, which was online at http://indernet. exit.mytoday.de/presentation/presentation.htm on December 26, 2000, when I started my documentation of the Internet portal. In the summer of 2006, the project description was rewritten, focusing more on "India" than on "Indians."
30. Indernet home page, http://www.theinder.net/ (accessed September 6, 2006).
31. For pitfalls of the concept of diaspora, see Rogers Brubaker, "The 'Diaspora' Diaspora," *Ethnic and Racial Studies* 28, no. 1 (2005): 1–19.
32. Compare with Gottlieb's discussion of Japanese as a nationalistic symbol in Chapter 5 in this volume.

33. For a discussion of language use on "ethno portals" in "Germany," see Jannis Androutsopolous, "Multilingualism, Diaspora, and the Internet: Codes and Identities on German-Based Diaspora Websites," *Journal of Sociolinguistics* 10, no. 4 (2006): 520–547, and "Language Choice and Code Switching in German-Based Diasporic Web Forums," in *The Multilingual Internet*, ed. Brenda Danet and Susan Herring (Oxford: Oxford University Press, 2007).

34. For a discussion of "spaces of the second generation," see Kathleen Heft and Urmila Goel, *Räume der zweiten Generation: Dokumentation eines Workshops* (Frankfurt/Oder: Viadrina, 2006; also available at http://www.urmila.de/UDG/Biblio/Raeume_der_zweiten_Generation.pdf). For a discussion of the Indernet as a space for the "Indians of the second generation," see, in particular, Goel, "Fatima and theinder.net."

35. The research project was funded by the Volkswagenstiftung and is affiliated with the Department of Social and Cultural Anthropology at the European University Viadrina in Frankfurt/Oder, Germany. The details of the project can be found at http://www.urmila.de/forschung.

36. For this chapter, I have chosen to draw a macro picture that does not focus on the individual parts, which are the basis of the mosaic. Those who are more interested in the ethnographic material should refer to Goel, "Fatima and theinder.net," as well as my article: "'Kinder statt Inder'—Normen, Grenzen und das Indernet," in *Jugend, Zugehörigkeit und Migration: Subjektpositionierung im Kontext von Jugendkultur, Ethnizitäts- und Geschlechterkonstruktionen*, ed. Christine Riegel and Thomas Giesen (Wiesbaden, Germany: VS Verlag für Sozialwissenschaften, 2007), 163–181; and "Imagining India Online: Second-Generation Indians in Germany," in *Mapping Channels*, ed. Joerg Esleben, Christina Kraenzle, and Sukanya Kulkarni (Toronto: University of Toronto Press, forthcoming).

37. cf. Oberkircher, "Die deutsche Greencard."

38. More information on the migration from "India" to "Germany" can be found at http://www.urmila.de.

39. cf. Mecheril, *Prekäre Verhältnisse*.

40. This translates to "Children instead of Indians," and demanded more investment in "White German" children, rather than encouraging the immigration of foreign specialists.

41. Compare with Gorny's description of the motivation of the webmaster of a "Russian" website in Chapter 6 of this volume.

42. Besides my own research, see, in particular, Jannis Androusopolous's "Multilingualism, Diaspora, and the Internet" and "Language Choice and Code Switching."

43. The term was established by Mecheril in *Prekäre Verhältnisse* to analyze the belongingness determined through "national," "ethnic," and "cultural" notions of belonging.

44. cf. Paul Mecheril, "Andere Deutsche gibt es nicht: Zusammenhänge zwischen subalterner Erfahrung und diskursiver Praxis," in *The Black Book: Deutschlands Häutungen*, ed. AntiDiskriminierungsbüro Köln and cybernomads (Frankfurt: 2004), 82–90.

45. This is my translation of the German original, which was available online at http://indernet.exit.mytoday.de/presentation/presentation.htm

46. Mecheril, *Prekäre Verhältnisse*, 211–212.

47. Since the first draft of this article published in the summer of 2006, this focus seems to have changed somewhat. The editors seem to increasingly target "white" users.

48. cf. Miller and Slater, *The Internet*, 3.

49. cf. Döring, *Sozialpsychologie des Internet*, 186–198.

50. For the norm of univocal belongingness, and the impossibility of multiple belongingness within it, see Mecheril, *Prekäre Verhältnisse*. The following analysis is based on his theoretical approach and its arguments. More on the discriminating functions of the unnamed norm can be found in the Critical Whiteness Studies. See Eggers et al., *Mythen, Masken, Subjekte*, and Moreton-Robison, *Talkin' up to the White Women.*

51. "Other Germans" was first developed by Paul Mecheril and Thomas Teo in their *Andere Deutsche*. The concept has been further developed by Mecheril in "Rassismuserfahrungen von Anderen Deutschen," *Prekäre Verhältnisse.*

52. For ethnographic material on the Indernet as a refuge, see Goel, "Fatima and theinder.net."

53. For a detailed analysis of this user's interview, see Goel, "Fatima and theinder.net."

54. cf. Kalpana Ram, "Phantom Limbs: South Indian Dance and Immigrant Reification of the Female Body," *Journal of Intercultural Studies* 26, no. 1–2 (2005): 121–137.

55. For the dichomoties inherent in racist structures, see, for example, Eggers et al., *Mythen, Masken, Subjekte.*

56. Santina Battaglia, "Interaktive Konstruktion von Fremdheit. Alltagskommunikation von Menschen binationaler Abstammung," *Journal für Psychologie* 3, no. 3 (1995): 16–23.

57. For a detailed analysis of the norms and boundaries challenged and reproduced on the Indernet, refer to Goel, "'Kinder statt Inder.'"

58. Mareile Paske, *"Andere Deutsche": Strategien des Umgangs mit Rassismuserfahrungen* (Frankfurt/Oder: Viadrina, 2006; also available online at http://www.urmila.de/UDG/Forschung/publikationen/Paske2006.pdf), analyzed two interviews with "Indians of the second generation." One is the perfect example of this, while the other shows that there are also "Indians of the second generation" who distance themselves from any such ethnicizing.

59. cf. Miller and Slater, *The Internet*, 85–116.

10 Serbian Minority/Refugees on the Internet

In the Midst of Denial and Acceptance of Reality

Ljiljana Gavrilović

POLITICAL FRAMEWORK

During the 1990s, while the world was engaged in the processes of globalization and intense Internet development, the former Yugoslavia experienced a process of transition and, at the same time, state wrecking. In the wars of 1991–1996, two new states were created (Croatia and Bosnia and Herzegovina), while Macedonia and Slovenia separated without military conflict, and Serbia and Montenegro remained in a joint state until 2006. Until the wars in Croatia, a large percentage of Serbs lived in Bosnia and Herzegovina, sharing geographical as well as cultural space with Croatians and Muslims (today called Bosniaks). After the wars, many of these Serbs were forced to move out from their native areas and start living in Serbia, Western European countries, or on other continents (Australia, the United States). The wars in the former Yugoslavia have produced more than three milion refugees and displaced individuals, where Serbs alone make up around 1.5 milion of them.

In the last fifteen years or so, the whole public rhetoric in the former Yugoslavia was based solely on national and nationalistic discourse; its function was to rebuild national identities and promote the formation of new states. On the other hand, ever since the nineteenth century and the rise of Romantic ideas about an uber-Slavic culture,[1] the national rhetoric was the foundation of all these programs involving political reconstruction of societes in all southern Slavic countries (divided, at that time, among the Austro-Hungarian Empire, Turkey, and Serbia). Even during the communist period (1945–1990), when the nationalistic discourse was in direct opposition with a desired order (the ruling ideology), this was built into the consciousness of every individual who went through a formal educational system, due to the fact that the educational system was, in its larger part, built on Romantic discourse (especially the programs in native language and history).[2]

The postcolonial and postmodern periods have brought about, as a consequence of reassesment and decomposition during the two centuries of official, normative, political/cultural reality, a crisis of identity on all levels.[3] The crisis is clearly recognized in the flourishing of new nationalism[4] movements worldwide, especially among communities that were left out of the nineteenth-century developments involving group homogenization and self-identification. These communities were either found outside of the European/Christian geopolitical framework that influenced the Romantic-era formations of nation-states; or even, sometimes, though they were included in nation-states, the comunities could not manage to build or create a desired identity. The third group includes those communities who have successfully built some new identity but in the nineteenth century, still unrecognized or unknown.

Identity problems stream from the present-day reality, which, according to Marc Augé, creates new solitude: an individual is alone, separated from the majority of others with whom he shares the same space, but remains disconnected from all social, interhuman, ritual, or any other relationships.[5] An identity is always built on relations to others, thus, if there are no relationships with others, it follows that there is no identity either. At the same time, different group identities make up an essential part of an individual, personal identity and *vice versa*; threatening to an individual (who am I?) also threatens all the other versions of the group identities (who are we?)—ethnic, cultural, political, and so on.

Most definitions of culture are based, explicitly or implicitly, on a culture's content, namely what can be perceived and described with relative ease. The content (text) encompasses elements of a given culture: language, alphabet, religion, kinship relations, dress code, esthetic criteria, ideal representations of thinking and behavior, concept of time, concept of universe, and so on. A culture defined in these terms is also given a "national" identity prefix—in fact, a common practice during the 1990s not only restricted to the southern European territory, but also worldwide, as one of the reactions to the processes of globalization.

If we define the culture/identity by its content, the question becomes, which elements are to be used in defining the same. Within the so-called "Serbian" culture, which is defined primarily by the language (Serbian) and religion (Christian Orthodox), there are numerous cultural models that diverge from each other by their other elements: social organization—which could be territorial or tribal in traditional areas or more open in new, urban centers of culture—ideal models of behavior and worldviews, subsistence economy, material culture habitations, diet, and dress.

At the same time, in multinational countries, such as the whole area of southeast Europe, the same real elements of culture appear among members of many groups, and even among all national groups within one particular area. Language, for example, in spite of the political intentions to separate and distinguish among groups, has remained a common thread for the Serbs, Croatians, Bosniaks, and Montenegrins.[6] The same traditional house types and the surroundings we find among the Serbs, Hungarians, and Slovaks in Vojvodina, Serbia, but also among the Serbs and Croatians in Croatia, the Serbs and Vlax in eastern Serbia, the Serbs and Muslims in Bosnia and Herzegovina, and the Serbs, Bulgarians, and Macedonians in the central Balkans area. Diet also appears to be the same or very similar, in spite of the differences prescribed by religon, subsistence means, and many other elements of culture, including some customs of non-Christian origin.

In the case of the southern Slavs, the language appears to be a distinctive mark in the process of national separation: in bi- or multinational areas, it is the language that serves as a primary element of identification (given by birth alone), while religion appears to be the secondary.[7] In monolingual but bi- or multinational areas, religion appears to be the primary element of identification, while in the case of the Serbian groups, the secondary element becomes use of the Cyrillic alphabet.

INTERNET: IDENTIFICATION VERSUS GHETTOIZATION

The Internet has allowed many cultures of the lesser-known, smaller states and people, who were always dependent on bigger, more powerful states in a financial and organizational sense, to be presented at the widest possible level. Through the internet these smaller cultures have an opportunity to present their total cultural inheritance, and in that way, to help the defining process of their role and place within the network of European and world cultures. This is also an opportunity for ethnic groups that were unable to create their own national state, such as Aromuns, Celts, Basks, Catalonians, and so on, as well as for those who live divided in many different states.

Although the Internet appears to be a global network, the space within is segmented in different ways, corresponding to the interests of potential visitors, users, and active participants in the creation of Internet contents. One of the possible means of segmentation is language usage: the sites using the languages of the smaller nations and groups are, in reality, closed spaces, available only to intergroup communication between people who can speak the language. In a way, this could represent a form of ghettoization, since the usage of a "small," rarely spoken language disables a dialogue or communication with speakers of the other language or followers of other cultural traditions. In fact, this very effectively limits the maneuvres of minority groups on the Internet. At the same time, the possibility of the presentation of a given culture worldwide becomes restricted; in addition, the communication among members of the same language/culture becomes facilitated, giving them a sense of belonging regardless of their actual place of residence.

However, in the case of the former Yugoslavia territories, division by language criteria is practically impossible, since the language differences are negligable. The local search engine, Pogodak.co.yu (http://www.pogodak.co.yu), reports around seven million pages in the Serbian language, in both the Cyrillic and Latin alphabets, along with declinations. At the same time, it is estimated that there are around 35,000 blogs (this is not entirely true, since these sites include not only Serbian, but also the Bosnian, Montenegrin, and Croatian Internet). They all function in the Serbian language, hence, it is not possible to obtain true data. Therefore, this requires new methodology for the determination of group/national boundaries in Internet space that would not rely solely on language distinction.

All Serbian "refugee" sites are defined as locations exclusively in Serbian language, and thus are made available to only Serbs worldwide, and even then, only to those who maintained the language—and are thus not available to emigrants from third, fourth, or even older generations who lost, forgot, or use the Serbian language with difficulties.

DOMAIN NAMES

The choice of the domain names of Serbian websites from Croatia and Bosnia and Herzegovina (Federation and Republic of Srpska), and websites of all the rest of the refugees from the former Yugoslavia, explicitly reflects a relationship of the authors toward the newly formed Balkans states where they originated, and thus are, their political attitudes. As a rule, the domains names contain the suffixes ".com," ".net," or ".info." Therefore, the names are registered in the domain names registry of the United States, considered today to be international, since they are commercial and available to users worldwide. The second largest group makes sites with suffixes such as ".co.yu," or ".org.yu," where the suffixes designate Serbian Internet space since they belong to the Serbian domain name registry,[8] although they refer to Yugoslavia (".yu"[9] was an official international mark for the former Yugoslavia, which existed until 1991, and for the reduced one, encompassing Serbia and Montenegro, in the period of 1991–2003). Locations with addresses from Croatian (".hr") or Bosnian and Hercegovinian (".ba") registers do not exist at all.

This choice of domain implies:

- A total rejection of the new political reality; a denial and rejection of the newly created states, and correspondingly, a rejection of one's own minority status within the new states (this is actually not valid for Bosnia and Herzegovina, since the Serbs make a constitutive people/parts of the state);[10]
- The ".yu" prefix is treated as a mark of Serbian language/cultural space on the Internet, similar to the understanding and usage of ".cat" and ".gal" prefixes.[11] Nevertheless, ".yu" is: "A country code top-level domain (ccTLD) . . . a top-level domain used and reserved for a *country* or a dependent *territory*,"[12] while three- letter suffixes—".gal" and ".cat"—are generic domains refering to language, but not to geographical and or geopolitical space.[13]

Therefore, the ".yu" top-level domain (TLD) is being used even today as an expression of the Serbian national and cultural identity. It is interesting, though, that the ".srb" TLD did not appear in some form, which could explicitly express a belonging to the Serbian culture and so mark the Serbian language space on the Internet. This could point out an implicit political attitude that the former Yugoslavia was a state where the Serbian national, and even language/cultural, rights were protected (more than they are now), but could also point out a degree of nostalgia for the former state.

REFUGEES' LOCATIONS

Serbian "minority" or "refugee" locations developed in three basic directions.

The largest group of websites represents a clear expression of nostalgia (for instance, http://www.kistanje.co.yu/, http://www.kistanje.net/, http://www.krajina.net/, and many similar others). The content is mostly limited to descriptions, photographs, customs, music and folklore, and images that the refugees see as a representation of selfness and their own culture of the lost homeland. These sites do not posses a high technical level nor do they have fulfilling contents, although an effort to present things nicely is clearly evident.

Here is some typical content characteristic of locations of this type:

> Greetings to my people (from Knin) and to all the rest from Republic of Srpska Krajina, wherever we are, our hearts are always at the same place, there near the hills and valleys of our gorgeous homeland. A 1000 "Storms" could not take this away from us, for WE ARE KRAJISNICI (people from Krajina) NOW AND FOREVER! (http://www.knin.org.yu/)

As a rule, these sites do not contain details about the refugees, such as where they live, what they do, what they think, know, and therefore, what they could offer to their homeland and the world. Instead, the sites offer images of the world that does not exist anymore, idealized by its own cessation and the fact that it will never come back. These sites represent the past, without the present or future. The insistence on history—mostly idealized in a romanticized manner—and on long-abandoned tradition clearly speaks to a lack of an idea that they exist today in the here and now (even if they are experiencing contemporary dislocation), hence, that there is no idea of a return to the homeland. Their message could be paraphrased as: Look, our homeland is wonderful, and we love it and remember it in the same way that we remember our customs. But, we have left, and that's forever, but a part of our heart has stayed on, even though our life in the homeland is history.

The second group is more concentrated on the present moment and communication in general, as evident from the content and presentation of the sites. The most important representative of this type of site is SerbianCaffe (http://serbiancaffe.com/), the most popular site for Serbo-Croatian languages for years. Since it's beginning in 1996, the site's aim was to gather not only people from Western Europe who were dislocated from the former Yugoslavia, but also to gather of all the rest who have stayed in the homeland. In other words, the site has maintained a high level of communication among people from the whole parts of the former Yugoslavia. Of a similar character are some other local sites, which try to keep former and present-day residents of a particular space in one place, such as Knin.org.yu (http://www.knin.org.yu) or Krajinanetwork (http://www.krajinanetwork.com). Such sites also gather all the others who might be interested in the particular culture of the area, understood not as a combination of idealized tradition and folklore, but as a totality. The central place of these sites is the forum, where visitors exchange opinions on various subjects, from politics and religion, to sports and gender relations. One of the characteristics of these locations is a considerably good technical level, accompanied by a high level of tolerance and respect; that is, maintenance of what is considered a code of behavior on the Internet.[14] Moderators of the forum help to maintain this kind of behavior by deleting messages with offensive notes, whether the offences are of a personal, national, gender-related, or intolerant (hatred) nature. The message of these locations is: Wherever we live, we know who we are; we want to respect others, and want others to respect us, our language, our culture, and our religion in kind. They represent the true, beautiful face of the Serbs, mature enough for European integration, without the fear of losing their identity and with a full consciousness of being carriers of the cultural model that has a lot to offer to European heritage.

The third group is made up of locations directed at maintaining intragroup cohesion, regardless of the actual residence of the group members. Sites such as Polaca.kom (http://www.polaca.com/) and 24casa.com (www.trebinje.com/) are the ideal examples. These sites gather dislocated people from Kninska Krajina, and the wider area of northern Dalmatia, whose main premise is to preserve the "native" tradition of all people from Krajina (Polaca); that is, the Serbs from Bosnia and Herzegovina (Trebinje), regardless of whether they live today in Croatia, the Republic of Srpska, Federation of Bosnia and Herzegovinia, or in other countries. These sites are well-designed and are visited very often. However, their bare existence is in opposition to the idea of intercultural communication because these sites insist on group cohesion and firm boundaries toward everybody outside the group; their basic premise is to maintain and preserve the "native" tradition of all Serbs from Krajina and Bosnia and Herzegovina. Considering the relatively high popularity of these sites, and the disharmony between the technical level and contents, these sites require more detailed analysis and description.

The front page of the site, Polaca.com, contains the description and defined aim of the site's existence:

> Polaca is one of the biggest villages in Kninska Krajina. This site is dedicated to the people of the area, who, during the centuries have managed to survive on the same spot, and manage to preserve its Orthodox religion, customs and traditions, until they got betrayed by heathens.

Then, there is a description of a few gatherings of the people from Polaca living outside their homeland and a song:

> In Canada, over the grey sea, there are many people from Polaca.
> Their hearths suffer for their native village, and they long to come
>   back to Polaca.
> In honour of their ancient customs and Saint day, they have built a
>   little church in Oakville.
> The church is nice, although small, and named after Saint Peter and Paul.
> When the summer comes, and the winter is gone, a lot of people
>   from Polaca gather at the church.
> All the people from Polaca are happy to be there, to drink some wine
>   and play cards.
> And when the roast meat smells, even more of the Polaca people come.
> They meet often to talk and play ball.

The site also contains a description of various customs:

> Petrovdan. A traditional Polaca' fair, organized every year on July 12th, in the church of Saints Paul and Peter. Folks would go to the church first, and attended graveyards afterwards.
>
> Young men and women used to play in *kolo* (a traditional dance), sing and enjoy. The men would watch girls, and at the end of the day, if their parents agree, some would have been taken to the men's homes.
>
> All people from Kininska Krajina would gather at this event. Billy and Ceko made the most of yearly profit. Mijo Masic brought some snow in a bag and sold ice water, saying: "Ice, snowy, cools the heart, sweets the mouth, come on people!

Also, there is a large collection of new songs, mostly sad songs and poems that long for Krajina, performed by freshly created bands, such as Srpska Tromedja or Jandrino Jato, with titles like: "A memory of Krajina," "Oh Krajina, bloody dress," and "Good for you Lasarus, in your grave!" These songs have lyrics such as:

> I went to Austria, Germany and Switzerland,
> but my heart still longs for where the people from Krajina are.
> I went to Romania, track to Rome,
> But such beauty is to be found only in Krajina.
> I went to America, went to Chicago,
> But there's nothing like one's home doorstep.
> Worldwide I have travelled, my destiny followed me everywhere,
> But my home in Krajina calls for me still.

Or:

> In a battle the Serbs heroes go, against their enemy,
> In a battle the fierce Serbs go against their enemy,
> For the cross, for the cross of Nemanjici, for the glory, for the
>   Obilic's glory.

Therefore, based on the site's contents, we can conclude that the maintenance of Krajina's traditional culture is made up of preserving the local language, Cyrillic, particular customs and elements of traditional culture that need not be established as rightly used, newly created folklore, heroic/fierce attitudes toward others, playing *balote*,[15] and roasting lamb. It could be assumed that these are the elements of the traditional culture that the refugees from Krajina wish and long for, even in their new environments, that are supposed to be the basis of their identity.

Nevertheless, it is obvious that the presented content of their traditional culture in fact corresponds to the mythical image of the Golden Age, placed, in this case, in Kninska Krajina, in some undetermined, undefined time before their dislocation. In a completely romanticized manner, these represent a longing for the safety and warmth of a patriarchal society, undisturbed by outside influences—a dream of a patriarchal paradise. A key question then is: what is not assumed by this ideal age and society? The idealized patriarchal paradise lacks the real images of mud, piggeries, blood feuds, a lack of an individual identity, and all the rest that make up an integral part of the rural, patriarchal Balkan traditions, including a substantial percent of functionally illiterate populations,[16] which, paradoxically, is in a total opposition with the idea of establishing communication via the Internet. However, such a vision is directed toward the members of the group wanting to maintain the *status quo* and have no desire or need to communicate with the rest of the world. These images do not contain a trace of a real-life economy, education, or social relationships. The site Polaca.kom is, in effect, a transposition of a traditional ideal model into a new form, with an effort to create a particular virtual environment corresponding to ideal type of culture/society[17] seen through the eyes of the refugees from Krajina.

The most interesting parts of these sites are the forums, where visitors and members talk about different subjects. This is the most explicitly shown on the 24casa.kom site (www.trebinje.com). As a rule, subjects discussing politics attract the most visitors (which is also the case for the entire former Yugoslavian domain, since the very beginning of Internet communication, in early 1990s).

Take, for example, the message of one of the site's moderators:

> The Government of Republic of Srpska is basing the report, given two months ago to the Committee for human rights in Bosnia and Herzegovina, on the data obtained from the Ministry of Defence, police and intelligence service. "In the period from July 14–17, a large number of Bosnian prisoners from Bratinac area were transported by buses and trucks to the area of Zvornik, where they were imprisoned at several locations . . . The locations were, among others, agricultural area of Vranjevo, elementary school Orahovac, Teskovci, Rodevici and House of culture in Pilica", stated the report. "At these places, a large number of prisoners were executed . . ."[18]

This provoked commentaries such as this one:

> Not efficient enough, too little, the next time we have to improve our deed, in order to get better grades. (Username *tupan* [dumb], location: Germany)

The participants in the discussion who disagreed with this comment got this answer:

> You just be polite, feel sorry for them and be ashamed, but you should know that you will not last very long, until the next time when they put a knife on your throat, you'll then remember mercenary and dumb (Username *tupan*)

The subject "Biljana Plavsic's health got worse"[19] provoked the following reactions:

> It is not a sin before God, nor it is a shame before people to kill a Muslim. God is punishing us for not killing them all. To leave a Muslim alive, it is a sin before God and a shame among people. We are only guilty for being alive, but never mind, we'll do it again, and we'll slay again, better us then them. (Username *tupan*, September 15, 2003)
>
> She didn't kill anybody, we, the young ones, did, but also not efficient enough, which could be seen from how many of them are surfing our Serbian forums! KNIFE, WIRE, SREBRENICA[20]!!! If God gives and a holly Sunday comes, Radovan[21] will walk down Brcko!!! (Username *Opa*, September 16, 2003)

As for B. Plavsic, she has had every opportunity to be a great states-man and Serbian people really loved her. From all the politicians, maybe she was liked the most. However, she fell into a trap and started to cooperate with European union, and slowly but for sure, started to sink into betrayal . . . she went from one betrayal to another, for she believed the West and even turned against Radovan. Every betrayal has to be paid for, so is this one too. What she did in Hague, those sluttish deals, I have no words for it . . . This is the example how from a hero one can become a betrayer, the worst one today. I sincerely wish that she dies in worst pains, and I'm not even angry . . . this is a pure fact. I will not remember her, nor will I tell my children about her. Sim-ply—she didn't even exist. (Username: *placenik* [mercenary], location: Sweden, October 3, 2003)

The obvious rigidity of the cultural model that is being presented here is supplemented with misogyny:

If we are to discuss with women about politics, nation and origins, we are not going to get very far. (Username: *placenik,* October 13, 2003)

These are also the xenophobic attitudes, which lead to refuse the con-nection with the homeland, while establishing local, unique identity as a national identity:

One thing is for sure: we from Republic of Srpska and those from SER are not the same people, nor we could ever be. We from Republic of Srpska have fought bravely for our future, with honour and decency. (Username: *placenik,* October 10, 2003)

On locations like SerbianCaffe we do not encounter comments like these, since they were discouraged and deleted from the very beginning, in early 1990s. On locations such as 24casa.kom and Polaca.kom, there is a pos-sibility of petition and even a message for posters to be respectful:

Please, do respect all participants in discussions and do not offend each other on any basis. (www.trebinje.com)

However, these types of messages are allowed, implying that the attitude of those who run the locations, as well as their users, are permissible and open to this kind of content. This way, the sites become new places of hatred and intolerance for the whole world to see.

Still, hatred is not the general message of these sites, or it is only at first glance. Their true message is: We are not entirely sure who we are, or where we belong. We are afraid of everything not foreign and alien, for we don't understand ourselves and understand others even less.

Xenophobia, and the aggression that springs from it, represents crisis of an identity at all levels. These messages reflect a total political blindness, since they can excommunicate the whole group, not just from the actual state, but from the framework of the whole world. They are in direct opposition to the efforts to establish any kind of minority rights (national, ethnic, cultural). This kind of self-isolation on a psychological plan affords the members of the group a sense of false power and safety, firmly closed in the frames of self-pity and conspiracy theory.

LANGUAGE AND ALPHABET

On all the sites that maintain forums, there is an intense discussion on the subject of the Cyrillic versus the Roman alphabet, with an emphatic attitude that Cyrillic is the only true alphabet for anyone considering him- or herself a Serb, and that all Serbs worldwide should, in intracommunication, use only Cyrillic.

Serbian, Croatian, and Bosnian languages (as well as the not-yet-firmly-established Montenegrin) are, in practice, one and the same language—used until the 1990s under the names of Serbo-Croatian or Croatian-Serb—which became officially divided and distinguished into several languages only after the fall of the former Yugoslavia. This forced "multilingual" situation cannot prevent users of the new languages from understanding and communicating with each other, in spite of the fact that they live in different states and have acquired different ethnic and national identities. The only factual difference between the languages is that the Serbs use the Cyrillic alphabet, which is never used much outside Serbia (though it is taught in schools in areas that speak the Serbo-Croatian language).[22] This is the reason for the insistence on the saying, "be a Serb and use Cyrillic," which is one of the main nationalistic sayings in Serbia, and is something that was established officially by the new constitution in 2006, when the official usage of the Roman alphabet was banned. The practice of Cyrillic alphabet usage is not so widespread, not even among the refugees living in Serbia[23]—most Serbians use the Roman alphabet in everyday life, while Cyrillic is used only when they want to emphasize their ethnic and national belonging.

While the first two groups of the Serbian refugee sites are mostly in Roman or in both alphabets, the third group of sites is written exclusively in Cyrillic—although many of their respective members are not able to obtain the suport needed for these languages on their computers; thus, instead of Cyrilic letters, they see unintelligible diacritic signs. A girl in Japan even requested an adjustment for the computer she was using in an Internet café so she could participate in communication. This situation limits the space to those who use and read Cyrillic, which excludes the most part of older Serbian diaspora—and eventually all younger users from Croatia and Bosnia, who never had a chance to learn Cyrillic in school and do not consider themselves members of the Serbian ethnic/national/cultural community. However, the authors of these sites expect their users to make an effort, through which they would enable themselves an access to "the real Serbian" Internet content, corresponding with the assumed group and ethnic identification. It is paradoxical that this actually stimulates people to better learn about the technical possibilities, and to use the Internet and compters with more self-confidence. These discussions regarding the alphabet are, after all, a subject where there are no offenses or threats to the others, even if the boundary of ethnic/national group identification is equated with the boundary of using the alphabet in everyday life worldwide.

It is also interesting how these three groups use the language. While the sites from the second group use mostly literature in the Serbian language (east or west; that is, officially recognized *ekavica* or *ijekavica* dialects of language), the first and the third group insist on particular local versions and speech. In the case of the first group, a local version of the language is one of the elements of reminiscence of the life in the old homeland, while among the third group, the explicit marker of ethnic identification is equalized with the narrow-group identification, which separates them even from Serbs from other areas, and acts as a factor of preservation of in-group cohesion, regardless of the actual place of residence.

PERSPECTIVES

At the present moment, it is obvious that the first and the second categories of the refugees' sites fulfill contemporary world and European standards (as defined by declarations of the United Nations and regulations of the European Union),[24] but they also comply to the unwritten rules on Internet behaviors, which assume respect and acknowledgment of respected differences (cultural, ethnic, language, and all others).[25] The first category is internally directed, nevertheless: toward the ones who can recognize themselves as a part of the group (many of the refugees associated with a local area) who share nostalgia for the lost native land. They deal exclusively with memories of the idealized past, but these sites do not endanger in any way the present, taken for granted and unspoken of. They do not speak about the others; the others are just implicitly present: the ones who do not belong to the group (that is, they are not Serbs from the "native land"). So, there is no discussion on others, and it follows that there is no hatred or intolerance, even though these sites' locations show certain exclusivity: all who do not belong to "us" or "our worldview" are not worth mentioning. The reality of a refugee's life, in contrast with the nostalgia expressed in the sites, is after all what defines an identity of the members of the group: it reveals to them what they are, in the light of what they are not.[26]

The second category is directed both inward and outward, and is totally integrated in the present time/reality, the way it is or the way the participants see it. It tells about obstacles of life in a new environment, and also about life values. The communication is not limited to the Serbs alone, but there are Croatians, Bosniaks (also Macedonians and, to a lesser degree, Slovenians)—all who once lived and shared life in the former Yugoslavia, regardless of their present place of residence (in some of the newly created states in the West, regardless of whether they moved out or remained in the native area). These locations stimulate multicultural dialogue between members of different cultural, ethnic, and national groups from the native land, as well with the people who surround them in the new environment. Therefore, the locations encourage meetings and respect and hence offer a solid condition for respect of the cultures they belong to and promote at the widest level. Even though they are in the Serbian language, they do contain places in English language, which allows many people to get to know and become familiar with their contents, though to a lesser degree. In this way, these locations, by their content and form, are the true promoters of the Serbian culture on the Internet, which helps maintain and protect the cultures of Serbian minority groups, not only in Europe where they exist in large numbers, but wherever they exist.

The third group shows intolerance toward all others who do not see the category "we" as often including Serbs from Serbia. They are extremly inward-oriented, intolerant, xenophobic, and reflect hatred toward their differences and all who differ in any way. These attitudes imply a denial of reality—the one in the new environment, as well as of a political situation that has made them to move out. It is possible that these attitudes could be slowly changed by overcoming cultural conflicts and being educated on different cultures. This kind of knowledge is acquired through means of general cultural education and familiarity of different cultures and their values, which in turn should help avoid application of cultural stereotypes of behavior and values inside others (but also one's own) cultural models. This kind of understanding of culture, including the global one, restricts a fear of losing one's own language, alphabet, and religion—that is, cultural identity in general—and at the same time, allows a precondition for dialogue with people who might hold different opinions. That is why, in this moment of confusing disharmony and discontinuity of contents, a seed of transformation can be found. Namely, all of their visitors and participants in discussions, regardless of how deeply they are emotionally connected to the image of their former life where they cannot or will not go back, are forced to become advanced users of the Internet. Sooner or later, they will start to look for new content on the Internet (even in the Serbian language, but constructed from a very different discourse). By doing so, they will start to learn about others and will soon realize that the differences are not big as they seemed; they will learn that no one is there to take away their ideal image of themselves, or their language, religion, and alphabet, which are all the basic markers of their identity. They will become a part of a growing group of liberated individuals who, regardless of their race, language, place of living, or cultural background, safely and self-confidently meet with McLuhan and Gibson in cyberspace,[27] paving the way to the new, world, truly global culture, whose development cannot prevent a sorrow for a mythical past, or efforts to become closed in narrow frames of tradition and ghettoization. In that moment, every one of them, individually, will understand that the world of peace, static condition, and long-lasting time is fading away, along with the people who contentedly survive in a familiar and safe environment.

At the same time, and in order to promote a culture of Serbs outside Serbia, it would be useful to provide institutional help (currently not given); that is, the stimulation of Serbian minorities to represent themselves more on the Internet. Such help could be financial or technical and the Ministry for Diaspora of the Republic of Serbia should handle it. In this way, an influence of the still-existing locations that promote international intolerance, even hatred and agression, would be reduced by limiting their presence on the Internet. Also, this could represent a contribution to the general public (global) image—but only in the case where they would, in their own representations, respect others in full (such as Serbian refugees and minority groups). Only in these terms they would obtain total respect and acceptance of their cultural models at the global level, and at the same time, better conditions for the protection and further development of the cultural models not only in Serbia, but also in all other countries where they reside.

The example of representation of Serbian refugees on Internet is symptomatic in many ways. It shows how:

> in the contemporary moment various identities (ethnic, group) are being constructed on the Internet independent of the community residing in the same space, but dependent from a discourse, based on totally different symbols (language, alphabet, memories, traditions, hatred against others, nostalgia);
>
> language and alphabet should not necessary be seen as boundaries between groups, as they should not be taken as cohesive element among those who use them—the core boundary is in discourse, that is, one's own perception of oneself in relationship with all others; and
>
> even in cases of "closed" groups, based on refusal to communicate with others, the technology itself creates a possibility of overcoming, step by step, the obstacles between ourselves and others.

NOTES

1. The romanticized pan-Slavic idea insisted on unity of all Slavic cultures (the same as pan-Germanic for German cultures), which in a political sense, assumed unity and cooperation of all Slavic states, as opposed to

those German states and others. This, in turn, corresponded to the political interests in Christian Era Europe in the nineteenth century.

2. Ljiljana Gavrilović, "Multikulturalizam u Vojvodini," *Zbornik radova "Susreti kultura"* (Novi Sad, Serbia: Filozofski fakultet, 2006), 195–203.

3. Both postcolonial and postmodern attitudes question the basic foundations of the modern world: the postcolonial introduces the discourse of the colonized and questions the power–identity relationship; and the postmodern deconstructs all big metanarratives, which served as foundations of modern societies, including all varieties of identity.

4. G.M. Tamas, "Ethnarchy and Ethno-Anarchism: Nationalism Reexamined," http://www.encyclopedia.com/doc/1G1–18501092.html

5. MarkOže, *Nemesta: Uvod u antropologiju nadmodernost* (Beograd, Serbia: XX vek, 2005), 73–101.

6. Đokica Jovanović, Jasmina Petrović, and Saša Madić, *Parodija tragičnog (kič kao konstituens političke i kulturne ideologije)* (Niš, 2002), 75–79.

7. Bojan Žikić, "Konstrukcija identiteta u dualnoj etnokulturnoj zajednici—Bečej i okolina," in *Tradicionalno i savremeno u kulturi Srba* (Beograd, Serbia: EI SANU Posebna izdanja 49, 2003), 294.

8. There have been numerous efforts to change the country code top-level doman (ccTLD) since 2003, when the state was called Državna zajednica Srbija i Crna Gora (SCG), but this was done only after the separation of the two states (Wikipedia, ".rs," http://en.wikipedia.org/wiki/.rs).

9. Even before the formation of its independent state, Montenegro had its own mark had within SCG, ".cg.yu," and in 2006, a mark ".me" ccTLD was established (Wikipedia, ".me," http://en.wikipedia.org/wiki/.me).

10. For more on domain names as indicators of national identity, see Erica Wass, *Addressing the World: National Identity and Internet Country Code Domains* (Lanham, MD: Rowman & Littlefield, 2003). Also available at http://www.addressingtheworld.info/intro.pdf

11. Josep Lluís Micó and Pere MasipChapter 8 in this volume. However, the ".cat" TLD is a generic domain; that is, not defined in terms of a territory like the ccTLDs (Wikipedia, ".cat," http://en.wikipedia.org/wiki/.cat).

12. Wikipedia, "Country Code Top-Level Domain," http://en.wikipedia.org/wiki/CcTLD

13. Since June 2006, the ccTLD for Serbia is ".rs," which is supposed to be applied in 2007 (http://arhiva.elitesecurity.org/t20025-Srbija-Crna-Gora-koje-ce-biti-ime-domena-Internet-domen-Srbije-RS-SS-SP-SQ-SW-ili-SX).

14. S. Hambridge, "Netiquette Guidelines," Intel Corp, *http://www.cybernothing.org/cno/docs/rfc1855.html* (1995).

15. A traditional game similar to bowling.

16. According to data from 2003, around 25 percent of the population in Serbia was illiterate; women make up around 80 percent of that number.

17. This is carried to such extremes that a forum or message board is called "prelo" (a traditional way of gathering).

18. "Lista foruma > Politika > Izvještaj Vlade RS o Srebrenici prvi put u javnosti, diskusija od," 3–6 novembra 2003 ["The report of The Government of Republic of Srpska on Srebrenica the First Time in Public," discussion from November 3–6, 2003].

19. Biljana Plavsic was a president of The Republic Srpska during the war years. She voluntarily surrendered herself to The Hague Tribunal.

20. Srebrenica is a place in Bosnia and Herzegovina where the Serbs committed war crimes against the Muslim population. According to various sources, it is estimated that during only a few days, around 6,000 to 8,000 people were killed.

21. Radovan Karadzic, the former president of The Republic Srpska. He is accused of war crimes, and has been in hiding since the foundation of The Hague Tribunal.
22. The area of the Cyrillic alphabet included the whole area of the former Yugoslavia, except for Macedonia and Slovenia, but there, too, the Serbo-Croatian language was taught alongside the mother tongue, which included both alphabets.
23. This analysis draws on data gathered by the Red Cross on the social and health status of refugees from Croatia and Bosnia and Herzegovina, who immigrated to Novi Banovci in the period from 1991 to 1995. Out of 474 questionnaires, only 92 (19.4 percent) were filled in using Cyrillic, even though the questionnaire was itself in Cyrillic. In the structured interviews with immigrants, Cyrillic was stated to be a distinct ethnic indicator in the homeland areas. Still, since they were using the Roman alphabet more in everyday life, in a situation where there is no need to emphasize ethnic belongings or cultural and ethnic preferences, the learned behavior prevails over the desired one.
24. "The European Convention on Human Rights," *http://www.hri.org/docs/ECHR50.html* (1950–1966); "International Covenant on Economic, Social and Cultural Rights," *http://www1.umn.edu/humanrts/instree/b2esc.htm* (1976); Council of Europe, "Recommendation No. R (97) 20 of the Committee of Ministers to Member States on 'Hate Speech'," *http://www.medialaw.ru/laws/other_laws/european/r97(20)-e.htm* (1997). For a wider collection of regulations, recommendations, and examples, see "The Tolerance and Non-Discrimination Information System," http://tandis.odihr.pl
25. Article 10 of the European Convention of Human Rights provides that everyone has the right to freedom of expression. But some kinds of expression—for example, Holocaust denial—are excluded from Article 10 by Article 17 (prohibition of abuse of rights). On the question of freedom of speech and hate speech restriction on the Internet, see David I. Shapiro, "Free Speech, Hate Speech," http://www.sjberwin.com/publication/download/index.php?publication=free_speech_hate_speech_and_incitement&published=2006_06_30; see also Morris Lipson, "Regulating Hate Speech Content for the Internet: the Legal Jurisdiction Puzzle," http://www.osce.org/documents/rfm/2004/08/3425_en.pdf
26. Pierre Nora, "Between Memory and History," *Realms of Memory I* (New York: Columbia University Press, 1996), 20.
27. Michael E. Doherty Jr., "Marshall McLuhan Meets William Gibson in 'Cyberspace', " *CMC Magazine*, September 1995, 4.

Part III

Islam, Modernity, and the Internet

11 Modems, Malaysia, and Modernity
Characteristics and Policy Challenges in Internet-Led Development

Nasya Bahfen

INTRODUCTION

> The Internet will be a part of the fabric of our daily life, changing the way we do things and look at issues such as trade and intellectual property. For Malaysia, the Internet can help groom a lot of the untapped human potential and capacity we have as a nation.[1]

The use of the Internet in Malaysia reflects competing themes—a culture of technological *nous* exemplified by young, upwardly mobile users keen to adopt new communication forms as a result of specific social engineering policies, versus the cyberpresence of vibrant political activists who have embraced Internet publishing, networking, and the blogosphere as weapons in the battle for *reformasi* and to counter the carefully sculpted representation of Malaysian identity in the docile print and broadcast media.

The overwhelmingly young Malaysian population that turns to the Internet as part and parcel of their daily lives—to form and maintain friendships, to consume goods and services, to study, and to complete work tasks—are the representatives of the new Malaysia. The Malaysia of today is symbolized by the conjoined monoliths of 450 meters of glass and steel that make up the Petronas Twin Towers in central Kuala Lumpur and stand as a proud, gleaming monument to Malaysian endeavor. Half of the Twin Towers' eighty-eight stories house the national petroleum company, Petronas, and the other half, an ultramodern shopping mall, a tourist viewing deck, and several office suites within a large complex called the Kuala Lumpur City Centre (KLCC). The KLCC also includes a concert hall for the Malaysian Philharmonic Orchestra, a luxury hotel, a park, and more office towers. The KLCC and the Twin Towers epitomize Malaysia's vision of itself, representing both the journey to where it stands today and the road it wishes to embark upon in the future. Modern, multicultural, and Muslim-majority Malaysia is positioning itself as a high-tech Southeast Asian tourist and business haven, and the Internet is playing a significant role in its modernity project.

At the same time, Internet adaptation by the country's political, religious, youth, and media communities has not been without teething problems. So far, Malaysia has been able to grasp the economic and cultural potential of the Internet while acknowledging its capacity to build communities of shared interests and challenge established political thought. The introduction of the Internet in Malaysia took place amidst a growing movement of change across several Southeast Asian countries. How the Internet helped the opposition activists and journalists of Kuala Lumpur and Kelantan reflected the increasingly important role played by technology in political reform, not just in Malaysia, but also in its nearest neighbors. While not as tumultuous as the overthrow of President Suharto in neighboring Indonesia, nor as muted as nearby Singapore's restricted nurturing of its public sphere, a steady increase of Malaysian voices urging social and political change took place. These voices reached a crescendo with the dismissal, imprisonment, and charging of former Deputy Prime Minister, Anwar Ibrahim. The Anwar Ibrahim case, the online experiences of opposition parties Keadilan (the Justice Party) and Partai Se-Islam Malaysia (PAS), and the establishment of the web-only newspaper *Malaysiakini* ("Malaysia Now"), collectively illustrate the critical part played by the Internet as Malaysia recovers from the 1997 financial crisis, and as its growing middle class calls for reformasi.

The themes of Malaysian Internet use—the adaptation of the Internet by the young for business, study, and social purposes and by opposition figures and independent journalists for political purposes—can be seen through the Malaysian cyberpresence. Malaysian national identity is discernible online as a reflection of Malaysia's societal composition, government policies, and the manifestations of religious and racial diversity online. On one hand, Malaysian-related online media sites and blogs demonstrate how the Internet has been successfully appropriated by a Malaysian readership as an alternative news source. Because of the country's strictly regulated print and broadcast media industry, the Internet has been effectively used by opposition parties and publications critical of the ruling party (including underground media and opposition groups, such as PAS, supporters of Anwar Ibrahim, and the malaysiakini publication) to distribute material that would not normally be published or aired, thus circumventing the cycle of regulations that governs the older media. On the other hand, Malaysian Internet users—particularly young Malaysian Internet users—have become avid online consumers and online citizens, using websites for social networking and shopping, demonstrating how the country's middle class, broadband take-up rates, and public wireless connectivity are all on the rise.

TRULY ASIA ON THE INTERNET

Tourism Malaysia's print and television advertisements in countries such as Singapore, Indonesia, and Australia emphasize the tagline, "Malaysia . . .

truly Asia." The advertisements show a mélange of cultural vistas—Indian dancers, Chinese food, Malay musicians, and colorful costumes worn by the *orang asli*, or indigenous people of Sarawak on the island of Borneo. As in Singapore, images of multiracial harmony are integral to the Malaysian image of self. Accordingly, and not surprisingly, the cultural dimension of Internet usage in Malaysia reflects the fact that the country has a population comprised of various ethnic groups.[2] Malays consist of just over 50 percent of the people of Malaysia; the Chinese (at nearly 27 percent of the population) and Indians (at nearly 8 percent of the population) comprise the most sizeable minorities; and the remainder consists of indigenous, Eurasian, and other ethnic groups.[3] To an extent, the practice of defining ethnicity at a bureaucratic or official level was introduced by the British.[4] The categorization of racial sets in Malaysia was largely a byproduct of colonial practice. Different subgroups existed within the main groupings used by British colonialists to lump residents of the Malay Peninsula. For example, within the Chinese population, there were linguistic and ethnic divisions among the Teochew, Cantonese, or Hokkien Chinese. Similarly, within the overriding grouping of "Malays" there were Malays of Buginese, Kelantan, or Minangkabau origins. In other words, the broad categories of "Malay," "Chinese," or "Indian" contained people who did not necessarily identify themselves with the ethnic label ascribed to them. Nevertheless, in the case of the Malays, "what different Malay groups had in common was their orientation towards Islam."[5] Being of Malay origin was equal to professing the Muslim faith. Islam is the only religion to which the Malay majority subscribes and is the religion of a substantial portion of the Indian minority; it is also a defining factor in the construction of Malay identity.[6]

Recent years have witnessed a resurgence of Islam in the politics of Southeast Asian countries—a process to which Malaysia was not immune. By the turn of the twentieth century, Malaysian political Islam was observed as being pluralistic and pro-democratic.[7] The increasing importance of Islam in the Malaysian public and political eye reflects the critical role it plays in the lives of Malays, for whom Islam represents stability, solidarity, moral direction, and an alternative to secular modernity. In the post-September 11 world, many Malays in Malaysia are cognizant of the fact that there is an increased focus on Islam in the world media. This in turn may have resulted in a heightened sense of awareness about being Muslim, and for some Malays in Malaysia, to identify him- or herself as Muslim first and Malaysian second.[8] But constitutionally, the factors that make someone "Malay" are a belief in Islam, the customary use of Bahasa Melayu, and practice and devotion to *adat*, or Malay custom.[9] So while self-identification takes place through religious before national parameters, the concept of being Malay is more complicated than a matter of faith: "Malayness" is both an ethnic marker and a social construct.

Although Muslim Malays numerically make up the majority of Malaysians, economically the country is dominated by the ethnic Chinese. Former

Prime Minister Mahathir Mohammad was scathing in his criticisms of his fellow Malays, arguing that "the main impediments to Malay progress" were "their mind-set, more specifically their 'inadequate attitudes to money, property and time'."[10] The New Economic Policy (NEP), adopted in 1971, attempted to "redress imbalances in the educational and economic position of the Malays."[11] The NEP was promoted in the wider context of encouraging a new Malay business class and culture. It was introduced in Malaysia along with the establishment of the Council of Trust for the People (Majelis Amanah Rakyat, or MARA)—a body that encouraged ownership and investment in business by the *bumiputra*, or native Malays.

The NEP also coincided with the idea of the *Melayu Baru* or New Malay, which is an interesting conflagration of identity, encompassing as it does a modern, successful business vision in harmony with notions of Malay identity and Islamic principles.[12] The New Malay is "an attempt at social engineering, the objective of which is to create a modern Malay middle class".[13] It was the response of the government to the perception that the progress of the Malay people had fallen short of the ambitions of Mahathir.

The cultural dimension of Internet usage in Malaysia is also indicative of a society that embraces technological development. Malaysia sees information as an integral aspect of the path to modernity. Mahathir's imposing vision for the development of both his people and his country were thus articulated in the *Malaysia Boleh* ("Malaysia Can") campaign, along with Vision 2020, the ambitious economic blueprint with the goal of turning Malaysia into a fully developed country by the year 2020.[14] The New Malay thus plays an important role that "complements his [Mahathir's] social engineering efforts by creating a 'middle-class subject' representing a 'spiritual fit between Malaysian "can-doism" . . . and Islamic modernity'."[15]

Critics of the NEP argued that such a brazen affirmative action policy would not work. However, by 1990, Malaysia's economy did reflect more accurately the diversity of the country's societal composition. Most of the targets set by the NEP to increase the proportion of Malay-owned investments and the number of Malays in professional and managerial roles had been fulfilled.[16] In addition, the rise of the middle classes across all races in Malaysia could be seen in the country's seemingly unending push toward modernity: for example, in increased consumer demand for products and services and an accompanying rise in shopping venues. Against this backdrop of Malaysia's journey toward the goals of Vision 2020, the introduction of the Internet in Malaysia took place with the opening in 1990 of the country's first Internet service provider, JARING.

Malaysia's population appears to have embraced the government's push for technology-driven development, with large numbers of Malaysians taking up Internet access, the overwhelming majority of whom are young people below thirty years of age.[17] Since 1990, the use of the Internet in Malaysia has echoed the racial/cultural plurality of the offline population, as well as the change in attitudes alluded to by Malaysian leaders, such as

Mahathir, who through his policies encouraged Malaysians to adopt the lifestyle of "the future that he has termed 'technotribalism', important elements of which include creativity, imagination and freedom."[18] Both government Internet sites as well as those challenging the government—such as web presences set up by supporters of former Deputy Prime Minister Anwar Ibrahim, and the sites of human rights groups, such as Aliran—are reflective of this "technotribalism," with detailed and well-maintained portals of information reaching out to readers with similar inclinations. The users of such Internet websites can be read as members of technotribes: cybercommunities whose reason for being relates to the grouping of individuals with a commonality in shared interests instead of the geographical, cultural, or linguistic ties that bind offline communities.

THE CYBER PUBLIC SPHERE

Frequent observations have been made of the links between state-initiated or -supported ideologies of conflict, identity, or modernity and the support that such ideologies receive throughout the national media.[19] In the search for Malaysia's modernity-related identity, the hegemonic discourse of traditional media plays an active part. The official vision of Malaysia is promoted and supported by the content found in mainstream newspapers and broadcasters (a situation that is similar to most countries). For instance, in a *New Straits Times* article entitled "Shop! Shop! Shop!," Malaysia's image as a high-tech, developed, and modern consumer haven is demonstrated through subheadings focusing on the appeal of "shopping morning, noon and night for Arab tourists who have arrived here in droves—and it's not just the prices they find attractive."[20] The Malaysian sense of self is further emphasized in paragraphs that discuss how the country has become an Asian shopping hub for Arabs and well-heeled Indonesian women due to the quality of products and competitive prices. In Malaysia, it is clear that given a situation where the established center of power plays an important gate-keeping role, the output of mainstream newspapers and broadcasters is closely linked to processes of identity construction and nation-building. The utilization of the media for the purposes of giving credence to government-established programs and principles can also be found elsewhere, for example, in neighboring Singapore,[21] so that the "blending of mediascapes and ideoscapes is by no means unique to Malaysia."[22]

The website *Malaysiakini* illustrates how the Internet has been used by independent journalists, opposition parties, and political activists as an alternative to the information found in the major media organizations, such as the *New Straits Times*. Against this backdrop, the most well-known example in foreign circles is the *Malaysiakini* publication. The opinion of its founder is that "[in Malaysia] we have a plethora of publications . . . but we don't have a free press."[23] As a cybernews organization that published material that was questioning of the government, malaysiakini was subject to raids in 2003 in which its computers were seized, and its journalists were denied entry to Malaysian ministers' press conferences. The raids were condemned by people within Malaysia as well as external observers as being antithetical in spirit to the commitment by the government not to censor the Internet. *Malaysiakini* continues to function today despite having reinvented itself from a free Malaysian news and information portal, to one operating on a paid-access basis. The *Malaysiakini* story is a key example of the Internet's role in assisting in the development of the Malaysian public sphere, and in providing new paradigms of critical perspective with which to engage with the legislative bodies tasked with engineering the development of Malaysian modernity. Given that the publication was not available offline (as are a number of Malaysian newspapers), *Malaysiakini*'s success indicates the crucial part played by the Internet in today's Malaysia. The founders of *Malaysiakini* gambled on the existence of an audience sited within and outside of Malaysia that was eager to consume its critical perspective on domestic issues. Indeed:

> . . . e-journalism has been much celebrated in Malaysia, particularly by those who craved alternative perspectives and adventurous encounters with ideas in their news consumption.[24]

There are several possible reasons for malaysiakini's popularity in some circles. Its editor attributes the publication's success to an increase in "political conscience" among Malaysians,[25] traditional media's more conservative reporting, and the Malaysian authorities' commitment to avoid Internet censorship:

> to promote the Multimedia Super Corridor, Malaysia's own Silicon Valley, the government has pledged not to censor the Internet. To its credit, the government has kept very much to its promise.[26]

The political crisis that engulfed Malaysia in 1998, resulting from the dismissal and arrest of former Deputy Prime Minister Anwar Ibrahim, also illustrates the political activism present in Malaysian Internet use. Supporters of Anwar turned *en masse* to blogs, web publishing, and e-mail. The Anwar case was the trigger that "sparked off on-line activism in Malaysia. Within months of his dismissal on 2 September 1998, dozens of reformasi web sites emerged."[27] However, the role of the Internet was not merely to act as a catalyst in this instance, for the activism of the pro-Anwar reformasi sites extended beyond cyberspace. The Anwar Ibrahim case and its championing through websites strengthened the networks of Malaysian reformasi activists[28] and in many ways, the fallout from these websites extended offline. The readership of alternative news sites and pro-reformasi or pro-Anwar sites was largely underestimated, given that it was not limited to those who read the contents of these sites online. Thanks to printing, photocopying, faxing, and snail mail,[29] the information contained in pro-reformasi websites made its way to a readership outside of the 700,000–800,000 estimated Internet subscribers in Malaysia in 1998.

Before the phenomenon of blogging made it possible for the players in newsworthy incidents to broadcast their thoughts to the world, Anwar Ibrahim's ideas and views during his incarceration were expressed via the Internet as visitors and supporters transcribed and then uploaded them: "mass access to his contemporaneous writings from prison was immediately enabled online."[30] Knowledge of the Anwar Ibrahim case, as well as his status today as a respected figurehead in Muslim circles not just in Malaysia, but elsewhere, can be attributed to the wealth of information and opinion that his supporters published online. The use of the Internet to disseminate such news and opinions in favor of the *reformasi* groups affected public opinion and the results of elections. The Keadilan, which lent strong support to Anwar Ibrahim's case and counted his wife, Dr. Wan Azizah Wan Ismail, as one of its founders and main spokespeople, gained a number of seats in parliament, which the party attributed to online campaigning efforts: the view of its media coordinator was that Keadilan "would never have reached the same success if it were not for the Internet, a medium that allowed to reach an estimated 25 percent of the voting population."[31] The opposition PAS has also used the Internet as an effective means of communication.[32]

There are fundamental differences in the way the Internet mediates meaning.[33] In creating a public sphere in which users can dissect and join in debates about current issues of interest, the online environment brings down the constraints that frame and limit offline discourse. Because of this dismantling of barriers, it is possible to discern elements of Mahathir's social engineering in the success of malaysiakini and the reformasi online movement, placing this success within a general context of widespread acceptance of the Internet by today's "New Malays" and other Malaysian ethnic groups. In addition to *Malaysiakini*, the mainstream newspapers (which Steven Gan's Internet news site tried to differentiate itself from) have set up shop in cyberspace with Internet versions of their print editions

> in order to establish their corporate presence in wired journalism as well as to attract a young generation of enthusiastic information technology-skilled Malaysians[34].

Since Anwar Ibrahim's release from prison, he and his supporters have continued their embrace of the Internet, setting up his official website, in English and the Bahasa Melayu language, and blog (only in Bahasa Melayu). Joining *Malaysiakini* and other Malaysian information sources online, such as human-rights-oriented nongovernmental organizations, Aliran and Suaram, these publications utilize the web's unique "management of meaning" to develop urbane, mature, and information-rich websites for the consumption of a growing, technologically literate Malaysian intelligentsia with an interest in politics and independent journalism. But there is another half of the Malaysian Internet presence who are also products of the Malaysian government's social engineering and pro-technological stance—the overwhelmingly young urban members of the Malaysian middle class, who venture online for the consumption of goods and services and make and maintain friendships and love in cyberspace.

SOCIALIZING AND SHOPPING ONLINE

From her profile on Friendster.com, it can be seen that twenty-year-old student, Uffa, hails from Pahang. She wears a headscarf and lists her hobbies as shopping, eating, sleeping, and traveling. Uffa's favorite television shows are *Smallville*, *Roswell*, and the Thai drama series, *The Princess*. Her favorite movies include *Pirates of the Caribbean* and the Indonesian teen romance, *Eiffel I'm in Love*. Nineteen-year-old Syazwin is one of Uffa's friends. Syazwin is single, likes chatting on the Internet, and camping, and also comes from Pahang. She likes reading the *Chronicles of Narnia* and manga comics. Over on the Malaysian social networking site, Ahmoi.com, users can find Kent—a young financial dealer living in Selangor. Kent is a nonsmoker who works long hours. He has put a profile on Ahmoi hoping to increase his social network.

Statistics from the Malaysian Communications and Multimedia Commission on the age demographics of Malaysian Internet users reflect a youth bias: 70 percent of the country's Internet users are below 40 years of age, while nearly half (40 percent) are below the age of 25.[35] The youth market is seen as the test bed for many information technology (IT)-related markets—for example, young people are the pioneers in the take-up of developments in mobile communications technology.[36] Uffa, Syazwin, and Kent exemplify the Malaysian cybercitizen—young, either studying or working, born after the launch of the NEP in 1971, and incorporating the Internet into their daily lives. Given the Malaysian government's endorsement and support of technology, the promotion of IT-savvy citizenry, and the country's developed multimedia and communications infrastructure, it is not surprising that the social and business lives of young people, who comprise one-fifth of the population of Malaysia[37] revolve around their various uses of the Internet.

With its Islamic majority and traditional societal customs, Malaysia had railed against the onslaught of globalized (which usually referred to American or Western) influences on the country's young people. In a situation reflective of its neighbor, Singapore (whose government and society had tried to support the maintenance of Confucian values and endorsed filial piety on behalf of the youth), Malaysia's government condemned the influx of foreign culture as a threat to Asian values, with former Prime Minister Mahathir Mohamad deriding young Japanese as "blondes" because of what he perceived to be their worship of Western lifestyles.[38] However, in the absence of any widespread support (in both Singapore and Malaysia) for local or indigenous musicians, artists, movies, and television shows, foreign cultural products and their conspicuous consumption were seen as desired and necessary trappings of modern life. The Internet helped to bring facets of Western culture (songs, films, television shows) into the living rooms of young Malaysians. Because the development of Malaysian youth culture was not encouraged, the adoption of Western youth culture took its place.[39] Like their counterparts in many second- and third-world countries, Malaysian youth are not immune to the attractiveness of the lifestyle of Western capitalism. Global consumerism has become imbued in Malaysian youth culture[40]—a consumerism mediated by the provision of transnational satellite broadcasting services that bring the likes of MTV into the homes of Malaysian youth, third- and fourth-generation mobile services, and broadband Internet availability.

As citizens of a country with a stable, growing economy and widespread Internet use, young Malaysians turn to the Internet as a source of information and as a networking tool. They can make or maintain links through web presence—this could incorporate instant messaging services, like g-mail chat or MSN Messenger, putting up detailed profiles on global social networking sites, like Friendster and Myspace, or specifically Malaysian ones. A cursory glance at the profiles on Ahmoi (one of Malaysia's biggest social networking sites) reveals that it is a popular place for Chinese Malaysians to gather and meet new friends. FriendX, another oft-visited Malaysian site, uses profiles similar to Friendster or MySpace, but also resembles the Korean supersite, Cyworld's minihompy, in its use of "rooms," which users can decorate with items (see Chapters 14 [Yoo] and 15 [Hjorth], this volume). Whereas Cyworld uses purchasable "acorns" as "currency," which can be used to buy goods for the user's cyberroom, FriendX uses a points system. Users can engage in activities to earn free points, or they can buy the points. In addition to a profile that can be linked to friends' profiles, sites like FriendX, Ahmoi, and Friendster also offer blogs and photo uploading, reducing the need to put digital photos on one site, the blog on another, and the friend network on a third.

Cognizant of the fact that young people are increasingly turning to sites like MySpace to consolidate their online presence, and aware that information accessible to young people can be used to decide purchasing decisions, government and commercial organizations in Malaysia have decided to reach out to the increasingly important youth market on their turf. Recognizing the power of the youth market, organizations make use of the hypermediated lifestyles of Malaysia's young people to present information, given that "it's a cinch reaching the under-25s: they are media junkies."[41] For example, consumer product manufacturer Procter and Gamble, together with two Malaysian partners, launched an official Friendster profile of its Head & Shoulders® shampoo brand, citing the demographics of the social networking site, which is said to receive 800,000 hits monthly from Malaysia, and whose members are described as overwhelmingly in the sixteen- to twenty-four-year-old age group.[42] The profile is called "H'n'S" and takes on the character of a young, single female whose hometown is Kuala Lumpur. Under "Hobbies," the profile lists "fighting the 5 signs of dandruff to give you the confidence of flake free, soft, smooth & itch-free hair."[43] As an official product profile, the Head & Shoulders Friendster profile has "friends" and "fans." At the time of writing, more than 24,000 people had linked to the profile as a fan. But major companies are not the only ones seeking brand loyalty or awareness through social networking sites. For instance, a Malaysian businesswoman runs a highly successful and extremely detailed website called Graduan for fresh graduates seeking work. It focuses specifically on domestic and returning Malaysian international students who are about to enter the job market. Run by a private company, it takes into account the local business context, such as what to do when employers ask about expected salary, or whether a graduate is able to apply for an administrative job when his or her degree is in Islamic studies. The print version of Graduan is distributed to universities where Malaysian students can be found both domestically and overseas.

The development of a wired nation was one of the cornerstones of Malaysia's modernity project, in which the goal of Vision 2020 is to make the country a fully developed and first-world nation within a set timeframe. As a product of this wired nation, the young people of Malaysia are active cybercitizens and cyberconsumers, connected by profiles on Friendster or Ahmoi, Internet messenger services, and blogs at the same time as they use the Internet to help in their professional and business duties. Online life is second nature to young Malaysians, but in a different manner to the way it complements the political activists who use it to promote *reformasi*. The Internet reflects public policy on its desirability in the lives of Malaysians as a way of leapfrogging into first-worlddom. What happens once that goal is achieved, and once the government's Internet-related development aims are reached, where the young cyber consumers and political bloggers take Malaysian modernity, is open to conjecture.

FUTURE CHALLENGES

The new electronic space created by the Internet's widespread adoption has collectively resulted in a more active Malaysian public sphere, and access to this sphere by those outside of Malaysia. At the same time, dedicated initiatives have been implemented by the government to attract Internet-related development. These initiatives, started while Dr. Mahathir was at the helm, will be continued by his successor, Abdullah Ahmad Badawi, who has a degree in Islamic studies and comes from a family of Islamic scholars—credentials that boosted his standing in the eyes of many devout

Malaysian Muslims. Yet, Mr. Abdullah has so far managed to retain both his focus on religious duty and identity, and an emphasis on Malaysia's status as one of the most developed Muslim-majority countries. The challenge for Mr. Abdullah, and for Malaysia, will be to maintain the impetus of the first few years, in which the Internet made a dramatic impact in the country's political and youth culture without turning back on the Mahathir government's promise to keep the Internet censorship-free. Future challenges for Malaysian policy makers include Internet usage by alternative media, such as *Malaysiakini*, and opposition parties and figures, such as the PAS (an Islamic party that controls the northern state of Kelantan) and Anwar Ibrahim's Keadilan. Like other Asian countries, such as China and Singapore, Malaysia recognizes that the Internet needs to be incorporated into the daily life of its citizens in order for the country to avoid being left behind in the information era. But unlike these other countries, Malaysia has made an explicit commitment to avoid censorship of the Internet.[44] This has resulted in a challenge for the government because, while the wholesale embracing of the Internet is crucial for the success of the Malaysian economy, it has opened up avenues for effective political resistance. The Malaysian government supported the use of the Internet among the business sector, young people, and the expanding middle classes, as part of a wider quest for economic progress. But it also saw the Internet as a traditional media form subject to the regulations used with newspapers and broadcasters—encouraging a culture of acceptance of technological developments, but restricting it "within the parameters of established means of cultural management."[45] Thus, the benefits of adaptation of the Internet came with a catch—the "proliferation of Malaysian websites dedicated to political challenge and social reform."[46]

The roots of this dilemma could be traced to an economic and a political crisis: the Asian financial meltdown of 1997 and the arrest of Anwar Ibrahim when he was the Deputy Prime Minister in 1998. As the region's economies recovered from the 1997 crisis, the call for political change spread amongst Southeast Asian countries, including Malaysia and Indonesia where, with their cultural and linguistic similarities, the translation of the word *reform* (which was the same in both countries) became a catchcry for a newer and more open future: a future of *reformasi*. Demands for *reformasi* amongst the Malay middle classes could be seen as a reaction to the 1997 crisis[47] and mirrored the events taking place in neighboring Indonesia: the call for change came from the "educated, (sub)urban students and professionals who took to the streets with unprecedented fervour."[48]

In response to the growing readership and popularity of the pro-*reformasi* movement online (and offline), the government reacted by using the mainstream media to counter the criticisms spelled out in Internet publications. The accuracy of the online *reformasi* news sources was brought up as an issue, with users being warned that, given the ease of publishing on the Internet, misinformation could easily be passed off as accurate reporting. Anyone could simply set up a website and post information that was difficult to verify as fact. The response of *reformasi* sites was to provide online, detailed information relating to political sources that supported their version of events, such as international news agencies. The Malaysian administration quickly learned that limiting the fallout from Internet-based challenges to governments is difficult. This is partly because of the inherent nature of the medium (a decentralized technology that can publish content from overseas servers does not lend itself to domestic surveillance very well). The resolution of the issues surrounding Internet adaptation and the ramifications for a new era of Malaysian political and media freedom remain a work in progress.

CONCLUSION

The current Prime Minister of Malaysia is someone known for both his economically forward outlook and his strong Islamic credentials. The introduction of the Internet in Malaysia was set against a tumultuous backdrop in domestic and regional affairs. A rising movement in support of political reform swept across several Southeast Asian countries, to which Malaysia was not immune. It was assumed that the careful selection of distributed information would still be possible, so that opposition parties and nongovernmental organizations critical of the ruling coalition would remain in the background, and new Internet technology could assist in Malaysia's economic development without causing political instability. These assumptions turned out to be shaky. The Internet did turn out to be a critical factor in Malaysia's development—but in ways no one could have predicted. Anwar Ibrahim's case galvanized *reformasi* groups online, while opposition parties, such as Keadilan and PAS, turned to the Internet in search of an audience—the same reason that alternative news sites, such as *Malaysiakini*, and human rights groups, such as Aliran, established online presences. As Malaysia recovered from the 1997 financial crisis, it was clear that two themes had emerged in Malaysian Internet use: the political presence of opposition and independent activists and journalists, and the presence of young tech-savvy Internet citizens who shopped, studied, worked, and interacted socially online. Cultural dimensions were discernible through the online manifestation of Malaysia's diverse ethnic composition and the promotion and support from official levels for a computer-literate Malaysian society that would embrace the wired world. While it was possible to see the development of an alternative component to the country's existing public sphere, with the Internet being actively used as a source of independent, nongovernment-sanctioned news, it was also possible to see young Malaysians in particular avidly use the Internet to trade, shop, do business, and make new friends, resulting in the rise of specific social network sites.

Just like Prime Minister Badawi has to maintain a balancing act (in his devotion to traditional religious duty alongside his commitment to modernization) his cabinet and government will also juggle critically important goals: the need for technology-led economic development spearheaded by young, educated cybercitizens, and the importance of a vibrant, flourishing, and free Malaysian Internet environment.

NOTES

1. Mohamed Sharil Tarmizi, cited in Edwin Yap, "Our Man in Icann," *The Star Online*, June 23, 2005, http://star-techcentral.com/tech/story. asp?file=/2005/6/23/itfeature/11240312&sec=itfeature
2. Don Zuraidah Mohd, "Language-Dialect Code-Switching: Kelantanese in a Multilingual Context," *Multilingua* 22, no. 1 (2003): 21–40.
3. Terence Lee, "Internet Use in Singapore: Politics and Policy Implications," *Media International Australia Incorporating Culture & Policy* 107 (2003): 75–88.
4. Alice Nah, "Negotiating Indigenous Identity in Postcolonial Malaysia: Beyond Being 'Not Quite/Not Malay'," *Social Identities* 9, no. 4 (2003): 511–534; Rudiger Korff, "Globalisation and Communal Identities in the Plural Society of Malaysia," *Singapore Journal of Tropical Geography* 22, no. 3 (2001): 270–283.
5. Korff, "Globalisation and Communal Identities," 274.
6. Cynthia Joseph, "Researching Teenage Girls and Schooling in Malaysia: Bridging Theoretical Issues of Gender Identity, Culture, Ethnicity and Education," *Journal of Intercultural Studies* 21, no. 2 (2000): 177–192; Bertil Lintner, "Terror in Southeast Asia," Asia Pacific Media Services Limited, *http://www.asiapacificms.com/articles/southeast_asia_terror* (2006).
7. Meredith Weiss, "The Changing Shape of Islamic Politics in Malaysia," *Journal of East Asian Studies* 4, no. 1 (2004): 139–173.
8. Patricia Martinez, "Thumbs up to Living in Malaysian Diversity," *New Straits Times*, August 10, 2006, 20.
9. Judith Nagata, "What Is a Malay? Situational Selection of Ethnic Identity in a Plural Society," *American Ethnologist* 1, no. 2 (1974): 331–350.
10. Paula Uimonen, "Mediated Management of Meaning: On-Line Nation Building in Malaysia," *Global Networks* 3, no. 3 (2003): 299–315, 300.
11. William Stoever, "Malaysia, the Bumiputra Policy, and Foreign Investors: An Evaluation," *Studies in Comparative International Development* 20, no. 6 (1985): 86–107, 86.
12. Korff, "Globalisation and Communal Identities," 277.
13. Paula Uimonen, op. cit.
14. Mohamad Mahathir, "Malaysia on Track for 2020 Vision," *http://www. perdana.org.my/antarctica/?newsid=5287* (1999); H. S. Barlow, "Malaysia—Swettenham's Legacy," *Asian Affairs* 28, no. 3 (1997): 325–334.
15. Uimonen, "Mediated Management of Meaning," 300.
16. Christine Chin, "The State of the 'State' in Globalization: Social Order and Economic Restructuring in Malaysia," *Third World Quarterly* 21, no. 6 (2000): 1035–1057; Barlow, "Malaysia—Swettenham's Legacy," 326.
17. Rahmah Hashim and Arfah Yusof, "Internet in Malaysia," *Informatik Forum* 13 no. 1 (1999) 49-51.
18. Uimonen, "Mediated Management of Meaning," 302.

19. Linda Dittmar, "Fending Off the Barbarians: Agit-Media and the Middle East," *Cinema Journal* 43, no. 4 (2004): 108–114; Kevin Carragee, "Evaluating Polysemy: An Analysis of the *New York Times'* Coverage of the End of the Cold War," *Political Communication* 20, no. 3 (2003): 287–308; Karmen Erjavec, "Media Construction of Identity through Moral Panics: Discourses of Immigration in Slovenia," *Journal of Ethnic & Migration Studies* 29, no. 1 (2003): 83–101; Shelah Burney, "Manufacturing Nationalism: Post-September 11 Discourse in United States Media," *Simile* 2, no. 2 (2002): 1–16; also available online at http://utpjournals.metapress.com/content/w3j1nur41833/?p=0644028e32ff449a97041a453a0a997d&pi=21%20

20. Lay Chin Koh, "Shop! Shop! Shop!," *New Straits Times*, June 20, 2005, 11.

21. Wendy Bokhorst-Heng, "Newspapers in Singapore: A Mass Ceremony in the Imagining of the Nation," *Media, Culture & Society* 24, no. 4 (2002): 559–569.

22. Uimonen, "Mediated Management of Meaning," 305.

23. Steven Gan, "Virtual Democracy in Malaysia," *Nieman Reports* 56, no. 2 (2002): 65–67.

24. Tony Wilson, Azizah Hamzah, and Umi Khattab, "The 'Cultural Technology of Clicking' in the Hypertext Era: Electronic Journalism Reception in Malaysia," *New Media & Society* 5, no. 4 (2003): 523–545.

25. Gan, "Virtual Democracy in Malaysia," 66.

26. Ibid.

27. Uimonen, "Mediated Management of Meaning," 307.

28. Jason Abbott, "Democracy@Internet.Asia? The Challenges to the Emancipatory Potential of the Net: Lessons from China and Malaysia," *Third World Quarterly* 22, no. 1 (2001): 99–114.

29. Abbott, "Democracy@Internet.Asia?," 105.

30. Len Holmes and Margaret Grieco, "The Internet, Email, and the Malaysian Political Crisis: The Power of Transparency," *Asia Pacific Business Review* 8, no. 2 (2001): 59–72.

31. Uimonen, "Mediated Management of Meaning," 309.

32. Abbott, "Democracy@Internet.Asia?," 105

33. Uimonen, "Mediated Management of Meaning," 310.

34. Wilson et al., "The 'Cultural Technology of Clicking'," 527.

35. Amy White, "Will Going Bahasa Help Latecomer to Make up for Lost Time?," *Media Asia*, January 27, 2006, 18.

36. Chin Chin Wong and Pang Liang Hiew, "Factors Influencing the Adoption of Mobile Entertainment: Empirical Evidence from a Malaysian Survey," *Proceedings of the International Conference on Mobile Business* (Sydney: Mobile Business, 2005), 682–685.

37. Samsudin Rahmin and Latiffah Pawanteh, "The Emerging Lifestyle of Malaysian Youth: Implications of a Changing Media Environment" (World Communication Association, 17th World Communication Association Conference, Haninge, Sweden, July 2003; available online at http://facstaff.uww.edu/. wca/Conferences/2003Conference/WCAfinalPawanteh7A_Paper.doc).

38. Asian Market Research News, "Thai Teens Get Serious: New Market Research on the Thailand Youth Market," Asian Market Research.com, *http://www.asiamarketresearch.com/news/000258.htm* (2002).

39. Asia Pacific Management News, "Asian Teen Idols: Better than Western?," Asian Business Strategy and Street Intelligence Ezine, *http://www.apmforum.com/news/ap230302.htm* (2002).

40. Farish Noor, "Youth Culture & Islamic Intelligentsia: Ignoring the Popular Cultural Discourse," Muslimedia, http://www.muslimedia.com/ARCHIVES/sea98/youth.htm (1996).

41. Sharon Shaw, "Rise of Malaysia's Under-25s," *Media Asia*, July 30, 2004, 10.
42. Atifah Hargrave-Silk, "H&S Gets Personality Online with Friendster," *Media Asia*, December 16, 2005, 14.
43. Procter and Gamble, "'H'n'S' Friendster Profile," *http://www.friendster. com/user.php?uid=22794179* (2005).
44. Abbott, "Democracy@Internet.Asia?"
45. Uimonen, "Mediated Management of Meaning," 307.
46. Holmes and Grieco, "The Internet, Email, and the Malaysian Political Crisis," 61.
47. Surain Subramaniam, "The Dual Narrative of 'Good Governance': Lessons for Understanding Political and Cultural Change in Malaysia and Singapore," *Contemporary Southeast Asia: A Journal of International & Strategic Affairs* 23, no. 1 (2001): 65–80; Uimonen, "Mediated Management of Meaning," 303–304.
48. Uimonen, "Mediated Management of Meaning," 304.

12 Muslim Voices in the Blogosphere
Mosaics of Local–Global Discourses

Merlyna Lim

INTRODUCTION

In the aftermath of the terrorist attacks of September 11, 2001, the effect of globalization on Islam has not only become a hot topic, but also more of a reality. Other world events following that day, such as the United States' war on terror and the Israel–Hezbollah conflict have awakened a consciousness among Muslims all over the world to unite and stand up for themselves. The concept of *Ummah*—a universal community of those who profess the Islamic faith, a community that transcends race, ethnicity, nationality, and class—has become more important in the minds of many Muslims.[1]

The proliferation of new information and communication technologies, such as satellite television and the Internet, is also promoting a greater Ummah consciousness, a heightened sense of belonging to a global community of believers. Global networks can potentially become vehicles that transform local concerns into global causes and vice versa. The recent development of Internet applications, such as blogs and other social exchange and networking software, has enabled more people to engage in global conversations. Blogs, in particular, can potentially be a venue for global dialogue and the formation of a global community.

Through a comparative study of the Indonesian and Iranian blogospheres, this chapter shows that these platforms and the messages they promote do not, however, result in a single global metanarrative[2] or the advocacy for a single course of action. The local contextualization of globally circulating discourses results in a diverse mosaic of interpretations, positions, and identifications of sources of discontent.

From this perspective, blogging and the blogosphere can be seen as being self-organized into nodes, networks, and streams that, while they overlap, cannot readily be molded into a hegemonic voice or viewpoint. The importance of this finding to the study of new media, particularly the blogosphere, is that while certain moments, such as the *Jyllands-Posten* Muhammad cartoons controversy,[3] are volatile and spread throughout the globe through electronic information technologies, they can neither be said to embolden resistance uniformly everywhere nor be imagined as fostering a "contest of civilizations." Yet, the technologies of the Internet and the advent of the blogosphere offer a decisively innovative set of interconnected pathways toward a public sphere that reaches far below and rises high above the territorial level of the nation-state. In this sense, it creates key conditions for civil society and allows collective voices to move from the local to the global and back again, no matter how disparate these voices might be.

Before moving to look in detail at the cases of the Iranian and Indonesian blogospheres, the following section will provide some background on how blogging emerged as one of most popular social activities currently undertaken in cyberspace, and how blogging and politics have become increasingly interrelated.

BLOGGING AND POLITICS

Wikipedia defines a *weblog* (usually shortened to *blog*) as "a web-based publication consisting primarily of periodic articles (normally in reverse chronological order)."[4] Blogs allow for the instant, chronological, and frequently updated communication of information, such as personal thoughts, news, and events. Blogs not only create an online journal that remains archived online, they are also indexed and searchable by search engines. With millions now online, blogs offer a new way for communicating and discovering social metadata and provide advantages over other web-based information sites, such as conventional websites, e-mails, forums, and mailing lists.

In the domain of politics, the rise of blogging has provoked discourse on incommodious issues. However, until early 2004, blogs were not yet perceived as playing any significant political role. Compared to other players in domestic politics and mainstream or mass media, bloggers and their blogs did not appear to be either powerful or visible, as underscored by statistics showing that even the most popular blogs received only a tiny proportion of the web traffic that the major media outlets attracted. The 2003 Pew Internet Survey reported that only 4 percent of Americans reported going to blogs for information and opinions.[5] With this in mind, the *New York Times* quipped, "Never have so many people written so much to be read by so few."[6]

But that perception changed with the rapid and progressive deployment of the Internet during the 2004 United States Presidential campaign. Even with only 9 percent of Internet users reporting that they frequently or sometimes read political blogs during the election campaign, blogs started to be seen as of potential significance to politics. Several candidates and political parties set up blogs during the campaign. Among the more notable was Howard Dean's *Blog for America*, which was exemplary in showing how a blog could be used for building social networks of political support. By

September 2003, Dean's campaign had raised $7.4 million via the Internet, out of a total of $14.8 million, with a remarkably modest average donation of under $100.

Dean's blogging phenomenon and a rapid rise in the popularity and proliferation of blogs marked 2004 as an important year in the history of the blogosphere. By the end of that year, the term *blog* had been chosen as the top word of 2004 by Merriam-Webster, a US dictionary publisher.[7] And in subsequent years, blogging has become much more popular. The 2006 Pew Internet survey[8] reports that 8 percent of Internet users, or about 12 million American adults, keep a blog, while 39 percent of Internet users, or about 57 million American adults, read blogs, and the numbers have shown a significant increase since the fall of 2005. The popularity of blogging is also increasing in other countries, including Iran and Indonesia.

While the biggest portion of the blogosphere is devoted to personal stories/journals, political blogs do exist and some of them are among the most popular. Dubbed a catalyst for change and the people's media, some argue that blogs could be an empowering tool for society, especially in countries where strict media censorship and surveillance is conducted. Dan Gillmor, a veteran journalist, hails the rise of blogs as the beginning of a citizen journalism era, where the marginalized can at last play a greater role in making rather than merely consuming news.[9] Some observers strongly believe that if politicians would all start blogging, public debate would be dramatically revitalized.

However, as previously hinted, even in the United States, the blogosphere suffers from the unequal distribution of readers across an array of blogs. While there are over one million bloggers in the United States posting approximately 275,000 new items daily, the average blogger has almost no political influence, as measured by traffic or hyperlinks. The distribution of links and traffic is heavily skewed, with only a handful bloggers getting most readers.[10] Presumably, the blogospheres in other countries would be found to suffer even more from the same problem. If the blogosphere is to be seen as an exemplary public sphere where everybody's voice can be heard, then this tendency shows that not to be the case. Yet, this could also be seen as a selection process weeding out the "bad" from the "desirable," although a limited observation shows that the top bloggers are not necessarily better than the rest.

Another constraint is that most blogs are not maintained professionally. Most bloggers are part-time, and blogging is almost exclusively a voluntarily venture. This means that, unlike professional journalists, bloggers mostly do not have the capacity to do any research or investigation prior to publishing their opinions. The credibility of blog entries, in this regard, is lower than articles in mainstream media. This does not mean that postings in the blogosphere are not as critical as those in the mainstream media, if not more so. Being a voluntary activity, blogging also can be seen as a positive force for regular people to voice their opinions without having to go through the exhaustive filtering of traditional journalism that often excludes some critical, unconventional, or controversial voices from the professional media sphere.

Also, there is no central organization to the blogosphere. No consensus exists among the bloggers/readers with regard to many key issues. This contributes to the pessimistic view that the blogosphere strengthens the Tower of Babel tendency[11] in cyberspace, where voices tend to be so idiosyncratic as to be meaningless to casual readers. Through a more positive lens, however, this could also mean that the blogosphere can potentially encourage more genuine individual voices to emerge and real dialogues to be created.

With these dynamics of the blogosphere in mind, this chapter investigates the cases of Indonesian and Iranian bloggers in relation to selected global political issues related to Islam in an effort to show how the general features of the blogosphere do not always have the same outcomes, even in societies with similar religious orientations. Instead, the convivial[12] nature of the Internet that is unreservedly amplified in the blogosphere, and the local contextualization of information, knowledge, and ideas, together resist the emergence of a single storyline put forth by any single powerful player. However, in this milieu of free-flowing ideas, at any one moment, a limited number of popular or preferred storylines is likely to appear, as manifested by increased numbers of hits or visits to certain blogs. Yet these, too, vary from setting to setting, as the Indonesian and Iranian cases reveal.

The cases of Indonesia and Iran were chosen not merely because both societies are predominantly Muslim and both offer rich examples and illustrate how Muslim society and Internet technology are mutually interacting. Both are examples of different political systems, Indonesia being the world's most populous Muslim country, but with a secular democratic government, and Iran being an undemocratic Islamic state. The cases also offer formidable challenges to some variants of Western modernization theory— the assumption of a declining role for religion—by showcasing how religion can couple with technology to force society to move in the direction of modernization. In both countries, religious sentiment and leadership, and not the secular intelligentsia, have lent coherence and force to the modernization and development project, particularly through information and communication technology.

THE INTERNET AND BLOGOSPHERES
IN INDONESIA AND IRAN

To fully understand the dynamics of the Muslim blogospheres in Iran and Indonesia, one has to understand the sociopolitical histories of Internet development in both countries. This section will narrate the brief histories of the Iranian and Indonesian Internets to provide a backdrop to understanding the development, uses, and impacts of blogs in both countries.

INDONESIA

Although the Internet arrived in Indonesia in the early 1980s, when the first connection from the University of Indonesia was made to the service provider UUNet, because of a lack of basic infrastructure, no permanent Internet link was established until 1994. With the arrival of private commercial Internet service providers (ISPs), the Internet attained a public presence by 1995, followed by a boom in ISPs at the end of 1997. The mushrooming of ISPs, however, did not lead to the Internet being widely used, since most Indonesians could not afford to pay the subscription fees in combination with the telephone-line rental necessary to connect.

It was not household connections but *warnet*, or Internet cafés, a grassroots form of commercial Internet connection that developed without government intervention, which played a significant role in popularizing Internet use among society at large. From 1996 onward, warnet became the main access points for more than 50 percent of Indonesian Internet users. For most users, the warnet facilitate not only online social relationships, but also function as places for extending online relationships into offline settings. With the expansion of warnet, telecenters, and campus/school-based access points, Indonesia has experienced a dramatic growth in Internet usage, from only 20,000 users in 1995 to 16 million users in 2005. Yet, more than a decade since the Internet first entered the nation, it is still only available to less than 1 percent of the total population. It is the price of Internet access, in addition to a lack of basic infrastructure, rather than political concerns, that are the primary barriers to the widespread usage of fast Internet connections.

Historically, the Internet in Indonesia has always been entangled with politics, and its development has very much run in tandem with discourses of democratization. During the Suharto era, Internet development in Indonesia provided a much more democratic media environment when compared to other media spheres, such as television, radio, and print. In addition, political experiences of the 1990s show how the substantially unregulated Internet contributed to the political reforms that led to the downfall of Order Baru.[13]

The Indonesian Internet operates in a reasonably free sociopolitical environment, under a relatively new government that is still trying to recover from the sociopolitical damage resulting from a long period under an undemocratic and authoritarian system. No censorship, surveillance, or control over self-expression either on- or offline have been formally applied in Indonesia since the overthrow of Suharto's New Order government, which lasted from 1965 to 1998. The people of Indonesia can now freely access all forms of media, and media are also free from outright censorship by the government. The blogosphere thus emerged in an unregulated Internet environment in Indonesia.

While some Indonesian bloggers started their first blogs as early as 2001, blogging only became popular in 2004, mostly due to the progressive campaigns of some early bloggers, such as Enda Nasution,[14] known as the father of Indonesian blogging, Priyadi,[15] and A. Fatih Syuhud,[16] as well as the availability of (currently) free blogging platforms, such as blogger, live-journal, blogdrive, wordpress, multiply, and Friendster's blog. The number of Indonesian bloggers is not well documented, as shown by estimates ranging from 100,000 to 1,000,000. While the list of the top 100 Indonesian bloggers is dominated by male Internet users, a significant percentage of female bloggers can also be observed in the Indonesian blogosphere. Most female bloggers are not into blogs dedicated specifically to politics, but they do intersperse politics into their stories and conversations about everyday life experience.

Based on my observations, Indonesian bloggers seem to need to be networked in communities. Big clusters of networked blogs are commonly found in the Indonesian blogosphere. Among the biggest blogging communities is that of Muslim bloggers,[17] where the community leaders (moderators) actively endorse some community (Islamic) values and encourage the members to address issues related to Islam and the Muslim world.

Iran

The origins of the Iranian Internet date back to 1987, with the establishment of the first dial-up connection from the Institute for Studies in Theoretical Physics and Mathematics through the co-operative U.S. university network BITNET network and Iran's membership in the European Academic Research Network. The link later developed into a national network with five hundred assigned Internet Protocol addresses. The first primary users of the connection were academics and research institutions.

The internal data network, though, was only established in 1993 by the Telecommunication Company of Iran (TCI), which planned to build a nationwide packet-switched network based on the X.25 protocol, Iran-Pac. In 1995, however, the government took over IranPac, clamped down on private information services, and advanced the development of its own data communication network. Over subsequent years, Iran witnessed a very rapid growth in its Internet network, as the Internet quickly became embedded in the sociopolitics of Iranian society. In the May 1997 elections, two leading presidential candidates, President Khatami[18] and the conservative candidate, Ali Akbar Nategh Nouri,[19] both used websites to get their message across, and the election results were announced online on the Iranian government's website.[20] The Iranian Internet continued to experience a remarkable growth, increasing from about one million users in 2001 to approximately five million users in 2005. With more than 1,500 cybercafés (in Tehran alone), around 5,000 Internet hosts (in 2003), and 650 ISPs, the number is expected to reach 25 million in 2009.[21]

Unlike other media, which are subject to harsh Iranian government censorship, initially the Internet was relatively free. This resulted in the Internet becoming one of the most important information resources in Iran. Polls show that people rely more on the Internet than any other media as a source of information, and beginning in 2000, more Iranians began to use the technology to circumvent the state's control over conventional media sources; this was marked by a burst of growth in online content in the Farsi and English languages. The state responded by applying a sophisticated state-mandated filtering system. The OpenNet Initiative's testing shows that more than 30 percent of websites are blocked by this filter. The Iranian government has effectively blocked access to:

> pornographic online sites, most anonymizer tools (which allow users to surf the Internet without detection), a large number of sites with gay and lesbian content, some politically sensitive sites, women's rights sites, and certain targeted blogs, among other types of sites.[22]

While there is no specific regulation regarding Internet content, the government does enforce strict controls on Internet materials under the country's Press Law.[23] For example, individuals who subscribe to ISPs must promise, in writing, not to access "non-Islamic" sites. However, the state apparently does not monitor the content of pages that users access. Yet, in some cities, judges have announced that they do intend to monitor usage in cybercafés while on the lookout for prohibited activities, which includes viewing non-Islamic material. Even in the face of such threats, Iranians still perceive the Internet as a relatively freer sphere for expressing opinions in comparison with other media spheres.

Thus, unlike the case in Indonesia, blogging in Iran operates under particular circumstances, as the Iranian government tends to discourage self-expression. A heavily censored, state-controlled mainstream media have created an environment for the Iranian blog to be potentially more important than blogs in the United States, Western Europe, and other more democratic countries, such as Indonesia, since blogs in general tend to be relatively unregulated compared to other forms of expression in Iranian society.

In April 2005, the BBC reported that Massih Ali-Nejad, an Iranian investigative journalist, had been barred by the conservative-controlled parliament of Iran after she exposed parliament members' huge pay and bonuses.[24] Ali-Nejad turned to blogging and continues to write about Iranian Members of Parliament in her blog. Mohammad Ali Abtahi, a former chief of staff of President Khatami, a vice president of legal and parliamentary affairs, and one of Khatami's advisors, also turned to blogging to voice his political opinions and views. He said that blogs "let me be myself . . . regardless of my official and governmental status." These two very different examples represent but a fraction of the Iranian blogosphere, which is perhaps among the most exciting in any language or cultural context.

In a country that has a population of about seventy million, almost three-quarters of which are under the age of thirty, apart from journalists like

Ali-Nejad and politicians like Ali Abtahi, many students have also turned to blogging. Among the most prominent student bloggers is a Toronto-based Iranian, Hossein Derakhshan, aka, Hoder. He has actively promoted blogging in Iran by explaining the steps necessary to start a blog and encouraging Iranians to use the available platforms to create their own blogs.[25]

As of October 2005, there were estimated to be about 700,000 Iranian blogs out of an estimated total of 100 million worldwide, of which about 40,000–110,000 are active and mostly written in the Persian language, the official language of Iran. Among the active blogs, many are available in both Persian and English versions. Through their bilingual blogs, users share their lives and perceptions with the world. Hossein Derakhshan argues that the Iranian blogosphere is a window to look into another culture, a café where Iranians can meet to discuss matters in ways not possible in the offline world due to geography, politics, or language, and thus blogs form a bridge for people or groups from different communities to interact and communicate.

In July 2006, Iran's President Ahmadinejad launched his own blog.[26] Well-designed and written in four languages, the blog attracts many visitors, not only from Iran, but also from other places in the world. The President's decision to start a blog lends official sanction to the importance of the blogosphere in Iran's political realm.

GLOBAL ISSUES IN THE INDONESIAN AND IRANIAN BLOGOSPHERES: NARRATIVES OF CONSPIRACY/VICTIMIZATION

As countries whose populations are predominantly Muslim, both Indonesia and Iran share some similar political narratives, yet with different iterations. One of the grandest narratives shared is related to Jewish conspiracies and the existence of Israel as a nation-state, which is closely connected to the narrative of a global Western–Israel (or Zionists–Crusaders, US–Israel, or Christians–Jews) conspiracy against Islam that is more widespread around the globe.

Historically, this narrative has been associated with two important lines of reasoning. First, radical fundamentalists in both Indonesia and Iran believe that none of the many aspects of modernization, including secularization and rationalization, the shift from traditional values to more liberal ones, and the global economy and its culture of individualism and hedonism, can be seen as independent processes, but rather should be viewed as interlocking aspects of a plot against Islam. This behind-the-scenes conspiracy with the purpose of destroying Islam is identified with Jews and Zionism, and anybody who is considered to be "helping" this conspiracy—no matter from what religion or background—can be called a Zionist.[27]

Second, the conspiracy theories and the tendency to scapegoat Jews originally came from the Middle East, especially Saudi Arabia, Kuwait, and

Egypt,[28] whose hatred of Israel is directly related to the Palestine case. In addition, the belief in a Jewish conspiracy to destroy Islam and to dictate to the whole world is not only a reaction to Israel's existence, but is also exacerbated by the dissemination of anti-Semitism from the West, including Russia, to Arabic countries. The source that is frequently referred to is *Al-Maka id Al-Yahudiyah*, or *The Protocol of the Elders of Zion*,[29] which is seen as proof of this conspiracy. In the 1950s, an Arabic version was published. This piece of writing was translated and adapted into Indonesian in the 1980s.[30]

For today's Muslim world, though, these past stories do not matter that much. More contemporary events, such as the lengthy Israeli–Palestinian conflict (which is perceived as a religious war rather than a territorial one), the "victimization" of Muslims all over the world (Bosnia, Kashmir, Chechnya, and Iraq are prominent cases), and moreover, the aggressive "War on Terrorism" by the United States and other governments, now have more significant meaning. They are seen as underlying the global narrative of conspiracy against Islam.

Previous studies on cyberradical fundamentalism in Indonesia show that many Muslims have become sensitized to issues affecting Muslims worldwide via the Internet and have developed a collective sense of identity and resistance through it. Yet, there is no evidence that any of these users have gone straight to a Palestinian or Iraqi training camp from an Internet café.[31] *Jihad,* in the form of physical war, is neither simply a blind and bloody-minded scrabble for temporal power nor solely a door through which to pass into the hereafter. Rather, it is a form of political action in which the pursuit of immortality is inextricably linked to a profoundly this-worldly endeavor—the founding or recreation of a just community on earth.[32]

Other studies confirm that the majority of Muslims are moderate and are not prone to joining radical *jihadi* groups.[33] Most Muslims cannot be categorized as being capable of "killing for politics or religion." Yet, similar studies have found that the belief that the West and Israel (Zionists–Crusaders or Jews–Christians) are conspiring against Islam is prevalent even among moderate Muslims worldwide, including those in Indonesia and Iran. In the last five years, after the September 11th attacks and the launch of George W. Bush's War on Terrorism, the "Zionist–Crusader/Jewish–Christian/Israel–US conspiracy against Islam" has become an extremely popular topic, and narratives on this theme fly around the blogospheres, and elsewhere in cyberspace, print media, and daily conversations in Indonesia and Iran.

At the same time, from within the body of Islam itself, much effort has been devoted by reformist believers to a struggle against the growth of radical fundamentalism and anti-Americanism in the post-September 11th context. Reformists, too, use the media, including the Internet, to spread their message of tolerance and peace, as Islam does profess itself as a religion of peace. The voices of these moderate and tolerant Muslims, however, are subdued by the fact that US foreign policy is lacking in sensitivity and nuance to its effects on the ground in the Muslim world. For example, in Indonesia and Iran, just like in any other part of the Muslim world, US policies toward Palestine and Israel are not seen as mutually supportive. The policy of the United States toward Israel is interpreted essentially as an anti-Muslim policy. In this manner, the discontent that US policies create in a place like Jerusalem, and places like the West Bank and Gaza, becomes indistinguishable from the policies of Israel. The Afghanistan invasion, and especially the Iraq invasion, has only strengthened this perception. The persistence of this conspiracy theory in today's deeply polarized world of politics has created a situation where Muslims who access global information through selected sites cannot help but frame world events—especially those related to Islam/Muslims—within this framework of conspiracy, which has now become a metanarrative underlying many Muslim believers' interpretations, perceptions, and analyses of current events.

Focusing on two recent issues related to the Muslim world, the following discussion provides some snapshots of how two blogospheres, in two different Muslim countries, on different continents, and with different political systems, but that do share some similar concerns have responded. The cases under investigation are the *Jyllands-Posten* Muhammad cartoons controversy and the letter sent by President Ahmadinejad of the Iranian Republic to President Bush of the United States.

THE *JYLLANDS-POSTEN* MUHAMMAD CARTOONS CONTROVERSY

The Muhammad cartoons controversy began after the Danish newspaper. *Jylllands-Posten*, published twelve editorial cartoons, most of which depicted the Islamic prophet Muhammad, on September 30, 2005.[34] The controversy spilled out onto the blogosphere on February 8, 2006, when the "Freedom for Egyptians" blog[35] published scans reportedly showing six of the cartoons, including the "turban bomb" image that had been reprinted in the October 17, 2005 issue of *El Faqr*, an Egyptian newspaper. On the same day, the "Egyptian Sandmonkey" blog[36] followed this by publishing a different version of the scanned pages from *El Faqr*.

Following these Egyptian bloggers, Muslim bloggers all over the world reacted to the controversy by posting various entries. On this issue, the Iranian blogosphere displayed both more polarized, as well as more nuanced opinions, when compared with the Indonesian reaction. In the Indonesian blogosphere, a large number of bloggers accused *Jyllands-Posten* of blasphemy and an abuse of freedom of expression. Among this group, some condemning *Jyllands-Posten* believed this blasphemous act to be proof of the hatred of the West for Islam and linked it to the global conspiracy metanarrative. They suggested that Muslims in Indonesia and all over the world should boycott Danish products. From February 2006 onward, banners proclaiming "Boycott Danish products" were pervasive in the Indonesian blogosphere.

In the Iranian blogosphere, however, such sentiments were not so pervasive. Although Ahmadinejad, the president of Iran, ordered a ban on Danish products (the Indonesian president did not do the same), Iranian bloggers were not keen on boycotting Danish products and did not think that such action was necessary. Regarding this issue, an Iranian commented in his blog:

> So much about these Danish cartoons these days that finally got here in Iran. Members of the government oriented Malissia groups together with some hard-line clerics attacked the Danish embassy. Ahmadinejad ordered the ban of Danish goods although I have not seen a significant reaction from the body of people. The fact that Iran did all these after most of the other Muslim countries is kind of odd! Seems that Iran suddenly woke up and sensed a competition from others around the world and feared that Iran might have called not Muslim [sic] enough by others! But I am sure Danish pastry that is very popular in every and each pastry shop in Tehran, will be there although some stupids suggested it's [sic] name to be changed![37]

There was a small group of Indonesian bloggers who tried to be more critical about this issue. While they also thought that the Danish cartoons were proof of the abuse of freedom of expression, they did not necessarily link this to any conspiracy. They also deemed that the extreme actions taken by some Muslims, who turned to protest and violent acts, were not rightful and went against the core of Islamic teaching. Some Iranians shared similar opinions with this Indonesian group.

Unsurprisingly, there was no known Indonesian blogger who defended the *Jyllands-Posten* nor had the courage to display the cartoons. According to the discussion carried on via the comment boxes of some blogs, many of those who condemned the Danish cartoonists never actually saw the cartoons.

Two Indonesian bloggers who declared themselves to be moderate–liberal Muslims articulated that they did not publish the cartoons in their blogs based on the belief that it is forbidden to depict Muhammad in the form of cartoons. Their hesitance was more rooted in the feeling that they would have been threatened had they done so. One blogger commented:

> There are *preman berjubah*,[38] moral police, everywhere, including in cyberspace. I do not want to jeopardize myself just by voicing my opinion about this cartoon or about anything related to Islam generally in my blog. Not worth it.

One thing that was not paralleled in the Indonesian blogosphere is that, in the Iranian blogosphere, there were some bloggers who fully supported the

Danish cartoonists. As Muslims (and Iranians), they stood firm in defending the freedom of expression. This does not mean that there were no Indonesian bloggers who shared similar opinions with these Iranian "freedom of expression" defenders. There might have been some, but they did not support this position in their blogs. As hinted at in the comment of the moderate Muslim cited above, self-censorship could have been among the reasons for their silence. Meanwhile, something cultural lies behind "not saying anything" in the Indonesian context.[39] The absence of a reaction can actually be interpreted as a sign of disagreement. Thus, in this context, the fact that there were many Indonesian bloggers who did not say anything about the issue does not automatically exclude them from the discourse. Many of them might have actually been expressing their disagreement with the majority opinion through expressing no reaction.

One important aspect that should be brought into consideration is the fact that most Indonesian Muslims belong to the Sunni tradition, while Iranians are mostly Shia/Shiite. The Shia tradition does recognize the graphical representation of the Prophet Muhammad—something not recognized in the Sunni tradition. Thus, it might have been easier for the Iranian Shiites to tolerate the cartoons when compared to the Indonesian Sunnis.

AHMADINEJAD: A HERO OR A FAILURE?

In May 2006, Iranian President Mahmoud Ahmadinejad sent President George Bush an eighteen-page letter discussing religious values, history, and international relations.[40] In it, Ahmadinejad criticized the US invasion of Iraq and urged Bush to return to religious principles. This long, well-written letter was quickly circulated in the blogosphere and translated into English, as well as various other languages, including Indonesian.

Indonesian Muslim bloggers cheerfully welcomed this letter as a gem that had emerged from the Islamic world. Ahmadinejad, a name that was formerly unknown to most Indonesians, has suddenly become an icon of the rise of Islam against the West. Many Indonesian bloggers now perceive Ahmadinejad as an ideal president, and romanticize his being a future leader of the Muslim world, the global Ummah. Many Indonesians, especially female bloggers, have become emotionally attached to the speeches of Ahmadinejad. In their blogs, many Indonesian Muslims state that Ahmadinejad is speaking for them, and his speech is described as "inspiring," "touching," and "making me cry."

When Ahmadinejad made a visit to Indonesia, he was enthusiastically and passionately welcomed as a new hero by Indonesians, especially young Muslims. His visit was covered in a large number of blogs. Glowing personal stories about Ahmadinejad—his choice of living a simple (poor) lifestyle, his piety, and his courage—were conspicuous in many of these postings. As reflected in some blogs, the Indonesians' romantic view of Ahmadinejad's leadership may be related to the frustration among Indonesian Muslims with multiple ongoing crises in their country. Faced with an unstable socio-political–economic situation and many unresolved problems marking the transition from authoritarian to democratic governance, many Indonesians have turned to religion as a magic wand for transforming the country.

Ironically, the Iranians themselves mostly do not share the same opinion about their president. While there are some bloggers who support Ahmadinejad, most of the top Iranian bloggers do not think that he is a good, let alone ideal, president. Some perceive Ahmadinejad through his controversial policies, especially those dealing with foreign affairs, as having failed to place Iran in a better position in the world of international politics. Others suggest that he would be better off using his energy and brainpower to fix domestic socioeconomic problems, rather than attempting to gain international attention by making controversial statements.

Concerning Ahmadinejad, one Iranian blogger, who calls himself Mr. Behi griped:

> I am going mad for everything he does [sic], from his one post blog, to the denial of holocaust, to his suggestion for debate with Bush, to his claims about being protected by hidden forces and the lies that he gives people about the rate of inflation, freedom of speech and rights of people. He is a little ignored individual that loves to be seen no matter positive or negative, he does not care.[41]

For most of the Iranian bloggers surveyed, who know much better than Indonesians how it is to live under the governance of Ahmadinejad, their president is little more than a failure. Iranian bloggers do recognize the growing popularity of their president in the world, although they suggest that Ahmadinejad's popularity is not due to his own qualities, but is more related to his enemy's, US President Bush, incompetence. They also opine that Ahmadinejad tries to shift the attention of his own people and that of the world from his own failures by pointing out of the damage that the Bush administration has done in the international arena. With this in mind, one Iranian blogger states:

> Imagine, without Bush Ahmadinejad would be forced to account for growing unemployment in Iran, for significant economic decline, stricter social controls, greater repression for free speech and thought and press. In other words, if there wasn't so much hatred for Bush and his own totalitarianism, there would be more pressure on Ahmadinejad to account for his own abuses.[42]

In contrast, no Indonesian blogger was observed to care about what Iranian bloggers themselves thought about their president. There are no known references made by Indonesian bloggers to any Iranian blogs concerning Ahmadinejad.

The snapshots presented here show how both Indonesian and Iranian bloggers take up certain global issues that tap into their interests and their Islamic identity. However, the examples also show that there are distinct differences between the two. Certainly, the majority of both Indonesian and Iranian blogs are mostly personal. They address communal and public issues, including those on a global scale, but in a personal mode. Still, the examples display how there is more common feeling among individual opinions in the Indonesian blogosphere when compared with the Iranian one. Indonesian bloggers seem to consider more overtly "what others think of him/herself" when expressing opinions. In attempts to voice personal opinions, Indonesian bloggers also show a tendency to filter out some aspects that would be uncomfortable for their friends, networks, community, and country if spoken about. In this manner, a hidden social self-censoring of the blogosphere can be said to take place in Indonesia.

Iranian bloggers, on the other hand, are observed to not be so uniformly concerned about this kind of issue. As the blogosphere is one of few spaces where Iranians can freely express their personal opinions, Iranian bloggers take this opportunity to voice their opinions in full. Richer and more colorful voices thus emerge out of the Iranian blogosphere.

CONCLUSION

The cases of the Indonesian and Iranian blogospheres clearly show how blogs function as a means for organizing and assimilating experience, as well as voicing opinions. While global issues and ideas of global community, such as Ummah, do resonate beyond nation-states, community boundaries still remain. Even for those who are writing/reading in the same language (English), there does not appear to be any cross-cultural communication between Iranians and Indonesians. Yet, while there is no significant dialogue or cross-cultural communication, contrary to polarization theory,[43] there is no example of deep polarization in either the Indonesian or Iranian blogospheres. What do exist are the many timbered voices not previously found in traditional media.

The blogosphere exists in the nexus of state–civil social relations that are contextualized by local histories and still affected by the power of the nation-state in a global era. Thus, although practice might still depart from the ideal, in the case of Indonesia, a secular, democratic form of governance has been wrested from an authoritarian regime. In this context, the discourse on Islam in the world does not present itself as a contest between civil society and the state. As such, it might seem to be less diverse because it tends to cater more to social than political pressures concerning what can and cannot be said in the blogosphere.

In contrast, Iranians live under a conservative religious government that is itself entangled in global Islam and, at the same time, engaged in a contest with many elements of civil society over basic rights of voice and expression in the public sphere. The fact that the Iranian blogosphere mixes critiques of the world at large with the government there is thus not surprising.

These observations return the discussion to the main theme of this chapter: the very technology of the Internet, which defies central management and control, and also defies global metanarratives. To be sure, such metanarratives do emerge and do have their moments of currency, but as this discussion has shown, the mix of the distant global and the intimately lived local in the context of the Internet-based blogosphere soon allows for nuances, differences, and even counterhegemonic voices. Whether this should be celebrated or not is yet another matter about which many voices can speak.

The cases discussed here also show that while cyberspace can promote a greater *Ummah* consciousness, it does not remove its users from their localities. The territorial-based localities retain their relevance. The cases presented also show that Islam is not monolithic. Just as it is uniquely and culturally practiced in Indonesia, Iran, and other places, Islam is personalized, contextualized, and territorialized in the blogosphere, too.

The blogosphere is indeed one of those spheres where global or postnational identity, such as Islamic identity, and ideas of community, such as a global electronic *Ummah*, can be molded and formed. However, postnational identity is not a matter of disavowing national difference, but rather of "constituting a discursive device which represent difference as . . . identity."[44] In the case of religious identity, identity can also recognize the national nature of communities while, at the same time, projecting them beyond the nation. In this regard, the common generalization about religious identity being in opposition to the nation state is misleading. Rather, in a network society, postnational types of identity are fluid and can take different forms according to social–political–historical contexts, moving from being nationalist, to challenging nationalism, or to a mixture of both. More specifically, at the current juncture in history when the nation-state is still a basic unit of territorial power and popular identity, seizing the nation-state and placing it under the aegis of postnational identity can be viewed as a practical approach toward ideologically, as well as politically, assembling the building blocks for global communities having that identity.

As the Internet becomes more internationalized and globalized, the technology does not homogenize the social and political experiences of those who inhabit cyberspace as if they were in one big "global village" with a singular dominant language and imagination. Global networks do indeed enable individuals to communicate beyond the boundaries of their locales—neighborhoods, hamlets, cities, counties, states, and nation-states—to join a global community and partake in global discourses. But their global social experiences always co-exist, connected, overlapping with, and extended to and from their local experiences. Cyberspace is another zone in which real world events are apprehended in a manner that is connected to the corporality of its users. This also implies that the existence and power relations of nation-states and other entities persist in cyberspace; yet, cyberspace offers more flexible boundaries for social identities to be amalgamated.

NOTES

1. For more on the concept of *Ummah*, see Wikipedia, "Ummah," http://en.wikipedia.org/wiki/Ummah (accessed May 20, 2007).
2. A *metanarrative* is a big story, a story of mythic proportions that claims to account for, explain, and subordinate all lesser, smaller, and local narratives. See Jean-Francois Lyotard, *The Postmodern Condition: A Report on Knowledge* (Manchester, UK: Manchester University Press, 1984); Michel Foucault, *The Archeology of Knowledge and the Discourse on Language* (New York: Pantheon Books, 1972), associates the concept of metanarrative with legitimacy, as it can be used as a tool for social and political mobilization against perceived antagonistic, hegemonic forces while it also seeks to create its own hegemony.
3. For a summary of this controversy, see Wikipedia, "Jyllands-Posten Muhammad Cartoons Controversy," http://en.wikipedia.org/wiki/Jyllands-Posten_Muhammad_cartoons_controversy (accessed May 18, 2007).
4. See Wikipedia, "Blogs," http://en.wikipedia.org/wiki/Blog (accessed May 20, 2007).
5. Pew Internet Project, "Blogs Gain a Small Foothold," http://www.pewinternet.org/reports/reports.asp?Report=87&Section=ReportLevel2&Field=Level2ID&ID=662
6. Katie Hafner, "For Some, the Blogging Never Stops," *New York Times*, May 27, 2004 http://www.nytimes.com
7. BBC News, "'Blog' Picked as Word of the Year," http://news.bbc.co.uk/2/hi/technology/4059291.stm (December 1, 2004).
8. Amanda Lenhart and Susannah Fox, *"Bloggers: A Picture of the Internet's New Storytellers,"* Report (Washington, DC: Pew Internet and American Life Project, 2006; also available at http://www.pewinternet.org/PPF/r/186/report display.asp).
9. Dan Gillmor, *We the Media* (Cambridge, MA: O'Reilly, 2004).
10. Matthew Hindmann, Kostas Tsiotsiouliklis, and Judy Johnson, "Googlearchy: How a Few Heavily-linked Sites Dominate Politics Online" (paper presented at the annual meeting of the American Political Science Association, Philadelphia, PA, August 2003).
11. Cass Sunnstein, *Republic.com* (Princeton, NJ: Princeton University Press, 2001); Anthony Wilhelm, *Democracy in the Digital Age: Challenges to Political Life in Cyberspace* (London: Routledge, 2000).
12. Characterized by convergence, low cost, broad availability, and resistance to control, the Internet is a "convivial medium" that affords a greater scope for freedom, autonomy, creativity, and collaboration than previous media. The first use of the term *conviviality* to describe the sociotechnical landscape of the Internet is found in Merlyna Lim, "The Internet, Social Network and Reform in Indonesia," in *Contesting Media Power: Alternative Media in A Networked World*, ed. Nick Couldry and James Curran (Lanham, MD: Rowan & Littlefield, 2003), 274.
13. Merlyna Lim, "Cyber-Civic Space in Indonesia: From Panopticon to Pandemonium?," *International Development Planning Review* 4, no. 24 (2002): 383–400; Krishna Sen and David Hill, *The Internet and Democracy in Indonesia* (London: Routledge, 2005).

14. Enda Nasution's Weblog, http://enda.goblogmedia.com
15. Priyadi's Place, http://www.priyadi.net
16. http://afsyuhud.blogspot.com
17. Komunitas Blogger Muslim, http://komunitas.muslimblog.net/
18. Khatami.com, http://www.khatami.com
19. http://www.netiran.com
20.
21. See CIA, "The World Factbook—Iran," https://www.cia.gov/library/publications/the-world-factbook/geos/ir.html (accessed May 11, 2008); and Telecommunication Company of Iran, "TCI at a Glance," http://www.tci.ir/eng.asp?sm=0&page=18&code=1
22. OpenNet Initiative, "Internet Filtering in Iran in 2004–2005: A Country Study," http://www.opennetinitiative.net/studies/iran/
23. Islamic Republic of Iran, *Press Law*, Article 2, translation available at http://www.netiran.com/?fn=law14
24. Sadeq Saba, "Iran Bans Parliamentary Reporter," BBC News, http://news.bbc.co.uk/2/hi/middle_east/4414895.stm (April 6, 2005).
25. Editor: Myself. Hossein Derakhshan's Weblog, http://www.hoder.com/weblog/
26. Mahmoud Ahmadinejad—The Official Blog, http://www.ahmadinejad.ir/
27. Martin van Bruinessen, "Yahudi sebagai simbol dalam wacana Islam Indonesia masa kini" [The Jew as a Symbol in Contemporary Muslim Discourse in Indonesia], in *Spiritualitas baru: Agama dan Aspirasi Rakyat* (Seri Dian II Tahun I, Yogyakarta, Indonesia: Dian/Interfidei, 1993), 253–268.
28. Bruinessen, "Yahudi sebagai simbol."
29. Norman Cohn, *Warrant for Genocide: The Myth of the Jewish World-Conspiracy and the Protocols of the Elders of Zion* (Chicago, CA: Scholars Press, 1981).
30. Among these books are: Darouza, *Mengungkap tentang Yahudi: Watak, Jejak, Pijak dari Kasus-Kasus Lama Bani Israel* (Surabaya: Pustaka Progressif, 1982); Madjid Kailany, *Bahaya Zionisme terhadap Dunia Islam* (Solo: Pustaka Mantiq, 1984); Hizbul Haq, *Skenario Rahasia untuk Menguasai Dunia* (Bandung: Hizbul Haq Press, 1989); Pustakakarya, *Ayat-Ayat Setan Yahudi. Dokumen Rahasia Yahudi Menaklukkan Dunia dan Menghancurkan Agama* (Jakarta: PT, 1990); The Indonesian editors and publishers of these adaptations or translations believed (and shared the belief) that this book consists of secret plans of a Jewish organization to rule and dominate the world through capitalism, communism, democratization, authoritarianism, revolution, and economic liberation all rolled into one (see Bruinessen, "Yahudi sebagai simbol."). Indonesian editors and publishers do not realize that this book is not a historical document at all, but was a fabrication written by several anti-Jewish Russians.
31. Merlyna Lim, *Islamic Radicalism and Anti Americanism in Indonesia: The Role of the Internet* (Washington, DC: East-West Center, 2005).
32. Hannah Arendt, *Crises of the Republic* (New York: Harcourt Brace & Co, 1972).
33. Bruinessen, "Yahudi sebagai simbol."
34. The newspaper asserted that the publication of these cartoons was meant to contribute to public discourse about criticism of Islam and self-censorship. In response, Danish Muslim organizations held public protests and spread the publications worldwide. On October 17, 2005, the Egyptian newspaper, *El Faq*, was the first non-Scandinavian media to publish the cartoons. It published six of the images, along with an article strongly denouncing them. No known protests from either Egyptian religious authorities or the

Egyptian government emerged due to this publication. However, in early 2006, as examples of the cartoons were reprinted in newspapers in more than fifty other countries, the controversy grew and eventually led to protests, as well as rioting, particularly in the Muslim world.

35. Freedom for Egyptians, http://freedomforegyptians.blogspot.com
36. http://egyptiansandmonkey.com
37. http://mrbehi.blogs.com/i/2006/02/the_danish_pas.html
38. *Preman berjubah* (in Indonesian), literally translates as "mobs wearing robes." This term refers to several radical fundamentalist groups who use an Islamic face to fight against what they interpret as acts of the infidels (*khufur/kafir*) or morally wrong. These groups include Front Pembela Islam (Islamic Defender Front), Majelis Mujahidin Indonesia (Indonesian *Mujahedeen* Council), and some other lesser-known and smaller groups. In executing their projects, they usually wear robes and turbans.
39. In Indonesian custom, which is heavily influenced by Javanese culture, one can show his/her disagreement by saying nothing, as opposed to showing support (saying "yes"). Giving no reaction can actually signify disagreement or opposition.
40. CNN World, "Ahmadinejad's letter to Bush," http://edition.cnn.com/interactive/world/0605/transcript.lemonde.letter/
41. Adventures of Mr. Behi, http://mrbehi.blogs.com/i/2006/08/ahmadijacket_lo.html
42. Rami Yelda, "Money exchange in Hamadan," http://www.iranian.com/Shorts/2006/sept2006.html (September 30, 2006).
43. Sunnstein, *Republic.com*.
44. Stuart Hall, "The Question of Cultural Identity," in *Modernity and Its Futures*, ed. Stuart Hall, David Held, and Tony McGrew (Cambridge, UK: Polity, 1992), 292–297.

13 The Internet in Iran

The Battle Over an Emerging Virtual Public Sphere

Gholam Khiabany and Annabelle Sreberny

INTRODUCTION

Iran's Islamic Republic was established in 1979 after a short, popular, but not overly bloody revolution. Thus, all developments in relation to the Internet and cyberspace have occurred in a postrevolutionary and highly politicized environment, in which Shiite Islam became the ideology of the dominant theocratic state. Yet, the central issue is not the obvious and crude divide between a "traditional" and a "religious" state and a "modern," even "secular" technology, since that very state has—and many individual clergy have—adopted new information technologies. There are two more subtle lines of tension running through Internet development in Iran that drive this chapter. The first is the centralizing state's desire to control expression in a "new technology" environment that is highly conducive to widespread and popular participation. The second is the centralizing state's desire to orchestrate and manage the slow development of the private sector and the inhibitions placed on entrepreneurial ICT activity in a field that has made Internet millionaires in other parts of the world.

In spite of these two fault lines, the recent period has seen the rapid emergence of the communication industry in Iran as one of the fastest growing economic sectors, and various uses of "new media" now constitute one of the most dynamic and vibrant politico-cultural spaces. Beside the expansion of Iranian media channels, popular desire for access to informal channels of communication and for greater cultural consumption is evident in the increasing usage of mobile technology and the Internet, and the astonishing rise and popularity of weblogs, which have become a particular site of struggle.

This chapter locates the expansion of the Internet in Iran in its wider social context. We acknowledge the reality of global digital divides and the fact that Iran is lagging behind some of its richer regional neighbors with only 10.6 percent of its population of 70 million people online, albeit in actual numbers constituting 38.7 percent of all users in the Middle East.[1] But we suggest that limited access and usage only tells part of a more complex story of the communicative experiences in Iran. Internet use has started to challenge the state monopoly over the pricing and availability of long distance telephony. However, the more significant challenge lies in the use of the Internet as a channel of political and cultural communication. In the absence of genuinely free political parties, regular clampdowns on the semi-independent press, and the total control of broadcasting, the Internet has come to the fore as a space for various alternative political and cultural voices, and has created a strong link between activists inside and outside Iran. This chapter examines this trend in detail, with particular reference to individual and collective voices and the Iranian state's attempts to control this diverse and vibrant virtual public space. Rather than the Habermasian concept of "public sphere" rooted in European history and rationalist politics, we prefer the notion of "public space" as articulated by Mouffe. She argues for a politics that is multifaceted, passionate, and played out in a multiplicity of public spaces where dissent can be voiced.[2] The Internet as such a public space, albeit virtual and not face-to-face, presents particular challenges for authoritarian regimes regarding control, and we show the variety of controls by the state and the range of deviant responses by users that constitute the current complex Internet environment in Iran.

A BRIEF REPRISE OF CONTEMPORARY IRANIAN HISTORY PRODUCING AN ISLAMIC REVOLUTION

The Islamic Republic of Iran was, and remains, a contradictory entity. Brought into being in 1979 by a popular revolution that included diverse class and ideological components, the reins of state power were rapidly Islamicized to produce the world's only theocracy, with a *velayat-e-faqih* (Supreme Jurisprudent) as the religious head of an Islamic polity. Khomeini was, of course, the first, followed by Khamenei, the extant unelected leader. However, alongside this system of religious leadership through the acclaim of the clergy, exists a parallel modern political system of elections and formal political roles. All Iranians over the age of eighteen, including women, who were enfranchised in the 1930s by Reza Shah, elect a president, as well as representatives to the *Majles*, or the Parliament. Political groups and individuals are strictly vetted, with knowledge of Islam being a strong criteria for inclusion, so this political process is orchestrated by the overarching Guardian Council, yet still, the general enfranchisement, growth of political campaigning, strength of political debate, and public eagerness to participate mean that many analysts[3] acknowledge the dual political system and the existence of democratic elements of polity. The films of Bani-Etema'ad, especially *Roozegar-e Ma* (*Our Time*), are vivid explorations of contemporary political desires and imaginative possibilities, when even young women feel able to run for the presidency. However, there is a deep internal struggle for power between the appointed and elected elements, which has become particularly acute under Ahmadinejad's presidency.

Despite this internal power struggle, a chronic economic crisis, an eight-year war with Iraq that produced colossal death, injury, and destruction, a lack of clear and coherent policies, and a very volatile political atmosphere, the Islamic Republic has been a developmentalist state and, since the end of the war with Iraq in 1988, even a "liberalizing" state. The development of basic communications infrastructure, including telecommunication, has been emphasized and developed rapidly. Yet, the policies have been *ad hoc* and contradictory and therefore, the development and expansion of the Internet (as rapid as it has been in the last few years) is constrained by confusion in government policies, varied institutional interests, and above all, the dialectical tension between the imperative of the market and the "revolutionary" claims of the state.

A brief look at the status of telecommunications in Iran demonstrates the rate of expansion and growth. In 1977, the number of fixed telephone lines was only 850,800, a little over 2 percent of the population. Only 312 of the 60,000-plus villages in Iran were connected. The number of public telephone networks was 4,294, with only 82 long-distance-connected points. Three decades later, even including one long decade of war with Iraq that damaged much infrastructure and swallowed the resources of the country, the picture is one of rapid expansion and modernization.

By December 2007, the number of fixed line telephones had increased to 23,560,859, or 32 percent of the population. The number of mobile phones, which stood at just below 60,000 in 1995, has increased to 21,300,098, or about 30 percent of the population. In addition, the number of cities with mobile network coverage has increased from 34 in 1995 to 1,016 in December 2007. All the mobile subscribers are provided with Short Message Service (SMS) facility, and 264,000 were equipped with Voice Mail System (VMS). The international roaming connection with 80 countries (162 operators) has also been established. The number of villages with telephone service has also increased from 312 in 1997 to 52,522 in December 2007. The Telecommunication Company of Iran (TCI) predicts that this number will exceed 62,120 villages by 2009. The TCI also launched 3,668 rural offices in December 2007, which it plans to extend to 10,000 villages. The number of public phone booths has also increased from a mere 4,294 to 186,489.[4]

Internet access in Iran was provided for the first time in 1992 through a single line connecting the Institute for Studies in Theoretical Physics and Mathematics (IPM). The link was through the BITNET network system and Iran's membership in the Trans-European Research and Educational Networking Association.[5] A year later, the private use of modems was permitted. This single line was later expanded and developed further with the allocation by BITNET of 500 Internet protocol addresses to Iran. The main users of the Internet in the early days were academics and research institutions, which had their own connection to IPM. Even in 1993, Iran had no internal data networks. Early in 1993, the High Council of Informatics announced that it was discussing with the TCI the possibility of establishing data communications networks over the country's telephone lines. Lack of investment by the TCI, as well as the absence of any clear and coherent policy, meant that the market was left to itself, and private companies started to form and began to provide international links via lines leased by the TCI. In 1995, fearful of losing control over its monopoly in telecommunication, the government started both clamping down on private Internet service providers (ISPs) and improving its own data communication network.[6] Since then, the Iranian state has taken steps to expand and develop the required infrastructure[7]. According to the same report, the number of offices established to provide ICT services in rural areas has increased rapidly, and the TCI estimates that their number will increase to over 1,000 by 2010.

As a result, the number of people with access to the Internet has shown a rapid rise. By 1996, the number of people with access to the Internet was 2,000, and their usage was mostly limited to sending and receiving e-mails; this number increased to 48,000 in 1999. Since 2000, the increase in the number of Internet users has been significant: 132,000 users in 2000, 418,000 users in 2001, and finally, 1,326,000 in 2002.[8] A 2003 report suggested that the number of Internet users was seven million, although only half of these users have regular access.[9] By the end of 2006, according to the Ministry of Communication, 11 million had access to Internet, a 50 percent increase from the previous year.[10] The TCI expects that the number of users will reach twenty-five million by 2009.[11]

INTERNET IN IRAN: NEW TECHNOLOGY, OLD PROBLEMS

However, in Iran as elsewhere, access to media in general, and the Internet in particular, is regulated above all by disposable income. Because of the high-tech boycott and lack of investment in importing hardware[12] the cheapest computer in Iran costs around 4,500,000 Rials, or $450. Despite this, some reports suggest that hardware equipment was a profitable part of the country's ICT market, bringing a 25 percent annual income growth for hardware companies. Around 730 companies (yet another indication of persistence of petty production in Iran) are active in the hardware field, with an estimated value of $1200 million.[13] The average cost of Internet access is 350,000 Rials ($35.00) per month, and this does not include telephone line rentals. Iranians pay more for Internet access than Americans and Europeans, although the average annual urban household income is only 25,831,527 Rials ($2,583.00), and for rural households,15,200,149 Rials ($1,520.00).[14]

The cost of Internet access in general is linked to the density of a country's Internet population and the distance from the main servers. The politics of bandwidth and the very fact that the United States operates as the hub of Internet traffic, means countries must make payments for traffic exchanges and connectivity to international telecommunication carriers. For this reason, the cost of Internet access in developed countries is lower than the rest of the world. According to one early estimate, 1 Mpbs ADSL connection in London costs £80. For the same connection in Iran, the cost is a staggering £9,200.[15] In Iran, a computer costs twice the "average" monthly salary in urban areas and three times the "average" monthly salary in rural areas. In real terms, however, the cost is even higher. A better comparative measure of cost is purchasing power parity (PPP), which is:

> a rate of exchange that accounts for price differences across countries, allowing international comparison of real output and incomes . . . PPP US$1 has the same purchasing power in the domestic economy as $1 has in the United States.[16]

The PPP price of a computer is about 2,250$, access to the Internet from a netcafé costs 3.5$ per hour, a dial-up connection used by many in Iran costs 1$ per hour, and the price of using Asymmetric Digital Subscriber Line (ADSL) featuring 128–512 kpbs is around 1,200$ per month.[17] Such conditions price the Internet out of reach of the majority. The realities of the media markets in Iran illustrate further polarization of media consumers between urban and rural areas, between Tehran and smaller cities, and of course between those with differing levels of disposable income. The share of income/consumption of the poorest 30 percent in Iran is just 7.1 percent, while the "share" of the richest 30 percent is 83.6 percent.[18] In Iran, as in the rest of the world, access to communication resources is regulated through price mechanisms, and the current cost of Internet access remains a primary obstacle to wider use of the Internet.

CONTRADICTORY POLICIES AND INSTITUTIONAL INTERESTS

Besides the harsh economic realities of Iran, a number of other factors have prevented the more rapid penetration of the Internet. First of all, there is the well-known tension between the United States and Iran, and the effect of the United States embargo. As Arabshahi suggests, the embargo

> made the acquisition and maintenance of powerful servers, workstations, and satellite communication equipment difficult, if not impossible in certain cases.[19]

In addition, in the early stages of the development of the Internet in Iran, the political tension between Iran and the United States made an impact on the free flow of information between the two countries, despite the fact that the embargo did not include exchange of text. For that reason, the

US academic sites (on NSFNET) were not even recognizing Iranian IP addresses for telnet/ftp access. This problem resurfaced in 1996 only to be put swiftly to rest through the efforts of many people and organizations in the US, Europe, and Iran (including IPM, and the Electronic Frontier Foundation), who brought pressure on NSF to correct the situation.[20]

Access to the Internet is not altogether a national matter, since the United States, in hosting about 80 percent of Internet sites, is the undisputed gatekeeper of the so-called "superhighway." In addition to the difficulties of acquiring machinery and software (where Iran increasingly relies on Asia), Iran's Internet access to the United States can be blocked. Yet, despite clear tension between the two countries as well as American sanctions, Iranian companies and institutions are ready, as are American companies, to establish ventures through an intermediary. One notable example is the Data Communication Company of Iran's (DCI) agreement with GulfSat Kuwait (a joint venture between the Kuwaiti government and Hughes Network System of the United Sates). In addition, two of the early ISPs in Iran, *Virayeshgar* and *Pars Supaleh,* represented the American companies 3Com and AT&T, respectively. Many of the deals with American companies are done through their subsidiaries and joint ventures in Europe and Asia.[21] However, American embargoes prohibit software companies, such as Microsoft, from doing business in Iran, a factor that contributes to widespread software piracy in the country, and is helped by the fact that Iran is not a signatory to international copyright conventions.[22] Ironically, the software that the state uses to monitor and censor Internet participation is pirated from the United States.

The second crucial aspect of the development of the Internet in Iran is the competing agendas and conflicting interests within Iran's state apparatus. The Islamic state that came to power after 1979 defined itself predominantly in a "cultural" sense. The two aims of the cultural policy of the new state were based on destruction of an imposed "Western" and "alien" culture, and its replacement with a dignified, indigenous, and authentic Islamic culture, which they claimed had declined under the previous monarchical regime. As a result of such broad cultural aims, the state began to develop a whole range of institutions to implement and safeguard the "Islamic" culture of Iran.

The Supreme Council of the Cultural Revolution, established as early as 1980, was to oversee general cultural policy. Various other organizations were assigned the task of implementing such policies. The Ministry of Culture and Islamic Guidance was given the specific tasks of managing and running the press, the Iranian News Agency, as well as charities and religious endowments. Iranian Broadcasting—that is Islamic Republic of Iran Broadcasting (IRIB)—was brought under the direct control of the Supreme Leader in 1989. Two major Iranian publishing firms (*Keyhan* and *Etela'at*), which control and publish a number of newspapers and periodicals, became "public property," and were put under the control of both the

Ministry of Culture and Islamic Guidance and the representatives of the Supreme Leader. Telecommunications were put firmly under the control of the state through the TCI, a branch of the Ministry of Post, Telegraph and Telephone.

Since 1979, the media has been one of the key points of contestation under the Islamic Republic. As part of the program of controlled modernization, the Islamic Republic restricted private ownership in all aspects of Iran's communication system, except for the press. The Iranian state controls the rest of the media through legislation and nonlegal ploys: from providing subsidies, the passing of different acts, using the Constitution and the Press Law, and by setting up a variety of regulatory bodies. As Siavoshi points out, the plurality of these institutions subjected cultural developments and policies to power struggles among many factions within the state:

> Although every faction declared its commitment to Islamic cultural ideals, all consensus vanished when it came to the question of what these ideals were and which policies were required to achieve them.[23]

Friction and the competition between various factions of the regime, the institutional interests of various agencies involved in the process, and ultimately, the tension within the state as well as between the state and private sectors, is one of the many faces of the "digital divide" in Iran. Such tensions clearly illustrate the social dimension of the Internet. In particular, the concerns of the private sector and the "moderate" factions of the Iranian establishment echo recent global debates about the Internet as profoundly democratizing and competitive. Yet, the dominant conservative faction of the Islamic Republic, much like other authoritarian regimes, has been quick to try to limit the potential of the technology and to utilize it for its own benefit. Both sides of the divide do indeed present a highly political account of the role of communication technologies. If the private sector and advocates of "civil society" in Iran subscribe to the "common sense" view of the Internet as inherently decentralizing, democratic, progressive, and therefore unsuitable for public ownership, the Conservatives' agencies and officials regard it as a threat to their interests and future. What is at the center of the debate is the very institutional and technological structure of Iran's rapidly expanding communications, and the dispute over the definition of "public interest."

While the Islamic Republic of Iran (IRI) officially encourages the use of the Internet,[24] the issues of access, control, and content remain controversial and have prompted many to argue that the external as well as internal "wariness have hindered the importation of technology tools and slowed the integration of technical tools in daily lifestyles."[25] Despite the fact that the earliest effort to connect Iran to the Internet was made by IPM, the commercial imperatives and motives, as well as the desire for effective control of the

Internet, has meant that the government has taken the leading role in providing Internet access and services. As Rahimi suggests, the tension in the early 1990s between various agencies, including the DCI (a branch of the Ministry for Post, Telegraph and Telephone), the High Council of Information (HCI), and IPM were over the quality and availability of network access.[26]

Lack of resources, expertise, and clear policies, as well as the commitment to privatization, has meant that for a few years, especially after 1997 (with growing public access to the Internet), the private sector began to dominate the market. With more than 100 private ISPs and the increased use of low cost "Voice Over IP" (VOIP), popular among those with relatives abroad, revenues of the state-owned TCI were hit severely. In early 2000, as cyber-cafés (*cafenet*) began to mushroom in big cities competing with each other and the TCI, prices began to plummet, especially when some cafés began to offer "economy" or "saver" packages of ten- to twenty-hour blocks of Internet access. This forced the TCI to reduce the cost of international calls to avoid further losses.[27] According to a report by BBCPersian.com,[28] the TCI reported a $20 million profit in 1998, but in 2002, despite the staggering threefold increase in the number of people with access to telephone lines in this period, the TCI reported a loss of $32 million. Private Internet and telephone providers were blamed for this loss. The use of VOIP service became widespread, despite limited penetration of the Internet, simply because of the growing number of Internet cafés across the country.

Musavi Shafaee[29] suggests that, in 2000, there were no Internet cafés in Iran. Two years later, around seven thousand to eight thousand such establishments had mushroomed in Tehran alone. While the government has intervened at times, closing more than four hundred Internet cafés in Tehran in May 2001, cybercafés still offer easy access to the Internet in major cities, although the costs are still way above the average monthly wage.

Matters are further complicated by the dispute over policies and institutional responsibilities. Mostafa Mohammadi, managing director of Parnham (a private ISP), in an interview with the daily newspaper, *Hambastegi*, pointed at such confusion and tension:

> Right now IRIB [Islamic Republic of Iran Broadcasting] believes itself to be in charge of the Internet because it believes that it is a media. Also on the other hand, the Telecommunication Company, the Ministry of Culture and the Islamic Guidance as well as the Intelligence Ministry believe themselves to be responsible for the Internet, whereas none of these institutions have the power to support the Internet.[30]

The state-owned and controlled broadcaster IRIB has tried to influence state policies on the Internet. Hated by many, including reformist officials, for its constant campaign against intellectuals, students, women activists, and the reformist press, IRIB is one of the key political actors in Iran. In an interview with the now defunct reformist daily, *Norouz*, the then Minister of Communications and Modern Technology, Ahmad Moatamedi, responded to the question of whether IRIB sponsored Internet development by saying:

> We are strongly opposed to this measure of the IRIB. Their activities must be within the limits of the radio and television organization. Establishing two-way communications is among the duties of the Communications Ministry. In all bylaws (so far approved) all these duties have been entrusted to the Communications Ministry. Of course there are certain people who hold contrary views but we are fully opposed to this. Nothing has been approved to the effect that the IRIB can function like a ministry.[31]

He was proved wrong, as one of those "certain people who hold contrary views" was the Supreme Leader, Ayatollah Khamenei, who in a decree not only disappointed the private sector by putting the Internet under the control of the state, but reserved a role for IRIB in all policy-making decisions on the Internet.

The Internet also reveals, once again, the existence of many contradictory institutions, policies, and competing interests within the Islamic Republic. As we have suggested, by providing cheaper forms of communication, and especially much cheaper telephone connections that are especially popular among those with relatives abroad, the Internet has seriously threatened the state monopoly on long-distance calls. But more importantly, as broadcasting inside Iran remains a tightly-controlled state monopoly, and as one reformist and semi-independent newspaper after another is banned, more and more people—including publishers, writers, journalists, and ordinary readers—are turning to the Internet for information, debate, and as a platform for expression of concerns and discontent. News websites have proliferated, as have sites about technology, music, sports, entertainment, women's issues, and student matters.

Weblogs have become the most significant area of Internet growth. What initially started in September 2000 via Persian instructions posted by a young Iranian blogger has grown into a massive collective phenomenon, sometimes estimated to include around 700,000 blogs, making Persian one of the leading languages in the blogosphere, and increasing the share of Persian material online. A combination of factors paved the way for such a rapid growth of the blogosphere. These include the disabling factionalism of the central Iranian state and the ongoing conflicts between Islamism and Republicanism, the intense pressure from private capital in Iran (which for so long relied on the mediation of the state to exercise class domination) seeking a larger share in the expanding and lucrative cultural industries, and above all, the existence of an already dissatisfied young population challenging the Iranian state and actively seeking a new order. As a result, weblog service providers in Iran (weblog farms) have emerged as part of the economic liberalization in Iran's communication industries. Companies such as persianblog and blogfa have become leading and recognized online brand names in new media in Iran, and provide a range of services. Iranian sites and blogs have become new sources of information on various aspects of public life in the country, and provide a strong link between activists and intellectuals in Iran and the opposition abroad.

Elsewhere,[32] we have offered a rebuttal both to the simplistic argument to be found in Alavi's[33] book that all activity in the blogosphere is necessarily antistatist and emancipatory, but also to the stark divide that consigns religious figures and practices simply to the space of "tradition." It is not only "oppositional" politics of various kinds that find a presence in the Persian blogosphere. Some parts of the regime have actively embraced e-development, so that the Islamic Republic has a large presence online. Some of the formal politics of the regime have migrated to the web, with a great many government departments, public statistics, and material also available on the web, and some government officials have also started their own blog. One of the best-known and celebrated of such blogs is found at www.webnevesht.com, and is written by Mohammad Ali Abtahi, one of Iran's six vice presidents during Khatami's presidency. His site consists of daily articles and diaries, well-kept and extensive archives, articles about him in other media, interviews, and photographs. He pokes fun at himself, the government, friends, and especially his conservative rivals (one photograph shows a leading conservative journalist picking his nose). Proud of his latest mobile phone, he uses it to take pictures of his colleagues in informal situations and his trips abroad, including one to Venice. He writes commentary on cultural issues, including the controversial movie, *The Lizard*, and regularly criticizes any crackdown on weblogs and the Internet. Indeed, from early on, the Internet in general, and weblogs in particular, have been regarded as so influential that not only could the government no longer ignore them, but it began to endorse them to some extent, too. The Internet played a key role in the 2005 elections, with all candidates having their own dedicated sites/blogs, and many religious institutions and agencies have deemed it necessary to establish an online presence. A report by Mehdi Khalji in August 2005[34] went as far as to call the holy city of Qom the "IT Capital of Iran."[35]

Abtahi's blog is one of the few that contain no links to other bloggers, which raises an interesting question about whether blogs are simply individualized phenomena or part of a wider collective process. Much of the brouhaha about blogging in the West focuses on the massive desire for individual expression and global presentation of self that would have given Goffman sleepless nights; yet, even these are increasingly hosted by major weblog providers and many contain more links than material[36] to produce a more evident collective phenomenon. Undoubtedly, many Persian blogs are individual-centered, and express the aspirations, thoughts, and sentiments of individual bloggers.

Hossein Drakhshan's aptly named blog, Editor:Myself,[37] indicates the importance of an individual taking control over content and finding their own voice, free of editors (although it could be said that there are almost as many "editors" as there are bloggers). Many are locations for the presentation of individual lives, with family photos, love poems, laments about failed relationships, whimsy and wit, and all the accoutrements of bourgeois individualism that can be found on British or American blogger sites. But even the least-popular blogs are no longer about individuals as such, since even the most private and anonymous blogs have become part of a wider community of interests through the addition—and the significance of—links. Increasingly, there is a clear and visible sense of connections and networks among Persian bloggers, and there are trends toward establishing a sense of solidarity, camaraderie, and belonging. Thus, while weblogs are one of the most individual and private forms of expression in public space, there are visible trends toward collective efforts in producing a weblog, as well as the creation, through linkages, of networks of friends, professional colleagues, sympathizers, and other relevant blogs and sites.

One site, tahsilat.webialist.com, was created in order to introduce student blogs, and has compiled a list of more than seven hundred weblogs written and maintained by students. A feminist site, womeniniran.net, provides a rich list of more than one hundred women bloggers in Iran, some of whom are producing powerful critical observations on public life in Iran. This site has added a new section, "From Weblogs," and, in addition to existing links, has announced that it will provide links to any posted materials on blogs that deal with women's issues. It aims to provide a platform for wider coverage of "individual and independent voices," as well as contribute to the diversity and richness of the womeniniran site.

Creating collective blogs has become so popular that weblog service providers have announced that, as part of their services, they will cater to bloggers who intend to work as a group. Defining "collective" blogs, however, is as difficult as defining the blog itself. This is an evolving process and a movement that is just beginning to take shape, and it is important to watch this development. Undoubtedly, and as Saidabadi[38]—one of the founders of the collective blog, hanouz.com—has suggested, one of the key features of collective blogs is the speed in updating the blog and presenting new material and postings. Providing relevant information and analysis on a regular basis is a daunting task for individual bloggers, especially for those with a full-time job outside the blogosphere. Most weblog service providers terminate their services to bloggers if they fail to update, and usually "auction" the space to new clients. Since collective blogs rely on the commitment of more than one individual, they not only keep the blog running and lively, but by doing so, maintain their visitors.

However, collective blogs are more than just a pragmatic and practical solution to avoid losing visitors and web space. They provide a platform for more diverse sets of arguments, opinions, and analysis. This, as Saidabadi suggests, creates circles that can open up spaces for dialogue between bloggers and their readers. The highly individualized Iranian blogosphere has been the target of serious criticism. Daruish Ashuri, a well-known Iranian writer, has argued (somewhat ironically, it must be said, by posting on his own blog[39]) that the volume of bad, rushed, and ill-conceived opinions and ideas that are posted on thousands of blogs can be regarded as nothing but a sad waste of the time, energy, and intellectual abilities of many young Iranians. He argues that this is especially dangerous for a nation that needs to produce its own knowledge and develop its own ideas. Ashuri's own site is part of another circle, *halegheh malakut*,[40] which describes itself as "a collection of weblogs with diverse identity intended to produce critique, dialogue, and friendship." It also describes itself as a decentralized network, where the only condition of membership is accepting the rights and freedoms of individuals, respecting pluralism, and freedom of speech. Currently, this circle contains thirty-nine individual blogs, including a few in English.

The Internet has become the latest tool to offer alternative news channels to Iranian activists inside Iran, and much needed international support and solidarity, including from some Iranians living in exile. The battle to control the Internet, therefore, cannot be separated from the broader social movements and political concerns that produce the very contradictory developments and the ongoing conflict between "accelerations" and "breaks" in the Islamic Republic.

INTERNET POLICY AND CONTROL

The dominant faction's response to the Internet has been twofold. Firstly, they have recognized the usefulness of the Internet as a tool for propaganda and furthering their policies and aims. In that respect, they have embraced technology, and there are now many conservative websites, which challenge the more critical ones. The most fascinating examples come from religious centers in the holy cities of Qom and Mashhad, where websites are designed and launched to promote Islam and the teachings and values of the Islamic Republic. In one computer center in Qom, more than 2,000 Islamic texts were transferred onto CD-ROM, and later onto the Internet.[41] Sheikh Ali Korani, director of the center, argued that the Internet is a reality and Iran must learn to live with it: "Take a knife, for example. You can use it in the kitchen or you can use it to commit crimes."[42] This new technology, as Rahimi has suggested, allows the clergy to spread Islam and provide their own *tafsir* (interpretation). Official Internet cafés have been launched to tackle "alien" and "decadent" Western culture and provide a "safer" environment for religious Internet users.

Besides the attempt to colonize the Internet with their own materials, including news and analysis, the conservatives have tried to block access, as well as censor undesirable content. In addition to regular crackdowns on

Internet cafés, a number of web journalists, users, and bloggers have been arrested. According to BBCPersian.com, the DCI has spent more than 70 billion Rials ($70 million) on censoring the Internet in Iran. Another report by the BBC announced that a list of 15,000 sites had been drawn up by the government in 2003 and was sent to all Iranian ISPs for blocking.[43]

In May 2001, in an announcement entitled, "Overall policies on computer-based information-providing networks," the Supreme Leader, Ali Khamenei, put the state in charge of encouraging the use and development of the Internet, and reserved a big slice for IRIB, contrary to the initial plan for wider participation of the private sector and investment. He urged the government to "make access to the global information-providing networks only through authorized entities."[44] Following his direct instructions, the High Council of Cultural Revolution (which has no constitutional powers to issue a ruling on the Internet or other matters) contradicted its own previous policy, announced a year before, and passed a resolution regarding the regulation of the Internet.[45] In this document, published in November 2001 and announced on state-owned IRIB, the council ruled that, notwithstanding an emphasis on free access of people to information and facilitating free flow of information, Internet connections would be a state monopoly, and all connectivity would be provided through the TCI. Even though government organizations are required to get the permission of the HCI to connect independently from the TCI, IRIB was exempted from seeking HCI permission to broadcast their programs on the Internet. Applications for access provision would be assessed by the Ministry of Post, Telephone and Telegraph and the Ministry of Intelligence. In addition, the document required all access providers to prevent access to immoral or political websites, and to make available the data banks of their users' activity to the Ministry of Post, Telephone and Telegraph, which could be handed to the Ministry of Intelligence upon request.

As for the ISPs, the document states that the permission of the Ministry of Post, Telephone and Telegraph is needed to provide VOIP. The rest of the document deals with conditions, quality, and objectives of the ISPs, and is very similar to the existing repressive Press Law, one of the key reasons for the six-day students' revolt in the summer of 1999 in objection to the closure of a reformist daily newspaper, *Salaam*. Section B of the document states that the managers of the ISP companies have to be: Iranian citizens and committed to the Islamic Republic Constitution; at least twenty-five years old; free of incapacity, bankruptcy by fraud, or guilt; free of moral corruption and criminal conviction; a believer in one of the recognized faiths in the Constitution; and finally, not a member of illegal and "anti-revolutionary" organizations.

The ISPs, similar to the limits on the press in the Press Law, must desist from:

* publishing any atheistic articles/issues and items that undermine the Islamic Republic, Islam, and the teaching of Khomeini, and

are against the unity of the country, its constitutions, and its Islamic values;
* creating discord between and among social groups;
* encouraging acts against the security of the country;
* propagating luxury;
* publishing obscene and religiously forbidden articles and pictures;
* disclosing information;
* creating any broadcasting networks without the control of the IRIB.

Similar rules and limits are also duly listed in Section C dealing with Internet cafés. The only major difference is that those applying for a license to run an Internet café are required (in addition to the conditions listed for managers of ISP companies) to have finished their military service, be at least thirty years old, and married. One can only guess that the inclusion of marital commitment as a condition for Internet café owners is yet another indication of the paranoia over the perceived immoral dangers that are associated with the Internet.

In each *Ostan* (province), a committee consisting of representatives of the Telecommunication Company, the Office of Culture and Islamic Guidance, a district attorney, Internet cafés' official guilds, and a representative of IRIB will control the activities of Internet cafés. The committee's decision regarding any violations of the Internet law is final. In a separate announcement, the duty of observing all Internet-related matters at a national level was given to a committee of three members. According to Ali Kaynejad, spokesman for the High Council of Cultural Revolution, this committee will consist of a representative from the Council, a minister for Post, Telephone and Telegraph, and the Managing Director of IRIB.[46]

This resolution and subsequent announcement was yet another indication of the dilemma of the Islamic Republic, which is caught between the need for liberalization and its "revolutionary" claims. Both IRIB (threatened by satellite channels and calls for the introduction of private channels) and the TCI (threatened by the private sector) not only kept their grip on their respected fields, but were also given further opportunity to influence the development of the Internet in Iran. Iran's ISP Association (one of the newly established institutions of "civil society") criticized the decision requiring them to provide Internet access through the TCI.

Although these measures have not been strictly observed or implemented, various attempts have been made to control the Internet. With the help of the IRIB, the regime has gathered lists of hundreds of websites deemed un-Islamic, antirevolutionary, and immoral.[47] In addition to filtering a number of allegedly pornographic and immoral sites, a number of political and oppositional websites, including legal reformist sites, such as rouydad.ws and emrooz.ws, some news sites located outside Iran, such as BBCPersian. com on occasion, and all oppositional parties in exile were blocked. Recent legislation in place since 2001 intends to block those dissident voices that had found the web a useful way to get around Iran's repressive Press Law.

According to Iran Civil Society Organizations (CSO) Training and Research Center,[48] there are two layers and three methods of Internet censorship in Iran. In the first instance, the Internet in Iran is controlled and censored via access service points that remain the monopoly of the TCI. A recent report by Opennet Initiative[49] argues that Iran, along with China, is among a small group of states with the most sophisticated state-mandated filtering systems in the world. Iran and many other countries use the commercial filtering package SmartFilter—made by the US-based company, Secure Computing—as the primary technical engine of its filtering system. The second layer of control, as we have already argued, is the government regulation, which forces ICPs and ISPs to use filtering systems, take notice of regulation, and update themselves with the lists of banned sites provided by authorities. Delegating censorship to ISPs and obliging them to filter sites deemed "corrupt" and "un-Islamic" (which, ironically, includes many news sites run and maintained by factions *within* the Iranian state) allows the state to share the blame with companies and small businesses, such as Internet café owners.

In addition to these two main layers, the government also uses three known methods of censorship. One method is to close all ports that have been used by savvy Internet users to bypass filtering systems. In the past few years, Internet users have managed to break through the existing filtering system by using proxy servers. But since 2004, the committees set up to control and monitor the Internet (Committee in charge of determination of unauthorized websites) have provided ISPs with regular lists of proxy servers and have asked them to block and filter these servers. Another method is censoring keywords in URLs, yet another obligation that ICPs and ISPs have to meet. For example, many Iranians still use prepaid cards to access the Internet in Iran, but the cards are designed so that searching for words such as "women," "birth," or "sex" while using search engines such as Google is impossible. It matters not if the search is related to science, history, or literature. The banning of "women" in particular generated a campaign supported by many bloggers that employed the slogan, "censorship is indecent, not women." Using filtering systems also reduces the speed of Internet access. But in addition to and despite official approval of ADSL by the government, high-speed Internet remains a dream instead of reality, as the current speed of ADSL in Iran is less than 144 kps. Most Internet users still use dial-up services due to the limited availability and cost of broadband. Iran CSO's Training and Research Center believes that this is yet another form of censorship and another method used by the government to restrict access to the Internet. This organization suggests that increased availability of broadband will jeopardize the state monopoly in broadcasting. And, of course, such controls have spawned their opposite: an active and industrious hacker community that delights in creatively circumventing the controls that the regime erects.

CONCLUSION

"Internet Studies" throws up a number of questions and debates about the entanglement between media and society. Two significant questions revolve around the problem of access/social inequality and the nature of political participation and whether the new media has solved (or is capable of solving) some of the old problems. Undoubtedly the notion of "the Internet" remains problematic, not least because the singularity of "the Internet," as Livingston[50] reminds us, suppresses the diversity of technologies imbedded in "new media," as well as differential access (both socially and geographically) and different policies, and responses it has generated across the world.

In this chapter, we located the expansion of the Internet in Iran in its wider social context and, while we recognized the realities of digital divides and the fact that Iran is lagging behind some of its richer regional neighbors, we suggested that limited access and usage only tells part of a more complex story of communicative experiences in Iran. Internet use has started to challenge the state monopoly not only over long-distance telephone calls, but also as a channel of political and cultural communication. In the absence of genuinely free political parties, regular clampdown on the semi-independent press and the total control of broadcasting, the Internet has come to the fore as a space for various alternative political and cultural voices, and has created a strong link between activists inside and outside Iran. This chapter examined this trend in detail, with particular reference to individual and collective voices and the Iranian state's response to control this diverse and vibrant public space.

As we have tried to demonstrate, the fairly rapid Internet development in Iran has been enacted amid political, economic, and cultural contestation at both the national and international levels.

Internationally, US sanctions and Iranian avoidance of copyright legislation have their impacts. Internally, the state has faced different kinds of contestation. These include competition between the burgeoning cultural and communication industries of the private sector; by public demands for greater political and cultural openness, expressed most vehemently by intellectuals, women, and students (not mutually exclusive categories!); and by creative uses of these new technologies by those collectivities and others. Like China, the very dynamics of Iranian control bring it condemnation from within and from without, Amnesty's 2006 campaign being an example of the latter. And yet, the central paradox remains that, despite a top-heavy and controlling state, Iran enjoys a vibrant Persian-language cyberspace that is far more eclectic and disputatious than might be imagined. The realities of "digital divides" in Iran also suggests that, rather than seeing the relation between state and religion in terms of theological (ideological) consideration of the *ulema* (religious scholars), we need to acknowledge crucial institutional interests of divided *ulema* and the continuing struggle to claim the monopoly of economic capital and the means of symbolic violence. New technologies have to be studied within specific and complex skeins of political, economic, and social issues, as the case of Iran vividly shows.

NOTES

1. See Middle East Internet Users, http://www.Internetworldstats.com/stats5. htm#me, (accessed December 20, 2006).
2. Chantal Mouffe, interview by Nico Carpentier and Bart Cammaerts, "Hegemony, Democracy, Agonism and Journalism," *Journalism Studies* 7, no. 6 (2006): 964–975.
3. Ahmad Ashraf and Ali Banuazizi, "Iran's Tortuous Path Toward 'Islamic Liberalism'," *International Journal of Politics, Culture and Society* 15, no. 2 (2001): 237–256; Said Amir Arjomand, "Civil Society and the Rule of Law in the Constitutional Politics of Iran Under Khatami," *Social Research* 67, no. 2 (2000): 283–301; Charles Kurzman, "Critics Within: Islamic Scholars Protests Against the Islamic State in Iran," *International Journal of Politics, Culture and Society* 15, no. 2 (2001): 341–359.
4. "Performance Report: Telecommunication Company of Iran, December 2007," http://irantelecom.ir/pdfs/amar/gozaresh_2007.PDF (accessed February 29, 2008).
5. Payman Arabshahi, "The Internet in Iran: A Survey," www.iranian.com/ WebGuide/InternetIran (1997).
6. Grey Burkhart, "National Security and the Internet in the Persian Gulf Region," http://www.georgetown.edu/research/arabtech/pgi98-4.html (1998).
7. http://irantelecom.ir/eng.asp?sm=35&page=17&code=5
8. Mousavi Shafaee, "Globalization and Contradiction Between the Nation and the State in Iran: The Internet Case," *Critique* 12, no. (2003): 189–195.
9. http://news.gooya.com/technology/archives/2003/10/000045
10. http://www.bbc.co.uk/persian/iran/story/2007/02/070209_oh_Internet_itc. shtml
11. Opennet Initiative, "Internet Filtering in Iran 2004–2005," www.opennetinitiative.net.iran
12. http://www.ilna.ir/shownews.asp?code=216328&code1=20
13. http://www.systemgroup.net/web/en/itnews.aspx
14. The "average" annual income of course suppresses the harsh realities of Iran even further by inflating real wages and obscuring the fact that many Iranian families are on incomes of less than $50 per month.
15. www.ksajadi.com/IranLinks2.html
16. "A Report on the Status of the Internet in Iran," http://www.genderit. org/upload/ad6d215b74e2a8613f0cf5416c9f3865/A_Report_on_Internet_ Access_in_Iran_2_.pdf
17. GenderIT.org, www.genderit.org
18. UNDP, "Human Development Report 2005," 271 http://hdr.undp.com/en/ reports/global/hds2005/
19. Arabshahi, "The Internet in Iran."
20. Ibid.
21. The MOSAIC Group, "The Global Diffusion of Internet: Iran," http:// mosaic.unomaha.edu/GDI1998/7CIRAN.PDF (1998).
22. Ben Hammersley, "Iran Nets Another Revolt," *The Guardian,* February 21, 2002, http://technology.guardian.co.uk/online/story/0,3605,653282,00. html

23. Sussan Siavoshi, "Cultural Policies and the Islamic Republic: Cinema and Book Publication," *International Journal of Middle East Studies* 29 (1997): 513.
24. Babak Rahimi, "Cyberdissent: The Internet in Revolutionary Iran," *Middle East Review of International Affairs* 7, no. 3 (2003): 101–115; Farhang Rouhani, "The Spatial Politics of Leisure: Internet Use and Access in Tehran, Iran," http://nmit.georgetown.edu/papers/frouhani.htm
25. Laleh Ebrahimian, "Socio-Economic Development in Iran through Information and Communications Technologies," *Middle East Journal* 57, no. 1 (2003): 93–111.
26. Rahimi, "Cyberdissent," 102.
27. Ebrahimian, "Socio-Economic Development in Iran," 102.
28. BBCPersian, http://www.bbc.co.uk/persian/science/030510_h-banned-sites.shtml (accessed December 12, 2006).
29. Shafaee, "Globalization and Contradiction," 194.
30. "Iran Will Have 1,326,000 Internet Users in 2002," *Hambastegi*, 7.
31. B. Ahmadi, "Internet, Mobile and Satellite in Iran," *Norouz*, September 27, 2001, 10.
32. Annabelle Sreberny and Gholam Khiabany, "Becoming Intellectuals: The Blogistan and Public Political Space in the Islamic Republic," *British Journal of Middle Eastern Studies*, 34, no. 3 (2007): 267-286.
33. Nasrin Alavi, *We are Iran* (Washington, D.C.: Soft Skull Press, 2005).
34. http://www.bbc.co.uk/persian/iran/story/2005/08/050802_mj-mkhalaji-Internet-qom.shtml
35. President Ahmadinejad has also joined the long list of officials with their own blogs: http://www.ahmadinejad.ir/
36. A much-celebrated Persian blog, http://z8un.com/, has listed more than 350 blogs/sites under the title of *dostan* (friends).
37. Editor: Myself. Hossein Derakhshan's Weblog, http://www.hoder.com/
38. BBCPersian, http://www.bbc.co.uk/persian/iran/story/2004/11/041114_mj-asa-iran-web-logs-anniv.shtml
39. http://ashouri.malakut.org/archives/005873.shtml (accessed March 20, 2006).
40. Malakut.org, http://www.malakut.org/
41. Rahimi, "Cyberdissent."
42. CNN, "Islam, Iran and the Internet," www.cnn.com/WORLD/9705/22/iran.tech (1997).
43. See Stop Censoring Us: Watching Internet Censorship in Iran, http://stop.censoring.us/
44. www.genderit.org
45. Full text of the document is available at www.iranispassociation.com/ete-laiye/mosavabeh1.htm [in Farsi].
46. IT Iran, "A Committee of High Council of Cultural Revolution Will Supervise the Internet," www.itiran.com.news (December 19, 2002).
47. For the latest list of censored sites, see "A Censored Network: Iranian Social, Political and Religious Sites," http://www.govcom.org/maps/censorship/GCO_Maps_set_censorship_final.pdf
48. www.genderit.org
49. Opennet Initiative, "Internet Filtering in Iran."
50. Sonia Livingston "Critical Debates in Internet Studies: Reflections on an Emerging Field," in *Mass Media and Society*, 4th ed., ed. James Curran and Michael Gurevitch (London: Arnold, 2005), 9-20.

Part IV

Asian Cybercultures

14 Internet, Internet Culture, and Internet Communities of Korea
Overview and Research Directions

Seunghyun Yoo

INTRODUCTION

South Korea[1] is undeniably one of the most advanced countries in the world regarding the wide availability and use of information technology (IT). In less than two decades, the Internet and Internet culture has become a part of most Koreans' daily lives. Korea's IT advancement has occurred at an alarming speed indeed, outrunning the thirty-year rule, which states that it takes about thirty years for a new idea to be adopted and to settle in.[2] Research on Korean Internet communities and Internet culture is growing, particularly regarding blogs and other sole-authored media on the Internet. Even with the growth in research, however, it is challenging to keep up with the speed of advancement and changes in IT, Internet communities, and their cultures. Furthermore, most research on the Korean Internet is published in Korean and thus has limited opportunities to be shared worldwide. Therefore, this chapter aims to introduce the current trends in Korean Internet communities, culture, and research.

This chapter also recommends the need for more "community capacity" research into online communities. Community capacity is a well-established concept that is frequently applied to community development and betterment in conventional community health sciences. It has, however, rarely been applied to studies of Internet communities. This chapter attempts to outline how community capacity research can illuminate aspects of Internet communities, particularly in the Korean context.

INTERNET CULTURE AND COMMUNITY IN KOREA

Korea is a world leader in terms of high-speed Internet availability and accessibility. Among 30 member countries of the Organization for Economic Co-operation and Development (OECD), Korea ranks high in the category of broadband penetration per 100 inhabitants,[3] topping many other developed countries, including the United States, Canada, and Japan (Table 14.1.). In fact, Korea ranked even higher in the early 2000s, and is still the leading country among those with larger population sizes.

Table 14.1 Broadband Subscribers per 100 Inhabitants (OECD, June 2006)

Rank	Countries	Subscribers/ 100	Total Subscribers	Rank—Dec. 2005
1	Denmark	29.3	1,590,539	4
2	Netherlands	28.8	4,705,829	3
3	Iceland	27.3	80,672	1
4	Korea	26.4	12,770,911	2
5	Switzerland	26.2	1,945,358	5
9	Canada	22.4	7,161,872	8
12	USA	19.2	56,502,351	12
13	Japan	19.0	24,217,012	11

Source: OECD Broadband Statistics to June 2006.[4]

About a quarter of Korean residents are broadband subscribers, and over 60 percent of the population of 48 million own wireless Internet-capable mobile phones.[5] This IT power of Korea is a combined result of state-of-the-art infrastructure, led by technology-savvy Korean people, and government policy. Indeed, Korea was reported to have the best e-government in the world in a Brown University study.[6] The IT industry represented 15 percent of the gross domestic product of Korea in 2005.[7] Almost three-quarters of the population live in seven major cities that are dense with high-rise apartment complexes equipped with high-speed Internet lines.[8]

Koreans are online for 13.3 hours a week, and Internet use by older adults is on the rise.[9] According to the National Internet Development Agency of Korea (NIDA), information searching (80.4 percent) and e-mailing (80.9 percent) are the main reasons for using the Internet. More Koreans use the Internet to participate in blogs and mobile-enabled personal home pages known as "mini-hompys" (85.5 percent), online groups and communities (77.8 percent), and online shopping (71.3 percent) than in games (47.5 percent), listening to music (44.3 percent), and chatting and instant messaging (44.3 percent), which used to be the main Internet usage patterns in the past. That is, the Internet usage pattern of Koreans has changed from using already existing contents on the Internet to producing user-created contents (UCC), such as blogs and personal homepages.[10] This new trend of UCC is supported by Korean researchers.[11] Similarly, the NIDA classifies the new patterns into the following categories: online groups and communities, blogs and mini-hompys, transferring contents (that is, *per-na-ru-gi*, or "scooping"), UCC, and commenting.[12]

INTERNET CAFÉS

Internet cafés in Korea refer not to establishments offering Internet access, but to online groups or communities established around a topic of common

Table 14.2 Top Five Internet Café Categories (January 2007)

Daum		Naver	
Categories	*# of Cafés*	*Categories*	*# of Cafés*
1. Socialization	1,677,836	1. Games	299,967
2. Games	780,957	2. Socialization	265,616
3. Hobbies	598,156	3. Hobbies	232,117
4. Alumni	430,690	4. Comics/ Animation	157,580
5. Fan Clubs	379,505	5. Fan Clubs	152,563

interest.[13] Portal sites provide such Internet café services to registered members. Almost 80 percent of Korean Internet users participate in Internet cafés to share hobbies and to socialize with people who have common interests for around 6.1 hours a week.[14] As of January 2007, approximately 6.2 million Internet cafés operated on the Korean portal Daum in 22 categories. Another popular portal, Naver, hosts 1.9 million cafés in 21 categories. Table 14.2. shows the top five categories of Internet cafés in these portal sites.

About half of Korean Internet café users are members of two to three Internet cafés, which they visit frequently.[15] Ku identified that Korean college students participate in Internet cafés for the purposes of communication/relationship building, entertainment/leisure, and usefulness/efficiency.[16] It is often observed that Internet cafés expand their activities to offline environments; for example, face-to-face meetings, parties, group purchases, or trips.

MINI-HOMPYS

Through services provided by the internet portal Cyworld, registered members can create a personalized webpage called a *mini-hompy*. Mini-hompys are connected with digital and mobile technology for both posting and viewing. Users, therefore, can upload digital pictures, streaming videos, and digital sounds, as well as textual content. Cyworld member registration requires submission of national ID numbers, which are the equivalent of the social security numbers in the United States, in order to protect members from potential online predator problems. Despite the strict membership requirements accompanied by the sacrifice of online anonymity, Cyworld is very popular in Korea. Cyworld compensates for the sacrifice of anonymity through offering an option to make mini-hompys private. Those who are not Cyworld members themselves cannot request access to private mini-hompys. If a user decides to keep his or her mini-hompy private, visitors to the mini-hompy must first receive the permission of the mini-hompy owner to access it. A mini-hompy owner can view profiles of other Cyworld members who want access to his or her mini-hompy. Therefore, most of the Cyworld mini-hompy network is personal among those who know each other. This network is termed 1-*chon* in Cyworld, a familial term that refers to one degree of separation in family trees (see Hjorth, Chapter 15, this volume), for a description of the *chon* system).

According to Cyworld, 18 million Koreans have Cyworld accounts, which represents 30 percent of the population. For the age group of 20–29-year-olds, over 90 percent have Cyworld mini-hompys, and 92 percent of the mini-hompy owners in this age group use the service almost daily.[17] A national survey revealed that mini-hompys and blogs are utilized for socialization, archives of life events, and sharing information on common interests. About 70 percent of blog and mini-hompy users visit their own pages at least once a day to post digital pictures or update journals, spending around 4.4 hours a week and receiving around 9.7 visitors to the page each day.[18]

Cyworld membership is free, thus there is no charge for having a basic mini-hompy. To decorate a mini-hompy, however, Cyworld cybermoney called "acorns" must be purchased. With the acorns, Cyworld users can buy items such as streaming music, background wallpaper graphics called "skins," avatars, avatar accessories, mini-rooms where avatars reside, decorative cursors and fonts, and so on. These acorns can also be used to view comics and movies provided by Cyworld. At the Cyworld gift shop, anyone can buy gifts for other Cyworld users. Cyworld offers an alert system to inform the users about their 1-chon members' birthdays and anniversaries in order to encourage acorn purchase and gift-giving. An acorn is approximately 10 US cents, and the decorative items cost from 5 to 30 acorns a piece, depending on the terms of validity. The decorative items can expire in seven days to one year. An estimated 2.5 million acorn transactions are made a day. In 2006, real-world banks opened online acorn banks where Cyworld users can deposit and loan acorns in order to join the growing Cyworld market. Credit card companies also presented credit card products that give rewards to card users in Cyworld acorns.[19]

Since it started in Korea in 1999, the Cyworld service has spread to China, Japan, and Taiwan to serve millions of users, and its US service started in July 2006. Cyworld announced that it garnered revenue of more than 100 million US dollars a year in Korea, which is three times greater than the expected revenue of MySpace.[20] In January 2007, Cyworld released version 2 beta service that combined mini-hompys with other applications, such as blogs, search engines, address book, scheduler, shopping mall, and online clubs on one page by utilizing widgets.[21] Version 2 is designed with a focus on internationalization, to operate with both Windows and Mac operating systems, as well as with different types of web browsers, such as Internet Explorer and Mozilla Firefox. It is also designed to accommodate multiple languages for worldwide users.

Cyworld mini-hompys serve multiple purposes as online spaces for self-expression, self-promotion, life logs, personal and social networking, and digital entertainment. Mini-hompys are distinct from blogs in their visual aspects, include graphic decorations such as avatars, avatar rooms, animated cursors and fonts.[22] Personal networking through 1-chon network makes Cyworld mini-hompys attractive to many young Korean users who value social networking and communication on- and offline.[23] Interface with mobile technology also matches the needs and interest of young technology-savvy "netizens." Koreans do cy-*hada* or cy-*jil* (that is, have a Cyworld mini-hompy account and perform actively in Cyworld) in order to have fun, to express themselves, to socialize,[24] and to look for information.[25] Some mini-hompy users held negative perceptions or had bad experiences with Cyworld, but still, such negative experience did not affect their use of mini-hompys.[26] While blogs and mini-hompys are similar in some ways, regarding motivation for use, mini-hompys are perceived to be better for the purposes of self-expression, sharing experiences, and life-logging. In terms of user satisfaction, therefore, mini-hompys are more satisfactory than blogs.[27] Mini-hompys are now items that appear on individuals' resumes for self-promotion. Public figures and industries also utilize Cyworld mini-hompys and Cytown services (Cyworld services for e-commerce) for promotion and communication.

Addiction to "cy-ing" is often brought up for debate, as well as the issue of invasion of privacy. Adolescents and university students spend quite a lot of time in Cyworld, as Choi reports—almost 13 hours a week, during which they visit their own mini-hompys 22 times and visit others' 26 times.[28] It is common among users to exchange Cyworld IDs as they would exchange other contact information. Mini-hompy users are frequently found in public places taking digital pictures of what they see, eat, and do in order to upload the pictures on their mini-hompys. Those who spend a lot of time in Cyworld and post their lives on the mini-hompys are called *cy-holics* (or *cy-pye-in* in Korean). In fact, Korean schools and offices block access to Cyworld in order to prevent students and workers from connecting to mini-hompys during school/business hours. While Cyworld addiction, invasion of privacy, and segregation between Cyworld users and non-users are recognized to be problematic,[29] potential solutions or treatment based on research are at an early phase at this point.

BLOGS

Blogs first appeared in the United States in 1998, debuted in Korea in late 2001, and became generalized to the Korean public at large in 2003.[30] As of 2005, over 15 million Korean blogs are on the Internet,[31] which represent 30 percent of blogs worldwide. Korean portal sites host a great majority of Korean blogs: 6.5 million blogs on Naver, 1.2 million blogs on Daum, and 0.5 million blogs on Empas. Egloos is not a portal but a blog-only service in Korea that hosts 150,000 blogs.[32] In 2006, the parent company of Cyworld purchased Egloos for approximately US$1.5 million, which caused a great deal of debate among Egloos users. Some Egloos users left the service, as they were not happy about their blogs being affiliated with Cyworld, which they perceived as being too commercialized. They preferred Egloo's original policy of limiting membership to those whose age was 18 years and older, and of not putting advertisements on blog pages. The users chose Egloos because they did not like commercialized, visually-oriented blog services, thus the merge with Cyworld, which is known for such services, produced concern and disappointment among Egloos users.[33] This development increased bloggers' interest in installation blogs that can be operated on a personal Internet server account, instead of using blog services and templates.

Whether visually oriented or not, Korean blogs in general are regarded as an alternative communication channel[34] that is controlled by individuals and that allows multidirectional communication between producers and readers about topics that have not traditionally been discussed in public, such as politics, religion, personal finances, mental health, and sexuality. Kim argues that Korean blogs function as a socialization tool rather than as a venue for social activism.[35] In other words, blogs in Korea are used more for interaction with others and for passing the time rather than grassroots journalism. However, raising social awareness and the formation of public opinion are still recognizable functions of Korean blogs. Acknowledging such functions, the Korean government is in the process of reforming laws on press and media to include Internet portals under its jurisdiction in order to prevent tangible and intangible damages due to misinformation and misrepresentation by online media while protecting freedom of speech.[36]

Research on Korean blogs emerged in 2004,[37] mostly concentrating on blog usage patterns,[38] motivation for use,[39] and satisfaction with the use.[40] These research efforts agree that Korean blogs exist for purposes of self-expression, interpersonal communication, experience sharing, and information seeking. Noh and Lee concluded that relationship-oriented blogs were more satisfactory and competitive than e-mails and instant messaging.[41] Han, on the other hand, argues that communication via blogging tends to emphasize visuals, which are shown and shared with others, thus it risks becoming superficial.[42] Lee and Im conclude that bloggers voluntarily disclose their identities and personal information online to express themselves, to establish and maintain relationships, to keep up with trends, to seek and exchange information, and to increase the entertainment experience.[43] The results, in return, include improved relationships and satisfaction, but also addiction to blogging. Choi, Lee, and Kim differentiate blogs from Cyworld mini-hompys in several ways, including the fact that each blog post has its own individual, original address in cyberspace and that blog postings are interlinked by backtracking.[44] Korean blog research has reached a point where it needs to move beyond identifying blog types, usage patterns, and user satisfaction[45] and look at the blog phenomenon from the perspective of exhibitionism and voyeurism.[46]

CONTENT TRANSFER

Termed "scooping" in Korean, content transfer is a common practice among bloggers who take content from other blogs or web media and post them on their own blogs. A Korean national survey reports that 62 percent of Korean Internet users have experienced scooping.[47] Although one-person media and UCC are noticeable characteristics of Korean Internet culture, Yoon argues that Korean blogging consists more in the scrapbooking of the contents of others' sites rather than creating individual contents.[48] Therefore, some bloggers now add notes to their original content postings asking other bloggers to explicitly mark the source of the content when they scoop up the postings. At the same time, blog services provide a backtrack option, with which bloggers can link others' original postings to their blogs. However, scooping still prevails among bloggers and is often at the center of debate and conflict. There is a copy "left" (versus copyright) movement that opposes restrictions on the distribution of others' work on the Internet and that advocates the freedom to reproduce and modify existing online content.[49] However, Internet copyright and unauthorized content transfer or scooping remain debatable in Korea's blogging culture.

USER-CREATED CONTENT

Apart from blogs and mini-hompys, Korean portal sites are places where Internet users generate UCC. UCC refers to Internet media content, including digital photographs and video clips that are produced by Internet users who are not necessarily media professionals. Most Korean portal sites provide blog services, and in addition, they offer a so-called "knowledge" service. Indeed, Korea's number one portal, Naver's, success is attributable to its knowledge service that was launched in October 2002.[50] From 2001–2003, Naver's sales total increased sevenfold. Through the knowledge service, users can post questions and answers on literally any topic, and answers written with significant expertise are registered in the portal's encyclopedia. In comparison with Wikipedia, the knowledge services of Korean portals cover trivial questions that are searchable not only by keywords, but also by sentences. The knowledge services come with an "auto completion" feature; that is, the typing of commonly asked questions is automatically completed, thus informing users that many other people have asked the same questions before. Topics covered in the knowledge service ranges from phone directory to computer troubleshooting, shopping, consumer reviews, directions, news, people, gossip, wisdom of life, and much more academic and professional information. As online shopping is one of the main motivations for Internet use, product and shopping site reviews occupy a portion of UCC. A great majority of Internet users (79.3 percent) check the reviews and are influenced by the reviews (94.3 percent).[51]

Visual UCC are more popular than ever as mobile phones, digital cameras, and other graphic communication tools are connected with the Internet. Indeed, digital image composition, distortion, and graphic parodies are hugely popular among Korean Internet users, and the trend in UCC is shifting from texts to visuals.[52] Portal sites promote the production of UCC by providing specific sections for user-created streaming videos, comics, flash animation, original digital pictures, or pictures digitally altered by the users, respectively, on their sites. These contents can be linked to blog and bulletin postings on the same portal sites. The portals include voting features in these UCC sections so that viewers can give votes or thumbs-up/thumbs-down to each UCC posting. Popular UCC are then introduced on the front pages of these portals that receive hundreds and thousands of hits per day.

Internationalization is realized on portal sites where language barriers are reduced by allowing visual UCC and providing a translation service for free. The Korean portal site, Naver, for example, has an "Enjoy Japan" section where Korean and Japanese users can interact with visuals and texts on various topics that include travel and culture. Enjoy Japan comes with a translator program that offers short sentence translations in both languages for free. The translation is mostly a literal, word-by-word translation, but is still helpful in facilitating interaction between Internet users in Korea and Japan. Although amicable interactions are encouraged and the users self-monitor to maintain a mature atmosphere, flames are often generated in the Enjoy Japan bulletin boards due to the historical and cultural backgrounds of the two countries.

UCC has created a great deal of debate about various social, political, and cultural issues in Korea. Online petitioning is a common strategy when social issues are raised. For example, a digital video clip of a young couple received a large number of votes in portal sites and was disseminated widely in 2006. In the video, the couple exchanged vows in front of passengers in a subway train as they could not afford a wedding. The video received such a huge response online that it was suggested that there should be some support offered to the couple. Soon after, however, it turned out to be a stunt performed by theater students, and the students apologized for deceiving the public and causing a commotion.[53] Another well-known incident is that of the so-called "dog poop girl." A young woman left a subway train without cleaning up the mess that her dog made. A passenger in the same train recorded the scene, in which another passenger cleaned the floor. The video was spread through portal sites and the woman became the target of public criticism. It reached a point where her identity was revealed.[54] The same case was also covered in the *Washington Post*, generating online discussions about Internet lynching, digital scarlet letters, and the Internet as Big Brother.[55] In 2007, a politician was fined for a sexual misconduct case captured on video and disseminated online.[56]

The sixteenth Korean presidential election in 2002 was notable for the development of candidate support movements on the Internet. Given that the Korean National Election Commission (KNEC) has strict guidelines on the kind of campaigning that can be undertaken in the media, it announced that it would monitor UCC that were relevant to the seventeenth election, scheduled for late 2007. These UCC are mostly digital images and videos of potential presidential candidates that the KNEC interprets as unauthorized precampaign activities. Under current guidelines, in January 2007, the KNEC had already requested two portal sites to delete fourteen UCC postings associated with potential presidential candidates or their activities.[57] The KNEC explains that it applies comprehensive criteria when judging violations of election regulations by producing and disseminating UCC.[58] The KNEC regulation is, however, still being debated in terms of the suppression of the Internet culture and the practicality of monitoring a medium that is used by millions of netizens continuously and simultaneously.[59]

COMMENT CULTURE

In the early years of Internet bulletin boards, responses to a posting were added as separate postings following the original, creating a *thread*, or series of messages. Thus, viewers had to click to go back and forth between the original posting and its associated responses. However, the embedded comment feature of newer web message boards allows users to add comments to a posting on the same page. The users also can see how many comments have been given to a posting from post listings, which encourages more views when the number of comments is large. Providing a comment section is a now basic requirement for most bulletin boards, blogs, mini-hompys, and Internet cafés. Internet newspapers and portal sites in Korea also provide a comment section for almost every posting on their webpages. Now that UCC is a mainstream feature of the Korean Internet, UCC producers naturally anticipate viewer responses that are mainly expressed through comments. Comment writers post 2.5 comments per week to express their opinions, sympathize with others, or object to others' thoughts, and readers are interested in what the writers have to say in the comments, even though they do not necessarily agree with them. According to one survey, Internet comments can influence decision making (67.5 percent), but the reliability of the comments is low (35.7 percent).[60]

On Internet sites where comments are posted rapidly by a large number of participants, a unique culture develops around message formats, expressions, nicknaming, emoticons, images, and other features that are created and understood in particular ways by the participants. For instance, users of the "DC Inside" site are well-known in Korea for creating "DC" style expressions. DC style expressions are also used in other bulletin boards on the Internet, and responses are often mixed because the DC style tends to be extreme. DC style and other online expressions are criticized for "destroying" the Korean language by creating terms and expressions that are outside of conventional Korean spelling, that are disrespectful or obscene, that can be understood only within a very specific online culture, and thus can cause a disconnect between generations or cultural subgroups.

Internet comments are now progressively utilized in Korean entertainment programming. In a national survey, respondents answered that they read and write comments on entertainment and sports-related topics the most.[61] Popular evening entertainment programs on Korean network television depend hugely on viewer comments when selecting program contents and casting to an extent that far exceeds the viewer voting system popular in American reality television shows. The storylines of popular television drama series are often altered in response to viewer comments. Fun and witty online nicknames often receive attention in comment sections of television station websites, and some television programs developed program segments that introduce unique online nicknames.

Since viewer comments on many websites are posted anonymously, problematic negative and hateful comments sometimes become a public issue. In 2005, when news media reported the family tragedy of a former political figure, many posted malicious comments jeering the victim. Twenty-five respondents who had posted with their real-name online IDs, and who turned out to be educated professionals, were charged, and four of them were fined.[62] Four additional cases were reported in 2006, in which those who posted vicious comments about entertainers and political figures were prosecuted for libel and slander.[63] Those who post mean comments are called "keyboard warriors," for they argue aggressively online and even offline. Keyboard warriors became an issue again in early 2007 when they reacted with hostile, ridiculing comments to the death of a comedian who died in a car accident. Within a month, a young Korean singer who suffered from depression committed suicide. It was reported that she had struggled with hateful comments on the Internet about her.[64] While many posted condolences on Internet news reports about her death, some keyboard warriors still produced inappropriate comments.

Efforts are being made to reduce the hostile atmosphere on the Internet and to encourage a more mature Internet environment. A majority of adult Internet users consider Internet comment culture to have mostly negative effects because there are too many hostile, inappropriate comments on the Internet.[65] In response to the hostile comments on the deaths of the aforementioned entertainers, an Internet user initiated an online petition to encourage the "self-cleaning" of the Internet comment culture. About 1,400 people signed the online petition in 1 day.[66] The Korean Ministry of Information and Communication announced that it would require real-name use in postings to websites with 100,000 hits per day or greater, starting in July 2007.[67] There are currently 212 Korean websites, including 27 portal sites, which receive more than 100,000 hits a day. The effectiveness of this requirement, however, is in question because 10 of the 17 portal sites with 300,000 hits per day or greater already require their users to register with their real names in order to post comments. Similarly, nine of eleven news media websites currently require real-name registration for posting and commenting on their sites.[68]

COMMUNITY CAPACITY AND INTERNET COMMUNITIES

The previous section outlined the contexts in which Korean Internet communities are formed in terms of Internet cafés, mini-hompys, and blogs by those who want to express themselves and to connect with others through sharing experience and information. These communities are supported by Internet service providers who supply the templates and virtual spaces that enable users to participate in the Internet community via the applications outlined earlier. Internet community researchers have maintained that an online community can evolve on its own with a minimalist design,[69] just as offline communities do.[70] While it holds true that Korean Internet communities have self-developed through online interactions and processes that are just as real as those in the offline world,[71] the level of minimalist design has become more sophisticated over the last decade, so as to accommodate the rapid advancement of Internet applications and mobile technologies. Regardless of the level of design, however, it is the participation of people that is the starting point for building upon the minimal platform. Once participation begins, other aspects of community development should follow for a community to progress; for example, facilitation of communication between participants, the establishment of rules, networking, and leadership. These aspects can be evaluated in terms of community capacity.

Community capacity is a pivotal element in community development, defined as the ability of community participants "to come together, learn, make well-reasoned decisions about the community's present and future, *and* to work together to carry out those decisions".[72] In other words, community capacity is a necessary and sufficient condition for a community to form, continue to grow, and sustain itself in order to achieve its common goals. Community capacity is a comprehensive construct that should be understood in multiple dimensions. Goodman and colleagues catalogued ten dimensions of community capacity that are instrumental for community development. Although the authors acknowledged that community capacity may have more dimensions, these ten dimensions are the ones that are deemed essential in community development research.[73] The ten dimensions include: participation, leadership, skills, resources, social networks, sense of community, understanding of community history, community power, community values, and critical reflection.[74]

Despite these multiple facets, community capacity has been treated as a single-dimension construct in the Internet research arena, particularly regarding sense of community[75] and social networks.[76] Community capacity is largely a foreign term in Korean Internet community studies, which have mostly focused on the motivation for online community participation and usage patterns,[77] and on user satisfaction.[78] A few have attempted to investigate social and cultural implications of the blog phenomenon, but have not explained the dynamics in blog community development.[79] Anecdotal cases of Internet community activism have been reported in the news media about political supporters, apartment complex residents, and consumers. However, no links have been made between such instances of community activity and community capacity. Korean Internet communities and their current cultural environment offer opportunities for community capacity research, as they appear to demonstrate multiple capacities simultaneously. The growth of mini-hompys and blogs in Korea can be explained in terms of several of Goodman and colleagues' ten dimension of community capacity. Hostile comments on the Korean Internet may illustrate active participation, high level of Internet skills, the strong community power of keyboard warriors, and lack of positive leadership. Efforts to correct such negative culture can be an example of community reflection. The purchase of Egloos' blog service by Cyworld might have led Egloos users to realize their current level of community capacity and the new capacities needed to cope with the situation.

Recently, I attempted to apply the concept of Goodman et al.'s ten dimensions of community capacity[80] to an Internet community case.[81] This qualitative study followed a Korean online community of a comic book fan club with 150 members for 2 years in order to identify the fan club's capacity development process. Through the observation of signature events that the fan club organized, I identified that an online community could demonstrate all ten dimensions of community capacity. In addition, community capacities that were specific to Internet communities were identified. As demonstrated in a series of signature events, member *participation* and volunteerism fueled the online fan club's development. Concurrently, *leadership* was displayed, both by the webmaster who started the fan club and by newly emergent leaders in the fan club. For both leaders and participants, basic Internet navigation *skills* were required to participate in the fan club. Financial *resources* were provided by member contributions, while social capital developed as the members experienced satisfaction, gratitude, and confidence in their community and membership. The members set and maintained a mature tone in interacting online, which created shared *community values*, and *social networks* of the fan club and its members strengthened. A *sense of community* intensified as the members experienced and expressed a sense of belonging and connectedness in the fan club. *Community history* was established as the fan club continued over the years, and *community power* was recognized by the comic industry and the media. *Critical reflection* was exercised as the community evaluated their activities and refined its rules and guidelines. In addition to the ten dimensions of community capacity, the fan club demonstrated Internet-community-specific capacities. They include: *development of online identities, expansion of activities from online to offline*, and *site management*, which are supported by Rothaermel and Sugiyama.[82]

The Internet community capacity study described above is the first of its kind that applies the multiple dimensions of community capacity to an Internet community. It is valuable in identifying all ten dimensions of community capacity suggested by Goodman and colleagues[83] in an Internet community context, as well as identifying additional capacities that are specific to online communities. However, the study was of a website-based Internet community observed in a period preceding the growth of mini-hompys, blogs, and multimedia UCC. Unlike the centralized website-based community illustrated in my case study, where community members come together in a central space, Internet communities that evolve around mini-hompys and blogs consist of members who have their own individual online territories under their control. How does this new trend affect the development and demonstration of community capacities in mini-hompy/blog communities in comparison with website-based communities? How should participation be defined in Cyworld and the blogsphere when an individual participates only in his or her own blog, as opposed to when others participate not only in their own blog, but also in someone else's through guest commenting or engaging with portal sites? How would the leadership patterns and structure differ between website-based communities and mini-hompy/blog communities? Could there be other core capacities to be identified in the communities of mini-hompys and blogs other than those already documented? What are the interrelations between community capacities in the new world of mini-hompys, blogs, and UCC communities on portal sites on the Internet? How could such community capacities and their dynamics be utilized to promote a positive Internet culture and to discourage destructive, hostile behaviors online? How could they inform policies? As Internet community dynamics and culture increasingly influence various aspects of the offline world, Internet research should broaden its scope beyond the use of mini-hompy and blog use to include how Internet communities and culture develop, and how they interact with the offline world. Multidimensional community capacities deserve attention in such research. It should also be mentioned that such research requires mixed methods and interdisciplinary collaboration.

CONCLUSION

With the broad availability of high-speed Internet supported by the government in combination with active utilization by a technology- and communication-savvy population, Korea is experiencing changes on the Internet.

The Internet usage patterns of Koreans have diversified from information search and e-mailing to UCC in blogs, mini-hompys, Internet cafés, and bulletin boards. Korean portal sites have been instrumental in this diversification, since they are the platforms where most of these UCC services are provided. With the increasingly active use of the Internet for blogging, cy-ing, and other activities for social interaction, information seeking, self-expression, and leisure, Koreans are faced with the invasion of privacy, Internet lynching, and reckless hostility on the Internet in return.

In the arena of Korean Internet community research, mini-hompys and blogs have received the most attention, with a focus on the usage patterns and the factors that influence Internet usage. Multidimensional community capacity has received much less attention, although it is an important area of research of offline communities. The limited research available does illustrate that an Internet community develops and demonstrates multidimensional community capacities, but there is a lot more to be done to address the interrelations of community capacities. Korean Internet culture studies should also reflect the changes in trends of Korean Internet communities. As Yang and Park argue, Internet activities in Korea are shifting from interacting in online groups or central websites to creating personal media, such as blogs and mini-hompys.[84] For people who have their own online spaces, such as blogs or mini-hompys, where they create their original contents and then network with other bloggers or mini-hompy users, understanding of the process and dynamics in this context should consider types of community capacities and their interrelations. It is anticipated that community capacity research will contribute to further understanding the development of Internet communities and their culture. It is also expected to inform strategy development to respond to negative functions or counter the effects of hostile comments, obscenity, misinformation, and invasion of privacy. For future research, interdisciplinary collaboration is encouraged, as community development, Internet culture, and online behavior are all multifaceted phenomena. Mixed methods of qualitative and quantitative approaches will be useful in interdisciplinary studies. Cross-cultural comparisons of Internet community research are also recommended to address similarities and differences in acceptance and utilization of Internet technology, characteristics of Internet culture, development of Internet communities, and community capacities.

The continuing advancement of the Internet infrastructure and the enthusiastic utilization of the Internet will support energetic activities by Korean Internet communities. While some aspects of Korean Internet culture are specific to the Korean language and society, they are suggestive of dynamic community characteristics and capacities that can develop in an international cyberspace where the entire world is connected. An understanding of fast-paced, multidimensional evolution of Internet communities and culture in the present requires innovative approaches that take diversity into account. Community capacity is arguably one construct that adds to the innovative nature of Internet community research, and the application of this construct to Korean Internet community research will surely contribute to the widening of Internet studies.

NOTES

Disclaimer: Some of the original Korean author names and publication titles listed below are the author's translation into English. Since there is no common agreement on how to spell Korean names, they have been transliterated into English and marked with an asterisk (*); original Korean titles have also been transliterated, followed by the author's English translation in brackets.

1. Hereafter called Korea.
2. Sang Hee Kweon and Ji Su Woo, "Blog Media Research: A Study of Motivation, Gratification, and Cognitive Styles of the Blog Media," *Hankookbangsonghakbo* 19, no. 2 (2005): 419–460.
3. OECD, "OECD Broadband Statistics, June 2005," http://www.oecd.org/document/16/0,2340,en_2825_495656_35526608_1_1_1_1,00.html; and OECD, "OECD Broadband Statistics, December 2005," http://www.oecd.org/document/39/0,3343,en_2649_34225_36459431_1_1_1_1,00.html
4. OECD, "Broadband Statistics to June 2006," http://www.oecd.org/document/9/0,2340,en_2649_34223_37529673_1_1_1_1,00.html
5. Tae-Gyu Kim, "How Korea Became an Internet Powerhouse," http://www.koreatimes.co.kr/www/news/nation/news_view.asp?newsIdx=261313 (May 9, 2005).
6. Darrell M. West, *Global E-Government, 2006* (Providence, RI: Center for Public Policy, Brown University, 2006).
7. Ministry of Information and Communication, Republic of Korea, *IT Statistics* (Seoul: Ministry of Information and Communication, 2006).
8. Kim, "How Korea Became an Internet Powerhouse."
9. NIDA, *Information Systems Survey: First Half of 2006* (Seoul, Korea: National Internet Development Agency of Korea, 2006).
10. NIDA, *Web 2.0 sidae-eui netizen Internet yiyong hyunhwang: Chamyo-wa gongyu-eui Internet* [*Netizen Internet Use in the Web 2.0 Era: Internet for Participation and Sharing*] (Seoul, Korea: National Internet Development Agency of Korea, 2006).
11. Suk-Joon Yang and Yu-Jin Park, "A Study on the Motivation and the Influence of Using Personal Community," *Journal of Consumer Studies* 16, no. 4 (2005): 129–150; and Min-Sun Lee* and Chul Park*, "Hankookgwa Meekookeui blog yiyong yuhyoungeh gwanhan bigyo yonku" [Comparison of Blogging Patterns in Korea and the US], (paper presented at the Korean Society of Management Information Systems Semi-Annual International Conference, Seoul, Korea, Spring 2006).
12. NIDA, "Netizen Internet Usage," NIDA Press Release, http://www.nida.or.kr/doc/issue_sum_report.pdf (June 28, 2006).
13. Commercial facilities for the use of Internet-ready computers are called "PC Rooms" in Korea.
14. NIDA, *Web 2.0 sidae-eui netizen Internet.*
15. Ibid.
16. Gyo-Tae Ku, "A Study of Needs and Behavior on a Virtual Community: Focused on College Students' Internet Cafe Activities," *Journal of Korea Association for Communication and Information Studies* 30 (2005): 1–28.

17. Michael Kanellos, "Korean Social-Networking Site Hopes to Nab U.S. Fans," Zdnet India, http://www.zdnetindia.com/news/communication/stories/151524.html (August 14, 2006).
18. NIDA, *Web 2.0 sidae-eui netizen Internet.*
19. Jung-Hoon Kim*, "Dotori Yegum, Jukgum, Card: Geumyoongkwon Netizen Japki Gyungjaeng," [Acorn Banking and Credit Cards: Competitions of Financial Institutions to Attract Netizens], http://news.chosun.com/site/data/html_dir/2006/12/07/2006120700801.html (December, 7, 2006).
20. Kanellos, "Korean Social-Networking Site Hopes to Nab U.S. Fans."
21. Yoon-Jung Yoo*, "Cyworld2, Veil-Buhtta. Shibum Service Gonggae" [Cyworld2 Unveiled. Example Service Opened], http://www.zdnet.co.kr/news/spotnews/internet/portal/0,39040068,39155041,00.htm (January 30, 2007).
22. Hompys allow for greater customization, something that has been important throughout East Asia. See Hjorth (Chapter 15), in this volume.
23. Hangwoo Lee, "Mini-Hompy and the Condition of Informal Public Life: Negotiations of The Public and the Private on The Internet," *Korean Sociology* 40, no. 3 (2006): 124–154; Hwan Jin Choi, "A Study of the Motives and Processes of the Usage of Blogs by University Students," *The Korean Journal of Advertising* 17, no.3 (2006): 225–248; and Ji-Soo Kim*, "Blog-Eui Sahwaemunwhajuk Jinwhawa Issue" [Socio-Cultural Evolution and Issues of Blogs], *Jungbo Tongshin Jungchaek* 16, no. 8 (2004): 18–36.
24. Choi, "Usage of Blogs by University Students"; and Kweon and Woo, "Blog Media Research."
25. Kweon and Woo, "Blog Media Research."
26. Choi, "Usage of Blogs by University Students."
27. Jae-Woong Choi*, Joung-Hun Lee*, and Byoung-Cho Kim*, "Online community yiyong euido: Blog sayongjarul joongshimooro" [Intention to Use Online Communities: Among Bloggers], (paper presented at the Korean Society of Management Information Systems, Conference, Seoul, Korea, Spring 2006).
28. Choi, "Usage of Blogs by University Students."
29. Ibid; Kweon and Woo, "Blog Media Research"; Jang-Young Lee, Yong-Mi Park, and Eun-Sil Lee, "A Study of Influential Factors on Friendship Forming Behaviors through Individual Webpage: Focused on 'Neighborhood' Relationship of College Students Using 'Cyworld'," *Jungbowa Sahwae* 9 (2006): 1–33; and H. Lee, "Mini-Hompy and the Condition of Informal Public Life."
30. J. S. Kim, "Blog-Eui Sahwaemunwhajuk Jinwhawa Issue."
31. Young-Ju Kim, "A Study on the Blog as a Media: Focused on Media Function and the Problems of the Blog," *Korean Journal of Journalism and Communication Studies* 50, no. 2 (2006): 59–89.
32. Jae-Hee Suh*, "Blog jabon mujang—Blogger dduhnalkka malkka" [Blog Armed with Capital—Bloggers Contemplate Leaving or Staying], http://www3.seoul.co.kr/news/newsView.php?id=20060325005002&spage=59 (March 25, 2006).
33. J. H. Suh, "Blog jabon"; and Hyo-Sil Park*, "Egloos user-deul 'woowangjwawang'" [Egloos Users Lost Direction], http://news.naver.com/news/read.php?mode=LOD&office_id=073&article_id=0000022062 (March 13, 2006).
34. Ji-Soo Kim*, "Il-in media, blog-eui hwaksangua issue" [One-Person Media—Spread of Blogs], *Jungbo Tongshin Jungchaek* 16, no. 22 (2004): 31–43.
35. Y. J. Kim, "Blog as a Media."
36. Hwa-Young Shim*, "Portal, unron gwangyebup jukyong gyuje" [Portal, Regulated by Media Law], http://www.dt.co.kr/contents.htm?article_no=2006080902010151727002 (August 9, 2006).

37. Y. J. Kim, "Blog as a Media."
38. Sang Hee Kweon, "Blog Media Mode: An Analysis Study of Blog Genre by Communicator, Construction Form, Content, and Connection," *Cyber-communications Papers* 15, no. 1 (2005): 93–134; Y. J. Kim, "Blog as a Media"; Kweon and Woo, "Blog Media Research"; Ghee-Young Noh and Mi-Young Lee, "Media Competition between Blog and Internet Media," *Korean Journal of Journalism and Communication Studies* 49, no. 3 (2005): 318–345; J. S. Kim, "Blog-Eui Sahwaemunwhajuk Jinwhawa Issue"; J. S. Kim, "Il-in media, blog-eui hwaksangua issue"; Kyung-Hee Kim and Jin-Ah Bae, "A Study on The Typology of Blogs and Their Significance in Bloggers' Lives: With More Focus on the Bloggers in their Thirties," *Hankookunron-hakbo* 50, no. 5 (2006): 5–29; and Hye Jin Kim et al., "A Qualitative Study with Blog Users on the Interplay between Social Networking Structure and Relationship Building Behavior," *Kyungyoungbak Yonku* 35, no. 6 (2006): 1853–1884.
39. Kweon and Woo, "Blog Media Research"; Choi, Lee, and Kim, "Online community yiyong euido"; Choi, "Usage of Blogs by University Students"; and Kwang-Soon Park and Myoung-Hwy Cho, "A Study on the Motive and Satisfaction in Using the Web-Blog of Internet: Focused on University Students," *Korean Journal of Journalism and Communication Studies* 48, no. 5 (2004): 270–294.
40. Choi, Lee, and Kim, "Online community yiyong euido"; Kweon and Woo, "Blog Media Research"; Noh and Lee, "Media Competition"; and Park and Cho, "Motive and Satisfaction in Using the Web-Blog."
41. Noh and Lee, "Media Competition."
42. Sun Han, "A Study of Personal 'Meaning Practice' in Blog Communication," *Korean Journal of Journalism and Communication Studies* 50, no. 5 (2006): 354–383.
43. Doo-hee Lee and Seunghee Im, "The Motivations and Consequences of Voluntary Self-Disclosure by Blog Users," *The Korean Journal of Advertising* 17, no. 5 (2006): 227–240.
44. Choi, Lee, and Kim, "Online community yiyong euido."
45. Han, "Personal 'Meaning Practice' in Blog Communication."
46. H. Lee, "Mini-Hompy"; Choi, "Usage of Blogs by University Students"; and J. S. Kim, "Blog-Eui Sahwaemunwhajuk Jinwhawa Issue."
47. NIDA, "Netizen Internet Usage."
48. Myung-Hee Yoon*, "Il-in community-eui sahwaejuk boonyul" [Social Division of One-Person Community], (paper presented at the Korean Sociological Association Conference, Chonbuk University, Korea, June 15, 2006).
49. Wikipedia, "Copyleft," http://en.wikipedia.org/wiki/Copyleft
50. Ji-Hyun Kim*, "Hankook 1-deung portal, Naver-eui sungjang dongryukeun gumsaek" [Growth of Naver, Korea's No.1 portal, Driven by Online Search], http://korea.internet.com/channel/content.asp?kid=10&nid=39847&cid=74 (July 18, 2006).
51. NIDA, "Web 2.0 sidae-eui netizen Internet yiyong hyunhwang."
52. Yonhap News, "Portal-deuleui UCC service model-gwa jinwha gwajung" [Models and Progress of UCC Services on Portal Sites], http://news.naver.com/news/read.php?mode=LSD&office_id=098&article_id=0000167318&section_id=117&menu_id=117 (September 14, 2006).
53. Hyo-Sik Lee, "Faked Subway Wedding Baffles Internet Users," http://www.koreatimes.co.kr/www/news/nation/news_view.asp?newsIdx=2818743 (February 16, 2006).
54. Jonathan Krim, "Subway Fracas Escalates into Test of the Internet's Power to Shame," http://www.washingtonpost.com/wp-dyn/content/article/2005/07/06/

AR2005070601953.html (July 7, 2005); and Wikipedia, "Internet Vigilantism," http://en.wikipedia.org/wiki/Dog_poop_girl

55. Mi-Kyung Chung*, "Bada gunnuh gahn 'Gaeddongnyeoh Sagun'—American blogger-dul nonjaengguhriro" [Dog Poop Girl Incident Crossed the Ocean—Debated by American Bloggers], http://www.donga.com/fbin/output?sfrm=4&n=200507090122 (July 9, 2005).

56. "Lawmaker Fined for Sexual Harassment," *Korea Times*, June 14, 2007; also available online at http://www.koreatimes.co.kr/www/news/nation/2007/07/117_4714.html

57. Yun-ah Kae, "UCC Likely to Influence Election," http://www.asiamedia.ucla.edu/article.asp?parentid=63196 (February 7, 2007).

58. Min-Wook Bae*, "Joongang Sungwanwee, UCC-mul Jejak, pernarugi uhmgyok kijoon jeshi" [KNEC Suggests Strict Standards for UCC], http://news.naver.com/news/read.php?mode=LOD&office_id=003&article_id=0000303796 (February 1, 2007).

59. "Bunmyonghan kijooneuro UCC bujakyong makaya" [Clear Rules Needed to Prevent UCC Misuse and Adverse Effects], *Seoul Economic Daily*, February 2, 2007; also available online at http://economy.hankooki.com/lpage/opinion/200702/e2007020216501148010.htm; and YTN, "Sungwanwee, UCC chut jejae" [First Sanction on UCC by KNEC], http://www.ytn.co.kr/_ln/0101_200702012037024082 (February 1, 2007).

60. NIDA, "Web 2.0 sidae-eui netizen Internet."

61. Ibid.

62. Eun-Jin Shin*, "Internet 'Im Soo Kyung Akple' jungshik jaepando bulgeumhyung" [Sentenced to Fine for Im Soo Kyung Malicious Internet Comments], http://srchdb1.chosun.com/pdf/i_service/read_body.jsp?ID=2006031700062 (March 17, 2006); and Sung-Hyun Cho*, "'Akple'-eh 100-manwon yakshik kiso" [One Million Won Summary Indictment for Malicious Internet Comments], http://news.naver.com/news/read.php?mode=LSD&office_id=001&article_id=0001205384&section_id=105&menu_id=105 (January 26, 2006).

63. Je-Sung Hong*, "'Kim Tae Hee Akple' netizen 11-myung ipgun" [11 Netizens Indicted for Kim Tae Hee Malicious Internet Comments], http://news.naver.com/news/read.php?mode=LSD&office_id=001&article_id=0001404590&section_id=102&menu_id=102 (September 7, 2006).

64. Sung-Hoe Kim*, "Jookeumjocha joronghaneun keyboard warrior" [Keyboard Warriors even Ridicule Death], http://news.mk.co.kr/newsRead.php?year=2007&no=42619 (January 25, 2007).

65. Yong-Moon Lee*, "2,30-dae sungin 10-myong joong 7-myongeun aksung daeguleh bujungjuk" [7 Out of 10 Adults in their 20s and 30s Are Negative towards Malicious Comments Online], http://www.cbs.co.kr/Nocut/Show.asp?IDX=423449 (January 31, 2007).

66. Hyun-Chul Mo*, "Akple," http://www.imaeil.com/sub_news/sub_news_view.php?news_id=4127&yy=2007 (January 26, 2007).

67. Tae-gyu Kim, "Internet Real Name System to Start in July," http://www.koreatimes.co.kr/www/news/nation/news_view.asp?newsIdx=3051480 (January 9, 2007); and Yoon-mi Kim, "Busy Websites Need Real Name Registration," http://www.asiamedia.ucla.edu/article.asp?parentid=60686 (January 10, 2007).

68. Chang-Hyop Chun*, "Internet shilmyongje chilwol shilsi jukyong site manchi ahneuldut" [Not Many Internet Sites Seem to Be Subject to the Internet Real Name System Starting July], http://www.heraldbiz.com/SITE/data/html_dir/2007/01/11/200701110096.asp)January 11, 2007).

69. Etienne Wenger, *Community of Practice: Learning, Meaning, and Identity* (Cambridge: Cambridge University Press, 1998).

70. Wenger, *Community of Practice*; Sasha Barab et al., "Designing and Building an Online Community: The Struggle to Support Sociability in the Inquiry Learning Forum," *Educational Technology Research and Development* 49, no. 4 (2001): 71–96; Sasha Barab, Jim MaKinster, and Rebecca Scheckler, "Designing System Dualities: Characterizing a Web-Supported Professional Development Community," *The Information Society* 19 (2003): 237–256; and Amy Jo Kim, *Community Building: Secret Strategies for Successful Online Communities on the Web* (Berkeley, CA: Peachpit Press, 2000).

71. Kevin Johnston and Parminder Johal, "The Internet as a 'Virtual Cultural Region': Are Extant Cultural Classification Schemes Appropriate?," *Internet Research: Electronic Networking Application and Policy* 9, no. 3 (1999): 178–186.

72. The Aspen Institute, *Measuring Community Capacity: A Workbook-in-Progress for Rural Communities* (Washington, DC: Aspen Institute Rural Economic Development Policy Program, 1996), preface–1.

73. Robert Goodman et al., "Identifying and Defining the Dimension of Community Capacity to provide a Basis for Measurement," *Health Education & Behavior* 25, no. 3 (1998): 258–278.

74. Details of the ten dimensions of community capacity are found in Goodman et al., "Identifying and Defining the Dimension of Community Capacity"; and Seunghyun Yoo, "Online Community and Community Capacity," (paper presented at Internet Research 7.0: Internet Convergences—Annual Conference of the Association of Internet Researchers, Brisbane, Australia, October 2006).

75. Paul Harwood and Wayne McIntosh, "Virtual Distance and America's Changing Sense of Community," in *Democracy Online: The Prospects for Political Renewal through the Internet*, ed. Peter Shane (London: Routledge, 2004), 209–224; Seong-Yeon Park and Seung-Hyun Yoo, "The Effect of The Sense of On-Line Community on Website Loyalty and Purchase Intention," *Kyungyounghak Yonku* 32, no. 6 (2003): 1695–1713; and Hee-Sung Park*, Moon-Bong Lee*, and Kil-Soo Suh*, "Gasang gongdongche euishiki junja sanggoerae sobijaeui choongsungdoeh michineun younghyang" [Effects of the Sense of Virtual Communities on the Commitment of E-Commerce Consumers], (paper presented at the Korea Society of Management Information Systems Semi-Annual International Conference, Fall 1999).

76. Jeffrey Boaseet al., *The Strength of Internet Ties: The Internet and Email aid Users in Maintaining Their Social Networks and Provide Pathways to Help when People Face Big Decisions* (Washington, DC: PEW Internet and American Life Project, 2006); and Kim et al. "A Qualitative Study with Blog Users."

77. J. S. Kim, "Il-in media, blog-eui hwaksangua issue"; Young Bae, "Dynamics and Structure of Relations in Cyber Community," *Korean Sociology* 37, no. 3 (2003): 109–134; Young Bae, "Social Relations in Cyberspace," *Korean Sociology* 39, no. 5 (2005): 55–62; Yoo-Jung Kim, "The Use of Cyber Community on Uses and Gratification Perspectives," *The Korean Journal of Journalism & Communication Studies* 49, no. 3 (2005): 291–317; Choi, Lee, and Kim, "Online community yiyong euido"; Kook-Yong Lee, "A Study on the Users' Commitment in The Online Community," *Sanup Kyungje Yonku* 18, no. 1 (2005): 119–142; Moon-Bong Lee and Eun-Jung Kim, "A Study on the Effect of Participatory Motives and Social Influence in Online Community on Commitment," *Jungbo System Yonku*

14, no. 2 (2005): 191–214; KyungHee Kim and Joo Youn Kim, "A Study of the Launching and the Attributes of Internet Community," *Cybercommunications Papers* 13 (2004): 5–37; Eugene Park and JaeHwi Kim, "The Effect of Social Support in On-line Community on Community Involvement and Self-Esteem," *Korean Journal of Social and Personality Psychology* 19, no. 1 (2005): 13–25; Kunsoo Suh, "The Effects of the Characteristics of Internet Communities and Individuals on User Loyalty," *Journal of Management Information Systems* 13, no. 2 (2003): 2–21; Kim et al., "A Qualitative Study with Blog Users"; J. S. Kim, "Blog-eui sahwaemunwhajuk jinwhawa issue"; Kim and Bae, "Typology of Blogs"; Y. J. Kim, "Blog as a Media"; Kweon, "Blog Media Mode"; Kweon and Woo, "Blog Media Research"; and Noh and Lee, "Media Competition."

78. Choi, Lee, and Kim, "Online community yiyong euido"; Kweon and Woo, "Blog Media Research"; Noh and Lee, "Media Competition"; and Park and Cho, "Using the Web-Blog."
79. Han, "Personal 'Meaning Practice'."
80. Goodman et al., "Dimension of Community Capacity."
81. S. Yoo, "Online Community and Community Capacity."
82. Frank Rothaermel and Stephen Sugiyama, "Virtual Internet Communities and Commercial Success: Individual and Community-Level Theory Grounded in the Atypical Case of Timezone.Com," *Journal of Management* 27, no. 3 (2001): 297–312.
83. Goodman et al., "Dimension of Community Capacity."
84. Yang and Park, "Using Personal Community."

15 Gifts of Presence

A Case Study of a South Korean Virtual Community, Cyworld's Mini-hompy

Larissa Hjorth

INTRODUCTION

In a period marked by the rise of online communities and when user-created content (UCC) is increasingly becoming a part of daily life, one is left to question what effect this is having on online and offline relations. What types of social gift-giving are being created via the Internet? Does Rupert Murdoch's acquisition of popular networking site MySpace represent a new frontier in global media, where viral marketing is vicariously seeded in social capital? A world where identity is so flexible and mutable that online forms of individualism override offline forms of community, as is often the case in MySpace? Or do virtual communities, such as the South Korean (now global) Cyworld mini-hompy—that merges avatars and gaming, blogging, and forums—offer an alternative future?[1]

One of the marked features of the Internet is that for a "global" technology, its adaptation at the level of the local is far from homogeneous. While Western modes of social networking systems (SNS), such as MySpace, might dominate Western and Anglophonic discussion, outside of this context, we can find examples of divergent SNS models that inhabit the global space of the Internet. By drawing on case studies of SNS outside Western-centric models, we can reflect on the different ways in which the Internet is constituted by various online communities and how this inflects offline forms of locality.[2]

In the Asia–Pacific region, we can find many examples of differing online/offline relationships framed by governmental, cultural, and socio-economic factors. The growth in SNS has seen a variety of models developed in relation to specific forms of locality and sociocultural relationships to the Internet. In Japan, for instance, 2ch (2 channel, or *ni-ch*) is an anonymous discussion forum visited by millions per day (predominantly via their mobile phone, or *keitai*). In Korea, the success of the SNS, Cyworld mini-hompy, has seen over one-third (18 million) of the population of 48 million regularly accessing and updating their own and their friends' pages. Unlike such sites as MySpace, Cyworld's mini-hompy is dominated by cute customization—from avatars, cybergifts, and virtual spaces, such as the "mini-room," in which friends can hang out online together. As Seunghyun Yoo (Chapter 14, this volume) points out, the visual differences allude to distinctive modes of online performativity that diverge in important ways from Western models such as MySpace.

For Han Woo Park and Randy Kluver (Chapter 16, this volume), this rise of divergent models of SNS and blogging outside a Western context are indicative of emerging notions of community, sociality, and agency that are informed by the local. Through these practices, we see contesting ideas about what it means to be "online," eroding Western precepts about the techno-social space of the Internet. With the dominant Korean SNS Cyworld mini-hompy having launched versions in both the Asia–Pacific region and now in the United States, it seems fitting to revisit the particularities of this SNS as illustrative of an online Korean community. In the light of the current rhetoric surrounding the battle for global dominance between SNSs, such as MySpace and Cyworld, this chapter will reflect upon the particularities of Cyworld and the improbability of any one SNS gaining global domination. Rather, in the technosocial space of the Internet, any such homogenized notions of community, networking, and social capital are—as this collection demonstrates—continuously disavowed, disrupted, de-centered, and dynamic.

Focusing on the highly successful South Korean virtual community, Cyworld mini-hompy, this chapter will first discuss the popularity of Cyworld in South Korea and its potential adaptations in a global market. Can, as some media—including blogs such as Mashable—have asserted, Cyworld compete with MySpace? Or is Cyworld's success in South Korea too firmly linked to a localized relationship to the Internet and the specific technonational agenda of South Korea that has seen it dubbed the best example of e-government and the broadband center of the world?[3]

This chapter will draw upon case studies conducted with sample groups of South Korean mini-hompy users and consider how exchange, representation, and copresence are conceived. With the rise and hype around customization and UCC, this chapter will look at the integral role of cute aesthetics (a key feature of Cyworld) in the customizing practice of gift-giving, and how this is configuring online/offline identification. The chapter will also discuss the costs and benefits of Cyworld for Korean users and consider how the particular modes of gift-giving and copresence reflect a localized definition of the "gift economy" (as developed by the Creative Commons movement) of the Internet.

HOME PAGE: LOCATING CYWORLD IN
SOUTH KOREA AND BEYOND

Money pours in when the Cyworld population goes on a decorating, gift-buying, or music-downloading spree to adorn their "rooms." The more attractive and interesting the room, the more visitors it gets. Also in Cyworld, popularity equates to fame and success. The site even measures sexiness and friendliness, which it gauges by the number of gifts a person gives or receives.[4]

In August 2006, Cyworld launched its SNS, the mini-hompy, in the United States. Having already been launched in Asian locations, such as China, Japan, and Taiwan, Cyworld's entry into the United States marked a move toward a global web community. But can the success experienced by the site in South Korea be replicated elsewhere? In a March 2006 posting on the blog Mashable, participants responded to Pete Cashmore's provocative question: "Cyworld US Launched—Will it Topple MySpace?"[5] According to Moon Ihlwan in "E-Society: My World Is Cyworld," Cyworld's global plans will race head to head with Murdoch's News Corp's (NWS) expansion of MySpace.[6] And yet, according to other sources, Cyworld does not pose any real threat to MySpace.

For US users, the "cute" graphic style of Cyworld lends itself to adoption by children, as was the case with the US Gaia virtual community, which also deploys cute aesthetics. This Western model that identifies the cute as child's play runs counter to its context in South Korea, where over one-third of the population, both young and old, partake in the politics of cute.[7] In the world's most broadbanded country, the relationship between the online and offline is apparently seamless.

It is easy to forget that South Korea has undergone a rapid rise to become a global symbol of twenty-first century modernity. In South Korea, Internet and mobile telephonic spaces have been seen as facilitating Korean forms of democracy.[8] The antagonistic yet integral role of new technologies in the rise of new forms of democracy in South Korea is clearly outlined in Yoo's and Park and Kulver's chapters (Chapters 14 and 16, this volume). My interest in this lies in the often-contradictory experiences of the politics of personalization/customization,[9] which will shed some light on the oft-binary opposition between debates around the rise of "user as producer" or "prosumer."[10] On the one hand, the rise of convergent media and SNS has provided a vehicle for everyday users to express their opinions and develop their multimedia skills. On the other hand, we can see the exploitation of users' (free) time and (free) labor for the profit of global conglomerates (such as YouTube and MySpace). However, through the politics of customization—as both an aesthetic/stylistic mode and also as an ethical reflection of mediated realities—we can gain insight into how users' relationships to the Internet are informed by the local.

Over the last couple of years, South Korea has managed to eclipse Japan as an innovative superpower for technology and cultural products both in the region and globally.[11] The rise of K-wave (Korean wave, or *Hallyu*) in the region, in combination with the Korean technonationalist agenda (discussed by Yoo, Chapter 14, in this volume) has led to online SNS that are indicative of Chua's notion that the region has come to be comprised of trans-Asian "communities of consumers."[12] As the most broadbanded country in the world and one of the leaders in innovative convergent Information and Communication Technologies (ICT), such as Digital Multimedia Broadcasting, South Korea provides a fascinating model for studying the seamlessness of online/offline correlations. Unlike other, less broadbanded locations, activities such as online gaming and SNS are mainstream and not seen as "lesser" experiences of sociality. The consumption of South Korean cultural products in the form of the K-wave—from Korean TV dramas and films to online multiplayer games—seems unstoppable in the Asia–Pacific region, having already eclipsed Japan's stronghold on regional cultural capital (J-pop). In particular, markets such as Hong Kong, Taiwan, and mainland China have recently become key consumers of Korean popular culture.

Cute aesthetics is one of the defining features in the customization of technologies. In the Asia–Pacific region, the cute is all-pervasive and yet disjunctive in its signification. The use of cute capital (that is, cute characters) has long been viewed as a popular practice for both young and old to domesticate new technologies—a phenomenon that does not translate into other contexts, such as the United States.[13] I argue that by investigating customization techniques, as indicative of the sociocultural context, we can gain insight into the relationship between online and offline and attendant localized notions of individualism, community, and social capital. I assert that we must read this emerging phenomenon of customizing convergent Internet and mobile technologies in terms of reciting earlier forms of mediation—that is, all modes of intimacy and presence have always been mediated—by language, gestures, and memories:[14] customizing encourages users to conceive of the technology as remediated. As Bolter and Grusin note, "remediation" is a reworking of Marshall McLuhan's argument that the content of new technologies is recycled from previous, older technologies.[15]

In order to illustrate the localized and remediated nature of customization, I will begin within the context of Seoul, specifically focusing on the relationship between cute capital, social capital, and gift-giving in the world of mini-hompy. I will reflect upon the ambivalence that is the weight, or more aptly in terms of temporal disjuncture, the "wait," of personalization.

THE PRICE OF CUTE PRESENCE: CUTE CUSTOMIZATION AND THE POLITICS OF ONLINE/OFFLINE IDENTITY

In Seoul one can find two types of youth sociality centered on technologies. Firstly, there is the significance of the mobile phone (*haendup*).[16] Secondly, there is the interrelated role of the Internet and the high participation in mini-hompys and online multiplayer games that take place in the social space of personal computer (PC) *bangs* (PC rooms).[17] As Yoo and Park and Kluver (Chapters 14 and 16, this volume) demonstrat, the online is not about substituting the virtual for the actual, but rather online interaction is another vehicle to strengthen social capital. In Seoul, the Internet—and its attendant connectivity—is part of the offline practices of everyday life. This is ensured in part by Internet users having to register their "real" offline names in the form of citizen IDs (as discussed by Yoo in Chapter 14, this volume). However, the specter of the offline is forever present—from the uploading of camera phone images and music to one's mini-hompy to the fact that many users participate in these practices while in the social spaces of PC bangs—highlighting the correlation between online and offline social capital.

The emphasis on being true to one's offline identity has ensured the success of Cyworld in South Korea. Cyworld's reappropriation of the traditional Korean familial concept of *ilchon*—once used to denote degrees of separation in a family (that is, an uncle is three *chon* in distance from yourself)—to divide mini-hompy users into friends (*ilchon*) or non-friends (non-*chon*) could be seen as capitalizing on the "family" metaphor so important to Korean self-identity. Moreover, the gift-giving culture of Cyworld, where *ilchons* can buy fellow *ilchons* cheap cybergifts for their mini-room with the Cyworld currency *dotori* (meaning acorns), reflects already existing gift-giving cultures as discussed by Yoo (Chapter 14, in this volume).

Avatars, as Cyworld's mini-hompy attests, are quintessential to the investment—both financially and emotionally—of users and their maintenance of copresent communities. The role of the "cute" is pivotal in the aesthetics both of the avatars and the overall design landscape of the mini-hompy and attendant forms of customization. These cute landscapes clearly play into what Anne Allison—in the context of the Pokémon global phenomenon—characterized as the "postmodern" qualities of the cute that make it open to polysemic readings, contexts, and reappropriations.[18] However, while the cute may afford polysemic readings, this does not mean a loss of local specificity. Rather, with the rise of "global" social networking spaces, such as Cyworld, Gaia, and Habbo Hotel, the cute is linked to types of play that are informed by localized sociality. Play spaces are social spaces.[19] Behind the "cuteness" is a struggle to humanize—and socialize—technological spaces, to highlight the mediated role of intimacy (regardless of technological interference). Although the use of the cute in the West has been associated with child's play,[20] in the Asia–Pacific region, the cute is part of what Brian McVeigh has dubbed Japan's "techno-cute" culture—highlighting the role that cute plays in making warm the coldness of new technology.[21]

Despite new forms of cute emerging from locations outside of Japan, little research has been conducted into the ways in which the production and consumption of cute is tied to specific forms of locality. When the cute has been theorized in terms of trans-Asian flows in the region, it is often mistaken as a form of Japanization.[22] To the uninitiated, the cute graphic style of Cyworld mini-hompy may look the same as the characters in the Icelandic Habbo Hotel and the American Gaia, but in the case of Cyworld, the connection and investment in the avatar as an extension of self is vastly different.

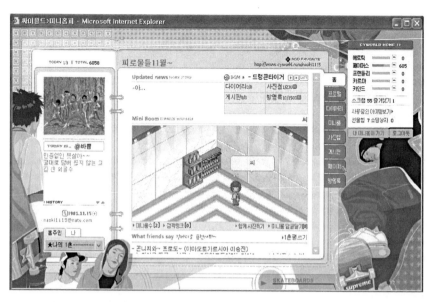

Figure 15.1 An example of a male respondent's mini-hompy.

In an early study, many users of mini-hompy discussed the importance of their cute mini-me avatars as representative of their offline identities.[23] For some, the cute "representative" could be read more playfully as an "ideal" or an emotional depiction of the user, while for others, the postmodern fluidity of the symbolism behind the cute avatar was a source of frustration, as it could be seen as confusing the online/offline correlation. While the dominant user demographic is in their twenties (90 percent of 20-year-olds use Cyworld), this does not mean that the logic of "cute" on the site is exclusive to young users, since it is not uncommon for parents and grandparents to start a mini-hompy to keep in contact with their children or grandchildren studying aboard (something discussed further below).

Note the "cute" avatar in the mini-room in Figure 15.1. In the top right corner, there is a gauge that measures his popularity, generosity, and charm in relation to how many cybergifts the user gives and receives, and how many users visit his home page. (This gauge was deleted from the interface early in 2007.)

THE WEIGHT/WAIT OF PERSONALIZATION: A CASE STUDY OF SOUTH KOREAN MINI-HOMPY USERS

Social networks and the norms of reciprocity and trustworthiness that arise from them are central to the logic of Cyworld. Gift-giving can operate on various levels. There can be the gift of visiting someone's mini-hompy, the gift of leaving a message in the visitors' book and then the return gift of answering it, the gift of asking someone to be your "cyberrelative" or cybuddy, the gift of sharing a photograph with someone, or the gifts of dotoris or buying cybergifts for friends' home pages. All these interactions can be seen as contributing to individual social capital.[24] Collectively, this may lead to growing social capital among Cyworld users. Yet, how much of the gift-giving occurs outside the acquisition of points for popularity, charm, and generosity on the Cyworld register?

As we move into a new epoch of the information age spoken of by Manuel Castells, the role of customization in the face of the increasing standardization of ICT becomes more and more prevalent.[25] With the hype around "prosumers," everyday users are becoming more and more savvy to media production and are even producing their own content (UCC). However, behind this rise of user agency is the double-edged sword of the symbolic weight—or, in terms of temporality, "wait" might be more appropriate—of customization. Many respondents expressed how much time customization took. Here, we see the downside to customization by way of the paradox of technology: rather than freeing us, it further enslaves us. Behind the politics of immediacy or fast-forwarding presence (the perpetual practice of almost immediate representation of offline experiences online) lie actual labor-intensive customization techniques.

For many of the twenty respondents (aged between twenty and forty years who were half male and half female) I interviewed between October and December 2005, the entry of mini-hompy into the mainstream of Korean life presented a problem. Specifically, university students expressed great concern about the value of mini-hompy and its community due to the fact that some of their professors had started their own mini-hompys. While a professor would only have limited access to any student's mini-hompy (s/he would have to be listed as an *ilchon* to have full access), what troubled the students was the potential of "their" community being disrupted by an authoritarian presence. Here, we see that the power relationships experienced offline are replicated online. Moreover, many respondents noted the various "costs"—both economic and personal—in maintaining one's mini-hompy and online reputation. The role of economic capital (that is perpetually updating and exchanging) and the amount of time needed to ensure popularity on Cyworld reflects offline realities. So, is there a price to these forms of presence? Can copresence be bought?

So much time can be spent maintaining connections through the various modes of gift-giving in order to maintain their online presence that users can feel enslaved to the community. In the 2005 study, respondents noted that they would often upload their camera-phone images of an event to their mini-hompy immediately for friends to view and share. However, this meant the user had to defer experience of the present, which could only be experienced later via its online mediation. This phenomenon of temporal disjuncture is what I have characterized elsewhere as a "fast-forwarding present." Here, we see that the presents—in the form of sharing of images, music, writing, and sending of texts—of copresence can jeopardize the experience of offline presence in the present.[26] This is the paradox of convergent media, whereby users find themselves devoting many modes of labor (social, creative, financial) to an attempt to maintain what Misa Matsuda described as "full-time intimacy."[27]

This labor of love was a dominant theme in many of the twenty respondents' comments. One female, aged twenty-eight years old, noted:

> At one stage I felt like all I was doing was taking pictures, editing and uploading them. This was initially fun because my friends enjoyed seeing them—especially when they were in them! However, I found the novelty wore off and then my friends came to expect me to be the photographer so that meant that I couldn't enjoy the event as much because I had to concentrate on getting "good" pictures of everyone. One time I pretended the camera wasn't sending pictures properly so someone else would take the responsibility.

When asked how much time they spent daily taking camera-phone images, customizing them, and uploading them to share, many respondents thought they spent at least one hour per day. The compulsion to continuously update, maintain, and check their own and others' mini-hompys was a time-consuming exercise, with many respondents claiming to spend at least three hours per day on these activities. This seems to reflect many of the stories in the media that have Cyholics confessing that they became addicted to mini-hompys, resulting in a strong emphasis on living predominantly online, in the world of Cyworld, rather than using the Internet to augment offline relationships and contacts.[28]

In the case of Cyworld, mobile phones, or *haendup* are often used to access and update Cyworld mini-hompy pages.[29] Yet, far from liberating users by allowing them to update and check their pages while on the run, many users expressed frustration over the constant pressure to be present in Cyworld. Hand phones, with their online capabilities, have created a paradoxical situation that Jack Qiu has dubbed the "wireless leash."[30] The so-called immediacy or "fast-forwarding presence" of haendup practices can often result in users spending more time documenting—rather than actually experiencing—the present. This fast-forwarding presence means that users are often documenting and sharing while experiencing; sometimes the documenting mediates the experience so much that users are only able to experience the moment afterward. Thus, the requirement to maintain online copresence can often put the present on hold.[31]

However, Cyworld does provide opportunities to extend social capital that may not be available to users in the offline world. Functions such as "people search" allow users to reconnect with long-lost friends. Another function allows users to request to become a stranger's Cybuddy if they like someone's mini-hompy (if they have similar tastes). Many respondents admitted to lurking on strangers' sites because they had overlapping social circles or similar interests. This sometimes leads to strangers leaving messages (that is, requesting to be a Cybuddy) and becoming friends—both online and offline—with the recipient. This vicarious networking has its price, especially as users grapple with becoming more and more guarded about what information they make visible to *ilchon*s and non-chons, and what they choose to leave unspoken. Sometimes, a user may accidentally not register offline friends marked as *ilchon*, thus causing much distress for the friends when they visit and realize they cannot gain access to *ilchon* material. The choice as to who is a non-*chon* or *ilchon* is a very sensitive issue, highlighting the palpable power relations involved, and that the Internet's architecture, like offline sociality, is deeply imbued with vertical hierarchies of capital—cultural, economic, and social.

Of the twenty respondents in the 2005 case study, none claimed to be addicted to Cyworld, noting the importance of offline meetings that could never be replicated online. However, a couple of respondents noted that they felt they could "perform" better online in Cyworld. While Cyworld is meant to be reflective of the offline social gift-giving gestures of friends, the user's indicator—which gauges how charming or popular a person is through how many times people hit their site or give or receive cybergifts—often created anxieties for users. Sometimes, the compulsion to look like a good friend meant that some respondents felt that their gift-giving tendencies—through visiting a friend's site, giving, and receiving presents—were sometimes more artificial than the more natural ones in offline relationships. As one female respondent, aged twenty-four years old, contended:

> My best friend gave me many items for my mini-room for my birthday. When it came to her birthday I wanted to give her even more gifts. Before long we were buying gifts for each other all the time. It went from a feeling of friendship to becoming an obsession that was almost competitive. Giving gifts in Cyworld isn't the same as in the real world, as the gifts in Cyworld are cheap. But it can really add up!

So, one wonders about what types of gift-giving rituals are being rewarded and taken up in Cyworld. Although respondents did not seem bothered by the relatively small material cost of such exchanges, one cannot help but wonder what logic of reciprocity is operating in the social network of Cyworld. Do users gift-give in the form of helping others to do their homework or find a job? Can the plethora of cyberitems purchased be reflective of emotional and intellectual support? One thing is certain: from the respondents interviewed, none gave greater importance to connection online over contact offline. In this way, Cyworld helps to develop relationships similar to that of older mediated forms of communication, like letter writing.

Many respondents noted that some mini-hompys were a form of art. A few of the male respondents claimed that female users cared more about the appearance of their mini-hompys. However, this stereotype was shifting, with some male users starting to spend more time on customizing and updating.

For a male respondent, aged twenty-five years old, mini-hompys are about identity. He states:

> . . . A lot of girls use the mini-hompy in a more obsessive manner. I think it can be a competition sometimes. I know a lot of girls who spend a lot of time on their mini-hompys. Some mini-hompys are amazing. In Korea, accessing the Internet all the time anywhere is part of everyday life.

As the above respondent notes, the Internet is very much "part of everyday life" and, thus, the offline/online distinction can seem artificial. One female respondent, aged thirty years old, stated:

> Many younger people like to spend a lot of time decorating and updating their mini-hompys. It is like a fashion. But then, isn't youth about great demonstrations of expression? If it weren't the mini-hompy, it would be clothes or music.

As this respondent observes, the role of the mini-hompy is a form of expression, just like music. And while highly engaged mini-hompy users may use up their funds (in the form of *dotori*) and time by constant customization, one could argue that they are not being exploited or duped but rather are participating in a creative and performative space. For another female respondent, aged twenty-eight years old, the cost of such performativity never outweighed the importance of the face-to-face. She suggests:

> I think the upkeep of a mini-hompy can become obsessive . . . I used to be more interested in my mini-hompy but now I just see it as one form in many to communicate with my friends and family. I'm not interested in spending too much time online. Neither are my friends. It's just what you do when you can't see each other.

For another female respondent, aged twenty-three years old, the mini-hompy was an important way to keep disparate groups of friends cohesive. She stated:

> I like to keep in contact with school friends and university friends. My mini-hompy is convenient in that way because I can put my recent images there and always keep friends involved. It has been a way for me to keep in contact even though we are all going different career paths.

Among those interviewed, none claimed to be obsessed with mini-hompy—and the attendant customization modes—to the point that they would classify themselves a Cyholic (Cyworld addicts). Many noted changes in their usage dependent upon the time of year and demands in the offline world. One male respondent, aged forty years old, who mainly used NATE (e-mail) services, saw the Internet in general as a bit of a "trap":

> South Korea is changing. The Internet is very important. It is part of the everyday. So whether you actively use mini-hompy or not, or whether you play lots of games or not, it is a noticeable fact . . . After all, actually seeing people is much more important but sometimes, life gets so busy, and so substitutes like the Internet are used. Sometimes, when my work schedule is difficult, I find myself just struggling to send an email to people close to me. But for non-close people, the Internet is perfect.

Here, the respondent identifies a recurring comment that, despite the ubiquity of "being connected" in South Korea, the Internet is never a substitute for offline contact. Moreover, the respondent pinpoints that, due to the overwhelming demands of work, vehicles such as the Internet just provide a window for reminding friends and family that one is thinking of them. This window is not mistaken for the world. Koreans traveling abroad especially acknowledge Korea's privileged position regarding connectivity and often take their world-class Internet connections for granted.[32]

CONCLUSION: GIFTS WITH PRESENCE

The growing importance of mediated forms of intimacy (and the underlining logic of gift-giving) through online social networks raises the question: is it presence or presents we want? Are we trading off actual contact with gestures of presence because our lives are too busy? The growth of SNS is indicative of what has been characterized by movements, such as the Creative Commons as the "gift economy" of the Internet. And yet, as the Internet continues to expand, we are reminded of how the definition of gift-giving is subject to localized practices.

The launch of Cyworld could well profit from the K-wave boom and its dominance in the Asian region. The fact that the popularity of Korean TV dramas has led to many middle-aged women from Hong Kong becoming Internet-savvy so they can actively chat online with other fans is indicative of the shifting role of sociotechnologies in the region.[33] As mentioned, this has led Chua to argue that the region can now be understood in terms of "communities of consumers," invoking Appadurai's notion of "communities of imagination and interest," rather than viewing it as a collection of nation-states, as in Anderson's "imagined communities."[34] One of the defining characteristics in technological usage in the region is the role of cute customization to humanize technological spaces. This form of customization differs dramatically from Western SNS, such as MySpace, reflecting localized notions of community, social capital, and gift-giving. While there is much gift-giving in Cyworld, measuring the ephemeral gestures between individuals and finding out what types of reciprocity operate to strengthen social capital can be hard, since authentic gestures of warmth and friendship are often masked by commoditization.

As can be evidenced by the specific customization and gift-giving practices of mini-hompy, the local informs this phenomenon. Returning to the aforementioned rivalry between MySpace and Cyworld—a clash between an "East" and "West" SNS—such a debate about global supremacy misses the point. The rise of the Internet has, as this collection demonstrates, been one marked by divergent formations informed by linguistic and sociocultural specificities that have disrupted any notion of the Internet as an homogeneous entity. The many different forms of what it means to be "online"—and its relationship to the offline—are indeed informed by already existing cultural practices and customs.

So, it is doubtful that mini-hompy will replace the likes of MySpace, as the use of the Internet in South Korea is dependent on ubiquitous, easy, and cheap access to high-speed connectivity unlikely to be replicated elsewhere in the near future. MySpace and mini-hompy represent two roads going in opposite directions. Mini-hompy is about the seamlessness between online and offline identity and community, whereas MySpace is devised around a Western notion of the individual in an age of self-confession, as exemplified by Wellman's "networked individualism."[35] In an age of copresence, communities such as Cyworld remind us that gifts with presence are indeed informed by localized notions of play, community, and social capital. Who said that cute was child's play?

ACKNOWLEDGEMENTS

I would like to thank the respondents interviewed in 2004, and Heewon Kim for our initial collaborative research in 2004. In addition, thanks to my Hallym University Mobile Media seminar students for their discussions about the role of mobile phone sharing in relation to their mini-hompys, as well as respondents interviewed in 2005.

NOTES

1. See Cyworld Factory, http://c2.cyworld.com/en/ (accessed May 15, 2007). John Borland and Michael Kanellos, "South Korea Leads the Way," CNET News.com, http://news.com.com/South+Korea+leads+the+way/2009-1034_3-5261393.html (July 28, 2004).
2. Here, I am drawing on Doreen Massey's notion of locality, in which she argues that a sense of place is defined through representational processes, a practice that is always mediated. See Doreen Massey, "Questions of Locality,"

Geography 78 (1993): 142–149. See also Doreen Massey and John Allen, eds., *Geographical Worlds* (Oxford: Oxford University Press, 1995).

3. Organisation for Economic Co-operation and Development, "OECD Broadband Statistics," http://www.oecd.org/sti/ict/broadband (2006).

4. Deborah Cameron, "Koreans Cybertrip to a Tailor-Made World," *The Age*, May 9, 2006.

5. Pete Cashmore, "Cyworld US Launches—Will it Topple MySpace?," Mashable blog, http://mashable.com/2006/03/30/cyworld-us-will-it-topple-myspace/ (March 30, 2006). This discussion was also taken up by David Jacobs in "Cyworld Lands on MySpace," *International Business Times*, http://ibtimes.com/articles/20060731/cyworld-myspace-sktelecom-news-corp.htm (July 3, 2006).

6. Moon Ihlwan, "E-Society: My World Is Cyworld," *BusinessWeek* Online, http://www.businessweek.com/magazine/content/05_39/b3952405.htm (September 26, 2005).

7. It should be noted that the dominant demographic is between 20 and 30 years old.

8. Shin Dong Kim, "The Shaping of New Politics in the Era of Mobile and Cyber Communication," in *Mobile Democracy*, ed. Kristof Nyiri (Vienna: Passagen Verlag, 2003), 325.

9. For the aforementioned first case study, conducted in 2004, see Larissa Hjorth and Heewon Kim, "Being There and Being Here: Gendered Customising of Mobile 3G Practices through a Case Study in Seoul," *Convergence* 11 (2005): 49–55. I still owe a great debt of gratitude to Heewon for introducing me to Cyworld and sharing her compelling insights as a user.

10. This idea of the consumer being transformed into a producer was first discussed by Alvin Toffler through the analogy of consumers having to fill their own petrol tanks. The prosumer concept was furthered by Don Tapscott in terms of the "promise and peril" of networked intelligence. See Alvin Toffler, *The Third Wave* (New York: William Morrow and Company, 1980) and Don Tapscott, *The Digital Economy: Promise and Peril in the Age of Networked Intelligence* (New York: McGraw-Hill Books, 1995).

11. Douglas McGray, "Japan's Gross National Cool," *Foreign Policy* May/June (2002)http://www.chass.utoronto.ca/~ikalmar/illustex/japfpmcgray.htm; Chua Beng-Huat, "East Asian Pop Culture: Consumer Communities and Politics of the National" (paper presented at Asia's Futures Initiative, Cultural Space and Public Sphere in Asia Conference, Seoul, South Korea, March 15–16, 2006).

12. Chua Beng-Huat, "East-Asian Pop Culture."

13. See Larissa Hjorth, "Odours of Mobility: Japanese Cute Customization in the Asia-Pacific Region," *Journal of Intercultural Studies* 26 (2005): 39–55, and "Playing at Being Mobile: Gaming, Cute Culture and Mobile Devices in South Korea," *Fibreculture Journal* 8, August (2006), http://journal.fibreculture.org/issue8/index.html

14. Margaret Morse, *Virtualities: Television, Media Art, and Cyberculture* (Bloomington: Indiana University Press, 1998).

15. McLuhan used the example of the TV and its adoption of the previous domestic technology—radio—through genres such as soap operas. See Jay Bolter and Richard Grusin, *Remediation: Understanding New Media* (Cambridge, MA: MIT Press, 1999); and Marshall McLuhan, *Understanding Media* (New York: Mentor, 1964).

16. The Korean word for mobile/cell phone is *haendup*, which is an abbreviation of the wird for "hand phone." For in-depth discussions of this phenomenon in South Korea, see Kyongwon Yoon, "Retraditionalizing the Mobile: Young

People's Sociality and Mobile Phone Use in Seoul, South Korea," *European Journal of Cultural Studies* 6, no. 3 (2003): 327–343. Also, see Shin Dong Kim, "Korea: Personal Meanings," in *Perpetual Contact: Mobile Communication, Private Talk, Public Performance*, ed. James Katz and Mark Aakhus (Cambridge: Cambridge University Press, 2003), 63–79.

17. The use of technologies in South Korea is a key example of sociotechnologies—that is, contemporary urban culture is permeated by technologies that are social in nature. In Florence Chee's ethnography on PC *bangs* (PC rooms where youths play online multiplayer games), these are social spaces that are viewed as "third spaces" between home and work. For the youth of South Korea—where most still live at home before getting married—these "third spaces" operate as places to connect with other like-minded people. See Florence Chee, "Understanding Korean Experiences of Online Game Hype, Identity, and the Menace of the 'Wang-tt'" (paper presented at DIGRA 2005 Conference: Changing Views—Worlds in Play, Canada, June 16-20, 2005).

18. Anne Allison, "Portable Monsters and Commodity Cuteness: Pokémon as Japan's New Global Power," *Postcolonial Studies* 6, no. 3 (2003): 381–398. See also Koichi Iwabuchi, *Recentring Globalization: Popular Culture and Japanese Transnationalism* (Durham, NC: Duke University Press, 2003). For the history of cute culture in Japan, see Sharon Kinsella, "Cuties in Japan," in *Women, Media and Consumption in Japan*, ed. Lisa Skov and Brian Moeran (Surrey, UK: Curzon Press, 1995), 220–254.

19. Brian Sutton-Smith, *The Ambiguity of Play* (London: Routledge, 1997). See Chee, "Understanding Korean Experiences of Online Game Hype," for a discussion of Sutton-Smith's notion of play and the "third space" in the context of Korean PC *bangs*.

20. Mary White, *The Material Child: Coming of Age in Japan and America* (New York: Free Press, 1993). See also Allison, "Portable Monsters."

21. Brian McVeigh, "How Hello Kitty Commodifies the Cute, Cool and Camp: 'Consumutopia' versus 'Control' in Japan," *Journal of Material Culture* 5, no. 2 (2000): 291–312.

22. Hjorth, "Odours of Mobility." See also Yu-fen Ko, "Consuming Differences: 'Hello Kitty' and the Identity Crisis in Taiwan," *Postcolonial Studies* 6, no. 2 (2003): 175–189.

23. Hjorth and Kim, "Being There and Being Here."

24. Ibid.

25. Manuel Castells, *The Internet Galaxy* (Oxford: Oxford University Press, 2001).

26. It is not accidental that research into mobile telephony has often referred to the technology as embedding and replicating already existing social rituals. As Taylor and Harper noted in their study of the usage of mobile phones among youth, the practices of phone-sharing and text-messaging create a level of reciprocity best understood as an extension of already existing gift-giving practices. See Alex Taylor and Richard Harper, "Age-Old Practices in the 'New World': A Study of Gift-Giving between Teenage Mobile Phone Users" in *Changing Our World, Changing Ourselves* (proceedings of the SIGCHI Conference on Human Factors in Computing Systems, Minneapolis, MN, April 20-25, 2002), 439–446. See also Yoon, "Retraditionalizing the Mobile."

27. Misa Matsuda, "Discourses of *Keitai* in Japan," in *Personal, Portable, Pedestrian: Mobile Phones in Japanese Life*, ed. Mizuko Ito, Daisuke Okabe, and Misa Matsuda (Cambridge, MA: MIT Press, 2005), 19–40.

28. Gift-giving evokes gestures of intimacy and affect experienced in modes of copresence in the context of the increasingly intertwined Internet and mobile-telephonic nodes. Mizuko Ito (in the context of Japan) has talked at

great length about the role of intimate or ambient copresence; Misa Matsuda has extended this argument to outline the costs of the increasing tendency for ICTs to create a sense of copresent "full-time" intimacy. Mizuko Ito, "Introduction: Personal, Portable, Pedestrian," in *Personal, Portable, Pedestrian: Mobile Phones in Japanese Life*, ed. Mizuko Ito, Daisuke Okabe, and Misa Matsuda (Cambridge, MA: MIT Press, 2005), 1–16; Mizuko Ito, "Mobiles and the Appropriation of Place," *Receiver* Magazine 8 (2002), www.receiver.vodafone.com; Misa Matsuda, "Discourses of *Keitai* in Japan."

29. Cyworld in the United States is holding off on its development of mobile nodes, instead watching to see the success of its parent company, SK Telecom's Mobile Virtual Network Operator (MVNO) Helio, with using mobile phones for MySpace.

30. Jack Qiu, "The Wireless Leash: Mobile Messaging Service as a Means of Control," *International Journal of Communication* 1 (2007): 74–91. See also Michael Arnold, "On the Phenomenology of Technology: the 'Janus-faces' of Mobile Phones," *Information and Organization* 13 (2003): 231–256.

31. These emerging practices of copresence should not be seen in isolation, and I am certainly not suggesting that we should concur with Robert Putnam's claims about the shrinking of social capital, or Habuchi's Japanese version, dubbed "telecocooning," in the case of Cyworld. See Robert Putnam, *Bowling Alone: The Collapse and Revival of American Community* (London: Simon & Schuster, 2000); Ichiyo Habuchi, "Accelerated Reflexivity," in *Personal, Portable, Pedestrian: Mobile Phones in Japanese Life*, ed. Mizuko Ito, Daisuke Okabe, and Misa Matsuda (Cambridge, MA: MIT Press, 2005), 165–182.

32. This point was evident in a case study of Korean students studying aboard in Melbourne, Australia, discussed in Larissa Hjorth, "Home and Away: A Case Study of Cyworld Minihompy by Korean Students Studying Abroad," in ed. Anne McLaren, special issue on "The Internet in East Asia,"*Asian Studies Review*, Vol 31, no. 4 (2007): 397–407.

33. Angel Lin, "Korean TV Dramas in Hong Kong" (paper presented at Asia's Futures Initiative, Cultural Space and Public Sphere in Asia Conference, Seoul, South Korea, March 15–16, 2006).

34. Chua, "East Asian Pop Culture"; Arjun Appadurai, *Modernity at Large: Cultural Dimensions of Globalization* (Minneapolis: University of Minnesota Press, 1996); Benedict Anderson, *Imagined Communities: Reflections on the Origin and Spread of Nationalism* (London: Verso, 1983).

35. Barry Wellman, "Little Boxes, Glocalization, and Networked Individualism," in *Digital Cities II: Computational and Sociological Approaches*, ed. Mitomo Tanabe, Peter van den Besselaar, and Tomoko Ishida (Berlin: Springer-Verlag, 2002), 10–25.

16 Affiliation in Political Blogs in South Korea

Comparing Online and Offline Social Networks

Han Woo Park and Randy Kluver

INTRODUCTION

While it is a true to say that the Internet has become an important repository of political information, it is also true that, because of the power of relational networking, the voices of a few individuals quickly become amplified. A frequently heard phrase in a networked society is, "It's not what you know; it's who you know." This is particularly true when it comes to a political culture where a politician's efficacy relies, to a large extent, on the ability to draw upon political relationships. In South Korean politics, personal and organizational ties (based on a shared regional, party, and gender backgrounds) have been critically important, as in contrast to many Western nations, where political efficacy is typically centered upon individual characteristics of candidates, in addition to party and regional affiliation. Previous studies of hyperlink networks demonstrate that online relationships expressed through hyperlinks between official websites are more or less associated with information flows among websites, as well as demonstrating linkages between the website producers.[1]

However, when politicians engage in a sort of "non-official" web publishing, such as personal blogs, do hyperlinks demonstrate similar sorts of political communities and ideological networks, or do other types of political imperatives drive those networks? Certainly there is an overabundance of discussion in the West on whether the Internet is a "disruptive" technology, creating a technological imperative and impetus to radically reshape social and cultural life, including politics. Particularly, much Internet literature focuses on the formation of new political alliances, especially in overcoming the impediments of distance.

But to what extent does the Internet overturn established political culture, and to what extent does it ultimately begin to resemble traditional political culture? In response to the rise of more "personal" and less official web presences by politicians, this chapter examines the communication networks of politicians, as expressed through the pattern of link connectivity contained on their (personal) blogs, rather than (official) campaign sites. In particular, the specific information we discover from the hyperlinks on a politician's blogroll can provide a glimpse into the social interaction patterns of that individual.

We are also interested in the ways in which "personal" blogging illustrates certain aspects of South Korean political culture. One of the authors[2] has previously argued that online behavior is a reflection of political culture, and the way in which web producers design and produce sites illustrates cultural values. We have previously shown[3] that this is indeed true in "official" political websites. But, do the same cultural values and patterns reproduce themselves when taken out of the context of regimented, and somewhat predictable, political expectation and patterns? To find out, we have conducted a comparative analysis of online and offline social ties to gain insights into how South Korean culture is manifested in this online behavior.

This study is particularly appropriate for understanding the internationalization of Internet studies, in that it ties together several significant strands of earlier research related to online behavior (politics, community, and social network analysis) and examines them in a context (South Korea) that has garnered precious little research. It is becoming increasingly apparent that many of the assumptions regarding online behavior arise from the habits, mindsets, and preconditions of Western nations. However, technological innovation, particularly the extension and pioneering application of new technologies, has largely shifted out of the large research parks of the United States and Western Europe, and into the populations, communities, and social networks of Asia (see Gottlieb, Chapter 5, this volume; Bahfen, Chapter 11, this volume; Hjorth, Chapter 14, this volume; and Koch et al., Chapter 17, this volume). The citizens of Japan, Korea, Singapore, Taiwan, and China have, in many ways, demonstrated an amazing capacity to redeploy and redefine technologies for novel social purposes that are largely unknown in many nations of the West. (See Yoo, Chapter 14, this volume, for a more detailed explanation of technological development and diffusion in South Korea.) For example, it will be very difficult for many researchers of mobile texting to gain any sense of the uses that can be made of this technology if their own experience is limited primarily to North America, where texting has not had a significant impact, as compared to some of the nations of East and Southeast Asia (as discussed by Koch et al., Chapter 17, this volume).

We also hope, with this study, to provide a more qualitative cultural perspective of a methodology (link analysis) that has heretofore been primarily oriented toward mathematical and statistically-oriented investigations.[4] Moreover, an examination of the use of the blog as an emerging communication network among political actors in Korea will provide an opportunity to identify and discern how new technologies have permeated society and become a driving force, changing organizational forms and social relations. Finally, this research will provide further analysis of the role of political culture in online politics, and the ways in which political culture both mediates and constrains online political action.[5]

The Internet is generally conceptualized as the "network of networks" due to its characteristic aspect of linking patterns of information flow to one another. Hyperlinks are one of the key technologies in this, and in so doing, have a role in delimiting and defining communication patterns. For a number of years, private individuals have used various forms of networking technology to connect to one another, and more recently, political figures have started to maintain their own websites, and offer political activities and services on the Internet. In some cases, politicians have created far more political space for themselves because of a strong presence in cyberspace, while others have found that strong networking activities *online* can help to complement the *offline* weakness of individual actors, as well as strengthen their competitive positions online.

A number of hyperlink studies[6] have found that civic and advocacy organizations communicate actively through hyperlinks with other institutions, whose missions and activities are similar to themselves. According to Garrido and Halavais,[7] the Zapatista's informational use of hyperlinks allowed citizens and activists in Mexico to afford their own individualized community, which was open, global, and completely free from governmental offline control. In another context, Burris and his colleagues[8] found that radical advocacy groups, such as the White Supremacists and the Italian extreme right, have formed hyperlink connections for information diffusion, as well as to form strong bonds.

A number of social network theories[9] argue that social entities (including people, groups, and nation-states) with similar attributes should be considerably connected in terms of having shared sociocommunicational ties. In other words, network theory claims that social members tend to form a community of "birds of a feather," where one communicates with others based on a shared trait.[10] Since group members in a homogeneous community employ various modes of communication to maintain their ties, communication and information flows reflect the configuration of social networks among group members. However, this network theory does not always sufficiently explain the way in which people build communication ties both online and offline. Is it necessary to illustrate social ties and relationships through all available modes of communication when one mode of communication is sufficient? Previous studies have only provided limiting help in discovering the answers to this question.

KOREAN POLITICAL CULTURE AND BLOGS

Although there have been a number of previous studies on the role of blogs in electioneering[11], and another set of studies that examine the blog as a social phenomenon, this chapter attempts to bridge these previous surveys by examining the relational structures between members of the South Korean National Assembly expressed in blogs. Korean political culture, heavily influenced by Confucianism, has provided a strongly hierarchical framework for social relations and a strong emphasis on homogeneity for over 2,000 years. This emphasis on homogeneity has contributed to political affiliation largely based upon relational, gender, school, or regional ties. Since traditional relationships are deeply rooted in every layer of Korean society, sharing a tie with somebody means much more than just being acquainted with someone. Moreover, these ties are considered binding, and there is little room for individual politicians to seek to establish a record of an individual or a maverick within a party, something that is often prized in Western politicians. Being a loyal party member means subsuming one's own policy ideas and one's own political identity to the larger collective.

Previous analysis seems to suggest that official political websites do indeed enact certain elements of Korean political culture. Park and his colleagues[12] have argued that the emerging Korean hyperlink network links together relevant websites (e.g., party, peer politician, government, assembly, press, nongovernmental organization, etc.) for two purposes: both to enhance their sites' navigability, as well as to reveal their own ideological orientation for visitors. When it comes to politicians, the endorsement of a political party is organized by a leader who is influential within their constituencies. This has enormous repercussions on maintaining political trajectories. Thus, it is extremely rare in South Korea for politicians to make an alliance with members of opposing parties.

However, South Korea as a society has undergone rapid change, including rapid political democratization and cultural transformation. Although these changes predate the widespread dissemination of the Internet, the diffusion of digital communication technologies, such as the Internet, does seem to have contributed greatly to the generation of a new cultural atmosphere, one which is largely detached from traditional political culture. Over the past ten years, there has been a dramatic increase in the use of the web among South Koreans. South Korea had the eleventh highest Internet penetration rate in the world by December of 2004, according to the most recent data available on Internet World Stats.[13] Almost two-thirds (63.3 percent) of the population accessed the Internet as of December 2004. If, as Kluver[14] argues, political culture mediates online politics, it is probably also true that online activity is helping to mediate political culture, and is one factor in the long-term transformation of political values and behavior.

One aspect of this transformation is that, in contrast to the highly collectivistic expectations of traditional Korean political culture, individual politicians and parities have started to run websites to enhance communication, opinion-sharing, and participation. Whereas in the past, it would have been highly unusual for party members to seek to highlight their individuality, the rise of the Internet seems to be facilitating just that trend. According to Park and Thelwall,[15] 268 out of 299 members of the Seventeenth National Assembly of

South Korea had websites (89.6 percent), in contrast to a previous era, when politicians were more likely to campaign exclusively via traditional media, such as pamphlets, which were much more centrally organized.

Political parties are often regarded as the most influential political actors in South Korea, in that the parliamentary election processes are generally dominated by a party, not individual candidates. While Koreans usually state that they will vote for candidates based on their qualifications, voters generally have tended to choose their Assembly members according to candidates' party affiliations.[16] Interestingly, the important criterion for Korean people to identify with a political party is not the party's social or political agenda, but rather whether the party leadership has personal or organizational ties with their own region. This is in contrast to Western countries, where political parties are typically considered to share certain political views and ideologies, and citizens usually vote for parties similar to their own political aims and opinions.

Another aspect of the changes in Korean political culture is the rise of virtual communities, called by names such as online café, Internet club, or Internet society (see Yoo Chapter 14, this volume). These communities are built to share common interests among participants. One important aspect of online mass community is that the community itself has become an important amplifier of political information, and a powerful source of relational networking. A community board is a key technical feature for facilitating communication, opinion-sharing, and participation for its members. Lee, Lancendorfer, and Lee[17] compared the agenda-setting effect between online and traditional media during the 2000 general election in South Korea, and found that the political discourse of Internet bulletin boards significantly influenced newspapers' campaign coverage.

Thus, one important aspect of the study presented in this chapter is to examine the extent to which the advent of the political web in Korea has usurped traditional Korean political culture. As it is technically easy for politicians to establish relational networks across traditional ties (such as region or party affiliation), the question arises as to how this technical ability undermines the traditional practices of political affiliation. Rather than affiliation by region or other forms of traditional political linkages, do politicians form social networks with those who share the same interests? Does the rise of hyperlinking as a form of social networking overcome the traditional markers of alliance, such as family relations, geography, gender, or school ties?

AN ONLINE REPRESENTATION OF SOCIAL NETWORKS AMONG KOREAN POLITICIANS

The purpose of this case study is to formulate an exploratory description of the social linkages embodied in personal blogs maintained by National Assembly members. In previous studies, we have examined "official" and campaign websites, but for this study, we wanted to examine sites that were defined less by a political role (Assembly member, party member, etc.) and more by the individual politician. Although many of the blogs are overtly political, they still embody a greater potential to feature nonpolitical content than their more formal websites. To obtain the data for this study, we examined the blogs of South Korea's 107 National Assembly members, who were elected in April 2004 (in other words, members of Seventeenth National Assembly). The 107 Assembly members used a blog engine provided by Naver, the most popular blog service in South Korea.

There were four major parties active at the time of this research, the ruling Uri Party (Uri; *Yeo-lin-uri* in Korean), the major opposition Grand National Party (GNP; *Han-na-ra* in Korean), and two other opposition parties, the Democratic Labor Party (DLP; *Min-joo-no-dong* in Korean) and the Democratic Party (*Min-joo* in Korean), which changed its name from the Millennium Democratic Party. The Uri and the GNP parties are the parties corresponding roughly to the Democratic and Republican parties, respectively, in the US system. While the Uri party is more or less liberal, the GNP is a conservative party. These two parties occupied 272 out of 299 seats in the Assembly at the time of this research. The Democratic Party is the recently ousted ruling liberal party, while the DLP has progressive (left-wing) policies.

We found that while 69 out of 130 opposition parties' members (45.39 percent) maintained blogs, only 38 out of 147 members (25.85 percent) of the ruling Uri party had blogs. The results of this are ironic, in that, after the 2003 presidential election, Uri party leader Moo-Hyun Roh openly expressed the belief that he was victorious because of his sophisticated use of the Internet. Since then, the Uri party has emphasized online campaigning, and expressed strong support for "electronic democracy." The Uri party even identifies itself on its website as an "e-party," to appeal to the young generation. Thus, the low rate of blog ownership among this party is striking indeed.

Even more striking, perhaps, is the tremendous gender gap between bloggers and nonbloggers within the ruling liberal Uri party. Whereas there was

Table 16.1 Blog Ownership of Assemblymen by Party and Gender

	Uri (Ruling Party)		Opposition Parties*	
	Male	*Female*	*Male*	*Female*
Blog	19%	78%	45%	50%
	(24)	(14)	(58)	(11)
No blog	81%	22%	55%	50%
	(105)	(4)	(72)	(11)
Total	129	18	130	22

* Opposition parties include three parties: Grand National Party, Democratic Labor Party, and Democratic Party.

a roughly equal percentage of female and male bloggers in the opposition parties, there was a three to one ratio between female and male bloggers in the Uri party.

One of the most important measures of hyperlink network analysis is to identify a central blog, generally defined as the node, which provides the most and/or shortest connections to other members within the group.[18] In traditional Korean politics, the "central node" would usually be a well-known and experienced party figure. The central node usually plays a role of hub and broker, and is typically an authoritative or prestigious actor. To understand the centrality structure of the blog network, we used Freeman's degree centrality to measure both in-degree (number of incoming links) and out-degree (number of outgoing links).

Freeman's[19] degree centrality measure is to identify the numbers and strength of online ties that a blogger has with other bloggers. In a social network, the concept of centrality is defined as the structural position of actors in the network, not an internal attribute of actors themselves.[20] Degree centrality measures a relational attribute of an actor in a network for popularity, activity, and prominence in the flow of information.

The degree centralities for the 107 blogging Assemblymen show that Moo-Sung Kim's blog is the most central in terms of in-degree. His blog was identified as a neighbor from thirty Assembly members. He was also central in out-degree measure (forty-nine outlinks), followed by Yeon-Hee Choi (fifty-three outlinks), and Tae-Whan Kim (fifty-one outlinks). But it should be noted here that the classification of specific Assemblymen's blogs as central or peripheral is open to debate. It can be questioned whether their high/low centralities fully reflect their perceived reputation or popularity in the offline world.

The number of in-degree and out-degree isolates, with no link either from or to another blog, is nineteen and sixty, respectively. This indicates that nineteen members are isolates, in that no other blog linked to their site. A close examination of the proportion of the nineteen isolates by their individual attributes demonstrates little variance by age, gender, hometown location, electoral constituency, and committee assignments. However, there was a striking variation in terms of party affiliation and experience. Fifteen of the nineteen isolates belonged to the ruling party, Uri. Moreover, twelve of the Uri bloggers were new to the Assembly, in that they had just been elected, for the first time, a year and three months prior to this analysis.

There are a number of out-degree isolates that do not render a clear explanation at this point. The large number of out-degree isolates cast doubt as to whether blogs have really permeated Korean political culture. Assemblymen without outgoing hyperlinks might have created their blogs just to avoid being behind the changing trends in communication with citizens in the digital age. In other words, the existence of a blog for a politician can be a symbol of the adoption of technological innovation, rather than as a useful communication device.

Moreover, by mapping the online network that emerges through hyperlinks, it is also possible to see the ways in which the bloggers differ in terms of interconnectedness. In this map, the arrows indicate directional links. As Figure 16.1 illustrates, there are several major subclusters in this data. Again, Moo-Sung Kim is located in the center of the GNP cluster, demonstrating that he is the most central blog in terms of degree centrality. Blogs of other Assembly members in the GNP aggregate around his blog. In contrast, the ruling Uri party's Assemblymen are scattered on the upper right side, showing that they have a less densely linked network with their peers. In the middle of the map, a few Assembly members with bridging roles are neatly interspersed, making a circle centered on the node "Jong-geel Je." Here, it is possible to see the few instances of cross-party linking. On the upper left corner, the four members of the progressive DLP party form a linear and thin cluster, indicating that they are hyperlinked mostly from the same node: the blog of Sang-Jeung Sim.

In order to answer the questions driving this study—to what extent the relational networks expressed on the blogs corresponded with the traditional bases of political affiliation—we assessed whether hyperlinking activities between blogs were related with bloggers' shared offline

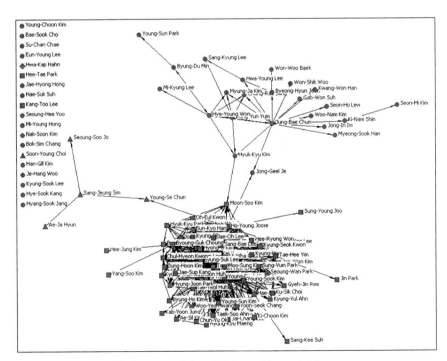

Figure 16.1 Network diagram of the 107 Assemblymen's blogs.

* Note: circle (Uri Party), square (Grand National Party), triangle (Democratic Labor Party), and diamond (Democratic Party).

backgrounds: age, gender, hometown, electoral constituency, party affiliation, experience, and committee assignments. We employed a quadratic assignment procedure using a standard routine from the social network software, UCINET.[21] In this chapter, we evaluated the strength of the connection between social relationships expressed through shared attributes and social relationships expressed through hyperlink interconnectivity among their blogs.

The results indicate that among these variables, party affiliation, gender, and hometown are significantly correlated with the structure of the blog links. In particular, a fairly strong correlation with party affiliation was found at the $p = .00$ level (Pearson's $r = 0.356$). The results have some important implications. First of all, the quadratic assignment procedure findings indicate that the links of more personalized and less official blogs do indeed demonstrate the continuity of traditional political networks among politicians. Politicians who blog express the traditional basis of political affiliation in the new media of weblogs, especially the relational ties of party affiliation, gender, and regional ties. In spite of the potential embodied in the Internet to create new political consortia and caucuses, the political communication structures that emerge online are but recreations of the traditional homophilous relationships among Assembly members. Moreover, in spite of the fact that these blogs are considered more personal and less official, political identity is still expressed according to traditional frameworks, such as regional background and party affiliation.

It could be that the traditional bonds resulting from the shared primary group affiliations, such as gender, locality, and party membership, influence both the allocation of information resources within cyberspace, just as they do in the offline realm, and the behavior and attitude of politicians. In addition, it seems that this data indicates that loyalty and respect for fellow politicians within the same party, which are typical political values within South Korea's political context, are the most important element in consolidating the information network. At least in the South Korean context, rather than creating new political constituencies and alliances, the Internet seems to reify existing networks, relationships, and political values.

CONCLUSION

This analysis of the linking patterns among Korean politicians' blogs reveals some interesting facets of how the advent of electronic media and Internet campaigning are intersecting with Korean political culture. Our findings demonstrate that online markers of homophily, in the form of hyperlinks, tend to follow the expectations established by centuries of Korean political tradition. In the context of personal blogs, politicians tend to link to other politicians who share the characteristics that drive many other phenomena in Korean politics, namely, affiliation based on party, gender, geographic origin, and so on.

There are significant implications of this finding for the task of internationalizing Internet studies. First, the Internet is by no means a "universalizing" phenomenon. Much of the analysis of the Internet in use in Asian political communities assumes that the technology will take on the values of Western democratic liberalism.[22] The Internet has been widely hailed as a liberating technology that would unleash forces that would overcome centuries-old traditions. This cyberutopianism has been influential in driving research agendas, as well as policy agendas of national governments, and plays no small role in global discussions of Internet governance. If the assumptions are that the Internet establishes a new social order by technologically restructuring social relations in the critical domains, such as politics, gender relations, racial relations, and so on, then it stands to reason that there are technological fixes to the world.

This analysis, as well as several others in this volume, points in a different direction. It indicates that culture matters when it comes to understanding the shapes, meanings, and manifestations of technology, and that culture mediates technological innovation and deployment as much, if not more, than the specific technologies themselves. In this case study, Korean social and political relations remain largely untouched by the technology, in spite of the vast potential, and the technological means, to reorder those relations.

In spite of the fact that electronic communication, and the advent of "e-campaigning," is indeed creating a new potential for democratic politics, it is clear from this analysis that, ultimately, technology is deployed by humans, who use it in ways that are familiar, and in ways that ultimately reify the political values and habits that are inherited from earlier generations of political expectations.

Social network analysis has become a significant form of Internet analysis, as the premise that we can map human relations through technological markers—the foundational premise to social network analysis via hyperlinks—finds itself embedded into the assumptions of Internet research. This analysis demonstrates significant promise for this form of quantifiable research when it is coupled with a qualitative approach to understanding the meaning of technological markers. This also raises another problematic issue for internationalizing Internet studies: to what extent can the meanings of technological indicators—or features, in this case—be said to "mean" something in a given culture? A hyperlink, for example, can have lots of meanings, as alluded to earlier. A hyperlink on a blog might mean agreement, disagreement, mockery, or any other range of human responses. The only thing that it does not "mean," is to ignore. To assess the real meaning of a technical feature, then, requires an in-depth, anthropological approach to assessing the motivation and meaning behind the technological feature.

On another project with which both of the present authors were involved—a cross-national exploration of the ways in which the Internet was used as a campaign device in election campaigns around the world—it became clear that because the political contexts and assumptions varied so much in each of the countries under review, it became difficult to make meaningful cross-national comparisons at all.[23] Although it was possible to identify the same technical features, such as hyperlinks, images, types of content, and so on, it was very difficult to assess the meaning of a feature in one country in comparison with another. This is not to say that it is not possible to understand the meaning of technology across cultural boundaries, but rather that it is critical to be aware of the variety of social meanings that might come into play.

There is another interesting finding of this study, which also speaks to the difficulty of understanding the role of the Internet across cultural boundaries. In this analysis, it is clear that the conservative GNP party, in every measure, dominated the Korean blogosphere in comparison to the ruling, progressive Uri party. To many Westerners, this finding seems puzzling, as the dominant discourse in the West is that the technology is itself "progressive," and provides tools to unmask the dominant mechanisms of state, media, and political organization. In fact, in the United States, organizations such as Moveon.org and the Daily Kos have banked much of their appeal on creating a synthesis between liberal-leaning politics and the "hipness" of information technologies, a meme that President Moo-Hyun Roh and his Uri party themselves stressed in 2004.

However, this analysis demonstrates that this synthesis is, in fact, artificial. The GNP, in the Korean context, is considered a conservative party, even bearing the legacy of the rightist, militaristic regime of the 1960s and 1970s. Yet, the GNP has demonstrated a greater commitment to fully deploying the technology than the left-leaning Uri party. Is there any meaning to this, other than that the GNP saw an effective campaign tool in the Internet that its opponents have not quite caught onto? Perhaps yes, perhaps no. But the point that we wish to stress is that the assumption that technology favors any particular ideological perspective or political value is just that: an assumption, and an unwarranted one at that. And yet, it is very, very difficult to approach a socially descriptive analysis of the Internet without making just such assumptions.

This analysis has not fully demarcated the intersection of politics, communication technologies, and Korean culture, but it has shed light on the ways in which, at least to some degree, hyperlinks have come to serve as a new type of social marker, used to mark group identity, raise one's prestige, or even just to demonstrate affinity. There are a number of related questions that this study raises that we have not been able to answer, including the extent to which hyperlinks reflect intentionality of purpose, whether to praise or to blame, or the meaning that audiences attribute to hyperlinks. However, it does provide a first step in determining the role of hyperlinks as a form of political action in the digital age.

ACKNOWLEDGMENT

A case study cited in this chapter is being extensively rewritten for international journal submission. The first author thanks his assistants at the New Media and Society Laboratory at YeungNam University. This research was supported by a Korea Research Foundation Grant (KRF-2004–042-H00004). This chapter is a part of the "Web Sphere Analysis for Political Websites" Project.

NOTES

1. Maria Garrido and Alexander Halavais, "Mapping Networks of Support for the Zapatista Movement: Applying Social-Networks Analysis to Study Contemporary Social Movements," in *Cyberactivism: Online Activism in Theory and Practice*, ed. Martha McCaughey and Michael Ayers (New York: Routledge, 2003), 165–184; Han Woo Park, Mike Thelwall, and Randolph Kluver, "Political Hyperlinking in South Korea: Technical Indicators of Ideology and Content," *Sociological Research Online* 10, no. 3 (2005), http://www.socresonline.org.uk/10/3/park.html
2. Randolph Kluver, "US and Chinese Policy Expectations of the Internet," *China Information* 19, no. 2 (2005): 299–324.
3. Park et al., "Political Hyperlinking in South Korea."
4. Mike Thelwall, "Interpreting Social Science Link Analysis Research: A Theoretical Framework," *Journal of the American Society for Information Science and Technology* 57, no. 1 (2005): 60–68.
5. Kluver, "US and Chinese Policy Expectations."
6. J. Patrick Biddix, "The Power of estudentprotest: A Study of Electronically-Enhanced Student Activism" (PhD diss., University of Missouri-St. Louis, 2006); Val Burris, Emery Smith, and Ann Strahm, "White Supremacist Networks on the Internet," *Sociological Focus* 33, (2000): 215–235; Garrido and Halavais, "Mapping Networks of Support"; C.L. Hsu, "International Politics and the Net: Making It Visible" (paper presented to the Asian Studies Conference—Japan Conference, International Christian University, Tokyo, Japan, June 24–25, 2006); Luca Tateo, "The Italian Extreme Right On-Line Network: An Exploratory Study Using an Integrated Social Network Analysis and Content Analysis Approach," *Journal of Computer-Mediated Communication* 10 (2005), http://jcmc.indiana.edu/vol10/issue2/tateo.html
7. Garrido and Halvais, "Mapping Networks of Support."
8. Burris et al., "White Supremacist Networks on the Internet"; Tateo, "The Italian Extreme Right On-Line."
9. Stanley Wasserman and Katherine Faust, *Social Network Analysis: Methods and Applications* (New York: Cambridge University Press, 1994).
10. Miller McPherson, Lynn Smith-Lovin, and James M. Cook, "Birds of a Feather: Homophily in Social Networks," *Annual Review of Sociology* 27 (2001): 415–444.
11. Lada Adamic and Natalie Glance, "The Political Blogosphere and the 2004 U.S. Election: Divided They Blog," http://www.blogpulse.com/papers/2005/AdamicGlanceBlogWWW.pdf (2005); Randolph Kluver, "The Internet and the Expansion of Political Discussion in Singapore Elections," in *Making a Difference: A Comparative View of the Role of the Internet in Election Politics*, ed. Richard Davis et al. (Lanham, MD: Lexington Publishers, 2007).

12. Han Woo Park, Chun-Sik Kim, and George A. Barnett, "Socio-Communicational Structure among Political Actors on the Web," *New Media & Society* 6 (2004): 403–423; Park et al., "Political Hyperlinking in South Korea."
13. Internet World Stats: Usage and Population Statistics, http://www.internetworldstats.com (accessed May 15, 2007).
14. Kluver, "US and Chinese Policy Expectations."
15. Han Woo Park and Mike Thelwall, "Link Analysis: Hyperlink Patterns and Social Structure on Politicians' Web Sites in South Korea," *Quality & Quantity*, May 2007.
16. C. S. Kim, "A Profile of Republic of Korea. INTERNET AND ELECTION PROJECT Workshop" CD-ROM; also available online at http://www.ntu.edu.sg/sci/sirc/internet&elections.html (2004).
17. Byoungkwan Lee, Karen Lancendorfer, and Ki Jung Lee, "Agenda-Setting and the Internet: The Intermedia Influence of Internet Bulletin Boards on Newspaper Coverage of the 2000 General Election in South Korea," *Asian Journal of Communication* 15, no. 1 (2005): 57–71.
18. Han Woo Park and Mike Thelwall, "Web Science Communication in the Age of Globalization," *New Media & Society* 8 (2006): 629–650; Wasserman and Faust, *Social Network Analysis*.
19. Linton C. Freeman, *Centrality in Social Networks: Conceptual Clarification, Social Networks*, vol. 1 (Lausanne: Elsevier Sequoia S.A., 1979), 215–239.
20. Wasserman and Faust, *Social Network Analysis*.
21. Steve Borgatti, Martin Everett, and Linton C. Freeman, *Ucinet for Windows: Software for Social Network Analysis* (Cambridge, MA: Analytic Technologies, 2002).
22. Randolph Kluver, "Political Culture in Online Politics," in *Internet Research Annual*, vol. 2, ed. Mia Consalvo and Matt Allen (Newbury Park, CA: Sage Publications, 2005), 75–84; Kluver, "US and Chinese Policy Expectations."
23. Ranolph Kluver et al., *The Internet and National Elections: A Comparative Study of Web Campaigning* (New York: Routledge, 2007).

17 Beauty Is in the Eye of the QQ User
Instant Messaging in China

Pamela T. Koch, Bradley J. Koch, Kun Huang, and Wei Chen

INTRODUCTION

> Once you turn on your computer, that little penguin with a red scarf, named QQ, will come into your sight as usual. (You have) a long name list of good friends there. You don't know where they come from and what their looks are. And you don't even know their real names. However, you consider them your good friends whom you can confide in. This is the life of the Q time.[1]

The Internet in China has deservedly been the focus of a great deal of research in recent years. Nonetheless, the majority of this research has been focused on the political implications of the Chinese Internet in general[2] and ignores other social implications. In addition, too much Internet research focusing on China or other venues caters to the assumption that the Internet is "an undifferentiable whole."[3] Little consideration is given to the fact that people interface with the Internet using particular applications and for particular purposes. Here, we look at the influence and interpretations associated with a specific Internet communication program, an instant messaging (IM) application developed by the Shenzen-based company Tencent known as QQ. The emergence of this local homegrown QQ software indicates that it plays an important role in Chinese society.

Hence, we seek to better understand the influence of this specific Internet platform as situated within Chinese culture. We are also interested in how the perception of QQ differs from perceptions of the Internet in general. Finally, we believe QQ has symbolic importance as a proud and nationalistic representation of China's technologically advanced society, while at the same time, being associated with negative social change perceived to threaten Chinese society. In the financial and political realms, the increasing importance of QQ and its associated virtual currency has led to recent arguments that it threatens China's real-world financial stability.[4]

In order to understand the emergence of an Internet firm lauded by society, even though its Internet application is perceived more negatively than the Internet as a whole, we first surveyed Chinese language news articles to determine underlying themes related to QQ use. Following this review, a survey of Chinese Internet and non-Internet users was conducted, focusing on QQ use and the perceived influence of QQ use. Finally, several in-depth interviews were conducted.

This study raises broader questions concerning the internationalization of the Internet by looking at how these factors work within the Chinese cultural context. QQ has grown to be so significant within China's online community that some discussion board participants attribute the failure of Macintosh and Linux to significantly penetrate the Chinese market as partly due to their inability to accommodate QQ.[5] Consequently, this study not only speaks to perceptions and uses of QQ, but it also has implications for understanding the Chinese Internet as a whole. In addition, it demonstrates the importance and ability of local software applications to not only dominate offers from large multinational companies, but also the ability of such applications to uniquely shape local content, usage, and attitudes.

QQ'S HISTORICAL DEVELOPMENT

QQ is an IM application that was developed by the Shenzhen, China-based company, Tencent. Since its introduction in 1999, it has become the most popular instant messaging service in China,[6] with some 70 percent of IM users chatting, playing games, and interacting via QQ.[7] QQ was one of the first programs aimed directly at Chinese Internet users, and its popularity and growth may in part be attributed to its "Chineseness." ChinaBYTE comments that, "If we want to choose a 'made in China' product that has changed our way of communication in the 21st century, Tencent's QQ must be on top of the list."[8] In fact, a 2004 survey indicated Tencent was ranked first among Chinese Internet companies in "creating the most social value," and "having the greatest social impact."[9] This influence has even been recognized in the business arena outside of China. QQ's developer, Ma Hua-teng, was named one of *Time Magazine*/CNN 's 25 influential businesspeople in 2005.[10]

QQ's history began in 1999, when Tencent's founder, Ma Hua-teng, began experimenting with developing an IM program suited to Chinese-language input. As Gottlieb (Chapter 5, this volume) comments, early Internet encoding technology was not suited for ideographic languages, such as Japanese and Chinese. Hence, there was a need for programs that could be used by such language users. Thus, OICQ _believed to have meant either Open ICQ or Oh, I seek you) came into being, modeled closely after the popular ICQ software, but based on Chinese encoding language, with a software interface that allowed users to easily and quickly input Chinese characters. The following year, AOL, which had bought out ICQ, sent a copyright infringement complaint to Tencent due to the similarity between the software names. Since the QQ name was already in some use as a short-ened version of OICQ, it was formally adopted shortly afterward. At the same time, the penguin icon was created and became the software's logo.[11]

The early QQ version launched in February 1999 allowed users to con-nect with wireless pagers and mobile phones. Almost immediately, many young Chinese users enthusiastically adopted this new software. By the end of 1999, more than one million users had created QQ accounts, and expo-nential growth continued into the next year, reaching 10 million accounts and more than 100,000 simultaneous users in May 2000. By early January 2001, the Tencent website was ranked as the sixth most-visited in China.

Over the next several years, Tencent sought to find ways to better profit from the QQ phenomenon, initiating fee-based accounts and restricting free account signups. Many people, however, still found ways to obtain free QQ accounts and, eventually, Tencent dropped the idea of a monthly user fee for basic accounts. By 2002, there were more than 100 million registered users.

During its growth, Tencent promoted QQ's use as central to Chinese youth and modern Chinese culture. In 2002, a star selection contest was held called "Q People and Q Life," which "further imprinted the QQ image on modern young people's lives."[12] In 2003, QQ games were launched. Gaming became a large part of QQ use, with more than 1 million simulta-neous online QQ game players in 2004, and more than 10 million in 2005. The QQ game website was ranked first among domestic Chinese game playing sites. "QQ currency," a special kind of virtual money, was intro-duced. This virtual currency could be bought or won by playing games and could be used to purchase games, avatars, and other online items.[13]

QQ's strong youth focus, unfortunately, was linked to concerns about Internet addiction and crime. Recognizing public concern about these issues, several of QQ's games were among those officially certified as suit-able for youngsters by the Ministry of Culture in 2006. Among these were QQ Tang, QQ Fantasy, and QQ Pet.[14]

In its 2005 annual report, Tencent claimed almost 500 million registered accounts, with some 200 million of these actively used. An average of 18.4 million simultaneous users logged on during peak times.[15] In September 2006, the QQ website was ranked by Alexa as the fifth most-accessed web-site in the world.[16] Arguably, this is the most commonly used communica-tion program in the most populous country in the world.

THE INTERNET IN CHINA

QQ influence and history must be understood within the context of the devel-opment of the Internet in China, as well as the growth of the Chinese Internet. Chinese Internet use has grown dramatically since the mid-1990s, when the regular public gained the privilege of opening Internet accounts. This growth in Internet use aided in QQ's popularity. In October 1997, when the first China Internet Network Information Center (CNNIC) report came out, there were 630,000 Internet users in China. In 1999, when QQ was first developed, there were approximately four million Internet users. This figure quadrupled over the next year. By 2003, sixty-eight million users were reported. The June 2006 CNNIC report indicated that some 123 million people used the Internet. Over 70 percent are under age 30, with some 35.1 percent between the ages of 18 and 24. Although most Internet users access the Internet at home, Internet cafés are used by some 27 percent of users.[17]

As more and more Chinese people became avid Internet and QQ users, the growth of the Chinese-language Internet has also boomed. Although the English language still dominates the Internet, with 30 percent of all Internet users communicating in this language, almost 14 percent of all users are Chinese-language speakers. And while English-language users increased 128 percent between 2000 and 2005, Chinese language users increased 347 percent.[18] In contrast to English-language Internet users, who are older, primarily use e-mail, and search the web for information, Chinese Internet users are young, like IM more than e-mail, and search the web for entertainment. Guo Liang, a researcher for the Chinese Academy of Social Sciences, said that the Chinese Internet user is interested not so much in the "information highway" but rather in the "entertainment highway."[19]

Another distinguishing factor of Chinese Internet users is the predominance of mobile phone use. Mobile use has almost reached a saturation point in urban China, with almost 90 percent of urban citizens owning a mobile phone. In raw numbers, this is more than double the amount of US mobile phone users. These mobile phone users are increasingly using their devices to access the Internet. In the January 2006 CNNIC survey, over 17 million users, or 12.4 percent, used their mobiles in this way. This tendency toward mobile phone use has helped spur the adoption of QQ, which, early in its development, made connectivity via mobile phones a central feature.

SOCIAL INFLUENCE OF THE INTERNET

The social influence of the Internet is arguably very important, particularly in reference to young people. Many Chinese reports have focused on the negative social influences associated with the Internet. In one large student survey of Internet use, Sheng, Liu, and Ding reported that more than 57 percent of those surveyed admitted to cheating on their coursework using the Internet, 86 percent had received abusive e-mails, and 36 percent had sent such e-mails. Forty-four percent had visited websites containing "pornography, violence and other illegality." Their summary was primarily negative, concluding that:

> College students' Internet behavior lacks enough rationality and stability. Keeping in touch with Internet for a long time, they are very apt to

be effected [sic] by different thought on Internet which make the college students wallowed in the net world desalinize [sic] to traditional culture and the values and even worse.[20]

Other research indicated that, in popular discourse, the prominence of sexual content on the web is emphasized. Use of terms such as "Internet girls" (*wang-ji*), indicating women using the Internet to solicit sex, are increasingly common. Parish and Pan wrote that,

> Changes in discourse alone are no proof of behavior change. Nevertheless, the proliferation of new terms and the revival of old terms in Internet chat rooms and on the street suggests the emergence of a new sexual culture.[21]

The emergence of such terms also suggests the perception that such things are an integral part of Internet use. As one interviewee commented, "What attracts many young people online is sex. I can say that in colleges and universities 99 percent of male students have visited erotic websites."

Notwithstanding such negative reports or the presumed increase in sexually oriented content, not all Chinese view the Internet with skeptical eyes. Views of the Internet are still primarily positive. The 13th CNNIC survey indicated that only some 20 percent of Internet users thought that the Internet at least partially resulted in delinquent association, while a slightly higher percentage of non-Internet users (26 percent) supported this assertion.[22] In his 2005 report, however, Liang found that positive attitudes toward the Internet had decreased, and he attributed this decrease to negative coverage in the popular press, which tended to focus on sexual crimes and the corrupting influence of Internet cafés.[23]

INTERNET CAFÉS

In China, the use of the Internet is primarily urban, as most rural users are too poor to purchase computers and the infrastructure to provide Internet service is nonexistent or poor. Even in urban areas, the less economically well-off do not have Internet access in their homes, but instead use Internet cafés,[24] and are also increasingly using mobile phones.[25] The 2003 CNNIC report indicated that some 20 percent of users regularly visited Internet cafés. Other reports put this figure as high as 27 percent.[26] While providing access to people who cannot afford Internet access or computers, these cafes have the reputation for being dark and corrupting places, as evidenced by the following commentary: "Most Internet cafes in China . . . do not have a decent environment. Basically, they are located in filthy spaces with bad lighting and crowded with customers."[27] The dank Internet café atmosphere is coupled with efforts by these cafés to avoid government taxes and regulations. Depending on the local enforcement of rules, there may be little supervision—hence, these bars may become popular even in more developed areas, as restrictions are looser than other places where public Internet access may be found.[28]

About 15 percent of kids in large cities use Internet cafés,[29] and parents often express concern about this situation. One 2003 study indicated that up to half of such student users are addicted,[30] with a Qingdao survey claiming that 7 percent of local students went to Internet cafés three times a week, staying late at night for gaming and surfing.[31]

Thus, the use and perceptions of QQ must be understood within a context of competing positive and negative influences. The Internet is considered a primary driver of the modern economy, education, and internationalization, and Tencent is considered an influential Chinese company. Nonetheless, there are strong concerns about youth Internet addiction and the use of the Internet for crime, and these have been regularly portrayed in the press.[32] These reports have been popularized such that they have even been covered in the international press. A recent *Times Online* article, for example, reported that there were more than two million Chinese teenagers addicted to the Internet, with these addicts being younger than those in the West by some ten years. This addiction is thought to contribute to rising crime.[33]

THE SOCIAL INFLUENCE AND USE OF QQ

Survey of News Reports

In order to better understand how QQ has been portrayed in the press, an online survey of Chinese-language news articles was conducted. Sample terms used include QQ's social impact (*QQ de shehui yinxiang*), QQ's influence on life (*QQ due shenghuode yinxiang*), QQ's merits (*QQde haochu*), and QQ and China (*QQ yu Zhongguo*). A total of seventy-one Chinese language news articles were gathered. We found that news coverage of QQ was dominated by negatively framed articles, which accounted for 48 percent of the total. In fact, although QQ's popularity indicates Chinese users are eager for the ability to use the anonymous accounts to interact, share information, and create relationships, the Chinese media have largely written stories regarding its negative social impact, including the "addiction" of underage youths, the victimization of youths who run away from home to meet online friends, the chat room live broadcast of sex shows, and sex workers' use of the service for client solicitation. Such negatively framed articles include stories titled, "Sex Chat Results in Rape," "A High School Student Killed His Classmate," and "What Has QQ Brought Us?"

In contrast, only 28 percent of the articles were coded as positive. These looked at the increasing influence of technology on Chinese society from a more positive viewpoint. Articles reporting how QQ was used to connect friends and help others fell within this category. Sample articles included "Online Social Life," which examined how the Internet enhances people's social life, and "Let Kids, Who are Lost in the Net, Get out of It," which looked at how a seventy-one-year-old-woman used QQ to help students fight Internet addiction. The remaining 25 percent of articles were coded as neutral or mixed. These included articles focusing on Tencent, its founder, and articles that examined QQ's influence on society from more nuanced, multifaceted perspectives.

Survey of QQ Use and Social Influence

After analyzing the news articles, we conducted a survey on QQ use and perceptions. The surveys were constructed based upon the themes identified in the news article analysis, as well as using themes and items from prior general Internet surveys done in China (e.g., CNNIC). This survey, however, specifically focused on the QQ program. The sample was collected using a network random sample method, gathering data from one network each in Chengdu, Shanghai, and Wuhan. A total of 347 surveys were collected, of which 271 were used for the present analysis.[34]

Survey Demographics

The mean age of respondents was thirty-seven, with a median of thirty-six. Fifty-three percent were women, and 66 percent were single. The sample was overweighted toward people with higher education—30 percent had at least a BA degree, 23 percent had 2 years of college, 27 percent were high school graduates, and only 20 percent had less than a high school education. Seventy percent of respondents were Internet users, and 66 percent used QQ. An additional 9 percent had heard of QQ, but were not QQ users, equaling a total of 75 percent who knew or used QQ.

When looking at QQ users only, these people reported that they used QQ for an average of 13.7 hours each week. Approximately one-half (47.6 percent) of that time was spent talking to existing friends, and almost 5 percent of that time was spent meeting new friends. Another 25 percent was spent playing games, and 3.8 percent of the time was used to read and post bulletin board articles. The remaining 13.3 percent of these hours were spent in miscellaneous "other" activities.

The average QQ users had fifty-six contacts on their "friends" list, about one-half of whom were only known via QQ. Twenty-nine percent of respondents indicated they added people to the list every month, while 26 percent deleted at least one contact monthly. QQ users admitted that about 76 percent of what they told their online contacts was true, but believed only 68 percent of what these same contacts told them. Almost half (49 percent) indicated that QQ was the first application they had ever used on the Internet.

QQ Usage Patterns and News Coverage

News reports indicated concern about sex crimes and murders when young people went to meet up with QQ friends they did not know. Fifty-five percent of QQ users in our survey indicated they had never met face-to-face someone they had first met online. Of the remaining 45 percent who had met up with their virtual QQ friends, more than 30 percent had done this more than once, and 13 percent indicated they did this often or very often. News reports also expressed concern with the use of the Internet for sexual solicitation and prostitution. Over 50 percent of our respondents had been solicited at least once via QQ, with 18 percent indicating that such solicitation occurred often or very often. In the related area of pornography, 14 percent of users admitted to downloading or viewing pornography at least occasionally.

Since harassment had been reported as a concern in the Chinese-language press, we asked respondents if they had harassed others using QQ. Most (75 percent) did not admit to engaging in such activities, but 31 percent had been on the receiving end of such harassment on several occasions. Deception in communication has also been written about with regard to the online presentation of self. Again, the survey results were biased in favor of self-presentation, but cynical with regard to reports about others. Although 65 percent said they never deceived QQ friends, only 25 percent believed their QQ friends never deceived them. Twenty-one percent admitted to occasionally or often engaging in deceptive communication, while 56 percent expected the same to be true of their online acquaintances. Finally, news articles reported QQ "cyberlove" and QQ "net marriages." Although most respondents did not participate in such online romantic relationships, 30 percent have engaged in a romantic online relationship at least once, and 11 percent formalized these online romantic relationships at least one time via QQ "net marriage."[35]

Virtual Uses and Reality Uses

We believe that to understand how QQ is used in China, it is helpful to conceptualize users as being virtual-only users, reality-only users, and virtual-to-reality users. Each of these three categories is comprised of about one-third of QQ users. Reality-only users use QQ to enhance their real relationships. They rarely play QQ games and never chat with people that they do not already know (see Table 17.1, Questions 1 and 2).

Virtual-to-reality users use QQ to first find new friends in the virtual world, and then transform these virtual friendships into real friendships. Many of these virtual relationships begin with a touch of reality, as 35 percent of QQ users often use web cams. Questions 4 and 5 reveal that 45 percent of the people have met someone in person that they first met online, and 23 percent have participated in a QQ group activity. In addition, QQ activity begins to supplement real-world activities, as 25 percent of QQ users often feel more comfortable expressing their emotions and opinions to friends.

Table 17.1 Results for QQ Usage Questions

	Question	Never	Rarely	Some-times	Often	Very often
1	Do you use QQ to chat in chat rooms with people you do not know personally?	35 percent	17 percent	28 percent	16 percent	4 percent
2	Do you use QQ to play games?	17 percent	12 percent	25 percent	24 percent	22 percent
3	Do you use QQ's web camera for live broadcast chatting?	30 percent	10 percent	27 percent	20 percent	14 percent
4	Have you ever met face-to-face someone you first met online via QQ?	55 percent	12 percent	19 percent	8 percent	5 percent
5	Have you ever partici-pated in an activity orga-nized via QQ (e.g., going to an entertainment, taking a trip?)	77 percent	8 percent	11 percent	3 percent	1 percent
6	Do you feel more com-fortable revealing your emotions and opinions to your virtual QQ friends than your other friends?	28 percent	14 percent	33 percent	18 percent	7 percent
7	Have you ever raised a QQ pet?	70 percent	8 percent	9 percent	7 percent	6 percent
8	Have you ever been part of a QQ "cyberlove"	70 percent	11 percent	10 percent	8 percent	2 percent
9	Have you ever been part of a QQ "net marriage"	89 percent	5 percent	5 percent	1 percent	0 percent
10	Do you ever deceive your QQ friends about yourself?	60 percent	13 percent	20 percent	4 percent	2 percent
11	Do you ever exaggerate when you chat with your QQ friends?	45 percent	18 percent	25 percent	11 percent	2 percent
12	Do you ever downplay your accomplishments when you chat with QQ friends?	31 percent	15 percent	27 percent	14 percent	3 percent
13	Do you believe your QQ friends ever deceive you?	25 percent	20 percent	28 percent	16 percent	10 percent
14	Do you believe your QQ friends ever exaggerate when they chat with you?	21 percent	15 percent	29 percent	25 percent	10 percent

(continued)

Table 17.1 Results for QQ Usage Questions (continued)

	Question	Never	Rarely	Some-times	Often	Very often
15	Do you believe your QQ friends ever downplay their accomplishments when they chat with you?	24 percent	16 percent	47 percent	11 percent	2 percent
16	Do you use multiple QQ accounts to take on multiple identities or personalities?	58 percent	16 percent	18 percent	5 percent	3 percent
17	Do you log on to multiple QQ accounts simultaneously?	53 percent	13 percent	16 percent	10 percent	8 percent
18	Have you ever been harassed by any of your QQ contacts?	52 percent	16 percent	25 percent	5 percent	3 percent
19	Have you ever used QQ to harass other people?	76 percent	12 percent	6 percent	3 percent	3 percent
20	Have you ever used QQ to look at erotic pictures or shows?	75 percent	10 percent	13 percent	2 percent	0 percent
21	Have you ever been solicited by sex workers via QQ?	50 percent	18 percent	16 percent	13 percent	3 percent

Virtual-only users enter the QQ world and cut links with the real world and engage in real-world activities in the virtual QQ world. The results for Questions 7 and 8 show that about 30 percent of QQ users have raised a QQ pet and have been in cyberlove. Another 11 percent have been involved in a QQ marriage, where they participated in an online wedding ceremony, invited QQ guests, and "married" a "web friend." In addition, virtual-only users tend to engage in various levels of deception and expect others in the virtual world to do the same (see Questions 10–15). At a higher level of deception, about 40 percent of QQ users have simultaneously used multiple QQ accounts and engaged in multiple online personalities. One QQ user interviewed explained how he had multiple QQ accounts and that he would use them to interact with a QQ friend using two different personalities—one male and one female—at the same time.

For virtual-to-reality and virtual-only users, the QQ world can be a very harsh environment, where users either act out baser instincts or are unintentionally exposed to these behaviors (see Questions 18–21). With the immunity provided in QQ cyberspace, many users are less inhibited about engaging in behaviors that they would not partake of in the real world.

Consequently, 48 percent of QQ users feel that they have been harassed by other users, and 24 percent openly admitted to harassing other users. In addition, the QQ world has become the roaming ground for sex workers selling their virtual and real-world services, with 50 percent of QQ users saying that they have been solicited. One person interviewed was solicited within his first two hours of using QQ.

Perceptions of QQ

Finally, we looked at perceptions of QQ's influence on society. We measured these perceptions of influence by asking respondents to rate the influence that the Internet has had on individual users, Chinese society, families,

Table 17.2 Perception of QQ and Internet Influence among People Familiar with QQ

People familiar with QQ	N	Internet mean	QQ mean	Difference	T-stat	P-value
Individual users	190	3.78	3.55	.23**	3.239	.001
Chinese society	190	3.90	3.37	.53**	6.997	.000
Families	190	3.32	3.10	.22**	3.086	.002
Marriages	189	2.99	3.01	−.02	−.330	.742
Young people	188	3.74	3.47	.27**	2.969	.003
Children	188	2.84	2.65	.19*	2.096	.037
Friendships	190	3.63	3.58	.05	.812	.418
Chinese culture	190	3.76	3.14	.62**	7.968	.000
China's government	190	3.66	3.13	.53**	6.893	.000
Schools	189	3.67	3.16	.51**	6.180	.000
Work organizations	186	3.91	3.34	.57**	7.019	.000
My life	189	3.58	3.40	.18**	3.036	.003
My family	186	3.32	3.09	.23**	3.805	.000
My marriage	84	3.14	3.06	.08*	2.219	.030
My children	94	3.14	3.12	.02	.000	1.000
My friendships	185	3.65	3.50	.15**	2.853	.005
My school	115	3.75	3.17	.58**	5.459	.000
My work organization	138	3.80	3.15	.65**	8.572	.000

marriages, young people, children, friendships, Chinese culture, China's government, schools, and work organizations on a 5-point scale (1 = very negative and 5 = very positive). In addition, respondents were asked how QQ influenced them personally with regard to their life, family, marriage, children, friendships, school, and work organization.

The N column of the table is the number of respondents who indicated the impact of both the Internet's and QQ's influence on society for each category. Although everyone can give an opinion on the Internet's and QQ's influence on society for each of the categories, they can only express their opinions with regard to their own lives, for the categories that are applicable to their lives. Thus, N for "My Children" and "My Marriage" is relatively smaller than the N for the "Children" and "Marriage" categories.

Overall, the results from the survey indicate that, despite the negative news portrayals, people in general still have a relatively positive view of QQ. Notably, however, respondents indicated that the influence of QQ on children is quite negative (2.65). The influence on marriage in general was thought to be neutral, while the influence of QQ on individual users, Chinese society, young people, friendships, work organizations, one's own life, and one's own friendships was considered reasonably positive. Respondents indicated slightly positive attitudes toward the influence of QQ on families, Chinese culture, China's government, schools, one's own family, one's own marriage, one's own children, one's own school, and one's own work organization.

The results presented in Table 17.2 also reveal that people do differentiate between the influence of specific Internet platforms, such as QQ, and the Internet in general. Overall, the results from the survey indicate that although people in general have a relatively positive view of the Internet and QQ, these respondents view QQ more negatively than the Internet. An examination of the "Difference" column in Table 17.2 reveals that the social influence of QQ and the Internet are perceived to be different at the .05 level of statistical significance in 15 out of the 18 social influence categories. All of these differences indicate that respondents view QQ as having a less-positive influence on society than the Internet in general.

INTERVIEWEE COMMENTS

In order to better interpret the survey results, informal semistructured interviews were conducted with ten informants. Interviews focused on media reports, QQ use, and perceptions of social influence. Interviews took place in person, and were conducted by a native Chinese speaker. Interviewees ranged from a sixteen-year-old secondary school student to a man in his forties.

The interviews revealed that many informants enjoyed QQ, using it to play games as well as interact with friends and strangers. A thirty-eight-year-old female commented that:

people with different nationalities and different religions, who have never met each other face to face before, can meet or get to know each other online. . . . they have nothing they could not talk about online (and) . . . feel like old friends at their first face-to-face meeting in real time.

Another twenty-five-year-old male evidenced pride in QQ:

I think it is a very epoch-making, very innovative or creative thing because there was no such thing before. There were IM tools like ICQ, MSN messenger and Yahoo messenger, but they were not as localized as QQ was. As QQ is more localized, it has attracted more young people in China. . . . For friends who haven't seen each other for a long time, for friends who are very far away from each other, they can chat or share through QQ. It's a very good help. It is very good.

At the same time, however, other informants clearly indicated they saw a negative side to QQ use. One commented that:

You can meet many bad people through it. There is a very wide or big group which is . . . How should I say? Anyway you can meet many bad people. If some people have a very weak distinguishing ability, those (bad) people will have a very bad influence on them. . . . . There's also nude chat. I have read reports. Very strange. . . . . QQ has just magnified people's bad morals so that you can see people's bad morals more clearly. The reason why I don't use it is because I think its harm is beyond its merit.

Another person had a specific negative example:

I have some friends around me. We were very good friends before. We always did and shared things together wherever we went. Ever since some of them started using the Internet, they had had no self-control or self-restraint ability. They had gradually become addicted to it. Finally, due to (his) financial situation, (one of them) did some illegal things in order to surf the net.

For another, the anonymity and opportunity for deception were problematic:

Too often people find that what net friends share is untrue. They didn't understand that actually people can be false. When they type words, they can invent many beautiful sentences or stories. They can pretend. When they really meet face to face, they find that actually the other side is not very good. But quite often some people have no distinguishing ability. They may go astray. There are too many bad examples especially about relationships between boys and girls.

When asked about media coverage of QQ, interviewees overwhelmingly cited negative stories. An interviewee commented that negative coverage was common, not only in the print news, but also on TV:

> I often hear about such things or reports on TV. For instance, in order to meet her net friend, a girl went to a very far place with money she had stolen from her parents. After she was cheated of her money, she had to come back. There are many such cases. I often see such reports on TV.

Notwithstanding such coverage, however, he added that he did not personally know anyone who had such negative experiences.

Interviewees were also asked how they perceived use of QQ versus use of the Internet. Several indicated that they saw the use of QQ as distinctly different. The Internet was used for information, while QQ was primarily an entertainment tool. As one commented:

> We use the Internet more for information, learning and growth in our characters and knowledge of all aspects. We can achieve growth in our knowledge of all aspects through the Internet. I'm not saying that we can't achieve such purposes through QQ, but it is much weaker than the Internet in achieving such purposes. QQ is more likely to make its users trapped in a virtual social relationship and or situation. It's more used by people for finding a sense of comfort there.

One Chengdu resident elaborated by focusing on the perception that QQ was primarily used by youth:

> (T)he majority of QQ users are kids and students. Many of them are crazy about QQ. They are addicted to it. They spend too much time chatting through QQ or playing online QQ games. It wastes their time and influences their studies negatively. Also, QQ has become a criminal or erotic tool. Some people with bad motives use it to commit crimes like defraud and rape. Some use QQ and webcams to offer erotic or pornographic services. As a result, it may poison adolescents, especially kids. So many people have a bad opinion of it. As for the Internet, it is more used by older people.

This line of thought appears to be a consistent opinion among the QQ-cognizant public. As one online blog commented, "by this time, QQ has basically become a young boys' or young girls' chatting tool," adding that older users were more likely to use MSN when communicating with each other.[36] Other bloggers indicated that QQ's orientation toward youth made its content and use more of a concern:

As the majority of Tencent QQ's user groups or users are adolescents or young people, experts point out that publishing bad information in such an irresponsible way will surely be unfavorable to adolescents' healthy growth, and will even possibly lure adolescents into committing crimes.[37]

Youth were also susceptible to addiction. One online research report argued that, "Nowadays, for high school students, playing QQ is not only a need for vogue, but also more importantly a psychological need."[38]

Informants indicated that these younger people were more susceptible to negative influences. QQ had a negative influence, as:

> its impact on kids is more negative. . . . This is because kids themselves have a very low self-control ability. If they spend too much time using the Internet, they may easily get trapped in it or addicted to it.

This concern about youth was connected by one informant to the importance of children in a society where one child is the norm. A college student said this about youth net addiction:

> There are kids who are addicted to surfing the net. The whole family of such a kid pin their hope on him or her. Since he or she is addicted to the Internet, the whole family's hope will be gone. How can I say. . . . They will have a conflict. Take my cousin, my eldest aunt's daughter, as an example. She loved surfing the net. Just because of this, they quarreled for a long time. She even left home, ran away from her home.

This interviewee added that older people would have better self-control and would be able to gain positive benefits from QQ and the Internet without becoming addicted. Nonetheless, parents were often thought to be ignorant of what their kids did while surfing the net. As one said:

> The parents' generation do not know what their kids are doing online and that uncertainty is reinforced by negative news stories. My mother is like that, when she worried that my niece will become bad if she is allowed online.

Another seconded this perception that parents were unable to provide adequate supervision:

> Most of the parents don't know about the Internet or how to use a computer, so they don't know how to help their children, how to form (or set up) a firewall to prevent those bad things from coming in.

In sum, while several informants focused on the positive contributions of QQ to their lives and Chinese cultural life, others believed that it had a negative influence. This perception appears connected to the entertainment and youth focus of QQ.

CONCLUSION

QQ is a very important part of Chinese Internet life. "No other Internet company in the world—not even Google—has achieved the dominance that Tencent commands in China"[39] via this entertainment and IM platform. Chinese users are proud of this home-grown software, and its use has permeated Chinese culture in varied and interesting ways, with a recent divorce case even being tried using video chat.[40] Its use, and interpretations of its use, also reflect Chinese life. QQ has capitalized on the youth and entertainment focus of modern Chinese Internet culture, while at the same time building on the social networking tendencies of its traditional collectivistic culture. It has done this so successfully that it is one of the central paths to the "entertainment highway" that Liang put forward as the central metaphor for Chinese Internet use. Tencent's ability to engage Chinese youth and understand their desires has made it an incredible success.

Based on the newspaper analysis and the survey data presented in this chapter, we have argued that even though Tencent is viewed favorably as a company, their QQ product is presented by the media as having a negative influence on society, and this perception is shared by the people we surveyed. QQ is viewed as being an essential part of the "entertainment highway" and is used most by teenagers and young adults to create varying degrees of virtual reality. This youth and entertainment focus, however, has contributed to the substantial criticism centered on QQ use found in the media and repeated by a number of our informants. Media commentary and interviewee perceptions indicate that children are thought to be particularly susceptible to its negative influences. This negative commentary must also be situated within the Chinese cultural space, where lightly supervised, "filthy spaces" in Internet cafés are a primary site for youth Internet access.

This study of QQ illuminates three important aspects of internationalizing Internet studies. First, although many Internet applications have diffused downward from developed Western nations, there is still considerable room for local Internet applications to develop and even flourish. This is especially interesting in the context of China's political environment, which has been promoting economic and technological development as a means to maintain political stability. Tencent, the creator of QQ, is a Chinese icon of economic and technological development, and a symbol of rising nationalistic feelings. Its QQ Internet application, however, provides a platform for political instability. Consequently, the QQ application is, on the one hand, a target of the state media's criticisms, while on the other hand, Tencent is a recipient of voluminous praise. Therefore, in the current political campaign to purify the Internet, Tencent works with the government to make QQ comply with the ever-evolving regulations and thus maintains its place in national lore while QQ and its users are labeled as problematic.

Second, the generation gaps that often emerge in developing nations' societies are further acerbated by technology and result in an indistinguishable amalgamation of criticism directed at technology and youths. Developing nations' societies as a whole are often under great strain from the rapid pace of change, which results in drastic differences between the daily lives of the younger and older generations. In this environment, criticism of the Internet can become an indirect criticism of the younger generation. In China, QQ is a symbol of the younger urban generation, and this symbol is associated with pornography, illicit sex, crime, addiction, and dreary Internet cafés. Consequently, criticism and regulation of QQ and Internet cafes may partly symbolize an intergenerational struggle in the face of rapid social change.

Finally, we believe this study supports our contention that understanding the Internet necessitates understanding how and why people use specific Internet platforms. The Internet cannot be viewed as an undifferentiable whole, but rather as comprising unique users and platforms. In China, the development of QQ by a Chinese company, and its popularity and use by young people, provides insights into Chinese society and culture that go beyond the typical focus on the political control of the Internet to look at Internet use, public perceptions, and concerns about youth addiction and corruption.

NOTES

1. "Ma Hua-teng: Did You Q today?" *Hangzhou Daily,*www.hangzhou.com. cn/20020127/ca168411.htm (November 3, 2002).
2. Jens Damm and Simona Thomas, *Chinese Cyberspaces: Technological Changes and Political Effects* (London: Routledge, 2006).
3. Irina Shklovski, Robert Kraut, and Lee Rainie, "The Internet and Social Participation: Contrasting Cross-Sectional and Longitudinal Analyses," *Journal of Computer Mediated Communication* 10, no. 1 (2004), http://jcmc. indiana.edu/vol10/issue1/shklovski_kraut.html
4. David Barboza, "Internet Boom in China Is Built on Virtual Fun," *New York Times,* http://www.nytimes.com/2007/02/05/world/asia/05virtual. html?ex=1328331600&en=92496de3170c3303&ei=5088&partner=rssnyt &emc=rss (February 5, 2007).
5. One Linux discussion board participant, Lanchongzhi, indicated that a major drawback associated with Linux was that "QQ doesn't really work under LINUX (and that is like the most important chat client used in China)," comment posted March 15, 2007, http://forums.fedoraforum. org/showthread.php?t=146840 (accessed March 18, 2007). A Macintosh discussion board post by David Feng contained this as number five in his list of problems with Macintosh service in China: "Finally, anyone heard of QQ? Were it not for the heroes of Sinomac, Mac users would be stuck without QQ. One of our members gave the Tencent crew quite a lesson and

got them to hire someone that would develop a Mac version of QQ. It's the trend, by the way—more and more Macs are being sold in China, and the one big barrier prior to liberation (as in Mac liberation) is the 'Will I be able to run QQ?' question. Yes, QQ has them Big Mamas take out the not-so-secure words you say, but most of us use QQ for legal intents and purposes and there is, in fact, quite a gathering behind QQ. One of our gang at our sister club, BeiPod (the iPod group), says that if there is a version of QQ that's natively developed by Tencent, we could see a massive surge in Mac users as they finally realize that the computer for the rest of us runs their most frequently used IM software," comment on "Sod the iPhone: Give us Mac Service in China," Danwei, comment posted January 31, 2007, http://www.danwei.org/trends_and_buzz/sod_the_iphone_i_ want_a_mac_br.php (accessed May 14, 2008).

6. Guo Liang, "Surveying Internet Usage and Impact in Five Chinese Cities," Research Center for Social Development, Chinese Academy of Social Sciences (2005).

7. "Structure of China's Instant Messaging Market Changing Dramatically," *People's Daily* Online, http://english.people.com.cn/200607/07/eng20060707_281020.html (July 7, 2006).

8. Rong Chun, "QQ: The Emperor Penguin that Has Changed Our Life," ChinaBYTE, http://www.chinabyte.com (November 10, 2005).

9. Chun, "QQ: The Emperor Penguin."

10. Daniel Kadlec et al., "The New Breed," *Time Magazine*, December 13, 2004. Also available online at http://www.time.com/time/magazine/article/0,9171,1101041220-1006663,00.html

11. Previously, popular, well-known comic and cartoon figures—such as Donald Duck, Pikachu, and Snoopy—had been used. It is probable that this change was made out of concern for copyright infringement. The QQ penguin itself, however, has now become an incredibly popular icon, with a shop opening in Guangzhou devoted to selling QQ penguin-related items.

12. Tencent, www.tencent.com/about/history_2002.shtml (accessed January 22, 2007).

13. Recent news reports indicate that China's Central Bank has expressed concern about the use of QQ currency and its influence on the Chinese *yuan*, as well as its possible use to launder money for crime. See www.enet.com.cn/article/2006/1103/A20061103281578.shtml; Barboza, "Internet Boom in China."

14. Information about the historical development of QQ may be found at http://blog.phoenixtv.com/user3/alexwork/archives/2006/341204.html (accessed September 15, 2006); Ma Hua-teng, "The Story of a Young Man from ChaoZhou, Who Has Built His Career in Shenzhen," *Shenzhen Commercial News*, http://sznewjob.sznews.com/n/ca1842431.htm (April 5, 2005); Tencent's historical events, http://www.tencent.com/about/history_2002.shtml (accessed January 22, 2007).

15. Tencent, "Annual Report 2006," http://www.tencent.hk/ir/pdf/news20060322a_e.pdf (March 22, 2006).

16. In February 2007, this ranking had dropped four positions, to ninth.

17. CNNIC, "17th Statistical Survey Report on The Internet Development in China," http://www.cnnic.net.cn (January 2006).

18. Miniwatts Marketing Group, "Internet World Statistics: Internet World Users by Language," http://www.Internetworldstats.com/stats7.htm (accessed September 10, 2006).

19. Guo Liang, "Plenary Talk" (lecture, Chinese Internet Conference, Singapore, July 2006).

20. Huanye Sheng, Zhiqiang Liu, and Peng Ding, "College Students' Internet Behavior Traits and Instructional Design in Digital City," http://www.digitalcity.jst.go.jp/conferences/pdf/1S-5.pdf (n.d.), 6.
21. William Parish and Suiming Pan, "Sexual Partners in China: Risk Patterns for Infection by HIV and Possible Interventions," in *Social Policy and HIV/AIDS in China*, ed. Joan Kaufman, Arthur Kleinman, and Tony Saich (Cambridge, MA: Harvard University Press, 2006).
22. CNNIC, "China's Internet Development and Usage Report," http://www.cnnic.net.cn (2003).
23. Liang, "Surveying Internet Usage."
24. Jack Qiu, "The Internet in China: Data and Issues" (paper presented at the Annenberg Research Seminar on International Communication, Los Angeles, October 1, 2003).
25. CNNIC, "17th Statistical Survey Report."
26. Ibid.
27. Junhao Hong and Li Huang, "A Split and Swaying Approach to Building Information Society: The Case of Internet Cafes in China," *Telematics and Informatics* 22, no. 4 (2005): 377–393, 378.
28. Hong and Huang, "A Split and Swaying Approach."
29. CNNIC, "China's Internet Development and Usage Report."
30. Li Huang, *On Internet Cafes* (Chengdu, China: Shichuan Publishing House, 2002), as cited in Hong and Huang, "A Split and Swaying Approach."
31. *The Southern Weekend* (2004), as reported in Hong and Huang, "A Split and Swaying Approach."
32. Liang, "Surveying Internet Usage."
33. Jane MacCartney, "Two Million Teenagers Hooked on Internet," *Times Online*, www.timesonline.co.uk/tol/news/world/asia/article1294058.ece (January 18, 2007).
34. We chose to use the network collection method to offset problems with survey response. An initial survey had less than a 20 percent response rate, greatly biasing the data collected. Nonetheless, collecting data through networks is also not likely to reflect the larger population. Typically, people from the same network have homogenous characteristics and attitudes—the closer the ties, the more homogeneous the attitudes. We attempted to offset this bias by incorporating a randomizing technique into the selection process. Respondents were recruited by the network heads to participate in a survey about "China's Social Progress" without knowing more information about the topic. After they agreed to participate, they randomly drew numbers (1–100) out of a hat that matched the percentile breakdown of China's urban population by age, education, and gender categories. After the contacts drew a category (e.g., female, education of high school and below, or thirty to forty years old), they would try to think of a person within this category. If they could not think of anyone in this category, they would choose another category from the hat. This process was repeated until the contact expressed a desire to end the selection process either verbally or nonverbally. After the contacts had selected the categories and assigned names of people they knew to each category, the contacts were given additional instructions. The contacts were given the appropriate number of surveys, and envelopes to put the surveys in. The respondents' numbers were written on the envelopes to facilitate tracking. The contacts were instructed to tell their contacts to complete the survey, put it in the envelope, seal it, and return it to the contact, who would return it unopened to the network head. The overall response rate for the survey was 83 percent.
35. Several news articles also reference a "net divorce" phenomenon.

36. Shenzhe, "My Road as A Programmer—Crazy QQ," January 26, 2006, URL no longer active.
37. "QQ Plays Edge Balls with Erotic Advertisements," http://www.jz88.net/bbs/index.php?showtopic=821 (June 18, 2004).
38. Contributed by 364070301 (QQ number), "Survey Report on High School Students Playing QQ," August 25, 2005, http://www.zuowen.com.cn/List.asp?ID=22468 (accessed February 13, 2006).
39. MacCartney, "Two Million Teenagers Hooked on Internet," paragraph 3.
40. "The Courtroom Was Moved to QQ and an International Divorce Was Tried while 'Chatting,'" *Chengdu Business News*, www.chengdu.gov.cn/news/detail.jsp?id=113373&ClassID=02060104 (January 8, 2007).

18 That Global Feeling

Sexual Subjectivities and Imagined Geographies in Chinese-Language Lesbian Cyberspaces

Fran Martin

INTRODUCTION

This chapter arises from an Internet-based survey of users of Chinese-language lesbian websites conducted between 2003 and 2004.[1] Lesbian-themed websites in Chinese-character formats have blossomed since the mid-1990s, and present varying degrees of complexity, incorporating some or all of chat rooms; guest books; news updates; bulletin board systems; celebrity gossip columns; news on local political and community events; personal ads; advice columns; blogs; Internet fiction; poetry and artwork archives; lesbian-themed films, comics, music, and TV programs available for download; and so on. The first such sites appeared in Taiwan (and to a lesser extent, Hong Kong) beginning around 1995, and a more recent wave was set up on mainland Chinese servers from the late 1990s.[2] Taken together, this group of sites constitutes a significant new area of Internet culture. As well as making antihomophobic information on homosexuality to contest the stigmatizing medical accounts still dominant in mainstream print media in some parts of the Chinese-speaking world (especially non-metropolitan areas in mainland China) freely available, the new Internet culture makes up a substantial, lively, and expanding Chinese-language electronic network potentially linking women of diverse social backgrounds who are widely geographically dispersed. Given the potential for transnational linkage apparent in these relatively recent developments, the aim of my survey was to investigate whether these developments are producing new kinds of "minor transnationalism" and "virtual community," linking women across the region and the globe on the twin bases of sexual (lesbian) and cultural/ethnic (Chinese) identification.[3] On a more conceptual level, the survey aimed to produce a kind of sketch-map of how experiences of sexual identification intersected with the ways in which the users of these sites imagined their own geocultural place in the world.

My starting point in this study is a 2000 essay entitled, "Grassroots Globalization and the Research Imagination," by Arjun Appadurai. Here,

Appadurai extends his earlier work on globalization's disjunctive flows with new thoughts on two related issues. The first is what Appadurai calls "grassroots globalization" or "globalization from below": forms of globalization advanced by the global economic underclass on its own behalf, against the interests of global capital. I would like to bend this framework slightly to consider whether the growth of the Chinese-language lesbian Internet could be considered another form of grassroots globalization: a way in which variously minoritized people (same-sex-attracted women in the People's Republic of China [PRC], Taiwan, Hong Kong, and Southeast Asia, as well as ethnically Chinese lesbians in Europe, the United States, Australia, and New Zealand) network *transnationally* on their own behalf as a way of dealing with, and actively challenging, the necessarily *local* experiences of their own minoritization.

Second, related to Appadurai's interest in globalization from below is his reemphasis on the new social role of the imagination. One new development, which Appadurai proposes entails the need to rethink the ways in which post-Cold War area studies have imagined the parceling-up of the globe into cultural "areas," is the globalization of "the capacity to imagine regions and worlds."[4] He asks: "How does the world look—as a congeries of areas—from other locations (social, cultural, national)?"[5] It is this question that inspires my study's interest in "imagined geographies." If Anderson has taught us to see modern nations as imagined communities, then how, in this era of accelerated transnational flows of information and culture, do people in different locations imagine transnational units (such as geocultural regions; transnational cultural affiliations, like "Chineseness"; and "the global")?

In exploring these questions through the survey of users of Chinese-language lesbian-themed Internet sites, this project addresses transnational Internet studies in two ways. First and most simply, it aims to highlight the interest and importance of paying critical attention to the lively and ever-expanding world of Chinese-language Internet-based communication, given that, at the time of writing, Chinese is the second most-used Internet language after English, and gaining rapidly.[6] Second, by investigating the relationship between Internet sociality and imagined geographies, the project also asks how Internet communications facilitate particular ways of conceiving the very category of the transnational. In these ways, this chapter aims to engage the question of the transnational in Internet studies in both material and imaginative dimensions.

CHINESE INTERNET: BACKGROUND

Complicating the common perception that, due to the history of its development, the Internet is somehow bound to remain inherently American, Chinese-language web content, used by "netizens" across mainland China,

Hong Kong, Taiwan, and the worldwide Chinese diaspora, is now second only to English content, and with 123 million Internet users by June 2006, the PRC (including Hong Kong) had the second largest Internet-using population of any nation in the world after the United States.[7] Internet usage in mainland China is marked by some notable geographic and demographic divides. In particular, there is a strong bias toward urban areas (16.9 percent penetration rate in cities versus a mere 2.6 percent in rural areas) and the eastern seaboard region. Gender and age biases remain notable, with 58.7 percent of all users being male, and 71 percent under 30 years of age. In Hong Kong and Taiwan, the demographics differ significantly. The overall penetration rate in Hong Kong is a far higher 61 percent, with a less significant gender bias (51 percent of users are male). In Taiwan, the Internet penetration rate (by household) was calculated at 66.6 percent for 2005, with the highest rates in Taipei City (77 percent) and the urbanized north of the island, decreasing to 53.6 percent for the mountainous east coast region.[8] There appears to be virtual gender parity in Taiwanese Internet users, with exactly 58 percent of both men and women island-wide being general users (although 60 percent of those classified as heavy users are male). The youth bias remains, however, with the highest percentage of users being between fifteen and twenty-four years of age.

"CHINESE" INTERNET?

But what precisely is meant by "Chinese" Internet? Recent writing on the question of Chinese cultural identity reveals two seemingly contradictory tendencies. On the one hand, scholars, including Allen Chun, Rey Chow, Ien Ang and others, have vigorously contested nationally, ethnically, or culturally absolutist accounts of Chinese identity.[9] Their work underscores the irreducible multiplicity of the various accounts of Chinese identity given by differently positioned speakers (in the PRC, Hong Kong, Taiwan, or various locations within the Chinese diaspora), with their widely variant historical, linguistic, cultural, and political identifications (and disidentifications) with the idea of China. Terri He's discussion in Chapter 19 of this volume on homosexual rights defense as a rhetorical actively taken up by Taiwan's government in an attempt to construct Taiwan as a liberal, Chinese-style democracy, in contrast to the cultural authoritarianism of the PRC, is one concrete example of the conflicts and contestations over the cultural and political meanings of Chineseness today. Even leaving aside the question of Chinese-reading Internet users' cultural identifications (discussed more below), the multiplicity and complexity of Chineseness is materially inscribed in Internet cultures through differences in orthography and character-set encoding. It is relatively easy for a moderately educated reader of simplified characters (used in the PRC and Singapore) to understand complex characters (used in Taiwan and Hong Kong) and *vice versa*.

Additionally, modern written Chinese is equally comprehensible to literate speakers of Cantonese, Mandarin, and Hokkien languages, and is the standard medium of written communication across mainland China, Taiwan, and Hong Kong. However, the distinct character-sets used for complex versus simplified orthography mean that frequently, technical constraints, such as not having the right software to decode the "other" character-set, mean that the degree of cross-communication between these different communities is less than one might expect.[10]

Interestingly, however, it is in studies of the Chinese Internet and other contemporary cultural crossflows that a tendency has recently emerged that seems to run against arguments about the increasingly multiple and disjunctive character of contemporary Chinese identities. This work speculates on the formation of a new form of the transnational Chinese public sphere where geographically dispersed publics come together in a new sense of Chinese community for the global era.[11] Sociologist Guobin Yang's work is exemplary of this trend. Based on a study of a range of issues-based, Chinese-language Internet forums, he proposes the emergence of "the online Chinese cultural sphere," which is transnational in scope, drawing on publics across the PRC, Taiwan, Hong Kong, and the diaspora, and yet seems, in his account, to produce a remarkably unproblematized sense of shared Chineseness for its participants, as they come together in cyberspace to debate questions of Chinese cultural life and citizenship.[12] The questions about imagined geography and subjectivity among users of the Chinese-language lesbian Internet that this project raises speak directly to the tension between these two competing tendencies in the existing scholarship. Do the cybercultures taking shape around this group of users bear out the centripetal tendencies hypothesized by Yang and others, creating a new and relatively unitary form of transnational public sphere? Or do they instead reflect and exacerbate existing fractures within postmodern experiences of Chineseness? I return to these questions in the analysis of respondents' cultural identifications in the following sections.

"LESBIAN" INTERNET?

As much of the extant research in cross-cultural sexuality studies has shown, the sexological categories that have become dominant in the modern West—heterosexual, homosexual, bisexual—and the post-Stonewall nonstraight identities that indirectly grow out of these—gay, lesbian, bi, queer, and so on—cannot be assumed to have cross-cultural currency, and the business of translating sexual terms from one cultural context and language to another is always a tricky one.[13] Modern written Chinese has several technical terms for female homosexuality, most commonly, *nütongxinglian* and *nütongxing'ai*: direct and comparably pathologizing translations of the English sexological term *female homosexuality*.

The term used in my survey, however, was *nütongzhi*, a neologism of the early 1990s that arose along with organized lesbian, gay, bi, transsexual (LGBT) political movements and literally translates as "female comrade," but is used commonly in LGBT activism and subculture throughout Hong Kong, Taiwan, and the PRC to translate "lesbian." While in some contexts, *nütongzhi* can be interpreted as notably culturally *distinct* from the Euro-American notion of lesbian identity, due to its common use in LGBT activism, the term is also (contradictorily) used as a practical *equivalent* to the Euro-American idea of the lesbian (and/or female bisexual) as a politicized social minority.[14] My usage of the term in my survey was closer to this latter sense, since my target response group was precisely women who self-consciously considered themselves to possess a distinct sexual identity based on same-sex erotic desire, which shaped their patterns of Internet usage. Many respondents echoed my usage of *nütongzhi* (or a colloquial abbreviation, *nütong*) in their responses to questions, but some other terms were also used, most notably a series of related subcultural terms that have gained popularity specifically within Chinese-language lesbian Internet cultures: these are *les* or *lez* (an abbreviation of the English term lesbian), *lazi* (a cute Mandarin transliteration of "les"), and *lala* (a derivative of *lazi*).[15] Occasionally, women referred to themselves as *nütongxinglian* (female homosexuals) or as *ku'er* (Mandarin transliteration of "queer"); some respondents also identified as *T* (an abbreviation of the English term "tomboy," and a Taiwan-derived expression for a secondary lesbian gender that is similar, though not identical, to the English "butch") or *kuaxingbie* (a Taiwan-derived translation of the English "transgender"). To help the reader keep in mind the complexity of this linguistic field, I have specified in brackets which terms have been translated as "lesbian" in each of the direct quotes from respondents as follows.

THE SURVEY: GENERAL TRENDS

The survey was carried out over five months between September 2003 and January 2004. It consisted of an extensive anonymous questionnaire, with calls for respondents—and in some cases, the full text of the questionnaire—posted in Chinese at five major lesbian websites based in mainland China, one lesbian website and one dedicated listserv in Hong Kong, five lesbian websites and text-only bulletin board systems in Taiwan, and one lesbian website in Singapore.[16] Completed questionnaires were returned to me via e-mail. The survey consisted of two major sections: the first was a series of short-answer or multiple choice questions covering basic demographic information, and the history and current practices of both Internet usage and other lesbian-related social practices. The second section consisted of fifteen long-answer questions probing respondents' subjective experiences of their usage of the Internet for activities related to sexual preference or identity. A total of 116 responses were received: 53 from mainland China, 29 from Taiwan, 28 from the diaspora, and 6 from Hong Kong.[17] This sample is too small to be of statistical significance; however, the qualitative material contained in the long-answers section of the completed question-naires provides a rich source of information about the subjective experience of Internet use for this group of users. It is the qualitative aspect that this chapter concentrates on, following a brief summary of demographics.

The basic demographic information confirmed common views of Inter-net users in general as predominantly urban, middle-class youth. The data confirm a strong urban bias in all areas. In Taiwan, a bias toward Tai-pei City and Taipei County in the North of the island is pronounced.[18] In the PRC, the data on respondents' area of residence corroborates existing studies of the relative penetration of Internet infrastructure along the east-ern seaboard and the East–West division of mainland China according to Internet access.[19] Forty-five respondents out of fifty-three specified the city or town in which they live; of these, only seven live outside of provincial capital cities, Municipalities (Shanghai, Beijing, Chongqing), or Special Economic Zones (Shenzhen).

ONLINE COMMUNITY: AN IMAGINATIVE RESOURCE FOR "REAL-LIFE" PROBLEMS

In terms of their usage of the Internet to pursue activities they deemed related to their sexual preference or identity, this was a very active sample. A majority of respondents in both Taiwan and the diaspora participated in Internet activities connected with same-sex attraction or lesbian iden-tity *at least daily*, and a majority in China did this at least two to three times per week. In any reckoning, these activities appear to constitute a significant part of the respondents' personal and social lives. This is cor-roborated by the long-answer respondents of the women themselves, who were all but unanimous on the high level of importance they attached to their participation in lesbian-related Internet activities in Chinese. As the responses quoted below show, for many women, the sense of being part of a lesbian (*nütongzhi*, *lazi*, or *les*) online community was a particularly use-ful emotional resource to draw on when dealing with "real-life" problems associated with their sexual preference. A twenty-three-year-old research assistant in Taiwan offered the following thoughtful response, which elo-quently expresses how, although it may not constitute a community in the traditional sense, this form of "imagined community" has tremendous affective importance for its users:[20]

> The so-called "lesbian [*nütongzhi*] community" is a very big concept, since individuals within this community may have different interests, different social positions, different family backgrounds, and may live

very far away from each other [. . .]. But the web joins this group of people together, it connects these "women loving women" into a community, allowing them to see each other, and to see the many different faces lesbians [*nütongzhi*] have. To me this is very important, because it lets me find lesbians [*nütongzhi*] who in real life remain anonymous. We may never see each other, or even know each other, but I know that they truly do exist, and are living their lives truthfully.

Illustrating the practical uses of this sense of imagined community in more detail, the following responses highlight a series of specific difficulties that the Chinese-language lesbian Internet has helped these respondents deal with.

A twenty-year-old student in Lanzhou, the provincial capital of Gansu in far western China, wrote:

It's extremely important to me [to feel part of the online community]. Because I live in a fairly remote area, and there are many pressures on me externally as well as imposed on me by myself, this kind of information comes to me almost entirely via the Web. [. . .] When I'm feeling down, I just go on the Web, and see that people just like myself are conscientiously, actively living out their lives—I find that very comforting, and it makes me proud. [Using the Chinese-language lesbian Internet] does give me this feeling [of being part of a community of lesbians], and that's very important. On one level, I'm still quite confused about my identity right now, and to a certain extent I haven't really accepted it. On the Web, I feel as if we're all in it together, which makes me feel a bit better. Sometimes I get to thinking: there are so many of us, what is there we can't achieve?

A twenty-two-year-old student in Changsha wrote:

I started using [the Chinese-language lesbian Internet] because of my own internal confusion. Over three years of middle school, my love for a female classmate had caused me a lot of pain. After I started using the Internet and found out that there were so many other people like me, I felt a lot better, and my former depression lifted to a great degree. [. . .] Before [I began using the Internet], I thought I was a "freak." And because of this, all my friends (including one friend I'd been close to ever since we were little) deserted me. On the net, I've met a lot of good people [. . .] who've told me to love and respect myself, and understand myself; that it's just like how some people like to eat meat and others like radishes (when I heard this analogy I laughed out loud. At that time, for me to be able to laugh about this topic was extremely unusual).

A thirty-four-year-old teacher in Guiyang, the provincial capital of the impoverished province of Guizhou in southwestern China, wrote:

Yes, it has helped a lot. I'm a very independent thinker, and when I was at university, the question of my own sexual orientation prompted me to hunt down and read a huge quantity of reading matter on the subject (but it was all very out of date). I always felt suspicious of the term "sickness" that kept cropping up in those books, so through it all I somehow managed to stay true to myself. Later on, being able to access the latest scientific research/breakthroughs about *tongzhi* on the Internet was a tremendous help to my own internal identity/ confidence/ stress-relief.

A fifteen-year-old student in Taipei wrote:

A: [The Chinese-language lesbian Internet is] extremely important [to me]. Even though my young age means I can't go to bars and it'd be inappropriate for me to make friends with lesbians [*nütongzhi*] too much older than myself, I still log onto lesbian websites from home to find out about what they're all up to! I guess if I had the time and age was no barrier, I'd often go along with my girlfriend to the events they organize. If I turn on my computer without taking a look at those lesbian sites, I guess I just feel all wrong!

A Chinese entertainment worker in Kagawa, Japan, wrote:

After my lover of seven years and I split up in the summer of 1998 (more precisely, after she dumped me because of social pressure), I had trouble getting over it and passed my days amid pain and loneliness, with no-one I could talk to about it—not even my own family. During the first two years, I was like a walking corpse. Then I met my present husband, and I'm grateful to this lovable "big kid" for putting an end to my loneliness. But I'm even more grateful to the lesbian [*nütong*] Internet, as it made me understand that there were so many others like me, and they were out there too, hurting, loving. [. . .] I am grateful to each one of those *tongzhi* articles [I found online]; they enabled me to walk away from my pain and say goodbye to my loneliness.

A thirty-year-old teacher in Hong Kong (original in English), wrote:

I used to frequent US glbt sites e.g PlanetOut. But at those sites, I find it hard to get to know people who truly understand the situations that Chinese lesbians are in. About 2 1/2 years ago, I started to visit Chinese sites (I had never visited any sites in Chinese before that) and took part in discussions on message boards. I also knew a few lesbian friends. I first communicated with them via email and later we met up for gatherings. Though I just met a few people this way and didn't really make any close friends, it was a comfort to meet like-minded peers.

These responses draw attention to a wide range of everyday difficulties encountered by the respondents in their own local contexts: lack of access to other forms of lesbian culture and resources; internal struggles with sexual orientation, linked to high levels of ambient homophobia and the resultant social pressure; failed or terminated love affairs; conflicts with family; and, especially for women in the diaspora, a lack of connection with western LGBT culture and a desire to connect specifically with other Chinese lesbians. The community of Chinese-speaking lesbians on the Internet is an imagined one in the fairly precise sense that, even compared with the imagined community of the modern nation as discussed by Anderson, its members have an even smaller chance of meeting each other "in real life." Nevertheless, it is clear that the *idea* of belonging to such a community, abstract though it is, provides a significant imaginative resource for these respondents in tackling the material obstacles thrown up by everyday "real" life in their various local contexts.

But to what extent are lesbian-identified Internet users in China, Hong Kong, Taiwan, and the Chinese diaspora using the Internet as a new means of communicating *with each other*, across geopolitical boundaries? Does the Internet facilitate forms of personal identification through the category "Chinese lesbian" that could override geopolitical identification with a particular nation-state or locality? To progress further with the analysis of these complex questions, it is necessary to turn to a qualitative analysis of respondents' experience of sexual subjectivity and imagined geography.

IMAGINED GEOGRAPHIES 1: CONTESTED CHINESENESS

The several long-answer questions that asked respondents to reflect on how their sexual subjectivity related to their sense of geocultural location yielded a wide variety of answers. For some people, identification as lesbian (*nütongzhi*) meant principally identifying with other lesbians only inside their nation-state of citizenship (or residence); for others, it meant identification with other lesbians worldwide who share their Chinese ethnicity and culture, but not with Japanese or American lesbians; for many others, the category *nütongzhi* seemed to have an inherently global feel. This last category of responses is considered in detail below; for the moment, I present a range of other responses to questions of the perceived relationship between sexual identification and imagined geography:

> Q: Do you feel you have many things in common with other Chinese-speaking lesbians you meet through the Internet who live in territories other than your own? Or do you feel you are very different from them? Please explain.

A: [From a twenty-six-year-old unemployed graduate in Guangzhou]: Aside from the fact that we have the same sexual orientation, I feel that there are many differences, which are to do with the different cultural conditions in each place. In mainland China, lesbians [*nütong*] from different provinces all have different cultural backgrounds. Lesbians [*nütong*] who live close to Hong Kong and Taiwan bear virtually no relation to my own sense of sexual identity, and lesbians [*nütongzhi*] from the interior have to face far greater levels of pressure, pressure that comes from all quarters in relation to all kinds of issues. Personally I feel that what we have in common mainly reflects the information and culture available through the lesbian [*nütong*] Internet.

Q: If you use lesbian-related sites in Chinese situated in territories other than where you live (EG: if you live in Beijing and use sites in Hong Kong; or live in Taiwan and use sites in mainland China, etc.), do you feel that this makes you feel part of a regional community of Chinese lesbians, or not?

A: [From a twenty-one-year-old government bureaucrat in northeastern China]: No, because I feel like it's too far. If it's just across provinces or across cities, that's not so bad, but Taiwan and Hong Kong feel too far away, to me.

A: [From a thirty-one-year-old Taiwanese professional working in Shanghai]: Yes, I've discovered that the *tongzhi* communities in Taiwan, Hong Kong and mainland China have been able to engage in a considerable degree of communication and exchange as a result of the Internet. Even many aspects of language usage are becoming similar, like the identity-roles of T [tomboy, similar to "butch"], P [similar to "femme"] and *bu fen* [similar to "no roles"] and the term *lazi*, etc. I was really shocked to discover this after arriving in Shanghai: it turned out that lots of mainland Chinese *lazi* had begun the initial process of self-identification after visiting Taiwanese *lazi* websites. And on Shanghai-based *lazi* websites, I've also been able to get to know friends in Hong Kong, and discovered that we have no problems at all in communicating—it's great ☺.

Q: If you use lesbian-related sites in English or other languages, does this make you feel part of a world-wide community of lesbians, or not?

A: [From a thirty-two-year-old teacher in Taipei]: I very seldom go to non-Chinese sites—it's too hard on the eyes, the print is so small. But often overseas Chinese post their articles or thoughts in English, and only then do I feel that I'm just a little *lez* on a tiny, tiny little island, and all the corners of the world are full of many, many *lezes* living out their lives—it turns out that the people of the world are all connected and our blood flows into one!

A: [From a twenty-three-year-old administrator in Chongqing]: I can't read any languages other than Chinese. I only feel that I am part of the circle of lesbians [*nütongzhi*] inside China, not that I am part of a global community.

A: [From a twenty-five-year-old transgender university administrator in Taipei]: The [non-Chinese] sites I most often use are English ones, so my thoughts below are specifically in relation to using English sites. Since the theoretical language that I have studied, and its translated vocabulary (such as transgender/ *kuaxingbie*; queer/ *ku'er*, etc) has all been translated from English, when I read information on English sites, I do indeed feel somewhat like part of a global community. But Taiwan's Ts and *pos* also have many local particularities which the English sites never touch upon; there are certain cultural differences that have a definite localness to them (for example, breast binding [among Ts]); and that in turn decreases my feeling of belonging in globalization.

A: [From a thirty-one-year-old Taiwanese researcher in upstate New York; original response in English]: NO. I don't think so. I feel: in US lesbian community, they are all white. No lesbian of color. When I'm in the gender topic conference, I always feel my race is prior to my sexuality. And such feeling leads me NOT feel like I'm a part of global les. community.

Q: Do you think that in general, you have more in common with other Chinese lesbians than you do, for example, with American or Japanese lesbians? Why or why not?

A: [From the same Taiwanese teacher quoted above]: Since we're from the same cultural background, our parents have been inculcated with similar views. The whole of Chinese (*huarende*) society keeps on reproducing the same range of stuff: continue the family line, worship your ancestors, filial piety is more important than the self, parents are not to be educated [by their children], and so on. To put it simply, patriarchy still maintains a firm grasp on the sexual orientation and sexual desires of sons and daughters. And, confronted with these traditional ethics and the shadow of the patriarchy, Chinese sons and daughters often choose escapism, deception or self-sacrifice. It's this kind of tragic situation that makes us sense the commonality between us.

A: [From a thirty-year-old Chinese lecturer in upstate New York; original in English]: Yes. American lesbians are more sporty, environmentalist and health-conscious. Born citizens of the U.S., they have some kind of 'safety net' around them, so they can afford to stand up to discrimination and oppression. Chinese lesbians here are mostly first-generation immigrants. With jobs and green cards at stake, they have to go back to the closet and endure. Maybe that's why a tightly knit lesbian network (be it virtual or real) is so important for us—that's the only place where we can be ourselves without worry. American lesbians may not place such high values on the lesbian community and tend not to 'fuss' over their sexual orientation.

As noted above, when commencing this study, I was motivated in part by the question of whether the Chinese-language lesbian Internet was facilitating the formation of a sort of queer version of the narrative of transnational Chinese identity. As the very wide range of responses quoted previously indicates, the answer to this question cannot be seen as affirmative in any simple sense. Rather than creating a unified Chinese identity, the confluence of Internet technology and sexual identification instead seem, in this case, to have reflected and reinforced the fractal, shifting, multiple, and contested array of forms of "imagined Chineseness" that exists in and between mainland China, Taiwan, Hong Kong, and the diaspora. "Lesbian cyber-China," then, appears like a kind of electronic ghost nation, floating above the solid ground of the territorial China(s), yet maintaining an unpredictably complex and shifting web of imagined links with them, as well as with the imagined globe, "the West," "Asia," and among the different parts of itself.[21]

IMAGINED GEOGRAPHIES 2: LESBIAN GLOBALISM

While the responses to this survey thus notably did not indicate a widely shared idea of a singular or cohesive Chinese *cultural* identity, in contrast, many of the responses to questions about people's subjective experiences of *sexual* identity did reveal a strongly globalist discourse. As the responses quoted below demonstrate, the "global feeling" that many respondents described as a result of accessing lesbian-related materials on the Internet seems to result less from simply using the Internet than from a globalist association carried, in large part, by the idea of lesbian, or *nütongzhi*, identity itself.

Q: If you use lesbian-related sites in Chinese situated in territories other than where you live, do you feel that this makes you feel part of a regional community of Chinese lesbians, or not?

A: [From a thirty-two-year-old journalist in Wuhan]: When using Chinese lesbian [*nütong*] websites outside the territory where I live, I [. . .] feel that [the people there] are one with the people in my own local area. Because, as a lesbian [*nütongzhi*], I feel that lesbians [*nütong*] the world over are as one; as a *tongzhi*, I feel that *tongzhi* the world over (regardless of whether male or female) are as one.

A: [From an eighteen-year-old student in Taichung]: Well, not really . . . I live in Taiwan, and most of the websites I go to are Taiwanese . . . Lesbians [*nütongzhi*] . . . well, lesbians are lesbians! It doesn't matter where they're from . . . I feel a sort of intimacy with all of them!

Q: If you use lesbian-related sites in English or other languages, does this make you feel part of a worldwide community of lesbians, or not?

A: [From a twenty-five-year-old advertising company employee in Zhongshan, Guangdong]: Yes. If my English got to a certain level, I'd use English-language websites just the same, and make even more friends that way. After all, lesbians [*nütongzhi*] the world over are as one.

A: [From the fifteen-year-old student in Taipei cited earlier]: I've never used lesbian [*nütongzhi*] websites in any other languages! But to tell the truth, even though right now I only use Chinese-language lesbian websites in Taiwan, I still feel like I'm part of a worldwide lesbian community, because all of us as individual units are united by this grouping.

A: [From the thirty-two-year-old entertainment worker from China living in Japan cited earlier]: I've never used lesbian [*nütong*] websites in languages other than Chinese, but this definitely doesn't hinder my own sense of identification as a lesbian [*nütongzhi*], which transcends nationality and race.

A: [From a twenty-year-old Taiwanese student in Chicago]: Yes. My personal opinion is that no matter what language lesbian [*nütongzhi*] websites are in, if you yourself identify as a lesbian, then you are already part of a global lesbian community.

A: [From a twenty-two-year-old import-export worker in Guangzhou]: Even though I don't use English websites, I still feel part of a global lesbian [*nütongzhi*] community. As a lesbian, I only feel that I am different from heterosexual women, toward other lesbians I have a kind of unconscious friendly feeling—I feel that lesbians the world over are all one big family, this has nothing to do with whether websites are in Chinese or English.

With their frequent references to the inherent oneness, affective intimacy, or quasi-familial ties of lesbians worldwide regardless of language, race, nationality, or geography, these responses show that, for many respondents, the category *nütongzhi* itself *feels* like a global category, and respondents frequently experience this global feeling even without ever having accessed—or even planned or wanted to access—a nonlocal or non-Chinese-language lesbian website.

CONCLUSION: LESBIAN GLOBALISM AS COUNTERDISCOURSE

How should we view the strongly globalist tendency in many of these respondents' experiences of sexual identification online? Does it reveal yet again the disturbing tendency for Euro-American-style, post-Stonewall gay and lesbian identity politics to take over the world, crushing all before it and creating the illusion that these geographically and culturally distant women share a culture and an identity with Western lesbians? Or, by framing the issue in those terms, are we perhaps asking the wrong question?

In his incisive critical review of *Mobile Cultures: New Media in Queer Asia*, Taiwanese gay scholar, Raymond Wei-cheng Chu, queries the pertinence of that volume's central interest in the question of:

> whether the impact of globalization is homogenizing—in its spread of a certain kind of (sub)cultural formations and identity politics that model on the metropolitan l/g/q existence—or in effect 'glocalizing'— in that any global trends, hegemonic as they are, inevitably hybridize as they become localized and indigenized.[22]

Chu remarks that "what is disturbing about this polemical framework is its conspicuous *tangentiality* to the various local subject cultures covered in the volume," which appear to be unconcerned with the debate as set out in these terms.[23] Instead, Chu notes,

> concerned only with the local adaptability of global influences and any possible pitfalls in their indigenous application, local l/g/q cultures basically favor globalization because its hegemony offers facilitating resources that are hard to come by domestically.[24]

Chu's point is extremely pertinent. Yet, one slight modification to his formulation is in order. I would suggest that, rather than it being the case that LGBT activists and communities in Asia favor the globalization of Euro-American models *as hegemony*, the point is precisely that Euro-American notions of LGBT identity, politics, rights, community, and so on, *are not necessarily hegemonic* in those local Asian contexts. At the local level, these models often remain, in Raymond William's terms, emergent rather than dominant, and their utility lies precisely in their capacity to be wielded as tactical tools to challenge the hegemonies of local regimes of sexual and gender regulation.

The results of this survey suggest that one such tactical tool used by this group of respondents is precisely the idea of a global lesbian community. Here, the global functions not as a material extension of actual Euro-American sexual cultures, but instead as an imaginative resource used to address the kinds of specific local problems detailed in the responses quoted in the first part of this chapter: isolation, family and other social pressures, and in some areas, stigmatization by locally dominant pathologizing models of homosexuality as illness.[25] The globalist lesbian discourse is a way of thinking and feeling about sexuality and community that provides emotional support to these women in their negotiation of the difficulties they face in their daily lives as same-sex-loving women in the local contexts in which they live.

Such a conclusion suggests an interesting articulation of the two new roles for the imagination in social life in the era of globalization suggested by Appadurai. To recap, Appadurai suggested that, on the one hand, the new social imagination is used in thinking forms of "grassroots globalization" on behalf of disenfranchised peoples into being; on the other hand, it is used in new ways of thinking about regions and worlds. My conclusion implies a joining of these two functions: an affective support network among minoritized peoples—the Chinese-language lesbian Internet as grassroots globalization—is sustained, in part, by new ways of imagining the world, in the idea of a global (or, less frequently, Chinese) lesbian community. Examples like the ones cited throughout this chapter perhaps give some sense of how transnational queer imaginaries operating outside the West, far from necessarily being symptoms of "Westernization" in any material sense, can provide imaginative resources for urgent and intensely local struggles.

NOTES

1. Special thanks to all of the webmasters who helped me with the survey (dongdong, Hui-tze, TC, Shuijing, Yue, Xiao Heng, Pizi, the webmaster at Tongnü Tiandi, AD, and Choo Lip Sin), and all the others who helped in various ways. Thanks to Mark McLelland for his invaluable suggestions on an earlier draft.
2. On Taiwanese queer bulletin board systems (BBS) cultures, see Terri He's chapter in this volume (Chapter 19).
3. The use of written Chinese in these Internet forums is commonly presumed to correlate with ethnic Chinese identity. Indeed, while interacting in these forums, the author was generally initially assumed by others to be of diasporic Chinese background.
4. Arjun Appadurai, "Grassroots Globalization and the Research Imagination," *Public Culture* 12, no. 1 (2000): 1–19.
5. Appadurai, "Grassroots," 8.

6. Internet World Statistics, "Internet World Users by Language," http://www. internetworldstats.com/stats7.htm (accessed May 17, 2007).

7. See Jon Stratton, "Cyberspace and the Globalization of Culture," in *The Cybercultures Reader*, ed. David Bell and Barbara Kennedy (London: Routledge, 2000), 721–731; Internet World Statistics, "Internet World Users by Language." Figures for the PRC and Hong Kong from China Internet Network Information Center's January 2006 report, "Zhongguo hulianwangluo fazhan zhuangkuang tongji baogao," http://www.cnnic.net.cn/en/index/0O/02/index.htm

8. Figures for Taiwan from the FIND research team (Focus on Internet News and Data) commissioned by Taiwan's Department of Industrial Technology, "2005 nian wo guo jiating kuanpin, xingdong yu wuxian yingyong xiankuang yu xuqiu diaocha," http://www.find.org.tw/find/home.aspx?page=many&id=126

9. Ien Ang, *On Not Speaking Chinese: Living between Asia and the West* (London: Routledge, 2001); Rey Chow, "On Chineseness as a Theoretical Problem," *boundary 2 25*, no. 3 (1998): 1–24; and Allen Chun, "Fuck Chineseness: On the Ambiguities of Ethnicity as Culture as Identity," *boundary 2 23*, no. 2 (1996): 111–138.

10. Technical constraints were the most frequent reason cited in my survey for mainland Chinese netizens not accessing Taiwanese and Hong Kong websites; it was a question neither of their access being officially restricted nor of an inability to read complex characters.

11. Ang, *On Not Speaking Chinese*, 75–92; Aihwa Ong, "Anthropology, China and Modernities: The Geopolitics of Cultural Knowledge," in *The Future of Anthropological Knowledge*, ed. Henrietta Moore (New York: Routledge, 1996), 60–93; Mayfair Yang, "Mass Media and Transnational Subjectivity in Shanghai: Notes on (Re)cosmopolitanism in a Chinese Metropolis," in *Ungrounded Empires: The Cultural Politics of Modern Chinese Transnationalism*, ed. Aihwa Ong and Donald Nonini (New York: Routledge, 1997):287–322.

12. Guobin Yang, "The Internet and the Rise of a Transnational Chinese Cultural Sphere," *Media, Culture and Society* 25 (2003): 169–190.

13. See Chris Berry, Fran Martin, and Audrey Yue, eds., *Mobile Cultures: New Media in Queer Asia* (Durham, NC: Duke University Press, 2003); and Fran Martin et al., eds., *AsiaPacifiQueer: Rethinking Gender and Sexuality* (Champaign: University of Illinois Press, 2008).

14. Fran Martin, *Situating Sexualities: Queer Representation in Taiwanese Fiction, Film and Public Cultures* (Hong Kong: Hong Kong University Press, 2003).

15. Chris Berry and Fran Martin, "Syncretism and Synchronicity: Queer 'n' Asian Cyberspace in 1990s Taiwan and Korea," in *Mobile Cultures: New Media in Queer Asia*, ed. Chris Berry, Fran Martin, and Audrey Yue (Durham, NC: Duke University Press, 2003), 87–114.

16. In China, *Shenqiu Xiao Wu* (http://www.leschina.com), *Tongnü Tiandi* (http://www.lesworld.net), *Les Ni Wo Jia* (http://www.lalahome.com), *Yuanfende Tiankong* (http://www.lalasky.net), and *Hua Kaide Difang* (http://www.lescn.net), plus several other sites, where respondents helped me out by crossposting. In Hong Kong, the call was distributed via the Lesway listserv, which has 200 recipients, and was posted at the Lesway website (http://www.lesway.com). In Taiwan, the call and/or questionnaire were posted to: *Lala Zidui* text-only BBS (http://www.lalainfo.com.tw), *Huai Nüer* text-only BBS (telnet://dawz.feminism.net), To-get-her Lez Cyberpub (http://www.to-get-her.org), *Ninü* BBS (http://bb/ttv/com.tw/bb/viewtopic.asp?forum=17), and *AD Wenzi Xiao Wo* (http://www.ariesdog.com); AD also kindly advertised

the survey on her web radio program. In Singapore, the call was posted at the Fridae website (http://www.fridae.com). All websites were accessed repeatedly between September 2003 and January 2004.

17. The number of respondents from Hong Kong was too low to analyze this data quantitatively, but the long-answer responses from these women have been considered.

18. This corroborates data obtained in the 2001 fourth Taiwanese lesbian Internet census, "Di si jie wanglu lazi renkou pucha," which obtained 1711 responses (http://98.to/lalasurvey/).

19. This division is based on Karsten Giese's definitions in "Internet Growth and the Digital Divide: Implications for Spatial Development," in *China and the Internet: Politics of the Digital Leap Forward*, ed. Christopher Hughes and Gudrun Wacker (London: RoutledgeCurzon, 2003), 30–57.

20. Responses quoted are my own translations of the Chinese, unless otherwise noted.

21. See Ananda Mitra, "Virtual Commonality: Looking for India on the Internet" in *The Cybercultures Reader*, ed. David Bell and Barbara Kennedy (London: Routledge, 2000), 676–694.

22. Wei-cheng Raymond Chu, "Review of *Mobile Cultures*," *Cultural Studies Review* 10, no. 2 (2004): 195.

23. Chu, "Review," 195.

24. Ibid., 196.

25. See Mark Johnson, "Global Desirings and Translocal Loves: Transgendering and Same-Sex Sexualities in the Southern Philippines," *American Ethnologist* 25, no. 4 (1998): 695–711.

19 Online *Tongzhi?*

Subcultural Practices in the Gay and Lesbian Community of Spiteful Tots[1]

Terri He

BACKGROUND TO TAIWANESE QUEER CULTURE

Lesbian, gay, and queer (LGQ) cultures in Taiwan first came into public view in the 1990s.[2] Since then, LGQ cultures in Taiwan have been greatly facilitated by the fast development of information and communication technology (ICT), particularly that of the Internet.[3] The surfacing of these cultures was concomitant with developments in late capitalism, consumer culture, and (urban) mobility.[4] Forces of urbanization and capitalist production—both developments can be argued to be based on Western models—favored a sense of liberalism and popularized Internet technology in Taiwan, making different forms of public discussions about homosexuality possible. With the help of the near-ubiquitous availability of computing and networked computers, LGQ cultures thus gained some visibility in public spheres, and were no longer hidden, criminalized, or blatantly pathologized.

After many years of effort, the first LGQ pride parade was made possible in 2003. While this queer event was certainly a result of many different forces, coincidences, and social/political circumstances at the time, it is undeniable that Internet technology played a significant part, especially in regard to instant communication and transregional coordination and cooperation. However, despite this partial assimilation of LGQ cultures into the mainstream via the power of technology, the linkage between LGQ cultures and Taiwan's politics remains an interesting one. It might be argued that everything on the islands of Taiwan is more or less related to Taiwan's unsettled business with mainland China, and LGQ cultures are no exception to this, in terms of their public emergence and social development. LGQ cultures embody a strong desire to distance Taiwan from its own forty-year period of martial law.[5] This attempt at distancing itself from Taiwan's authoritarian past is also about differentiating the current regime from the authoritarian treatment of homosexuality in neighboring countries, especially in mainland China. The intention of differentiating contemporary Taiwan from its own past, as well as from mainland China, is, according to Cindy Patton, a rather common strategy that has been utilized, for example, in South Africa, Israel, and the former East Germany in order for radical groups to establish a liberal self-image that runs against public imagination or expectations in these countries.[6] As such, LGQ cultures in Taiwan have, from the beginning, been very much conditioned by the particularities of their social, political, and cultural contexts, which may be summarized as related to late capitalism, the rise of the middle class, the prevalence of Internet technology, and Taiwan's political and diplomatic relations with its neighbors—among them, of course, China is especially significant.

My case study focuses on one online community named "Spiteful Tots,"[7] which involves some twenty people, aged from twenty-five to thirty-five years old, generally well educated, and middle class. Most of them are self-identified gay men and some are lesbians. Many of them would not have known each other were they not members of Spiteful Tots. The participants in Spiteful Tots are quite familiar with contemporary ideas deriving from gay and lesbian studies, queer theories from the West, Japanese popular culture, and their Chinese cultural and literary heritage. Their simultaneous and hybrid access to these various kinds of cultural and social resources gives shape to what they have become—what is termed nowadays as, "Taiwan *tongzhi*."[8]

To further illustrate the kind of cultural hybridity that characterizes Taiwan's tongzhi, I would like to briefly mention the Spiteful Tots community's offline participation in the 2003 and 2004 LGQ pride events. In 2003, the Spiteful Tots' members among the marching crowd wore masks of the leading female character, Shizuka, from the Japanese comic book and animated series, *Doraemon*. The Spiteful Tots portrayed themselves as Shizuka, as she is best known as a kind of girl-next-door figure. Wearing pink shirts, red skirts, and Shizuka masks, the Tots hoped to make the point that gay men are just like Shizuka—cute, friendly, and nice, and thus deserving of people's care and acceptance.

In the 2004 parade, however, the Spiteful Tots chose a very different character: a god known as Kwan-yin in Chinese Buddhist belief. Kwan-yin is a god who transforms into a tree, an animal, a woman, or a man in order to remind people of the importance of being kind and generous to all creatures. Kwan-yin is usually represented as a woman in a white robe, which was the image that the Spiteful Tots appropriated in the parade in order to demonstrate fluidity in identity—a prominent idea in queer theory. They also wished to convey a message reasserting that all people are equal, and that, as Kwan-yin is the god of mercy in Buddhism, his/her love for everyone lies in a spirit of tolerance and kindness.

THE HYBRID DISCOURSE OF TONGZHI IN TAIWAN

What, then, is tongzhi? Tongzhi is a transliteration of a Mandarin term that is used in Communist Chinese discourse to signify "comrade," and nowadays has ironically become politically charged for homosexual people in Taiwan. Since its debut in the Hong Kong Queer/Tongzhi Film Festival in 1992, tong-zhi has been appropriated as an equivalent term, designating homosexuality, queer, *and* LGQ.[9] In recent years, tongzhi has also been the very term that sexual dissidents have mobilized to address issues surrounding the politics of sexuality. Its use in the Taiwanese media has become interchangeable with LGQ, but, as Fran Martin indicates in Chapter 18 in this volume, there are, of course, a range of local significances and dynamics attached to this term, the discussion of which is beyond the scope of this chapter.

The most salient feature of tongzhi as an all-encompassing term for LGQ may be its relation to Communist China. This particular appropriation of tongzhi is ironic in that it satirizes, as well as criticizes, what is considered to be absent in China—that which underpins the pursuit of diversity in sexual-ity and the creation of "sexual citizenship"—namely, the primarily Western discourses of human rights.[10] Analyzing the underlying logic of this political efficacy in which tongzhi is grounded, I argue that one consequence of this logic is the construction of sexuality as a byproduct of the contemporary dis-course of modernity in Taiwan. While tongzhi is becoming more and more frequently utilized as a political identity for sexual minorities, it is also already about a strategic move to resist China by means of an alliance with Western-influenced notions of modernity and the kind of liberal attitudes modernity promotes. Under such circumstances, tongzhi is clearly politicized in a differ-ent way to Western LGQ identities and might be viewed as more "contami-nated" by issues unrelated to sexuality *per se*, but rather more closely allied with national identity and difference.

At the same time, tongzhi communities in Taiwan have been formulating a hybrid subculture, as they intermingle elements from mainstream popular culture derived from their Chinese heritage, Japan, and the West. Tongzhi subculture in Taiwan mixes different cultural representations and practices to promote their own tongzhi identity and to obtain more visibility. In this capacity, we are dealing with a hybrid subculture, and I believe that the analytic capacity of hybridity has not yet been fully developed.[11] The kind of hybridity that Taiwan tongzhi live with is a kind of everyday, ordinary hybridity, which facilitates a more practical understanding of the term. It is no longer about here or there, local or global, but rather a forever ongo-ing process of hybridization—both here and there and local and global, as shown in the previous examples of Shizuka and Kwan-yin, both cul-tural borrowings from Japanese cartoons, local deities and legends,[12] and Western theories of sexuality. What is more, this kind of hybridity is not particular to Taiwan because hybridity can and should be theorized with regard to the meeting and negotiating of different discourses and manners of perception between different geopolitical locations. On the one hand, all kinds of discourses might become hybrid during their mutual meeting and negotiation, and yet on the other hand, this process of negotiation also embodies games of power. As in the Foucauldian sense, one discourse or mode of perception eventually gains more legitimacy and becomes thought of as more "truthful" than others; the less "truthful" discourses that formulate different understandings about certain issues are subjugated to or dominated by the more powerful one.

In this vein of thought, then, there is a dualism at work. In his work, "The Wily Homosexual (First—and Necessarily Hasty—Notes)," Silviano Santiago, for instance, has elucidated this dualism between the more and less powerful:

> [p]eripheral," "subaltern," "particular" correspond semantically to the referent of the cosmopolitan question on the value of [local] culture, and these terms are respectively opposed to "metropolitan," "superior," and "universal," features associated with the place of utterance.[13]

In other words, hybridity is a result of being structured and placed by the "metropolitan," "superior," and "universal," its reality already embedded in an imbalanced power relationship, struggling for agency in its own right. The kind of hybridity that tongzhi demonstrates here cannot be entirely characterized as "a subversion of political and cultural domination," as contended by Homi Bhabha and May Joseph; or as a special quality of those who are privileged as third-world scholars, as argued by Jonathan Friedman; or as being "complicit with structures of inequality," as asserted by Aijaz Ahmad.[14] Rather, it is both "a sign of empowerment" and "a symptom of dominance."[15] It is a very concrete form of being and understanding one's own position in relation to others, and below I will illustrate what tongzhi does and does not do for participants in this case study of the Spiteful Tots community—and also how it is critical to the particularity of LGQ cultures. However, before doing so, it is necessary to say something about the online environment in Taiwan, within which the Spiteful Tots' community has developed.

OVERVIEW OF INTERNET USAGE IN TAIWAN

No doubt following the common belief in ICT as a major force bringing about advanced development in the economy, communications, and other crucial social infrastructures, Taiwan has been prompt in adopting new technologies. Starting from the mid-1990s, the state developed major infrastructure initiatives, such as the Taiwan Academic Network, which saw the spread of Internet access to all public senior-high and vocational schools, colleges, and universities throughout the island.[16]

Outside of educational sectors, around 61 percent of Taiwan's households are regular Internet users, and 47 percent of them are equipped with broadband hook-ups, ideal for 24-hour connection.[17] In other words, Internet access is generally easily available both in the urban and rural areas. At the very least, those connected to the telephone system can access a dial-up Internet connection.[18] As a consequence, residents in Taiwan have been exposed to the many possibilities enabled by multimedia-assisted forms of communication for the past decade.

Additionally, Internet cafés are very popular throughout Taiwan. The regular customers in Internet cafés are mainly students, the unemployed, and even the working-class (after working hours or in between jobs), who are likely to spend their days, evenings, or weekends chatting, surfing, and most likely of all, playing online games, such as Ultima Online™ or World of Warcraft. Due to its low costs and easy availability, Internet access in Taiwan does not seem to exclude as many people as in other societies. Hence, Nina Wakeford's reminder that we should pay close attention to "economic conditions of production and consumption"[19] while doing cultural analyses on studies of the queer net, does not seem to be a primary concern in the Taiwanese context. This is not because there are no socioeconomic differences among the Taiwanese population, but because the state's proactive participation has ensured more equitable access to the Internet for all.[20]

However, different groups do use the Internet differently.[21] Some tend to go for more text-based activities, such as chatting and message posting, as ways of bonding with friends, while others prefer searching for useful information or reading newspaper articles online. At any rate, using the Internet is an activity that focuses on users' textual experiences, which means that expressing oneself through words and symbols, for the most part, is an important skill that repeats itself again and again in cyberspace. This digital literacy that requires one to express oneself in such a way so as to attract a readership emphasizes the need for "verbal artistry and communicative competence that create and sustain 'community' through audience response."[22]

Perhaps then, it is this particular way of creating a loosely connected community via verbal mastery that has resulted in a generational divide in Taiwan, as this has not been an accustomed mode of communication for older generations. The contemporary online culture, to further emphasize this point, is formed and directed mostly by the younger generations, who have collectively invented, just to name a few, *zuyinwen* (the use of phonetic symbols to replace complex Chinese characters), combinations of symbols for conveying emotions and feelings, and new sets of terminology for online communications.[23] Of course, when making this statement, I do not wish to neglect the middle-aged generations in their thirties and forties, who still constitute an important part of the online population, though they do not seem to be as actively involved in the fads of popular cultural performances online. The dominant popular online (sub)culture seems, in most cases, to be created by younger online users, who range in age from teens to early twenties.

THE SPITEFUL TOTS COMMUNITY

Participants in the Spiteful Tots community occupy an awkward position in relation to Taiwan's mainstream popular cyberculture. Since most participants hold bachelor's degrees, they have been acquainted with networked computers and typing since they were first-year university students in their late teens. However, now that they are no longer students and have to split their time between work and play in a more practical way, the kind of subculture they form tends to be more outside the mainstream and on the edge. For example, they reject the use of zuyinwen, while embracing some symbol combinations, and remain suspicious of new and fashionable trends in terminology in online conversations. What seems to be central to this community, according to my observations over the past six years, is a forever ongoing attempt to position their subjectivity via formulating their own independent subculture against the mainstream.

The name Spiteful Tots[24] itself represents such an attempt. To call them "spiteful" is to imply that they are different from the majority in Taiwan, since they have little intention of being nice and kind to other people. While this may appear to imply a rather negative image of themselves, I argue that it is really meant as a rejection of false courtesy or sociality, which does not reveal kind-heartedness so much as a sense of false affection or even hypocrisy. This kind of false display of affection hurts them while it continues to be reciprocated widely among the major population in Taiwan as a way of life. On the flip side, then, the naming suggests a sense of frustration regarding the processes of socialization. For the participants, they feel they might be misunderstood and eventually excluded for not treating others in some of the "nice" ways people generally recognize as polite or social.

While this sense of frustration with regard to normal socialization might seem somewhat adolescent, it is, however, significant when it is considered that their dissident sexuality has kept them from full participation in institutions, such as marriage and the family. In the Chinese cultural context, all persons, irrespective of age, are considered immature until they have entered into marriage and started their own family. They maintain a mentality as daughters and sons who are still "kids," no matter how old they might be. The name Spiteful Tots, then, encapsulates the day-to-day reality of exclusion from mainstream, heteronormative modes of socialization and interaction since, in society's terms, they can never be fully mature.

SPITEFUL TOTS AND THE USE OF ZUYINWEN

The Spiteful Tots community is then a place where LGQ people with these kinds of sentiments and experiences can come together. It is made possible by its members reading, participating and interacting in many of the electronic bulletin boards they have collectively created. Each of the boards has its own theme and its own rules. Most of the boards are spaces for humorous posts and interesting discussions; others are rather personalized, meant for keeping an electronic diary, and usually made viewable only to online users with screen names known to the journal keepers. Below, I will give an example as I try to give a flavor of the community and back up my previous argument about the community being positioned against the mainstream online culture. Take, for example, the board "kindergarten." In April 2001, participants organized a discussion board titled "kindergarten" where they articulate their disapproval of the online fad of zuyinwen.

Zuyinwen is a contemporary Taiwanese way of producing online text that mixes complex Chinese characters and phonetic symbols. For instance, in regular typed text, a sentence in complex Chinese characters may look like this: 你吃東西沒啊 (have you eaten yet?); in zuyinwen, it may look instead like this: 你ㄔ東ㄒㄧ沒ㄚ. In the process of communication, zuyinwen oftentimes requires more guesswork on the receiver's end, since, before it became popular sometime between 1999 and 2000, zuyinwen was nonexistent. The difficulty of reading zuyinwen has to do with the fact that zuyinwen as a language is a highly contextualized and interpretative one, as the same phonetic symbol, ㄒ, without the other matching phonetic symbol and stress, can mean, just to name a few: "west," "wash," or "drama." The way to determine which meaning fits, of course, depends on the context.

On the "kindergarten" board, the Spiteful Tots participants create the imaginary backdrop of a "kindergarten," where typing/communicating in zuyinwen is seen as a remedial move that must be avoided. In the discussion, they frame their disapproval of zuyinwen by representing complex Chinese characters as something to be protected as part of the national heritage. By national heritage, the participants are convinced that complex Chinese characters should be considered historically as the authentic Chinese characters, unlike the simplified characters used in mainland China, which were produced as a result of the Cultural Revolution of 1966–1976. Therefore, upon entry to this board, the following statement appears:

> In order to develop soldiers tough as iron, our kindergarten will practice severe physical punishment on the pupils. Any pupil who violates the following rules will be prohibited from posting for three days. The director of the kindergarten will also have appropriate punishment tailor-made for each individual depending on how much zuyinwen is used. Pupils can only resume their status as pupils in the kindergarten after they have accepted as well as undergone the tailor-made punishment.

> Rules are to be updated irregularly. Please pay constant attention to the changes.

Ignorance is not an excuse.

The director of the kindergarten belongs to the managerial class, and so s/he does not have to observe the rules.

The rules are:

1. You can not use "I," and have to replace "I" with other ways of addressing yourself, such as nicknames etc.

2. For everyone's own good, this kindergarten promotes "knowing your own national characters" [author's note: in this case, complex Chinese characters] policy. No posts should include any zuyinwen.[25]

From these instructions, it can be inferred that the "kindergarten" board attempts to compare zuyinwen users to preschool pupils—those who have not yet learned complex Chinese characters, but have acquired phonetic symbols and started to express themselves in a basic way with these symbols. Kindergarten is a way of mocking online users who support the use of zuyinwen and rejecting the idea of making phonetic symbols—*zuyin*—a viable option for textual communication. Even in this online, imaginary kindergarten, as the previously cited rules indicate, zuyinwen is strongly discouraged. One of the posts clearly argues for the inappropriateness of zuyinwen: "You don't see Americans using K.K. phonetic symbols to communicate."[26] However, Spiteful Tots participants do not avoid zuyin entirely when they need to show the tone of speech, since there are usually no corresponding Chinese characters for the interjections found in daily speech. These participants are simply uncomfortable with using zuyin instead of complex Chinese characters as a general way of online communication. Zuyinwen violates their sense of appropriateness, and "does not respect complex Chinese characters,"[27] which is seen as a problem. Juxtaposed with this disapproval of zuyinwen is an attempt to make things more difficult by banning the pronoun "I" (*wuo*), underlining the unreasonableness of the "kindergarten," rendering this discussion board an unwelcoming place for zuyinwen users.

Zuyinwen is in itself a hybrid system of symbols. It is a product of complex Chinese characters, a legacy of historical and cultural China, and the Taiwanese phonetic symbol set that is unique to Taiwan. In other words, zuyinwen is a manifestation of Taiwan's cultural hybridity. In the context of the Spiteful Tots community, zuyinwen as a hybrid induces tensions. Before the board "kindergarten" came into being, the use of zuyinwen on Spiteful Tots' boards had caused some conflict between visitors and nonregular participants and the regulars, especially in terms of the old-timers' frustration and irritation with zuyinwen, since it is not as readily understandable as complex Chinese.[28] However, perhaps because members of Spiteful Tots would still like to maintain an atmosphere of democracy (considering that all the other boards have been created according to the majority opinion and are based on most of the participants' unanimous wishes), the rule-setting of "kindergarten" adopts an unreasonable and self-styled way of speaking, so as to establish a paradoxical rationale behind its unexplained rejection of zuyinwen. The idea of transforming "pupils in kindergarten" into "soldiers who are tough as iron" as stated in the rules, for example, denotes Spiteful Tots' self-mocking attitude as authoritarian by banning zuyinwen without further discussion or group voting. In this regard, the "kindergarten" board should be seen as an attempt to manage the rising discontent with some posts in zuyinwen composed by less well-known screen names in the community. It is, on the one hand, about the tension between visitors and regular participants, and on the other hand, about participants' frustration at reading this new type of online language, which is an unfamiliar hybrid—neither Chinese nor zuyin.

In a postmodern manner, moreover, the Spiteful Tots' self-mocking reminds me of the aforementioned forty-year period of martial law. The martial law era before 1986 required all students, no matter how young, to be potential fighters protecting the country from invasion by mainland China and communism, in order to maintain the nation's legitimacy and independent status. Decades later, this logic still exists in the form of two-year compulsory military service for all male citizens in Taiwan. The combining of students and military together via educational/training institutes (such as the board "kindergarten") becomes striking in this context of Spiteful Tots, where (inter)actions are all textually based. The discussion board specifically posits that complex Chinese characters are ordered, appropriate, and legitimized, as opposed to phonetic symbols, which are characterized as the meaningless babble of unruly and unlearned children. Words, and the images or metaphors the embody, unwittingly and yet powerfully reiterate the residues from the previous era of martial law, and remind one of the state's former high-handed measures for control.

SPITEFUL TOTS' REJECTION OF TONGZHI

An interesting aspect of Spiteful Tots for considering Internet communication lies in how zuyinwen serves as an example of how Spiteful Tots as a group deal with new terminology and fashionable ways of online communication in general. The act of mocking zuyinwen via the board "kindergarten" comes from, I believe, a very typical strategy for participants in Spiteful Tots who mock newly available ways of speaking and communicating online.

This is shown in how the term tongzhi is deployed by Spiteful Tots participants. From its inception, the Spiteful Tots community has expressed doubt and mistrust about the term tongzhi. Prior to 2000, tongzhi was still relatively uncommon in Taiwan, and most LGQ people did not wish to be labeled as tongzhi because it seemed both unfamiliar and too politicized (or perhaps too activist).[29] However, nowadays, tongzhi has become a localized name for homosexual people, and the term has been extended to other sexualities, such as straight tongzhi (*zi tongzhi*)—that is, heterosexual people who are friendly to homosexual people—or third-sex tongzhi (*di san xing tongzhi*)—that is, transgender people. While tongzhi remains politicized and related to activism, the term has also been represented in rather negative ways because mass media coverage of tongzhi often occurs in the context of drug use, promiscuity, home parties,[30] and AIDS. Thus, there are two distinct social discourses of tongzhi, one that stresses the modern, diversified society that respects variety and difference in personal relationships, and another that stresses drugs, social breakdown, and disease.

Postings to the Spiteful Tots community that express discomfort with the term tongzhi, however, do not necessarily relate to the latter association represented in the media. Rather, participants find tongzhi to be a term with limited relevance to their own lives and experience, partly because of its political implications, and partly because "homosexual" still seems to them the most "realistic" term to describe who they are. Frequent usages of *tongnan* (homo-man/men) and *tongnü* (homo-woman/women) also seem more acceptable, though both are perhaps less readily understood by people outside of the community. Tongnan and tongnü are shorthand, combining *tongxinglian* (homosexual) and *nanren* (male person)/ *nüren* (female person). These terms in Spiteful Tots are considered more neutral and to be without political implications.

Tongzhi, though politicized, has also developed differences in meaning and implication over the years. Upon achieving common parlance in public discourse, tongzhi appeared, at the time, new and inspiring, carrying political momentum and a hint of modernized liberalism. However, the way tongzhi is perceived nowadays does not necessarily confer the same optimistic nuance, as these positive implications of tongzhi have been overlaid with negative representations via the mainstream media. While at present, in Taiwan the term "homosexual" has been largely replaced by "tongzhi," the Spiteful Tots community does not embrace the identity of tongzhi and occasionally challenges the term as a "fashion" that people use because they want to feel "in." As a result, messages on the discussion boards in Spiteful Tots either skip over issues of self-designation or simply fall back on tongnan or tongnü, without fussing about these terms and their meanings. The community of Spiteful Tots has veered away from accepting the term tongzhi despite the widespread social acceptance of the term outside of the community. This ambivalence about the term tongzhi has, however, gradually reduced, since many members have taken part in the annual pride parades three times in a row, resulting in people feeling less awkward about the term, and the fact that tongzhi has also gradually lost its association of being "new" and "fashionable."

CONCLUSION: HYBRIDITY AS A STRATEGY FOR RESISTANCE

The analyses of Spiteful Tots members' strategies for dealing with names, terms, and ways of communication sheds light upon what the Internet provides for gay and lesbian participants in this online community. First, regular members of Spiteful Tots are in general not politically motivated, and do not view their sexuality as needing to be politicized. While it may be too much of a jump to designate these regular users as apathetic, it is perhaps appropriate to assume that the contemporary politics of sexuality is not constructed in such a way as to garner their support. In this regard, through the Internet, participants are able to express what they think of the current politics of sexuality in more creative ways, such as their collective decision to dress up as Shizuka and Kwan-yin in the recent parades. Despite the fact that they marched together under a rubric of respect for sexual diversity, they still maintain that a separation between life and politics is necessary and needs to be protected.

Both zuyinwen and tongzhi have incurred the dislike of the Spiteful Tots community, since both are seen as fads. While zuyinwen reflects some features of contemporary Taiwanese popular culture and is part of the debate over Taiwan's national distinction from mainland China, tongzhi shows that, even with a term meant to be liberal and politically empowering for LGQ subjects, the manner in which it gained currency is not far from the way fashions are created and fostered—as something advertised as desirable and symbolizing certain contemporary qualities.

From the community's apolitical perspective, they disagree with tongzhi as a euphemism for homosexuality, and recognize that the term results from many other political forces and aspirations that lie outside gay and lesbian people's daily lives. For the most part, then, tongzhi seems to be simply trendy, rather than useful for these participants. This is to say that, when something has been politicized as part of social discourse, encouraging and promoting ideas related to the "in" discourse may only be meaningful to those who actively and visibly seek more attention and resources, while simultaneously inferring negligence on the part of other LGQ groups who do not enjoy this kind of social attention or demand for political power.

In conclusion then, the contribution of this Internet-facilitated community of Spiteful Tots in Taiwan may be in the way it offers alternatives for representing sexual dissent outside of dominant paradigms. As participants' embrace of cultural hybrids such as Shizuka and Kwan-yin shows, they oppose contemporary perceptions and social understandings of sexual dissidence in Taiwan by refusing integration into a system of sexual politics that operates in ways unappealing to them. In this regard, the importance of the Internet can be found in allowing this subcultural manifestation that, via both hybridity and creativity, can make critical statements about dominant discourses.

NOTES

1. For the completion of this essay, I thank Dr. Ann Kaloski-Naylor for having read the first few drafts and given me feedback and comments.
2. Bisexual and transgender communities are not as developed and do not receive as much attention as do LGQ subjects in Taiwan. Although Professor Josephine Ho in the English Department of Central University has promoted transgender studies by holding events and activities, there does not seem to be much follow-up afterward.
3. Terri He, "Representations of Gayness: A Case Study of Spiteful Tots as an Online Community in Taiwan" (MA diss., Linköping Universitet, 2004); Chris Berry and Fran Martin, "Syncretism and Synchronicity: Queer 'n' Asian Cyberspace in 1990s Taiwan and Korea," in *Mobile Cultures: New Media in Queer Asia*, ed., Chris Berry, Fran Martin, and Audrey Yue (Durham, NC: Duke University Press, 2003), 87–114.
4. Berry and Martin, "Syncretism and Synchronicity," 87.
5. In Wei-cheng Chu's terms, this is called "a process of self-enlightenment"; Wei-cheng Chu, "Queer(ing) Taiwan and Its Future: From an Agenda of Mainstream Self-Enlightenment to One of Sexual Citizenship?" (paper presented at Sexualities, Genders, and Rights in Asia: 1st International Conference of Asian Queer Studies, Bangkok, Thailand, July 7–9, 2005).
6. Cindy Patton, "Stealth Bombers of Desire: The Globalization of 'Alterity' in Emerging Democracies," in *Queer Globalization: Citizenship and the Afterlife of Colonialism*, ed. Arnaldo Cruz-Malavé and Martin F. Manalansan IV (New York: New York University Press, 2002), 195. See also Berry and Martin, "Syncretism and Synchronicity," 93.
7. More details about the name of Spiteful Tots can be found in my chapter, "Why (Not) Queer? Ambivalence about 'Politics' and Queer Identification in an Online Community in Taiwan," in *Queer Popular Culture*, ed. Thomas Peele (New York: Palgrave Macmillan, 2007).
8. He, "Why (Not) Queer?," 309–315.
9. Ibid., 310.
10. As the BBC reported at the time of the first lesbian, gay, bisexual, transgender pride parade in Taipei, the Taiwanese government was preparing legislation for same-sex marriage, and if passed, Taiwan would be the first country in Asia to recognize gay marriages. The report also specifically pointed out that "[t]he proposals [were] part of a Human Rights Basic Law which is due to be debated by Taiwanese legislators before the end of the year [of 2003]." However, the legislation did not pass, and this Human Rights Basic Law is still pending. But, through boasting about legalizing same-sex marriages, Taiwan has obtained the desired publicity and earned a reputation for being radically progressive, in stark contrast to China, whose "problem" has been considered to be its lack of understanding about human rights (BBC News, "Taiwan Holds its First Gay Parade," http://news.bbc.co.uk/2/hi/asia-pacific/3233905.stm [November 1, 2003]).
11. Marwan M. Kraidy, *Hybridity, or the Cultural Logic of Globalization* (Philadelphia, PA: Temple University Press, 2005), 3.
12. Religious rituals and ideas about Kwan-yin have developed and thus altered in Taiwan in comparison with those in mainland China.
13. Silviano Santiago, "The Wily Homosexual (First—and Necessarily Hasty—Notes)," in *Queer Globalization: Citizenship and the Afterlife of Colonialism*, ed. Arnaldo Cruz-Malavé and Martin F. Manalansan IV (New York: New York University Press, 2002), 13.
14. Kraidy, *Hybridity*, 2.

15. Ibid., 5.
16. For more information, see FIND, "Internet in Taiwan," http://www.find.org.tw/eng/index.asp.
17. See Ibid.; or the survey posted on July 13, 2005, available online at http://www.find.org.tw/eng/news.asp?msgid=179&subjectid=2&pos=0. As these reports show, the obsession in scoring well in information and communication technology ranking is a defining feature of information and communication technology development in Taiwan.
18. There is, however, the exception that households in mountainous areas of Taiwan might not be able to be provided with such service.
19. Nina Wakeford, "Cyberqueer," in *The Cybercultures Reader*, ed. David Bell and Barbara M. Kennedy (London: Routledge, 2000), 413.
20. From FIND, "Internet in Taiwan," we can also see that the demographics of Internet users are quite well distributed in terms of gender and geographical location. For example, slightly more men (56 percent) than women (52 percent) used the Internet. Geographically speaking, moreover, Internet penetration rate was over 60 percent in northern Taiwan, while in other parts, it was between 40 and 50 percent. As for age groups, however, there is a greater divide: 95 percent of people between 15 and 24 years old were Internet users but only less than 10 percent of people over 60 used the Internet.
21. An interesting case that occurred in Taiwan toward the end of December 2006 may provide a good example in illustrating how the Internet has been utilized by people. According to the report in the *Taipei Times* on December 24, 2006, a suicide group online helped a person refrain from committing suicide. This story proves that a seemingly negatively-intended community, such as a suicide group, might actually facilitate public discussions on some taboo issues, and therein provide people necessary and timely help. For more details, consult the online archive at http://www.taipeitimes.com/News/taiwan/archives/2006/12/24/2003341724.
22. Kurt Lindemann, "Live(s) Online: Narrative Performance, Presence, and Community in LiveJournal.com," *Text and Performace Quarterly* 25, no. 4 (2005): 354–372.
23. First of all, *zuyinwen* (注音文) is a popular online phenomenon in Taiwan that serves as a manifestation of the *Taike* (台客) subculture. Zuyinwen means the mixture of complex Chinese characters and phonetic symbols, and has been widely discussed as part of the cultural production of Taike. For further studies and discussions on zuyinwen and Taike, see a research note in complex Chinese based on Pierre Bourdieu et al., http://www.cc.ncu.edu.tw/~csa/journal/52/journal_park397.htm. In addition, a transcription of a public discussion forum consisting of academics, postgraduate students, and online users is available at http://hermes.hrc.ntu.edu.tw/csa/journal/42/journal_forum32.htm. I have also presented a paper on zuyinwen in the Spiteful Tots community at the Annual Conference of the British Sociology Association in April 2006. Secondly, the combination of symbols used to express online users' emotions, or "emoticons," began as a kind of online subculture, but with the ubiquity of the Internet and mobile phones, they have become integrated into younger people's everyday use. More information is written in complex Chinese at http://zh.wikipedia.org/wiki/%E8%A1%A8%E6%83%85%E7%AC%A6%E5%8F%B7, and in English at http://en.wikipedia.org/wiki/Emoticon#Posture_emoticons. A list of illustrations can be found on http://pichuw.myweb.hinet.net/expression.htm, where the most frequently used combinations of symbols are offered. Lastly, the new set of terminology in Taiwan is mocked as the "Mars Language" (火星文), because the kind of typed language is not readily understood, but

needs to be decoded a little so as to be made meaningful. A good example may be the invention of "Orz," which is an entry in the English Wikipedia found at http://en.wikipedia.org/wiki/Orz.

24. I would like to make a point of Spiteful Tots *not* being something inspired by "queer" from the Western LGQ cultures. This argument is based on my own observation and participation in Spiteful Tots over the past years. One of the supporting reasons is that they oppose any kind of naming strategies that ultimately are applied to gain or increase political strength, which, as they understand, is how "queer" reappropriated in the 1990s as a way to cope with the fear and threat of AIDS. Another reason may be that "Spiteful Tots" is a name that conveys a sense of the real frustration they experience repeatedly in life. Their frustration, as explained in this paragraph, leads them to think that they are just spiteful and different from the majority of Taiwanese people. It stems from a rather sentimental and melancholic feeling of being "naturally" excluded due to their difference in social dealings.

25. This is my own translation from Chinese to English.

26. This comment was found in "kindergarten" but was part of a private online conversation on the board strictly for board masters.

27. Quoted from a post responding to the private discussions on zuyinwen on the board for board masters.

28. In various boards where nonregular participants left messages to let people know that they had enjoyed reading the discussion threads, zuyinwen was frequently used and soon caused much criticism and rejection from the regular users of the Spiteful Tots community.

29. See, for example, Antonia Yeng Ning Chao, "Lao Ti Banjia: Quanqiuhua Zhuangtai xia de Ku'er Wenhua Gongming Shenfen Chutan" (老T搬家:全球化狀態下的酷兒文化公民身分初探), in *Taiwan: A Radical Quarterly in Social Studies* (台灣社會研究季刊) 57 (2005): 48–51.

30. This is a local and colloquial way of saying "house parties," sometimes shortened to "home pa."

20 Going Mobile

The Mobile Internet, Ringtones, and the Music Market in Japan

Noriko Manabe

INTRODUCTION

It is January 2007. Steve Jobs has just announced the iPhone, and the CNN headline screams, "The iPhone is so Yesterday," for a segment showing the Japanese buying soda from vending machines and storing architectural plans with their cellular phones.[1] Indeed, Japan has been in the forefront of mobile phone applications. When NTT Docomo, Japan's largest carrier, introduced i-mode in February 1999, it was among the first in the world to offer Internet access through mobile phones. A boom in wallpapers (backgrounds to cellular-phone screens), ringtones, and avatars for mobile phones quickly followed—several years before they would become popular in the United States or Europe. Camera phones, which were first marketed by the Japanese manufacturer Kyocera in 1999, and were commonplace in Japan by 2001, only began to be marketed widely in the United States around 2003.[2]

Similarly, consumer acceptance of 3G, or broadband services over cellular phones, has been faster in Japan than in many countries in Europe or the Americas. Initially rolled out in 2001, 3G was used by two-thirds of Japan's mobile phone subscribers as of December 2006, compared with 8 percent of subscribers in the United States and 14 percent in the United Kingdom.[3] Maximum downlink speed in Japan as of 2006 was over 3MBps. Given that the mobile Internet has been readily available, at affordable rates and high speeds, for longer in Japan than in most other countries, it is not surprising that the mobile Internet is a more integral part of everyday life for the Japanese than for Europeans or Americans: 85 percent of all Japanese mobile users browsed the web over their phones on a daily basis, while only 12 percent of young Americans and 14 percent of young Brits had ever done so.[4]

This chapter will explore the consequences of this rapid take-up of the mobile Internet on one application in particular—music downloads. Ringtones and their sampled cousins, mastertones and full-track downloads, were not only a favored application before the advent of the mobile Internet, but were also a leading driver of 3G adoption in Japan, accounting for half of all content revenues. Furthermore, mobile downloads grew to become a major factor in the music business, comprising 13 percent of total music industry sales, and 90 percent of all music downloads in 2006.[5] I will first discuss the factors that led the mobile Internet to find such fertile ground in Japan, including a lower dependence on personal computers (PCs) than in the United States, and importantly, a business environment that was friendly to both users and content entrepreneurs. I will then explore how ringtones are changing how consumers come in contact with music and acquire it, and how the Japanese music industry has reacted.

THE GENESIS OF MOBILE PHONE CULTURE IN JAPAN

Japan was an early adopter of mobile technologies, particularly among its youth. In the early 1990s, the pager was a must-have item among high-school students, who created their own pager code for messaging each other.[6] By 1994, high schoolers were replacing pagers with the Personal Handyphone Service (PHS), which offered low-cost handsets that relied on existing fixed-line infrastructure. As cellular handsets came to approach the small size and weight of PHS handsets that had made them popular, young users began to switch over to cellular phones.[7] In addition, as the system shifted from leasing handsets to—from 1994 onward—selling them, prices of handsets fell sharply as carriers subsidized them heavily to attract new subscribers. This move to outright ownership also helped to change the *keitai*, or mobile phone, from a standard-issue corporate instrument to a personalized item that came in a myriad of pastel colors and could be decorated by straps and other accessories. By 1998—the eve of the introduction of i-mode—there were 1.5 times more mobile phones per person in Japan than in the United Kingdom or the United States.[8]

This high rate of ownership provided an excellent setting for NTT Docomo's launch of i-mode in February 1999. This service offered e-mail, a variety of content on an easily navigable menu supplied by the phone carrier, and direct web browsing. While its success was not a surprise, given the continuity between pagers and text messaging to e-mail over mobile phones, there were nonetheless several factors that boosted its demand. Its launch coincided with a policy change at Japan Railways, which started to prohibit talking on mobile phones in trains, making announcements and putting up stickers in trains to this effect; therefore, e-mailing offered a way to communicate during hour-long commutes without breaking accepted social norms.[9]

NTT Docomo and Japan's other primary carriers at the time—KDDI (au) and J-Phone (subsequently Vodafone [2001] and Softbank [2006])— also provided infrastructure that supported the burgeoning media. These carriers provided a settlement system, whereby a user could pay for content on his or her phone bill; such systems eliminated the need for credit cards that many young people, who form the core of mobile content users, do not have.[10] This system was already set up for the micropayments that would encompass many purchases for content.[11] Furthermore, the business models were favorable to content developers, who could take advantage of these settlement systems for a commission of only 9 percent, versus 20–30 percent for American and European carriers; such low rates allowed more content companies to survive, sustaining entrepreneurship in the sector.[12] Developing content was easy, as i-mode was built on compact-HTML, familiar to Internet programmers, rather than the new WML or WAP adopted by Europe. In addition, the carriers operated an open business model, whereupon content providers could be included on the carriers' wireless portal (after screening by the carrier). When i-mode first launched in February 1999, it had 67 such content partners; by June 2000, this number had grown to more than 500, and it also had more than 15,000 nonpartner sites.[13]

While e-mail was clearly the killer application of mobile Internet, content for entertainment was also an early driver. Content that personified the phone, such as wallpaper, characters (such as Bandai's *Kyarappa*),[14] and *chaku-mero* (or polyphonic ringtones), proved enormously popular, far exceeding use of other services, such as financial transactions, local information, and news.

As Japanese carriers upgraded their systems, they continued to subsidize handsets heavily, encouraging consumers to replace their handsets within short time frames, and as a result, to keep up with the latest capabilities. By 2002, it was no longer possible for a new cellular subscriber to acquire a handset without Internet capabilities. As of 2006, the average replacement cycle for a handset in Japan was two years versus over three years in the United States and Europe, while the cost of acquiring a new customer (largely through subsidizing handsets) was 38,000 yen ($317) in Japan versus $100 in the United States.[15] Grossly generalizing, Japanese consumers tend to have lighter handsets with larger color screens and greater capabilities than their Western counterparts.

The Japanese mobile Internet market was estimated to be six times the size of that in the United States in 2005.[16] The market for paid cellular phone content in Japan was 315 billion yen ($2.6 billion) in 2005, half of which came from music. Specifically, 105 billion yen came from polyphonic ringtones (*chaku-mero*), 46 billion yen from mastertones (ringtones sampled from the original recording, or *chaku-uta*), and 10 billion yen from full-track downloads (recording of the entire song, or *chaku-uta full*).[17] As of 2006, 55 percent of KDDI's content revenues came from music, with manga and e-books growing in revenue; for NTT Docomo, which was late in offering *chaku-uta full*, 20 percent of web access was for music, 24 percent for videogames, and 27 percent for other entertainment applications, such as sports and gambling simulations.[18]

INTERNET ACCESS THROUGH MOBILE PHONES VERSUS PCS

Mobile phones continued to be an important Internet access device for the Japanese. Part of this use was a matter of practicality: the average Tokyoite commutes for an hour each way using crowded public transportation, and the immediate start-up and smaller size of phones, relative to a PC, made them more practical as a way to communicate or kill time while commuting. Japan was also less inviting for the wandering PC user, with hotspots less numerous than in the United States, and cafés prohibiting customers from using electrical outlets.

Another reason was that Japanese individuals were less likely to have a PC to themselves than Americans. In 1998, Japan had half as many PCs per person as did the United States;[19] while this ratio increased after 2000, as of 2006, only 57 percent of Japanese households owned PCs,[20] whereas over 76 percent of Japanese individuals owned cellular phones; practically speaking, everyone other than very young children or the elderly had cellular phones.[21] Part of this slower take-up of PCs can be explained by Japan's shorter history with keyboard-driven word processing (see Gottlieb, Chapter 5 this volume), which was only introduced in 1978, without a prior phase with typewriters.[22] Furthermore, many households had only one PC for several users, and sometimes the husband and older children were deemed to have a greater "right" to use the PC than the housewife, who may have been told, or felt herself, that she was less technically proficient. For housewives, the *keitai* afforded a private sphere to access the Internet.[23] In contrast to PC culture, women and girls adopted many aspects of *keitai* culture before men, including ringtones.

RINGTONES IN JAPAN

Chakushin merodii (*chaku-mero*), or ringtones, were first offered by NTT Docomo, whose handsets offered preset ringtones, in May 1996. A few months later, IDO (now KDDI's au) offered a phone that would allow the programming of one's own ringtone by inputting it into the keypad. The personalized ringtone soon became popular as a way to personalize the *keitai*; in 1998, the *Keitai Chaku-mero Doremi Book*, which showed how to program melodies, sold 3.5 million copies.[24] In the same year, karaoke companies started to develop polyphonic MIDI ringtones. Astel Tokyo opened the first commercial *chaku-mero* download service in 1997, followed by J-Phone in 1998, and sound quality saw steady improvement, as Yamaha Corporation developed sound chips that could play an increasing number of chords. In late 1999, NTT Docomo added Xing and other polyphonic ringtone suppliers to its official menu, and the polyphonic ringtone rage was on, as consumers learned the utility of identifying ringtones for certain callers or different types of messages, or the pleasure of hearing music that one liked. According to Mobile Content Forum, the polyphonic ringtone market in Japan peaked at 116.7 billion yen ($1.1 billion) in 2004; in that year, the US and German markets were only one-fifth of the size, at $217 million[25] and $240 million,[26] respectively.

Chaku-uta, or mastertones, were introduced by KDDI in December 2002. These clips were originally set up as 30-second ringtones, which users could download for 100 yen each. However, ringtone portal sites, such as Faith, Index, and For-side.com, soon discovered that *chaku-uta* were not being used as ringtones, but for listening pleasure. Their research indicated that consumers were at first embarrassed to use *chaku-uta*, with their human voices, as ringtones because they were judged too "personal" and too revealing of one's tastes;[27] it took over two years for this stigma to be overcome, as teenage girls first adopted *chaku-uta* as ringtones *en masse*. Instead, consumers were listening to *chaku-uta* with earphones while walking around, or with friends, playing them through the phone's speakers. Some consumers were downloading *chaku-uta* to keep up with the latest hits or as a trial purchase, as CDs were relatively expensive at around 3,000 yen ($25). If they liked the song, they bought the whole song or album.

In response to this demand, KDDI launched its *chaku-uta full* service (full-track downloads), which downloaded directly to handsets for 300 yen ($2.50) a song, in November 2004. In the same year, it also offered a flat rate for data packet transmission services, without which the total cost of downloading would have been prohibitive. Within thirteen months, the service had already downloaded thirty million songs, and was pacing at four to five million songs per month in early 2006.[28] With quarterly revenues rising to over 3 billion yen in 15 months, *chaku-uta full* grew fastest among KDDI's content offerings, rivaling *chaku-mero* in absolute size. Leadership in these music-related applications helped KDDI to increase market share from 24.6 percent in March 2001 to 28.7 percent in April 2007; it was also the first carrier, by a wide margin, to convert practically all its subscribers to 3G. Industry watchers were expecting further growth in *chaku-uta full*, as market leader NTT Docomo started offering this service in the summer of 2006. Increasing storage capacity on cell phones, which had expanded from the 20 songs available with an extension card in 2005 to over 1,000 songs with a 2GB flash card by 2007, was also expected to spur demand.

CONSUMER BEHAVIOR WITH *CHAKU-UTA*

In December 2006, I conducted a survey of 100 junior college students,[29] mostly women from 18 to 20 years of age, in the northern city of Sapporo. Eighty-two percent of respondents used *chaku-uta*, while 26 percent used *chaku-uta full*. As a primary ringtone, 53 percent of respondents used vibration or silent mode, as required by Japanese cell phone etiquette in many public places, such as work, school, or on public transportation. Nonetheless, many respondents used audible ringtones at home, when out with friends, or on weekends; half of them used *chaku-uta*, and 20 percent used *chaku-mero* as ringtones. Most chose ringtones they simply liked (82 percent), often favoring current hits (37 percent) or songs that had a personal meaning for them (19 percent), rather than choosing songs that their friends liked (8 percent), or to show others what music they liked (6 percent). On average, they changed their ringtone once or twice a month, when their mood changed or they tired of the ringtone. The average respondent used 3.2 ringtones simultaneously, with over one-third of respondents using more than four ringtones to distinguish phone calls from text messages or e-mails, or to identify different callers. Eighty percent of respondents acquired ringtones by downloading them through their cellular phones.

The respondents downloaded an average of 3.5 *chaku-uta* and a median of 2 per month, with 9 percent downloading more than 10. While nearly all of them were downloading *chaku-uta* for practical use as ringtones, about half were also using them for listening pleasure. While continuing to favor listening to whole albums or songs on minidisk players or iPods, nearly 80 percent of respondents used cell phones to listen to music for short periods, often for the instant gratification of listening only to song hooks. They also used *chaku-uta* as trial purchases (61 percent), to play for friends (29 percent), or as an alarm.

For those using pay sites, using *chaku-uta full* may seem economically irrational, as at 300 yen a song, it is considerably more expensive than renting a CD, with about 12 songs, for 280 yen a week. Nonetheless, respondents (who used the service) downloaded an average of 4 *chaku-uta full* and a median of 1 per month, with 16 percent downloading 5 or more a month, and one person downloading 70 a month through pirate sites. Seventy-percent of *chaku-uta full* users liked the convenience of acquiring a song at any time, often buying a song immediately after having heard it.

Nonetheless, most *chaku-uta full* users also continued to use the shorter *chaku-uta* clips in order to use them as ringtones (88 percent), enjoy parts of songs at lower prices (24 percent), or isolate the hook (16 percent). Respondents who did not use *chaku-uta full* preferred to use iPods or minidisks for music, while others only wanted to hear their favorite parts of a song. As one user put it, "Full-track downloads take too long for the hook to come on. They're also too much data—they take up too much space on my phone and too much time to download." Another commented, "I don't need the whole song; I just want the hook."

THE JAPANESE MUSIC MARKET

Like many other developed music markets, the Japanese music market declined from the late 1990s to the mid-2000s, with revenues down 30 percent from the peak in 1998. Financial executives at Sony Music Japan and Avex, Japan's largest and second-largest record companies, respectively, attributed this decline to the saturation of the market for CD players, which had encouraged replacement of old formats; aging demographics, as 70 percent of Japanese music buyers were in their twenties or younger in the 1990s; and the recession of 2001 to 2003.

Most importantly, record companies blamed the copying of CDs through minidisks and PCs, the latter of which became widespread from 1998 onward, as new PC models facilitated such copying.[30] This trend was helped along by the existence of a CD rental market, which is two-thirds the size of outright retail sales, at 424 billion yen ($3.5 billion) in rental revenues of CDs and DVDs versus revenue from retail purchases of 724 billion yen ($6 billion).[31] Numbering over 3,000, these stores were conveniently located near major train stations, offered a wide selection, were often open until the wee hours of the morning, and charged only 280 yen ($2.33) to rent an album for a week. Some CD rental shops, such as the Tsutaya store in fashionable Roppongi Hills in Tokyo, even provided CD players on the premises for consumers to listen to the CDs. Moreover, this CD rental market was completely legal: as revised in 1984 and 1991, Japanese copyright law invoked the first-sale doctrine for musical recordings, allowing the purchaser of a legally obtained copy to sell or rent it, while the original rights holder was paid a compensatory fee.[32] Nationwide chains of rental stores were operated by stock-exchange-listed companies, such as Cultural Convenience Club, whose stores provided a one-stop entertainment shop, with DVD rentals and sales of CDs, DVDs, books, and videogames, along with CD rentals.

ROADBLOCKS TO DOWNLOADING TO PCS

These rental shops, which made CDs readily available at a low price, may have discouraged downloading to PCs. Despite high rates of broadband diffusion, at three-quarters of homes with Internet connectivity,[33] downloading of music to PCs was not a large market in Japan, at only one-tenth of the size of downloads to cellular phones. One explanation was that many young people did not own their own PCs, which also affected ownership of digital audio players, such as iPods. Recognizing this potential constraint, Sony, the second-largest maker of digital audio players, with a 20-percent share, introduced the Walkman S digital audio player, which recorded music directly from CD and minidisk players, in October 2006.

In addition, record company policies inhibited PC downloading. Initially, record companies showed little interest in downloads, with initial prices for a single-track download on Mora, the online site run by Sony and a consortium of record companies, being 400 yen—an unreasonable price compared with rental costs. It was only with iTunes' entry into the market, with prices of 150 to 200 yen a song ($1.25 to $1.67), in August 2005 that Japanese sites lowered their prices; by that time, mobile downloads had already been firmly established. Nonetheless, lower prices did spur the doubling of revenues from music downloads to PCs between the last quarter of 2005 and the same period in 2004, and to rise 3.7 times in the first 9 months of 2006. Demand appears likely to rise if prices were to be lowered further: 69 percent of my survey respondents said that they would download more if prices were lower. In addition, many young people did not have credit cards necessary to use PC sites; with *chaku-uta full,* the cost was added to the phone bill.

Another major stumbling block was the lack of offerings, also cited by several respondents. As of the end of 2006, iTunes was the top download site in Japan, helped by the iPod's top share, at 47 percent. Despite this dominance, as of February 2007, Sony Music, the largest record company in Japan, was not offering music on iTunes and supplied only to the online music store Mora, run by Label Mobile, the record consortium in which it had a stake. Warner Music Japan's artists were also not available on iTunes. Nonetheless, record companies appeared to be softening their stance about making songs available on iTunes; the available catalogue on the site doubled to two million in the last six months of 2006. Although some domestic labels, such as Pony Canyon, began to make their music available in the second half of 2006, other domestic labels, such as Crown, seemed to be waiting for Sony's lead on iTunes. Compatibility between Mora and iTunes was also an issue: iTunes in Japan only downloaded in AAC format to the iPod, and for a long time, Mora only downloaded in ATRAC3 format to Sony's digital walkman. In late 2006, Sony changed its strategy so that Mora also began to support downloads in the Windows WMA format.

Consequently, a minority of the iTunes Japan catalogue was Japanese, and as of early 2007, only about eight out of the top twenty songs on the best-selling CD charts could be found on the site. Hence, iTunes was running some risk of being seen as a site for a Western catalogue and Japanese independent releases, but not necessarily the hottest J-Pop hits, which comprised the majority of Japanese popular music sales. Meanwhile, Sony and other record companies used Mora to promote new songs, rather than present a comprehensive historical catalogue. Hence, while downloads to PCs were growing, they were not as compelling an alternative for consumers as they could have been, given the lack of a comprehensive lineup and high prices relative to rental shops, who benefited from the boom in digital music players.

Nonetheless, a minority of survey respondents used downloads to PCs quite heavily, downloading ten, twenty, or even a hundred songs a month; such users were often using person-to-person (P2P) sites, such as Limewire. P2P use was relatively low in Japan compared with the United States, with only 3.5 percent of PC owners using them actively as of 2006; industry observers believed that the existence of the CD rental market and the arrests and convictions of people, such as Kaneko Isamu, the developer of popular P2P site, Winny, discouraged P2P use. Nonetheless, 2006 saw a doubling of users who had some experience with P2P to 12 percent.[34]

REACTIONS OF THE MUSIC INDUSTRY TO *CHAKU-UTA*

Given a declining market and a small market for music downloads to PCs, music downloads to phones presented an important opportunity for music companies. Nonetheless, as with PC downloads, initial reactions were less proactive than they could have been. As with *karaoke*, record companies did not benefit greatly from *chaku-mero*; a MIDI rendition could be recorded by anyone, and the only royalty payment due was to the composer. With these royalties being a low 7–12 percent and with low barriers to entry, margins for polyphonic ringtones were potentially high, and many ringtone portal sites flourished, including Xing (run by Faith), For-side.com, and Dwango.

The tables turned with the transition to *chaku-uta*. Unlike *chaku-mero*, a *chaku-uta* was sampled from a recording, so that portal companies were obligated to obtain rights and pay royalties to the rights holder of the master recording. In Japan, rights ownership was negotiated with each artist on a case-by-case basis, and was often held by a production or artist management company; in the case of Sony, Avex, Victor, and Toshiba EMI, the record company itself or its management subsidiary usually held the rights.[35] In cases where content rights were controlled by artist management rather than the record company, the record companies had less incentive to increase digital distribution, as they would not have benefited directly from digital sales.

Miffed by their opportunity losses in *chaku-mero*, several record companies initially restricted distribution of *chaku-uta* to only a handful of portals; Sony Music only supplied Label Mobile, a joint venture among several record companies. Portal companies that had been highly successful in *chaku-mero*, such as Xing, found themselves less able to secure *chaku-uta* for the latest hits. Companies that were successful in securing this content did so at a price; Mobilephone Telecommunications International (MTI) spent 3 billion yen per annum on television advertisements that featured the record companies' artists.[36]

Consequently, as of mid-2006, Label Mobile had top share in *chaku-uta* at about 50 percent, while MTI's Music.co.jp was second at about 15 percent.

Meanwhile, royalties for *chaku-uta* ran at 40 to 70 percent of sales, depending on the song. Some companies, such as Nippon Enterprise, circumvented these high royalties and difficulties in procurement by creating "cover" *chaku-uta*, sung by aspiring singers, but such tactics risked the alienation of record companies in subsequent negotiations. As the uptake of *chaku-uta* on less content-rich sites failed to make up for the decline of *chaku-mero*, many portal sites found themselves financially squeezed.

IMPACT ON CD SALES AND CORPORATE PROFITS

One reason for the reluctance toward initiating an open policy among record companies was the fear that *chaku-uta full* (along with downloads to PCs) would cannibalize CD sales. A survey by Mobile Content Forum in September 2005 did show that about one-third of iPod and *chaku-uta full* users believed that they bought fewer CDs as a result of downloads.[37] On the other hand, the same survey showed that over half of these respondents felt that downloading had no impact on their CD purchases.

My own survey suggested that downloads were having a neutral-to-stimulatory effect. Seventy-four percent of respondents saw no change in their CD buying patterns due to downloading; and while 11 percent claimed that downloading had led to decreased CD purchases, primarily of singles, 15 percent had increased their purchases of CD singles and albums. In addition, 68 percent had purchased a CD after having downloaded a song. Of this number, 87 percent wanted to hear the whole album after having heard one song; 56 percent wanted to play it on a home or car stereo; and 30 percent wanted the accompanying sleeve notes or lyric sheet or the better sound quality of a CD.

Indeed, total music sales, including downloads, started to climb over last year's sales from April 2005 onward. In the first 9 months of 2006, total music sales were up 1.4 percent year-over-year, as a 52 percent rise in mobile downloads compensated for a 4 percent drop in CD and tape sales. By early 2006, sales of single CDs were equivalent to that of mobile and PC downloads, which totaled 14 percent of industry revenues. Both record companies and retailers credited *chaku-uta* for stimulating album sales.

The impact was particularly dramatic at Avex. Unlike most other record companies, it had embraced the new platforms early, making its music available on many mobile portals and on iTunes and other PC portals. The company's focus—pop idols for young women—also corresponded to the biggest market for *chaku-uta*, and sales were helped by the *chaku-uta* boom. In the fiscal year ending in March 2006—the first full year with *chaku-uta full*—Avex's sales rose 19 percent, and operating profits more than doubled over the same period last year, as downloading revenues increased 81 percent. In April–December 2006, its download revenues rose 39 percent to account for about one-quarter of the company's sales and profits. As downloads carry no inventory, and hence no losses from writing down inventories of CDs that do not sell and do not incur the costs of physical distribution and in-store promotions, profitability improved as the percentage of downloads increased.[38] The visible success of Avex eventually spurred other record companies to adopt progressively more open policies starting around mid-2005.

USING *CHAKU-UTA* TO PROMOTE SALES

Once record companies realized that *chaku-uta* could stimulate CD sales, they were eager to exploit it as a promotional device. They were particularly eager to create an alternative to television, which had a stranglehold on promoting music in Japan. Songs were promoted not only on long-running music programs, such as *Music Station*, but also as theme songs for television programs or commercials. While highly effective, opportunities for television exposure were limited in number, as they were focused on the five terrestrial networks rather than cable or satellite television, which had low diffusion rates relative to the United States.

My survey suggested that ringtones and mobile marketing had already garnered high levels of awareness; more respondents said they first heard new songs on ringtone portal sites or as other people's ringtones than on the radio or the Internet. Record companies typically issued a *chaku-uta* a week to two months before the release of an album; they used the sales data of *chaku-uta* to fine-tune their promotional strategy for the CD. Some made *chaku-uta* available on over 100 portals to create buzz at album launch. Record companies and retailers regularly offered a free *chaku-uta* download for consumers who bought an album. Toshiba EMI sent promotional emails to consumers who had registered on an artist's (mobile) fan site.

In addition, information services existed to support impulse purchases. KDDI's mobile sites had recommendation engines running on Google that kept track of songs that had been downloaded, responding with other songs liked by the people who downloaded that song (similar to Amazon) or matching playlists, while Label Mobile's site offered links to other artists and a "my page" with everything previously viewed.

More dramatic examples were the identification services. Should a user hear a song in a café or on television, he or she could identify it by punching in the name of the artist onto a music portal on the mobile phone. Phones could also identify songs being played on an FM radio, to which users could listen through their cell phones simply by the user hitting a menu button. If the consumer did not know the name of the performer, he or she could point the cell phone in the direction of the music, whereupon the phone would "hear" it and identify it through its sound-wave patterns. Once the song was identified, the consumer could immediately download it to his or her cell phone or buy the CD on a mobile Internet shopping site. According to KDDI, 30–40 percent of such searches results in a download.[39] About 30 percent of *chaku-uta* users in the survey employed these search functions, three-fourths of whom downloaded the song at least some of the time.

Even with this recognition of the importance of *chaku-uta*, some portal companies complained that the content available was often limited to current hits for promotional purposes, and that back catalogues could be more complete. On the other hand, portal sites concentrating on specific genres, such as rap, reggae, Cuban music, or Korean pop, could be found on KDDI's menu.

POTENTIAL IMPACT ON ALBUM AND SONG FORMATS

Many consumers preferred downloading to buying a CD because they could choose the songs they wanted, thereby saving both money and disk space.[40] In the first 9 months of 2006, 84 percent of CD sales came from albums, while singles accounted for 72 percent of PC downloads, and 100 percent of mobile downloads. If such trends were to continue, it would seem economically rational for record companies to produce singles rather than concept albums, hence eliminating the cost of producing tracks that would not generate revenue. As of mid-2006, record companies and retailers were still focused on albums, which were seen as more economically viable, given their higher prices. Meanwhile, artists saw albums as an opportunity to make artistic statements or experiment with ideas that were not suitable for a pop hit.

Nonetheless, some record companies and artists were looking at different conceptions of a successful album. Some albums by Avex were coming to resemble a "best-of" collection, producing five singles from one album. The company also released Koda Kumi's latest album in a series, where one single was released every week for twelve weeks. Independent labels, such as 247, were skipping CD singles entirely for *chaku-uta full*.

A more radical question could be asked of song formats, as the market for *chaku-uta* clips remained larger than that for the full song (*chaku-uta full*). While available clips included introductions, instrumentals, and verses, the survey respondents favored choruses by a wide margin. While some users were downloading clips rather than full songs because they were cheaper, some survey respondents chose *chaku-uta* to isolate the hook.

Given this behavior, one might expect songwriters to highlight choruses more while reducing verses and other sections. However, as of mid-2006, Japanese artists were not changing their style to suit *chaku-uta*. Many were reluctant to give up the opportunity for narrative afforded by the verse–chorus format. Furthermore, as many songs were promoted as commercials, Japanese songwriters were already consciously delivering hooks quickly or starting a song with the chorus. Nonetheless, the increasing importance of *chaku-uta* was changing what songs would be developed: a song by Nakama Yukie, which started as a thirty-second *chaku-uta* and commercial for KDDI, was expanded into a full-length song only when its appeal became clear through *chaku-uta* sales.

FREE SITES AND PIRATE SITES

Until 2006, the rate of piracy in *chaku-uta* and *chaku-uta full* was remark-ably low in Japan. Most users had been accessing the mobile web through the carrier's menu, which accepted or rejected websites for its official menu; to use unofficial or "free" sites, the user would have to type in a URL or have the URL sent directly to their cell phone. However, along with greater diffusion of 3G came more browsing of unofficial mobile websites. As of mid-2006, over 60 percent of mobile web activity was thought to be on "free" sites, not on the official carrier menu—up from 40 percent the previ-ous year. In July 2006, KDDI made a Google-run search engine available on its mobile service, which returned both on- and off-menu mobile sites, as well as PC sites. Perhaps as a result of this move to an open Internet system on mobile phones, free *chaku-uta* sites and bulletin boards mush-roomed in the course of 2006. Many of these free sites were legal, gaining revenues from advertising or point systems, based on a user's introduction of other users; one such site run by Yamaha—Gorgonzola—had over 1.3 million members in early 2007. My survey respondents who used such sites were by far the heaviest downloaders.

Illegal *chaku-uta* sites, based on file-sharing or unauthorized use of copyrighted material, also became commonplace. A survey of mobile users under age 40 by Recording Industry Association of Japan in November 2006 showed that 70 percent of users were aware of illegal *chaku-uta* sites, half of them had experience using them, and one-third used them regularly. Usage was particularly high among 12- to 15-year-olds, with over 70 per-cent using them regularly; these users downloaded an average of 6.4 *chaku-uta* and 2.5 *chaku-uta full* a month. Forty percent of users had stumbled onto these sites simply by surfing on the mobile Internet. The Recording Industry Association of Japan estimated that illegal downloads were pacing at 234 million *chaku-uta* and 53 million *chaku-uta full* per annum, and that while 5 percent of illegal site users said that they bought more CDs as a result of downloading, 16 percent said they bought fewer.[41] With 60 percent of respondents looking to use illegal sites in the future, business models for the music industry appeared on the brink of another change.

CONCLUSION

Important factors that differentiate the mobile Internet from PC-based Internet include: 1) the potential for a relatively small number of gatekeep-ers, that is, the carriers, to control access; 2) the fact that it can be used more readily from anywhere, unlike the PC-based Internet; 3) the small-ness of the screen and the need for a simple inputting mechanism; and 4) the greater likelihood that the access device will be owned by a single indi-vidual and is, therefore, more likely to be personalized. As demonstrated in this study, in Japan, the mobile Internet became as viable an Internet experience, if not more so, than the PC-based Internet, to a large extent because the telecommunications industry—the gatekeepers—provided a friendly environment for both users and entrepreneurs. While the mobile Internet in Japan, at the outset, was a natural development from pagers and PHS, the carriers directly stimulated its growth by providing user-friendly, menu-driven portals and settlement services at low commissions. This business model greatly improved the chances of success for start-ups, encouraging entrepreneurs to develop applications that capitalized on point 2 (ubiquitous and immediate access) or point 4 (a desire for personalization). Given the ambulatory nature of Japanese society and the high diffusion rate of cellular phones, ideas for such applications were abundant. In addition, the carriers helped make new applications viable by heavily subsidizing handsets, which encouraged upgrades.

Hence, the walled-garden approach worked well in Japan in the initial stages of the mobile Internet, and was far more successful there than, say, in the United States, where both business models and infrastructure were less optimal for content providers. While many observers have commented on the cultural factors leading to the popularity of the mobile Internet in Japan, many of the same applications, such as ringtones and camera phones, became popular in later years in the United States and Europe, once those applications were made available. Furthermore, these applications were used in much the same way in the West as they were in Japan, as my surveys of my American students suggested. It was the business model and technological infrastructure that made these Japanese innovations viable in the crucial experimental stages.

Similarly, *chaku-uta* provided an interesting case study of how corporate policies can stimulate or hinder the trajectory of a mobile Internet service. As the company with the most open policy toward the new service, Avex benefited spectacularly. In addition, the story of *chaku-uta* was an example of how unanticipated ways of using a service can redefine an industry. Originally meant as a ringtone, *chaku-uta* was detected early on as a product for listening pleasure, thus inspiring the rollout of *chaku-uta full* and a whole industry of search and download functions. These products grew despite their price premium relative to CD rentals, illustrating the power of the instant gratification offered by the anytime, anywhere mobile phone. *Chaku-uta* eventually became a major promotional tool for record companies.

As noted aerlier, the advent of 3G and more efficient search engines were shifting the mobile Internet business model away from the walled garden to an advertising- or member-driven model. With access to the carriers no longer necessarily a precursor to success, and with greater multimedia capabilities available, a new period in innovation on the mobile Internet had likely begun, requiring a whole new set of support mechanisms from both users and businesses.

NOTES

1. Eunice Yoon, "The iPhone is so Yesterday in Asia," CNN, www.cnn.com (January 13, 2007).
2. Gerard Goggin, *Cell Phone Culture: Mobile Technology in Everyday Life* (New York: Routledge, 2006), 144.
3. US and UK figures from M:Metrics, as quoted by International Federation of the Phonographic Industry, "Digital Music Report," http://www.ifpi.org/content/section_resources/digital-music-report.html, hereafter cited as IFPI. Japan figures from Telecommunications Carriers Association, http://www.tca.or.jp/eng/database/daisu/yymm/0612matu.html
4. Japanese figures from Internet Kyōkai, eds., *Internet Hakusho* (Internet White Paper), (Tokyo: Impress, 2006), 28, hereafter cited as *IWP*; UK figures from M:Metrics, "Teens Take User-Generated Content and Social Networking to Go," http://www.mmetrics.com/press/PressRelease.aspx?article=20061214-social-networking (December 14, 2006).
5. Record Industry Association of Japan, www.riaj.or.jp, hereafter cited as RIAJ.
6. Tomoyuki Okada, "Youth Culture and the Shaping of Japanese Mobile Media: Personalization and the *Keitai* Internet as Multimedia," in *Personal, Portable, Pedestrian: Mobile Phones in Japanese Life*, ed. Mizuko Ito, Daisuke Okabe, and Misa Matsuda (Cambridge, MA: MIT Press, 2005), 41–60, hereafter cited as *Ito*.
7. Kenji Kohiyama, "The Development of Mobile Communications in Japan," in *Ito*, 61–74.
8. Calculated by the author from data in "World Data," Encyclopaedia Britannica, www.britannica.com (accessed February 12, 2007). Specifically, there were 47.3 million cell phones for a population of 126.4 million in Japan in 1998, versus 14.9 million phones for 58.3 million people in the United Kingdom, and 69.2 million for 276 million people in the United States.
9. Daisuke Okabe and Mizuko Ito, "Keitai in Public Transportation," in *Ito*, 214.
10. Japan remains a cash-oriented society, with many smaller establishments not accepting credit cards or restricting their use (e.g., some restaurants will not accept credit cards for lunch, whereas this form of payment may be acceptable for dinner). In addition, most credit cards in Japan function more like charge cards, where one is billed for the entire amount of transactions at the end of the month rather than just the interest payment. For large transactions, stores will ask buyers if they would prefer to pay the bill in one or more installments, but a consumer will generally not be able to charge the full amount of the credit limit and pay only the interest for months on end. Hence, it is rare for young people to have credit cards.
11. Kohiyama, "The Development of Mobile Communications," 68.
12. Commission rates can vary widely for different content providers. However, the 9 percent figure for the Japanese carriers is a generally accepted figure in the industry, as stated by numerous executives of mobile portal companies interviewed between 2000 and 2006. It is also widely recognized by executives of portal companies operating internationally that commission rates are higher in the United States.
13. NTT Docomo, "Annual Report 2000," http://www.nttdocomo.co.jp/english/corporate/ir/binary/pdf/library/annual/fy1999/p04_c.pdf
14. Bandai's Kyarappa service provided downloads of characters, such as Hello Kitty, to the customers' cellular phones on a daily basis at the cost of 100 yen a month. By October 1999, the service had already attracted 180,000 subscribers (*Japan Internet Report*, no. 42 [1999]; also available at http://www.

jir.net/jir10_99.html). The rights to the characters, such as Hello Kitty, were owned by other companies (in Hello Kitty's case, by Sanrio).

15. Kazuyo Katsuma, JP Morgan, personal communication, June 28, 2006. Only 17 percent of Japanese subscribers have handsets that are more than 2 years old, and only 5 percent have handsets that are more than 3 years old (*IWP*, 38). Yen estimates made at 120 yen to the US dollar, the prevailing rate in January 2007. Japanese carriers can justify higher acquisition costs because monthly revenue per customer is higher, at 7,000 yen, versus $40 in the United States (Katsuma, personal communication, June 28, 2006).

16. Katsuma, p.c., June 28, 2006.

17. Mobile Contents Forum, http://www.mcf.to/press/images/2006_Mobile-Contents_market_scale.pdf (accessed February 16, 2007).

18. NTT Docomo, personal communication, June 29, 2006; KDDI, personal communication, July 7, 2006.

19. "World Data," Encyclopaedia Britannica.

20. *IWP*, 42.

21. Japan *Mobile Phone White Paper* 2007, (Tokyo: Impress, 2006) 15.

22. Japan has had a shorter history with keyboard-driven word processing, owing to the difficulties of Japanese script. There are three forms of script—two phonetic (*hiragana* and *katakana*) and the other pictorial (*kanji*, or Chinese characters). Because the language contains many homonyms, *kanji* are essential to convey meaning efficiently in written script. Typewriters were not popular in Japan, and it was only in 1978 that Fujitsu introduced the first commercial word processor. See Nanette Gottlieb, *Kanji and the Keyboard: Word Processing Technology in Japan* (Richmond, UK: Curzon, 2000). Japanese word-processing software for PCs has been available as early as 1983, with Just Systems' JS-Word for the PC-100. Even then, using a keyboard can be cumbersome: to enter a *kanji* in most word-processing software, the writer must toggle through a list of choices.

23. Shingo Dobashi, "The Gendered Use of Keitai in Domestic Contexts," in *Ito*, 230–232.

24. Wikipedia (Japanese), "Chakushin merodii," http://ja.wikipedia.org/wiki/ (accessed February 14, 2007).

25. Jupiter Media, "Jupiter Research Projects Ring Tone Revenues to Reach $724 Million and Mobile Game Revenues to Reach $430 Million in the U.S. by 2009," March 15, 2005, http://www.jupitermedia.com/corporate/releases/05.03.15-newjupresearch.html (accessed May 27, 2007).

26. Informa, quoted in Peter James and Rsoita Kürbis, *Introduction to the German Music Market* (Berlin: GermanSounds AG–Music Export Germany, n.d.), 139, http://www.wbm.be/dbfiles/doc249_MarketguideAllemagne.pdf

27. Personal communication, Dwango, Index, Faith, For-side.com, July 2005.

28. KDDI, "Analyst Meeting for the Fiscal Year Ending March 2006" (webcast at http://www.irwebcasting.com/060425/06/89eef34b9e/main/index01_hi.html).

29. Junior colleges offer two-year degrees. The college in question was affiliated with a four-year college.

30. Avex, personal communication, June 10, 2004.

31. Figures calculated by the author from numbers provided by Culture Convenience Club, which had calculated that, in the fiscal year ending in March 2004, it had 31.5 percent of the CD and DVD rental market at 133.5 billion yen, and 10.2 percent of the CD and DVD retail sales market at 73 billion yen, using filed financial statements of its competitors and data from Nikkei MJ and Teikoku Databank. These sales figures differ from other industry figures because they are retail values, rather than wholesale or manufacturer's production values.

32. CD rental stores generally refrain from renting a new CD for three weeks from its date of initial sale for a Japanese CD, and for one year for a foreign CD. In contrast, US law made renting of sound recordings (outside of educational institutions and nonprofit libraries) illegal in 1984. See Nihon kompakuto disuku bideo rentaru shōgyō kumiai, http://www.cdvnet.jp/
33. *IWP*, 39.
34. RIAJ.
35. RIAJ, p.c. there is no personal communication ref for RIAJ previously cited. Please check
36. The president of MTI's site, music.co.jp, was also known in the copyright industry and trusted by the music industry.
37. Mobile Content Forum 2005, 29.
38. Costs incurred by a digital model include the cost of converting the sound file to various mobile formats, online advertising on portal sites, and awareness-building advertising for Avex's own site.
39. KDDI, personal communication, July 7, 2006.
40. Mobile Content Forum 2005, 23. A survey I conducted among junior college students in Sapporo in December 2006 showed similar results.
41. RIAJ, http://www.riaj.or.jp/release/2007/pr070129.html

Contributors

Nasya Bahfen is a lecturer in journalism at the Royal Melbourne Institute of Technology University, and a reporter with Radio Australia. Her research interests include Islam and the media, the use of the Internet in Malaysia and other Southeast Asian Islamic societies, and diaspora Muslim communities in the West. Her PhD, which took a comparative look at the use of the Internet by Muslim tertiary students in Southeast Asia and Australia, was recently submitted at the University of Technology in Sydney, Australia. .

Wei Chen is an associate professor in the Department of Graduate English, School of Foreign Languages, Wuhan University of Technology in Wuhan, China (wei.chen@whut.edu.cn).

Daniel Cunliffe is a senior lecturer in Multimedia Computing and leads the Computing and Minority Languages (CaML) Group within the Faculty of Advanced Technology at the University of Glamorgan in Pontypridd, Wales. The CaML Group has been investigating aspects of the relationship between minority languages and Information Technology since 2000. Areas of current research include: minority language communities online, designing websites for bilingual users, the language behavior of bilingual users in online environments, and e-activism for minority languages. He has published on a variety of topics relating to the use of the Welsh language online. Recent publications have included "Minority Languages and the Internet: New Threats, New Opportunities" in *Minority Language Media: Concepts, Critiques and Case Studies*, ed Mike Cormack and Niamh Hourigan (Multilingual Matters, 2007).

Ljiljana Gavrilović is at the Institute of Ethnography, Serbian Academy of Sciences and Arts in Belgrade, Serbia. Her research interests include: traditional social organization of the Balkans societies and its applications in a contemporary society, especially in relation to common law; family; social stratification; identity; relationships of global–family/group–individual, costume; systems of meanings; and indicators of social stratification in traditional communities. She has a special focus on adaptations of the refugees from the 1991–1995 wars. Ljiljana also has an interest in contemporary popular culture, especially science fiction and the Internet.

Urmila Goel is a postdoctoral researcher in social and cultural anthropology based in Berlin, Germany, specializing in the experiences of people marked as South Asians in Germany. She has just completed the research project, "The Virtual Second Generation," about the negotiation of ethnic identities in virtual spaces at the European University Viadrina in Frankfurt/Oder, Germany, and has been a visiting researcher at the University of New England in Armidale, Australia, and the University of Bergen in Norway. Her research interests cover, in particular, strategies of dealing with experiences of racism and the interdependency of racism and heteronormativity. More information can be found on http://www.urmila.de.

Gerard Goggin is a professor of Digital Communication and deputy director of the Journalism and Media Research Centre at the University of New South Wales in Sydney, Australia. He is author of *Cell Phone Culture* (2006) and *Digital Disability* (2003, with Christopher Newell), as well as editor of *Mobile Technologies: From Telecommunications to Media* (2008; with Larissa Hjorth), *Internationalizing Internet Studies* (with Mark McLelland), *Mobile Phone Cultures* (2007), and *Virtual Nation: The Internet in Australia* (2004). Gerard is editor of the journal, *Media International Australia*.

Eugene Gorny was born in Novosibirsk, USSR. In 1991, he graduated from the University of Tartu, Estonia, with the equivalent of an MA in Russian Philology and Library Science. From 1996 to1998 he was editor-in-chief of Zhurnal.ru (www.zhurnal.ru). From 1998 to 2000 he worked for *Russkij Zhurnal* (www.russ.ru), where he edited the "Net Culture" section. He has also participated in a number of online literary projects, such as Setrevaja Slovesnost (www.netslova.ru), the Russian Virtual Library (www.rvb.ru), and the Fundamental Digital Library of Russian Literature and Folklore (www.feb-web.ru). The title of his PhD thesis (Goldsmith College, University of London, 2006) is "A Creative History of the Russian Internet."

Nanette Gottlieb is an ARC Professorial Fellow in the Japan Program, School of Languages and Comparative Cultural Studies at the University of Queensland in Brisbane, Australia. Her recent work includes *Japanese Cybercultures* (2003; with Mark McLelland) and *Language and Society in Japan* (2005).

Terri He currently serves as a visiting scholar at the Institute of Ethnography in Academia Sinica, Taiwan, while also a last-year PhD student at the University of York in York, United Kingdom. Her research on politics of dissident sexuality in contemporary Taiwan explores the relations between nationalism, ethnicity, sexuality, and the ways some sexual dissidents constitute an online community. Her work brings together studies and critiques of cyberculture; postcolonialist and feminist theorizing of nation and nationalism; and gay, lesbian, and queer studies.

Larissa Hjorth is a researcher and artist lecturing in Media Cultures in the Games and Digital Art program at Royal Melbourne Institute of Technology University in Melbourne, Australia. Over the last five years, she has been researching and publishing on he gendered customizing of mobile communication and virtual communities in the Asia–Pacific region. Hjorth has published widely on the topic in journals such as *Journal of Intercultural Studies, Convergence, Fibreculture Journal*, and *Southern Review*. Hjorth has been the recipient of an Australia Council Tokyo studio, an Asialink Seoul residency, and an Akiyoshidai International Village Residency, as well as received grants for cross-cultural art projects from th Besen Foundation, the Australia Council New Media Fund, the Asialink-Japan Foundation, the Pola Foundation, and the Noruma Foundation. Hjorth has a forthcoming monograph, *The Art of Being Mmobile: Gendered Customisation in the Asia–Pacific* (London: Routledge).

Kun Huang is an assistant professor in the Government Department at New Mexico State University in Las Cruces, NM (kunhuang@nmsu.edu). He is interested in the study of collaboration between government, nonprofit, and business organizations, particularly in health care.

Gholam Khiabany is in the Department of Applied Social Sciences at London Metropolitan University. He is author of *Blogestan: The Internet and Politics in Iran* (2008; with Annabelle Sreberny) and *Iranian Media and the Paradox of Modernity: Media, Religion and State since 1979* (2008).

Randy Kluver is the director of the Institute for Pacific Asia and a research professor in the Department of Communication at Texas A&M University in College Station, TX. Dr. Kluver has been on the faculty of universities in the United States, Singapore, and China; has published over thirty peer-reviewed journal articles and book chapters; and is the author, editor, or co-editor of four books. Dr. Kluver's current research interests include the role of the Internet in Asian societies, Asian political communication, globalization, and the political and social impact of information technologies.

Bradley J. Koch is an assistant professor of Management at Seidman College of Business, Grand Valley State University in Allendale, MI (kochb@gvsu.edu). His research focuses on the rapidly changing cognitive institutional environment in China and its impact on management logic, as well as joint venture strategies in Sichuan Province.

Pamela T. Koch is an adjunct faculty member at Seidman College of Business, Grand Valley State University in Allendale, MI. She is interested in issues at the intersection of work, technology, and society, and her research primarily focuses on China and East Asia.

Merlyna Lim is an assistant professor of Justice and Social Inquiry at Arizona State University in Tucson, with a joint appointment at the Consortium for Science, Policy and Outcomes. She was awarded a PhD in 2005 from the University of Twente in Enschede, The Netherlands, for a doctoral dissertation entitled, "@rchipelago online: The Internet and Political Activism in Indonesia." Her research interests include: political economy of space, globalization, identity politics, cyber and urban activism, and mutual shaping of technology and society. She holds the following awards: the Annenberg Netpublics Fellowships (2005), the Henry Luce Southeast Asia Fellowship (2004), the WOTRO Fellowship (2003), and the ASIST International Paper Contest Winner (2002). Recent publications include a monograph entitled *Islamic Fundamentalism and Anti-Americanism in Indonesia: Role of the Internet.*

Noriko Manabe is a PhD candidate in Ethnomusicology and Music Theory at City University of New York Graduate Center. She has published articles on Japanese rap, the music business, Mozart operas, and Cuban music in *Ethnomusicology, Asian Music, Trans,* and edited volumes, and presented papers at SEM, IASPM-América Latina, IASPM International, and IMS. She teaches at John Jay College and Brooklyn College, both in New York, and serves on the Investment Committee of SEM. She is currently pursuing work on her dissertation on Japanese popular music under a SSRC/JSPS Fellowship. Before re-entering academics, she was an Internet and media analyst for JP Morgan in Japan, ranking highly on surveys by Institutional Investor and Asiamoney.

Fran Martin is a lecturer in Cultural Studies at the University of Melbourne. Her publications include *Mobile Cultures: New Media in Queer Asia* (2003; co-edited with Chris Berry and Audrey Yue); *Situating Sexualities: Queer Representation in Taiwanese Fiction, Film and Public Culture* (HKUP, 2003); and *BackwardGlances: Transnational Chinese Cultures and the Female Homoerotic Imaginary* (forthcoming).

Pere Masip holds a PhD in communication from the University Ramon Llull in Barcelona, Spain, and teaches Journalism and Information Systems at the School of Communication there. His research focuses on the use of information and communication technologies in newsrooms, the impact of the Internet on journalistic routines, and the effects of the Internet on cultural identities. He is the author of books and articles on these topics. He has also taught at the University of Vic and the Open University of Catalonia.

Mark McLelland lectures in the Sociology Program in the School of Social Sciences, Media and Communication at the University of Wollongong, Australia. He is the author or editor of six books relating to Japanese cultural history, minority social groups, and new media. These include *Japanese Cybercultures* (2003) and *Queer Japan from the Pacific War to the Internet Age* (2005).

Josep Lluís Micó holds a PhD in communication from the University CEU San Pablo, and teaches Journalism at the School of Communication at the University Ramon Llull in Barcelona. His research focuses on journalists' use of information and communication technologies, the implementation of the Digital Terrestrial Television in Spain, and the impact of the internet on cultural identities. He is the author of several books and articles about journalism and technology, particularly broadcast journalism. He is also a journalist who works at the *Diari de Girona*, and he also edits the School of Communication student newspaper, *Nova Ciutat Vella*.

Susanna Paasonen is a research fellow at the Collegium for Advanced Studies, University of Helsinki in Finland. Her teaching and research interests include Internet research, feminist theory, pornography, and popular culture. She is the author of *Figures of Fantasy: Women, Internet and Cyberdiscourse* (2005), as well as the co-editor of *Women and Everyday Uses of the Internet: Agency & Identity* (2002) and *Pornification: Sex and Sexuality in Media Culture* (2007).

Han Woo Park is assistant professor at YeungNam University, Republic of Korea. He obtained his PhD in the Department of Communication at the State University of New York at Buffalo. He has also worked as a researcher for the Royal Netherlands Academy His research focuses on the social impact of new media, the e-science/research method, and social network analysis using weblink data. His research has appeared in international journals such as *New Media & Society, Journal of Computer-Mediated Communication,* and *Journal of American Society of Information Science and Technology.* His website is found at http:// www.hanpark.net.

Helga Tawil-Souri is assistant professor in the Department of Media, Culture, and Communication at New York University in New York City.

Her research focuses on various aspects of Palestinian and Arab media practices and spaces, including analyses of local broadcasting industries and cinema, the relationship between the Internet and national/economic development, and issues around social and political spaces. She is also a photographer and documentary filmmaker.

Annabelle Sreberny is a professor in Global Media and Communication, in the School of Oriental and African Studies at the University of London.

Seunghyun Yoo, PhD, is an assistant professor in the Department of Behavioral and Community Health Sciences at the Graduate School of Public Health, University of Pittsburgh, in Pittsburgh, PA. Dr. Yoo is a community health scientist whose areas of research include community-based participatory research and practice, community capacity building, and community empowerment. Her community research extends to online communities, particularly the process by which an online community evolves and develops community capacities. She has previously published work on community development and capacity building of Internet-based fan communities.

Index

LaVergne, TN USA
02 September 2010
195530LV00011B/22/P